Global Migration Governance

Global Migration Governance

Edited by
Alexander Betts

OXFORD
UNIVERSITY PRESS

OXFORD
UNIVERSITY PRESS

Great Clarendon Street, Oxford OX2 6DP

Oxford University Press is a department of the University of Oxford.
It furthers the University's objective of excellence in research, scholarship,
and education by publishing worldwide in

Oxford New York

Auckland Cape Town Dar es Salaam Hong Kong Karachi
Kuala Lumpur Madrid Melbourne Mexico City Nairobi
New Delhi Shanghai Taipei Toronto

With offices in

Argentina Austria Brazil Chile Czech Republic France Greece
Guatemala Hungary Italy Japan Poland Portugal Singapore
South Korea Switzerland Thailand Turkey Ukraine Vietnam

Oxford is a registered trade mark of Oxford University Press
in the UK and in certain other countries

Published in the United States
by Oxford University Press Inc., New York

British Library Cataloguing in Publication Data
Data available

Library of Congress Cataloging in Publication Data
Data available

Typeset by SPI Publisher Services, Pondicherry, India
Printed in Great Britain
on acid-free paper by
MPG Books Group, Bodmin and King's Lynn

ISBN 978–0–19–960045–8

3 5 7 9 10 8 6 4

Acknowledgements

This book represents one of the major outputs of the Global Migration Governance project, based in the Department of Politics and International Relations at the University of Oxford. The project, funded by the John D. and Catherine T. MacArthur Foundation, has had two core aims: to improve academic understanding of the international politics of migration and to contribute to policy debates by offering a vision of global migration governance that can simultaneously meet the interests of developed and developing countries while respecting the human rights of migrants.

As a starting point for thinking about these issues, a workshop was held in Oxford in October 2008, at which a group of the world's leading experts on migration were asked to consider three important questions relating to the global governance of the particular areas of migration on which they work. What, *institutionally*, is the global governance of migration? Why, *politically*, does that type of governance exist? How, *normatively*, can we ground claims about the type of global governance that should exist in that area? This book is the outcome of those workshop discussions.

The contributors to the volume were drawn predominantly from across the University of Oxford's existing three research centres on migration: the International Migration Institute (IMI), the Centre on Migration, Policy and Society (COMPAS), and the Refugee Studies Centre (RSC), and supplemented with a number of other leading international experts on migration, most of whom also have long-standing associations with migration studies in Oxford.

The provenance of the authors means that this volume offers a showcase of some of the Oxford's rich and diverse talent in migration research. It purposefully brings together a combination of established academics with a number of younger, emerging scholars. It also consciously brings together scholars from a range of disciplinary backgrounds including anthropology, economics, geography, law, political science, and sociology. But, far more than that, it attempts to draw them into a conversation on an area that has been systematically neglected within both migration studies and international relations: the international politics and global governance of migration.

Given the task of inviting a range of scholars from different disciplinary backgrounds, whose main commonality is that they all have in-depth expertise in a

Acknowledgements

particular area of migration, my first words of thanks must go to the contributors to the volume. I have been advised on many occasions by senior colleagues that preparing an edited volume can be a considerable challenge; but in this instance the contributing authors were all an immense pleasure to work with, submitting chapters on time, making revisions as requested, and offering generous input on other chapters in the volume. As ever, as well as being contributors, Nick Van Hear and Gil Loescher offered support, guidance and mentorship throughout the editing process. I believe that the result is a set of excellent chapters and I only hope that my editing does justice to the sum of the book's parts.

Given that the focus of the book has been on global governance, it has benefited enormously from the Global Migration Governance project's association with the Global Economic Governance Programme (GEG), based at University College, Oxford, and directed by Ngaire Woods. Ngaire has been a constant source of advice, encouragement, and inspiration. As administrator of the GEG, Reija Fanous has been incredibly supportive and contributed greatly to the organization of the workshop for this volume. The GEG has been a wonderful laboratory within which many of my ideas relating to global governance and international institutions have evolved in ways that have undoubtedly shaped this book. I am especially privileged to have had Arunabha Ghosh, Jochen Prantl, Devi Sridhar, and Jeni Whalan as GEG colleagues.

Elsewhere in Oxford, many of my excellent and inspirational colleagues in both migration studies and international relations have provided advice and feedback on the development of this volume and on my project in general. Others have simply been an indirect source of ideas through their own work. To name a few, I am particularly grateful for conversations with Matthew Albert, Oliver Bakewell, Robin Cohen, Matthew Eagleton-Pierce, Alice Edwards, Matthew Gibney, Guy Goodwin-Gill, Hein de Haas, Andrew Hurrell, Katy Long, Neil MacFarlane, Calum Nicholson, Kalypso Nicolaidis, Emily Paddon, Sarah Percy, Anne Roemler-Mahler, Heloise Ruaudel, Martin Ruhs, James Simeon, Helene Thiollet, and Roger Zetter.

Reflecting its relative neglect as an area of study, the community of academics working on the area is comparatively small. However, I have found that community to be an extremely supportive and encouraging group, many of whom have been generous with their ideas, time, and feedback in supporting this project and my other related work. In addition to the contributors to the book, I am grateful to Vincent Chetail, Michael Collyer, Ale Delano, Jerome Elie, Elspeth Guild, Jussi Hanhimaki, Randall Hansen, James Hollifield, Martin Jones, Susan Kneebone, Rahel Kunz, Gallya Lahav, Loren Landau, Sandra Lavenex, Susan McGrath, Kamal Sadiq, Anna Schmidt, Eiko Thielemann, and Darshan Vigneswaran.

Given the nature of the subject on which this book is focused, it would not have been possible to prepare without the generous support of a range of people from the policy community, who have been an enormous help and support in navigating my way around 'Global Migration Governance'. Whether through sharing their ideas and knowledge, making time to engage in conversations, helping me to set up interviews and fieldwork, or through inviting me to participate in meetings, a number of people outside of academia have supported my work in ways that make me optimistic for the future of global migration governance. I am especially thankful to T. Alexander Aleinikoff, Ibrahim Awad, John Bingham, Joe Chamie, Ryzard Cholewinski, Jeff Crisp, Sarah Cross, Jean-François Durieux, Erika Feller, Brian Gorlick, Rolf Jenny, Jobst Koehler, Bela Hovy, Thomas Linde, Gregory Maniatis, Sergio Marchi, Kathleen Newland, Angela Li Rosa, Michelle Klein Solomon, Kristof Tamas, and Colleen Thouez.

I also wish to acknowledge my excellent doctoral students working on aspects of the international politics of migration: Erin Court, Francesca Giovannini, and Nina Hall. Their work and ideas, and the conversations that we have, are a great source of inspiration in my work. Erin has also provided terrific research assistance as part of the Global Migration Governance project, which has contributed directly to this book.

At Oxford University Press, I am thankful to my editor, Dominic Byatt, for once again showing great belief in both me and the project. I am also extremely grateful to the John D. and Catherine T. MacArthur Foundation for funding the Global Migration Governance project and thereby making this book possible. In particular, I wish to thank Milena Novy-Marx and John Slocum at MacArthur for their personal support and guidance. I very much hope the book does justice to the belief they and the Foundation have shown in me. Last, but far from least, I am immensely grateful to Esra Kaytaz, who as Research Officer on the Global Migration Governance project has contributed both practically and intellectually to the development of this book.

Contents

Contents

List of Figures

List of Tables

List of Abbreviations

ACP	African, Caribbean, and Pacific Countries (EU)
AML	anti-money laundering
APC	Intergovernmental Asia-Pacific Consultation on Refugees, Displaced Persons and Migrants
API	advance passenger information
ASEAN	Association of South East Asian Nations
ASEM	Asian-European Meeting
CCEMA	Climate Change, Environment and Migration Alliance
CIREFI	Centre for Information, Discussion and Exchange on the Crossing of Borders and Immigration (EU)
CIS	Commonwealth of Independent States
DFID	Department for International Development (UK)
DHA	Department of Homeland Security (USA)
EAC	East African Community
EAP	Employee Assistance Programme
ECA	Economic Commission for Africa
ECOWAS	Economic Community of West African States
EMWU	European Migrant Workers Union
ESCAP	Nations Economic and Social Commission for Asia and the Pacific (UN)
ETA	electronic travel authorization system
EU	European Union
EUBAM	EU Border Assistance Mission
EURODAC	Europe-wide system for the identification of asylum seekers (EU)
ExCom	Executive Committee (UNHCR)
FADO	Data Bank for False and Authentic Documents (EU)
FATF	Financial Action Task Force
FDI	foreign direct investment
FRONTEX	European Union border agency
GATS	General Agreement on Trade in Services (WTO)
GATT	General Agreement on Tariffs and Trade
GCC	Gulf Cooperation Countries

GCIM	Global Commission on International Migration
GDP	gross domestic product
GFMD	Global Forum on Migration and Development
GMG	Global Migration Group
HLDMD	High-Level Dialogue on Migration and Development
HLWG	High-Level Working Group
HSLM	high-skilled labour migration
IADB	Inter-American Development Bank
IASC	Inter-Agency Standing Committee
IATA	International Air Transport Association
ICAO	International Civil Aviation Organization
ICARA	International Conferences on Assistance to Refugees in Africa
ICCPR	International Covenant on Civil and Political Rights
ICEM	Intergovernmental Committee for European Migration
ICISS	International Commission on Intervention and State Sovereignty
ICMC	International Catholic Migration Commission
ICMPD	International Centre for Migration Policy Development
ICPD	International Conference on Population and Development
ICRC	International Committee of the Red Cross
ICRMW	International Convention on the Protection of the Rights of All Migrant Workers and Members of their Families
IDP	internally displaced person
IFAD	International Fund for Agricultural Development
IGAD	Intergovernmental Authority on Development
IGC	Intergovernmental Consultations on Asylum, Refugees and Migration
IIRIR	Illegal Immigration Reform and Immigration Responsibility Act (USA)
IISD	International Institute for Sustainable Development
ILO	International Labour Organization
IMF	International Monetary Fund
IML	International Migration Law
IMO	International Maritime Organization
INS	Immigration and Naturalization Service (USA)
IO	international organization
IOM	International Organization for Migration
IPCC	Intergovernmental Panel on Climate Change
IRCA	Immigration Reform and Control Act (USA)
IRM	International Retirement Migration
ISO	International Standards Organization
IUOTO	International Union of Official Travel Organizations
JHA	Justice and Home Affairs (EU)

LDC	less developed country
LESC	Law Enforcement Support Centre (USA)
LICUS	Low-Income Country Under Stress (World Bank)
LM	lifestyle migration
LNHCR	League of Nations High Commissioner for Refugees
MIDSA	International Dialogue on Migration in Southern Africa
MIDWA	International Dialogue on Migration in West Africa
MIGRANT	Office for International Labour Migration (ILO)
MOIA	Ministry of Overseas Indian Affairs
MOU	memorandum of understanding
MPI	Migration Policy Institute
MRTD	machine readable travel documents
MTM Dialogue	Mediterranean Transit Migration Dialogue
NAFTA	North American Free Trade Agreement
NGO	non-governmental organization
NOVIB	Dutch Organization for International Development Coordination
NRIs	non-resident Indians
NSA	non-state actor
OAU	Organization of African Unity
OCHA	Office of the Coordinator for Humanitarian Affairs
OECD	Organisation for Economic Co-operation and Development
OHCHR	Office of the High Commissioner for Human Rights
OSCE	Organization for Security and Cooperation in Europe
PCU	Post-Conflict Unit (World Bank)
PICMME	Provisional Intergovernmental Committee for the Movements of Migrants from Europe
PNR	passenger name record
PSRP	Poverty Reduction Strategy Paper (World Bank)
PTK	professional, technical and kindred (workers)
R2P	Responsibility to Protect
RCM	regional consultative mechanism (Americas)
RCP	regional consultative process
REC	regional economic community
RFID	radio frequency identification
SADC	Southern African Development Community
SAP-FL	Special Assistance Programme to Combat Forced Labour (ILO)
SCIBA	Strategic Committee for Immigration, Border and Asylum (EU)
SIS	Schengen Information System (EU)
SME	small and medium sized enterprise
SOPEMI	OECD's reporting system on international migration
SPP	Security and Prosperity Partnership (USA)

SSHRC	Social Science and Humanities Research Council (Canada)
TAG/MRTD	Technical Advisory Group on Machine Readable Travel Documents (ICAO)
UAE	United Arab Emirates
UN	United Nations
UN.GIFT	United Nations Initiative to Fight Human Trafficking
UNAIDS	Joint United Nations Programme on HIV/AIDS
UNCTAD	United Nations Conference on Trade and Development
UNDESA	United Nations Department of Economic and Social Affairs
UNDOC	United Nations Office on Drugs and Crime
UNDP	United Nations Development Programme
UNEP	United Nations Environmental Programme
UNESCO	United Nations Education, Cultural and Scientific Organization
UNFPA	United Nations Population Fund
UNHCR	Office of the United Nations High Commissioner for Refugees
UNI	Union Network International
UNICEF	United Nations Children's Fund
UNIFEM	United Nations Development Fund for Women
UNITAR	United Nations Institute for Training and Research
UNODC	United Nations Office on Drugs and Crime
UNPAN	United Nations Public Administrations Network
UNTOC	United Nations Convention on Transnational Organized Crime
UNWTO	World Tourism Organization
USAID	United States Agency for International Development
US-VISIT	United States Visitor and Immigrant Status Indicator Technology
WCO	World Customs Organization
WFP	World Food Programme
WHO	World Health Organization
WTO	World Trade Organization

About the Contributors

Alexander Betts is the Hedley Bull Research Fellow in International Relations at the University of Oxford, where he is also Director of the MacArthur Foundation-funded Global Migration Governance project and a Fellow of Wadham College. His research focuses on the international politics of migration and refugee protection. He is the author of numerous books and articles, including *Protection by Persuasion: International Cooperation in the Refugee Regime* (Cornell University Press, 2009) and *Refugees in International Relations* (edited with Gil Loescher, Oxford University Press, 2010). Outside of academia, he has worked as a consultant to the United Nations High Commissioner for Refugees, the International Organization for Migration and the Council of Europe, and as an advisor to numerous governments and non-governmental organizations.

Amber Callaway works as an information officer in Washington, DC for USAID's Office of US Foreign Disaster Assistance (USAID/OFDA). She has been deployed to Pakistan, the Philippines, Kenya, Ethiopia, and the Democratic Republic of Congo. Prior to working as an information officer, Amber worked with USAID's Office of Civilian Response, USAID's Office of Conflict Management and Mitigation, and the US Embassy in Uganda. Amber received her BA in Sociology from Southwestern University in 2000 and her Master's Degree in Public Policy from Georgetown University in 2008, where she served as a Research Assistant at the Institute for the Study of International Migration.

Stephen Castles is Research Professor of Sociology at the University of Sydney and Associate Director of the International Migration Institute (IMI), University of Oxford. Until August 2009, he was Professor of Migration and Refugee Studies at the University of Oxford and Director of IMI. From 2001 to 2006, he was Director of the Refugee Studies Centre at Oxford University. His recent books include: *The Age of Migration: International Population Movements in the Modern World* (Palgrave-Macmillan, 2009), *Migration, Citizenship and the European Welfare State: A European Dilemma* (with Carl-Ulrik Schierup and Peo Hansen, Oxford University Press, 2006), and *Migration and Development: Perspectives from the South* (edited with Raúl Delgado Wise, IOM, 2008).

Lucie Cerna is an Anglo-German Postdoctoral Fellow in the Department of Politics at the University of Oxford, and a Research Associate at the Centre on Migration, Policy and Society (COMPAS), University of Oxford. Lucie's research focuses on the political economy of high-skilled migration, and regional and global governance. She holds a DPhil in Politics from the University of Oxford and has been a Lecturer in Politics at Merton College and Somerville College in Oxford, as well as a Consultant for the International Labour Organization. Her most recent publications have appeared in the *Journal of European Public Policy* and in an edited volume at Amsterdam University Press.

Franck Düvell is Senior Researcher at the Centre on Migration, Policy and Society (COMPAS), University of Oxford. He is also an Associate Fellow to the International Migration Institute (IMI), Oxford, and the Jean Monnet Centre for European Studies (CEuS), Bremen. His research focus is on irregular migration, mixed migration, European and international migration politics, and on the ethics of migration control. Amongst his publications are *Transit Migration and Transit Countries* (Moscow University Press, 2009, edited by Irina Molodikova), *Illegal Immigration in Europe* (Palgrave-MacMillan, 2006), *Migration. Boundaries of Equality and Justice* (Polity, 2003, with Bill Jordan), and *Irregular Migration. Dilemmas of Transnational Mobility* (Edward Elgar, 2002, with Bill Jordan).

Alan Gamlen is a Postdoctoral Fellow based at the International Migration Institute at the University of Oxford. He works on migration, diasporas, and transnationalism, with a specific focus on Asia-Pacific migration and on sending contexts more broadly. He holds a doctorate in Geography from Oxford University; his thesis focused on the diaspora engagement policies of migrant-sending states, and included a large cross-country comparison based around a new comparative framework, as well as in-depth case studies of New Zealand and Ireland. His articles include 'The Emigration State and the Modern Geopolitical Imagination' (in *Political Geography*) and 'The New Migration and Development Optimism' (in *Global Governance*).

Khalid Koser is Associate Dean, Head of the New Issues in Security Programme, and Director of the New Issues in Security Course (NISC) at the Geneva Centre for Security Policy. He is also Non-Resident Fellow in Foreign Policy Studies at the Brookings Institution and Research Associate at the Graduate Institute of International and Development Studies in Geneva. He is Chair of the UK's Independent Advisory Group on Country Information. He is co-editor of the *Journal of Refugee Studies*.

Rey Koslowski is Associate Professor of Political Science and Public Policy at the State University of New York at Albany (SUNY), where he is also Director of the Center for Policy Research Program on Border Control and Homeland Security. He is the author of *Migrants and Citizens: Demographic Change in the*

European States System (Cornell University Press, 2000), *Real Challenges for Virtual Borders: The Implementation of US-VISIT* (Washington: Migration Policy Institute, 2005), editor of *International Migration and the Globalization of Domestic Politics* (Routledge, 2005), and co-editor (with David Kyle) of *Global Human Smuggling: Comparative Perspectives* (Johns Hopkins University Press, 2001).

Christiane Kuptsch is Senior Specialist in Migration Policy, International Migration Programme, International Labour Organization (ILO) in Geneva, Switzerland. She is a political scientist, specialized in international relations (Graduate Institute of International Studies, Geneva), with a background in law (University of Hamburg). Her migration-related publications include edited books on migrant recruitment agents, the increasing competition for global talent, and the internationalization of labour markets; she is also co-author of *Managing Labor Migration in the Twenty-First Century* (Yale University Press, 2006).

Anna Lindley is a Lecturer in Development Studies at the School of Oriental and African Studies at the University of London. She completed her DPhil at the University of Oxford, where she was Research Officer at the Refugee Studies Centre. She specializes in migration and conflict-related issues, and is the author of *The Early Morning Phonecall: Somali Refugees' Remittances* (Berghahn Books, 2010).

Gil Loescher is Visiting Professor at the Refugee Studies Centre, University of Oxford. He was professor of International Relations at the University of Notre Dame and has held positions at Princeton University, the London School of Economics, and the Department of Humanitarian Affairs at the US State Department in Washington, DC. He has published numerous works on refugees, human rights, and conflict and security, including *UNHCR in World Politics: A Perilous Path* (Oxford University Press, 2001), *UNHCR: The Politics and Practice of Refugee Protection into the Twenty-First Century* (Routledge, 2008), and *Protracted Refugee Situations: Politics, Human Rights and Security Dimensions* (United Nations University Press, 2008).

Philip Martin is Professor of Agriculture and Resource Economics at the Department of Agricultural and Resource Economics at the University of California, Davis. Martin's research focuses on farm labour and rural poverty, labour migration and economic development, and immigration policy and guest worker issues; he has testified before Congress and state and local agencies numerous times on these issues. He has worked for the World Bank, International Monetary Fund, and United Nations agencies such as the International Labour Organization and United Nations Development Programme in countries around the world, and is the author of numerous articles and books on labour and immigration issues including *Managing Migration: The Promise of Cooperation* (Rowman and Littlefield, 2006).

Susan Martin is Donald G. Herzberg Chair in International Migration and is Director of the Institute for the Study of International Migration at Georgetown University. She served as the Executive Director of the US Commission on Immigration Reform. Her publications include *Managing Migration: The Promise of Cooperation* (Rowman and Littlefield, 2006), *The Uprooted: Improving Humanitarian Responses to Forced Migration* (Lexington, 2005), and numerous other works on immigration and refugee policy.

Jane McAdam is Associate Professor in the Faculty of Law at the University of NSW and a Research Associate at the Refugees Studies Centre, University of Oxford. She previously taught in the Faculty of Law at the University of Sydney and at Lincoln College at the University of Oxford, where she obtained her doctorate. She is author of *Complementary Protection in International Refugee Law* (Oxford University Press, 2007) and *The Refugee in International Law* (with Guy Goodwin-Gill, 3rd edn, Oxford University Press, 2007), and editor of *Forced Migration, Human Rights and Security* (Hart Publishing, 2008) and *Climate change and Displacements: Multidisciplinary Perspectives* (Hart Publishing, 2010). She is currently working on a monograph entitled *Climate Change, Displacement and International Law* (Oxford University Press, forthcoming 2011).

James Milner is Assistant Professor of Political Science at Carleton University. He was previously a Social Science and Humanities Research Council Postdoctoral Fellow at the Munk Centre for International Studies, University of Toronto, and has worked as a consultant for the United Nations High Commissioner for Refugees (UNHCR) in India, Cameroon, Guinea, and its Geneva Headquarters. He is author of *Refugees, the State and the Politics of Asylum in Africa* (Palgrave-Macmillan, forthcoming), co-author of *UNHCR: The Politics and Practice of Refugee Protection into the 21st Century* (Routledge, 2008), and co-editor of *Protracted Refugee Situations: Political, Human Rights and Security Implications* (United Nations University Press, 2008).

Caroline Oliver is a Research Associate at the Faculty of Education at the University of Cambridge. She completed her doctorate at the University of Hull (1998–2002) before working as a Lecturer in Sociology and Social Anthropology in the School of Geography, Politics and Sociology at the University of Newcastle (2002–5). She has published widely on lifestyle migration, including a book, *Retirement Migration. Paradoxes of Ageing* (Routledge, 2007).

Nicholas Van Hear is a Deputy Director and Senior Researcher at the Centre on Migration, Policy and Society (COMPAS), University of Oxford. His background is in Anthropology and Development Studies. He is the author of *New Diasporas* (Routledge, 1998), co-editor of *The Migration-Development Nexus*

(International Organisation for Migration, 2003) and *Catching Fire* (Rowman and Littlefield, 2006), as well as the author of numerous articles in journals, edited volumes, and practitioner publications. Nicholas has worked on forced migration, development, and related issues for many years, with field experience in Africa, the Middle East, Europe, and South Asia. Before joining COMPAS, he was a Senior Researcher at the Danish Centre for Development Research in Copenhagen. Prior to this, he was a Senior Researcher at the Refugee Studies Centre in Oxford.

Introduction: Global Migration Governance

Alexander Betts

International migration represents one of the most obvious contemporary manifestations of globalization. With growth in trans-boundary interconnections, there has been a rapid increase in human mobility across international borders. Between 1970 and 2005, the number of international migrants increased from 82 million to 200 million, comprising 3 per cent of the world's population (GCIM 2005). Given the range of social, economic, and political implications of migration, it has become increasingly politicized by states, and is emerging as an issue of great importance at the international level. States and non-state actors are increasingly concerned to find ways to manage migration in ways that enable them to maximize the benefits and minimize the costs of mobility.

In most policy fields which involve trans-boundary movements across borders, such as climate change, international trade, finance, and communicable disease, states have developed institutionalized cooperation, primarily through the United Nations (UN) system. In relation to these other trans-boundary issues, states have developed a range of international agreements, often overseen by international organizations. These have been created based on the recognition that collective action and cooperation are often more efficient in meeting states' interests than unilateralism and inter-state competition.

However, despite the inherently trans-boundary nature of international migration and the interdependence of states' migration policies, there is no formal or coherent multilateral institutional framework regulating states' responses to international migration. There is no UN Migration Organization and no international migration regime, and sovereign states retain a significant degree of autonomy in determining their migration policies. International migration divides into a range of different policy categories: low-skilled labour migration, high-skilled labour migration, irregular migration, international travel, lifestyle migration, environmental migration, human trafficking and smuggling, asylum and refugee protection, internally displaced people, diaspora, remittances, and root causes. Each of these is regulated differently at the global level. They vary along a spectrum in terms of the degree of formal institutional cooperation that exists—from asylum and refugee protection, which has a formal regime and a UN organization, to labour migration, which is largely unregulated at the global level. Although there is an International Migration Organization (IOM), it remains outside of the UN framework and has no explicitly normative mandate other than as a service provider to states. The degree of institutionalized cooperation that exists in relation to migration is therefore relatively limited in comparison to many other trans-boundary issue-areas.

Yet this is not to say that there is no global migration governance. Despite the absence of a 'top-down' multilateral framework, there is a rapidly emerging 'bottom-up' global migration governance framework. In the absence of coherent multilateral institutions, states are creating ad hoc forms of multi-level migration governance. An increasingly complex array of bilateral, regional, and inter-regional institutions is emerging, enabling states to selectively engage in different forms of informal cooperation with different partner states. Aside from the emerging bilateral and regional institutions, a number of multilateral institutions that regulate other policy areas have significant implications for states' responses to migration despite not explicitly being explicitly labelled as 'migration'. The global governance of trade, health, and human rights, for example, indirectly regulate states' responses to migration. The picture that emerges is of a complex and fragmented tapestry of overlapping, parallel, and nested institutions.

The recognition that global migration governance is relatively incoherent has contributed to the emergence of a debate on the international institutional framework governing international migration. Following calls by states for greater debate on the issue at the International Conference on Population and Development (ICPD) in Cairo in 1994, former UN Secretary General Kofi Annan invited Michael Doyle to reflect on the international institutions that exist in relation to migration. The 'Doyle Report' was completed in 2002 and recommended further reflection, leading to the creation of the Global Commission on International Migration (GCIM), which ran between 2003 and 2005, to assess in greater detail the nature of the issue and possible institutional responses. The GCIM's recommendations in turn led Kofi Annan to appoint a Special Representative on Migration and Development and to convene a UN High-Level Dialogue on Migration and Development in 2006, at which states openly reflected for the first time on the appropriate location for multilateral debate on migration. Given opposition from Northern states to the creation of a UN-based debate on migration, a new forum, the Global Forum on Migration and Development (GFMD), was created in 2007 and has subsequently held annual informal dialogues. This range of initiatives represents the beginning of an inter-state process for reflecting on how more coherent international cooperation might be developed in the area of migration.

In addition, a range of non-state actors have invited growing reflection on global migration governance. A number of academic projects have been convened to reflect upon issues relating to the international institutional architecture regulating migration. In 2000, Bimal Ghosh edited a book entitled *Managing Migration: Time for a New International Regime?*, in which he argued for a 'new international regime for the orderly movement of people'. Randall Hansen set up a project to examine International Cooperation and Migration in collaboration with IOM, while Rey Koslowski has established a project on Global Mobility Regimes with funding from the MacArthur Foundation, in which they argue for certain types of global migration governance. Meanwhile, in 2009, the International Catholic Migration Commission (ICMC) convened an initiative called 'Conversations on the Global Governance of Migration', bringing together a range of stakeholders from the policy and academic worlds to debate global migration governance.

However, despite the emergence of a debate on the global governance of migration, the issue remains poorly understood within both academic and policy circles. Claims are frequently made about 'improving' the international institutional framework regulating migration or having 'better' international cooperation on migration. However, the emerging debates on international institutions and migration lack a coherent understanding of, analytically, what global migration governance actually is and, normatively, the basis on which we can make claims about how global migration governance should look. Indeed, debate on global migration governance is simply meaningless unless one first reflects upon, three conceptual questions: *institutionally*, what is global migration governance; *politically*, why it is the way it is; and *normatively*, how might we ground claims about how it should look? In the absence of clear answers to these analytical and normative questions, the debate on global migration governance has unsurprisingly lacked coherent leadership and vision.

One of the reasons for this analytical gap in understanding global migration governance is that, international relations, as a sub-discipline of political science, has generally not focused on the international politics of migration. In contrast to the work that has been done on other trans-boundary issue-areas such as security, the environment, and trade, for example, there have been only small and relatively isolated pockets of international relations scholarship on migration (Zolberg 1981; Weiner 1985; Loescher 2001; Hollifield 2004; Koslowski 2004; Rudolph 2006; Sadiq 2008). This is regrettable because migration is inherently political in nature—involving states according rights to non-citizens—and inherently international—involving movements across borders.

This book therefore represents an attempt to address that gap. It brings together a group of the most prominent international migration scholars in the world to explore the institutional, political, and normative dimensions of global migration governance in relation to different aspects of international migration. In doing so, the book attempts to make two significant contributions. On an academic level, it attempts to provide a starting point for understanding how international migration is regulated at the global level and why politically it has emerged in the way it has. On a policy level, it attempts to work towards the development of a vision for a normatively desirable and politically feasible framework for global migration governance.

This introduction serves to contextualize and outline the approach of the book. It begins by explaining exactly what the book means by global governance and offers an overview of the global governance of migration. It then outlines the main three sets of analytical questions explored by the chapters in the book. It explains the institutions of global migration governance, the politics of global migration governance, and the normative implications of global migration governance. In each case, the introduction sets out the main concepts and analytical tools that the book uses in its analysis. Finally, the introduction concludes by outlining the chapters in the book.

Global governance

At the outset there is a need to clarify what the book means by 'global governance'. One of the central challenges of international relations emerges from the distinction between domestic politics and international politics. In domestic politics there is a sovereign who can uphold order within a state. In international politics there is no sovereign, and international politics has therefore been characterized by 'anarchy'—not in the sense of chaos but in the sense of the absence of world government (Morgenthau 1948). It is essentially this distinction between domestic and international, and the pursuit of order in the absence of world government that defines international relations as a distinct discipline.

'Global governance' is a murky and often poorly defined term. A working definition of global governance can be taken to be the 'norms, rules, principles and decision-making procedures that regulate the behaviour of states (and other transnational actors)'. Govern*ance* distinguishes itself from govern*ment* insofar as there is no single authoritative rule-maker. In that sense, it represents a process that is contested by a range of actors at several stages: agenda-setting, negotiation, implementation, monitoring, and enforcement (Abbott and Snidal 2009). What makes governance 'global' is not the 'level' at which it is identified—whether bilateral, regional, transnational, or supranational—but rather the fact that it is constraining or constitutive of the behaviour of states (and transnational actors).

The genesis of the concept of 'global governance' has roots in both policy and academia. The policy-level genealogy of global governance can be found in the

Global Commission on Global Governance, convened during the 1990s. Its role was to reflect on the emerging challenges stemming from an increasingly interconnected world in which trans-boundary issues cannot be adequately addressed by individual sovereign states acting in isolation. The 1994 report of the Commission, *Our Global Neighbourhood* set out an agenda for how states might cooperate in order to address a range of new threats and challenges in areas such as the environment, trade, transnational crime, finance, and conflict. Building on this report, 'global governance' has subsequently become part of the mainstream policy-level vocabulary used to describe the whole range of roles that international institutions and international organizations play in regulating processes that transcend the jurisdiction of the nation-state.

The academic-level genealogy of global governance emerges from attempts within international relations to understand the role of international institutions in world politics. In particular, regime theory represents a branch of international relations that attempted to understand the role that regimes—as norms, rules, principles, and decision-making procedures—play in influencing the behaviour of states in particular issue-areas (Krasner 1983; Hasenclever et al. 1997). It tried to explore questions relating to the emergence and effectiveness of regimes, and how they are negotiated, implemented, monitored, and enforced. However, from the late 1990s, dissatisfaction with the explanatory power of regime theory and its rationalist origins led to a focus on the broader concept of 'global governance' (Held and McGrew 2002; Woods 2002), within which specific research topics have emerged focusing on issues such as the role of international organizations (Barnett and Finnemore 2004), compliance (Raustiala and Slaughter 2002), global public goods theory (Kaul 2003; Barrett 2007), the rational design of institutions (Koremenos et al. 2003), and the role of international law in world politics (Chayes 1998; Goldstein et al. 2001).

The use of the phrase global governance is not unproblematic. In contemporary international relations, the policy and academic origins of the term have increasingly merged. The definition of global governance, the levels of governance and what it regulates, and how, are not always explicit in the burgeoning literature on the subject. The term also frequently carries with it an implicit normative bias, often assuming that 'more' governance is both necessary and desirable. These caveats highlight the need for analytical rigour in understanding what global migration governance is, and where it can be found, and what normative claims are implicit in making a case for particular types of governance. Nevertheless, the concept of global governance is useful insofar as it highlights the move away from individual nation-states having absolute authority over policy-making towards a situation in which the behaviour of states and other actors is constrained and shaped by a range of institutions which exist beyond the nation-state.

There has been a proliferation in global governance since the Second World War. The most obvious source of global governance is multilateral institutions

(Ruggie 1993). States have created a range of multilateral institutions to regulate a host of issue-areas. A dense tapestry of international agreements comprising public international law have been negotiated and implemented in areas ranging from security to human rights to trade. Furthermore, a range of international organizations have been created to oversee the implementation of these international agreements. The UN and its specialized agencies have been the most obvious source of multilateral institutions, representing the forums within which many agreements have been reached and the bodies with the mandate for overseeing implementation and enforcement. Beyond the immediate scope of the UN system, the affiliated institutions of the World Bank, International Monetary Fund (IMF), and the World Trade Organization (WTO) have been significant sources of multilateral global economic governance. In all of these areas, states have agreed to delegate sovereignty in exchange for other states reciprocating.

The logic underlying the creation of multilateral institutions has been to overcome so-called collective action problems, in which there is a disjuncture between a course of action that would be collectively rational, on the one hand, and how actors behave when they consider their interests in isolation from one another, on the other hand (Olson 1965). To take the example of climate change, the reasoning underlying the creation of international institutions is that cooperation to reduce greenhouse gas emissions is in states' collective interest but, acting in isolation, it would be individually rational for one state to free-ride on the emissions reductions of other states. International institutions contribute to overcoming collective action failure and enable joint gains to be derived from cooperation because they reduce the costs and increase the benefits of international cooperation. For example, by providing information, reducing the transaction costs of cooperation, providing surveillance, creating stable conditions for multilateral negotiations, increasing the value of reputation, and creating a context within which mutually beneficial issue-linkage can take place, institutions facilitate cooperation (Axelrod 1984; Keohane 1984; Hurrell 2007: 68).

It has also been increasingly recognized that the scope of global governance goes far beyond the formal multilateral institutions that exist within the structures of the UN. On a regional level, institutions have emerged to facilitate cooperation inside the regions and to enhance bargaining power outside (Fawcett and Hurrell 1996; Mattli 1999). Furthermore, global governance is not confined to inter-state cooperation. While some issue-areas are predominantly statist, being negotiated and implemented by states, an increasing range of issue-areas are characterized by what Scholte (2000) describes as a 'polycentric' mode of governance. In other words, they involve a growing range of non-state actors—including the private sector—in agenda-setting negotiation, implementation, monitoring, and enforcement (Biersteker and Hall 2002; Ruggie 2003; Sell 2003; Falkner 2008). Within this context, international administrative law is increasingly being used to describe standard setting at the international level that falls short of the definition of public international law but nevertheless serves as a significant form of regulation at the global level (Kingsbury 2009). An example of this type of standard setting is the work of International Standards Organization (ISO) (Mattli 2003).

As well as formal institutions, other sources of regulation may represent implicit forms of global governance. For example, under certain conditions, one state's domestic policies may represent an implicit form of global governance. This will be the case when policy interdependence means the behaviour of one state serves to constrain the behaviour or policy choices of another state. This is likely to be especially true in the case of migration policy in which, for example, one state's policy choice in relation to skilled labour immigration, the regulation of remittances, or its diaspora will necessarily represent a regulatory constraint on the behaviour of other states. Furthermore, dominant ideas—for example, about the nature of state sovereignty—may represent important sources of informal norms which maintain order and serve to regulate behaviour.

All of these examples serve to highlight that in looking for sources of global migration governance, it is necessary to go beyond simply describing the formal multilateral institutions that exist at the inter-state level. Global migration governance, as is explained in this chapter and throughout the book, comprises a complex range of formal and informal institutions existing on a range of levels of governance and involving a host of states and non-state actors.

Global governance and migration

Global governance has been developed particularly in response to the emergence of trans-boundary issues. A range of issues are inherently trans-boundary insofar as the nature of the problem is one that crosses borders and cannot be addressed by a single state acting in isolation. Climate change, international trade, communicable disease, transitional crime, international financial markets, and terrorism, for example, are amongst these trans-boundary issues and, as such, states have developed forms of institutionalized international cooperation to address these issues.

Globalization—in terms of growing trans-boundary interconnectivity—has therefore created a growing need for governance that goes beyond the nation-state. The demand for global governance is closely associated with globalization and the need to address cross-border spillovers and externalities. However, although international migration is one of the most striking contemporary manifestations of globalization, and it is, by definition, a trans-boundary issue that no state can address individually, it has not developed a coherent, multilateral global governance framework. Instead, it has remained largely the domain of sovereign states without a formal multilateral institutional framework.

This is not to say that there is no global migration governance—but that what exists is fragmented and incoherent in comparison to most trans-boundary issue-areas. Global migration governance is a complex picture. International migration is not regulated by a single formal multilateral structure in the way that health, monetary stability, or trade are regulated through the World Health Organization, IMF, and WTO frameworks, for example. Although the IOM exists in the area of migration, it exists outside of the UN system and mainly as a service provider to individual states that pay for its services. The IOM has no clear mandate provided by the international community, in the way that most UN agencies have a statute that provides them with normative authority. Perhaps more importantly, with the exception of asylum and refugee protection, there is no formal migration regime in the sense of a formal set of inter-state agreements. This contrasts with the global governance of most trans-boundary issue-areas in which the main international organizations' work is underpinned by a mandate to uphold a particular normative framework based on international law.

Global migration governance is instead based on a range of different formal and informal institutions, operating at different levels of governance (Koser 2010; Newland 2010; Hansen et al. 2011; Koslowski forthcoming; Kunz et al. 2011). States' responses to the various different categories of migration addressed in this book are regulated in different ways. The institutions that regulate states' responses to human trafficking and smuggling are not the same as those that regulate states' responses to skilled labour migration. In each category of migration, there is a complex range of multilateral, regional, inter-regional, and bilateral agreements, with different levels of governance having greater importance in relation to some categories of migration than others. For example, while refugee protection is predominantly regulated through multilateral governance, high-skilled labour migration is predominantly regulated through bilateral governance, and diaspora relations are predominantly regulated through the extra-territorial scope of individual states' policies. In different categories of migration, regulation in different issue-areas matters to a greater or lesser extent. In the case of environmental migration, for example, the global governance of climate change matters; in the case of labour migration, International Labour Organization (ILO) conventions on labour rights and WTO law matter; in the case of refugee protection and internally displaced persons (IDPs), human rights law matters. Furthermore, in the different areas of migration, different actors matter to different degrees. The relevant international organizations, private sector actors, and non-governmental organizations vary.

The complexity and variation in global migration governance makes mapping the institutional landscape at the global level an important but challenging task. One of the central purposes of this book is to provide a comprehensive overview of global migration governance. This is important because the way in which migration is regulated at the global level matters significantly for the international politics of migration, and this in turn has implications for both migrants and non-migratory communities. Indeed, the regulatory framework within which states determine their migration policies matters because it affects individuals' and communities' access to human rights, human development, and security.

Identifying and understanding the institutions that regulate states' responses to international migration also has wider implications for understanding global governance. The complexity of global migration governance points to a different type of global governance beyond the formal and inclusive multilateralism that characterized the post-Second World War consensus. In the absence of a comprehensive UN framework, it highlights an environment in which institutional proliferation has created a complex, multi-level tapestry of diverse and contested institutions. This form of plurilateralism, in which a range of institutions with different degrees of inclusivity and exclusivity coexist, is increasingly becoming the norm in a range of issue-areas, and global migration governance offers an extremely salient case study within which to explore international politics in the context of a dense framework of overlapping, parallel, and nested institutions.

One of the challenges of identifying and exploring global migration governance is to divide empirical analysis of 'migration'. Although human mobility within states is an important aspect of migration, the book's focus is on international migration. This is not because internal mobility is not significant but because it is analytically very distinct from both a global governance and a political perspective. With the exception of internal displacement, internal mobility is almost exclusively the domain of individual state sovereignty and domestic politics.

In focusing on the global governance of international migration, however, a key challenge is how to cut the cake of 'global migration governance' into analytically meaningful slices. While Koslowski (forthcoming) divides global migration governance into three 'global mobility regimes', focusing on the refugee, travel, and labour migration regimes, this book takes a slightly different approach. It instead divides international migration into a range of policy categories into which international migration is often divided: low-skilled labour migration, high-skilled labour migration, irregular migration, international travel, lifestyle migration, environmental migration, human trafficking and smuggling, asylum and refugee protection, internally displaced people, diaspora, remittances, and root causes, and has a chapter on the global governance of each.

This approach has both advantages and disadvantages. One advantage is that the approach offers comprehensive coverage of nearly all aspects of international migration. Another significant advantage is that, by following the dominant policy categories, it allows the different politics and governance of each area to be explored in ways that are excluded by aggregating the categories.

Because the categories themselves reflect differences in policy and governance across the areas of international migration, they are themselves indicative of the differences in institutions and politics that the book is trying to explore. The disadvantages are that the approach is less parsimonious than the 'global mobility regimes' approach and that the 'policy categories' approach risks overlap and repetition. For example, certain institutions and organizations will arise in similar ways in the governance of different policy categories. The 'policy categories' approach also risks reifying categories which may have been created for policy purposes but have far less empirical or analytical relevance (Zetter 1991). However, as a starting point for understanding a largely under-researched area, the book chooses to sacrifice parsimony for empirical depth.

The selection of contributing authors to the book is also a reflection of the desire for empirical depth. Rather than inviting political scientists or international relations scholars with a little or no knowledge of the empirical side of international migration, the book draws together scholars from a range of social science backgrounds who have in common an in-depth empirical knowledge of a given aspect of international migration. The authors have in common a background in migration studies rather than in international relations, and come from backgrounds in law, geography, anthropology, sociology, economics, political science, and international relations. The intention is that, as well as offering stand-alone overviews of the global governance of different areas of migration, the chapters will provide a rigorous and well-informed starting point which will serve as a starting point for more conceptual work on the global governance and international politics of migration.

Each of the empirical chapters in the book attempts to respond to the same three broad sets of questions, relating to the institutional, political, and normative dimensions of global migration governance. Firstly, on an institutional level, the chapters attempt to identify how states' behaviour is regulated at the global level. They explore three broad questions in relation to each area of migration:

1. What is the institutional framework regulating migration?
2. Why politically do these institutions exist in this way?
3. How normatively can one ground claims for or against alternative forms of institutionalized cooperation?

These questions are the logical building blocks on which any meaningful debate about global migration governance needs to take place. In relation to the first, until we have a conceptual understanding of what the existing institutional framework governing migration looks like, and what global migration governance is, it is not possible even to frame a debate about it. In relation to the second, until we understand the politics underlying different areas of migration, it is not possible to have a sense of the boundaries of the possible and the obstacles that might exist to reform. In relation to the third, until we have a basis on which to understand the assumptions, goals, and implicit trade-offs underlying different claims about migration governance, arguments about 'better' global governance will be arbitrary. Hence, far from being obscure and purely academic questions, these are the issues that must be resolved before a coherent vision for policy and practice can emerge.

The next three sections set out the questions in more detail and provide an overview of the institutional, political, and normative dimensions of global migration governance. They also set out the analytical tools available to shed light on these different aspects of global migration governance.

The institutions of global migration governance

The first and arguably most important task of the book is to map out global migration governance. There is a need to outline the institutional framework that regulates states' responses to the different areas of international migration. What are the core norms and actors in global migration governance? How important are different levels of governance? What are the different multilateral, regional, inter-regional, and bilateral institutions that shape governance? What role does the global governance of other issue-areas such as trade, human rights, and health play in regulating migration? To what extent are the institutions that regulate states' migration policies formal or informal? What are the most relevant actors in the governance of each area of migration? Which international organizations (IOs) and non-state actors (NSAs) are involved in agenda-setting, negotiation, implementation, monitoring, and enforcement of global migration governance?

This section provides an overview of institutions of global migration governance. It argues that in order to make sense of global migration governance, it is conceptually useful to identify three different levels at which it exists. It has become increasingly common to argue that there is no or limited global migration governance. While it may be true to suggest that global migration governance within a formal multilateral and UN context remains limited, and that progress on the 'migration and development' debate within the UN has been limited, this is not a basis on which to claim that there is no global migration governance. It is simply of a different and arguably more complex type than many issue-areas in which more neatly compartmentalized regimes emerged in the post-Second World War context. Indeed, it is possible to conceive of global migration governance as existing at three principal levels.

Multilateralism

There is no UN Migration Organization and no explicit migration regime (Ghosh 2000; Bhagwati 2003; Koser 2010). There are also very few binding multilateral treaties in the area of migration. However, although formal multilateral cooperation on migration is limited, the issue-area nevertheless does have elements of a thin multilateralism. These exist at two levels. Firstly, there is a basic multilateral framework—with its origins in the Inter-War Year period—regulating states' behaviour in relation to refugees, international travel, and labour migration. Secondly, there is a more recent and emerging form of 'facilitative multilateralism' which does not aspire to create formal multilateral collaboration but serves to enable states to engage in dialogue and information-sharing as a means through which to develop predominantly bilateral cooperation.

Koslowski (forthcoming) divides the global governance of migration into three broad 'global mobility regimes': the refugee, international travel, and labour migration regimes. He suggests that the former has the most developed multilateralism, the latter the least, with travel somewhere in between. However, in many ways, each of these regimes does provide a layer of multilateral global migration governance, primarily based on the legacy of cooperation initially developed in the Inter-War Years period. In each case, there are formal inter-state agreements and overseeing international organizations.

Firstly, the global refugee regime, based on the 1951 Convention on the Status of Refugees and the role of United Nations High Commissioner for Refugees (UNHCR), is arguably the strongest formal of formalized cooperation on migration (Loescher 2001; Loescher et al. 2008). It is the only area of migration with a specialized UN agency and a near universally ratified treaty that constrains states' sovereign discretion in their admissions policies. Secondly, the international travel regime, insofar as it is a regime, has developed common standards for passports and visas. Over time, cooperation on technical standards relating to travel document security has become ever more complex. The International Civil Aviation Organization (ICAO) has played an increasingly important role in standard setting at the multilateral level (Salter forthcoming; Koslowski forthcoming). Thirdly, the labour migration regime, although extremely limited, is nevertheless underpinned by a range of labour standards developed through the ILO treaties. In labour governance, the ILO has concluded a range of conventions relating to labour rights since its creation in 1919, which set out standards and principles on how states can treat labour—including migrant labour. In 1998, the ILO Labour Conference adopted the Declaration on Fundamental Principles and Rights at Work, which consolidated many of the previous ILO Conventions. In 2005, ILO produced the ILO Multilateral Framework on Labour Migration, as a non-binding framework for ensuring migrants' access to rights. Furthermore, the organization has an in-house unit focusing on migration called 'MIGRANT'. However, the formal treaty framework on the rights of migrant workers remains limited, being confined to the 1990 UN Convention on All Migrant Workers and Their Families, which so far has limited ratifications from migrant-receiving states.

What is notable about all of these three areas, though, is that while they have all developed and evolved over time, the formal multilateral cooperation that exists has its origins in the Inter-War Years. The most prolific era of the ILO was prior to the Second World War, when it was one of the largest and most influential of international organizations. The basis of the passport regime—which underpins the entire notion of a travel regime—was established before the Second World War. The origins of the refugee regime can also be traced to the Inter-War Years and the League of Nations High Commissioner for Refugees (LNHCR). New multilateral cooperation has built only incrementally on these long-standing agreements but in many ways has adapted conservatively. Even in the three global mobility regimes, powerful states have rarely sought to delegate additional authority in the areas of migration to a binding, multilateral framework.

In addition to these formal multilateral agreements, overseen by normative international organizations, a new and slightly different form of what might be called 'facilitative multilateralism' has emerged. The most notable forums for facilitative multilateralism have been some aspects of IOM's work and through the role of the GFMD. In neither case has there been any significant attempt to develop binding, multilateral norms on migration. However, both play a role—at the multilateral level—in enabling states to develop predominantly bilateral forms of cooperation.

IOM was created in 1950; however, since the 1990s it has grown rapidly from being a small members' organization for migrant-receiving states to being the most prominent international organization working on international migration. It is not a UN agency, and it does not have fully inclusive membership. It therefore has no normative basis for its work in the form of either a clear mandate or regime in the way that most UN organizations do. It exists mainly as a service provider to states, working on specific projects according to the demands and priorities of donor states. In many ways, IOM's approach is nearer to a private firm than a typical international organization. Beyond meeting its own institutional aims and providing services to meet states' own interests, it has very little normative vision of its own. One of the areas in which IOM has, however, acted very much like a typical international organization is in attempting to facilitate bilateral cooperation on migration, through enabling Northern donors to fund specific capacity-building projects in mainly Southern states.

Although it only began in 2007, the GFMD has become the most visible and high profile forum for inter-state dialogue on migration. It held its first meeting in Brussels in 2007 with the participation of 156 states and has subsequently met in Manila in 2008, Athens in 2009, and Mexico City in 2010. The Forum is formally outside of the UN system but is linked to it through the role if the UN Special Representative of the Secretary General on Migration and Development, who holds a responsibility for promoting the Forum. The focus of its work is not migration per se but rather 'Migration and Development', covering issues relating to remittances, 'brain drain', circular migration, and the relationship between migrant rights and development, for example. The Forum is not intended to result in formal inter-state agreements but rather aims to facilitate information-sharing and dialogue. It is a 'behind closed doors' dialogue and the Forum has no permanent secretariat, instead being run by a troika of current, past, and present host states with the support of a 'light support structure' provided by IOM. The GFMD can be conceived as a type of 'facilitative multi-lateralism' insofar as its purpose is not to develop multilateral cooperation per se but rather to enable like-minded states to develop bilateral partnerships on the basis of prior GFMD discussions.

Embeddedness

Although there is relatively limited formal multilateralism in the area of migration, this is not to say that there is limited global migration governance. Indeed, much of global migration governance is not explicitly labelled as 'migration' but nevertheless regulates how states can and do behave in relation to migration. Much of global governance, in issue-areas such as trade, security, and human rights, predates the post-Cold War international focus on migration. Rather than arriving on the international scene with an institutional blank slate, debate on international migration takes place against the backdrop of the extensive pre-existing structures of global governance that have emerged since the Second World War. In contrast to 1945, when much of the existing UN-based multilateral framework emerged, new issues and problems that arise at the international level are subject to the regulation and politics of a dense, pre-existing institutional framework. While these pre-existing institutions may not be explicitly labelled as covering 'migration', migration is nevertheless often implicitly regulated by these institutions.

The concept of 'embeddedness' is widely used in anthropology to refer to a situation when an area of social life does not exist as a recognized and compart-mentalized area but is an integrated part of the larger social system. In many communities, anthropologists have argued that issue-areas such as the 'economy' or 'law' do not exist as an explicitly identifiable or atomistic area of society but are instead an integrated part of a larger social structure (Sahlins 1974; Appadurai 1986; Wilk 1996). For example, people in a particular community may not be able to point to a particular area of social life called the 'economy' but it may instead be an integrated and implicit part of the community. The concept can be analogously applied to global governance to highlight situations in which there may be limited explicit governance in an issue-area but in which that issue-area is nevertheless implicitly regulated by institutions that were created to regulate other issue-areas.

At the level of norms, states' response to migration is regulated by their obligations in a host of other areas. A range of areas of public international law shape the boundaries of acceptable state behaviour in the area of migration.

International human rights law, international humanitarian law, WTO law, maritime law, labour law, for example, all represent important elements of global migration governance. It is as a result of these embedded institutions that some international lawyers have argued that one may conceive of the existence of international migration law (IML) based on these pre-existing bodies of law (Cholewinski et al. 2007). In that regard, Alexander Aleinikoff (2007) has spoken of the global governance of migration as comprising 'substance without architecture' insofar as the norms exist but they have no coherent institutional framework to apply them. The chapters in this volume serve to illustrate the embedded nature of the normative framework regulating states' responses to migration. The global governance of high-skilled labour migration draws upon WTO law through General Agreement on Trade in Services (GATS) Mode 4; the global governance of environmental migration draws heavily upon a range of other areas of public international law, not least international human rights law; remittances are indirectly shaped by the global governance of security; the root causes of migration are shaped by the governance of development, trade, and security.

At the deepest level, the sovereign state system defined by the seventeenth century Peace of Westphalia shaped the nature of how states perceive international migration by defining the nation-state structure that constitutes the very idea of international migration. Sovereignty represents the constitutive norm of the international system and creates the concept of exclusive political community, on which the very concept of international migration is premised. Without the system of institutions—including, for example, Article 2(4) and 2(7) of the UN Charter—that uphold the primacy of state sovereignty, states would not have a basis on which to legitimate the limitations that most states place on human mobility (Biersteker and Weber 1996).

In trade governance, the WTO's General Agreement on Trade in Services attempts to prevent WTO member states from discriminating against service providers on the basis of their country of origin. It sets out four 'Modes', which relate to four major groups of services. Mode 4 focuses on the temporary movement of natural persons—services are provided by individuals abroad (e.g. consultants travelling across borders) (Martin 2003). WTO GATS Mode 4 is unique in that it relates to the movement of individual service providers across borders and so implies a potentially binding obligation on states to admit non-nationals on to their territory (Lavenex 2003). In practice, Mode 4 is so far very limited in scope, applying only to a narrow group of people. Firstly, it is not 'a high-skilled migration clause' but is confined to temporary, skilled, contractual service providers engaged in intra-firm movement. Secondly, it is limited to the specific visa commitments that individual states are prepared to make in the context of broader WTO negotiations. Indeed up to now, these commitments have been extremely limited. However, it is often argued to have great potential to be expanded because of the binding and supranational nature of WTO commitments.

Similarly, even though states rarely openly acknowledge the fact, they have obligations to ensure that migrants' human rights are upheld. All international human rights law treaties have application to migrants just as they do to all other human beings. Meanwhile, customary international norms such as the principle of *non-refoulement* have application beyond 'recognized refugees'. These rights include the procedural guarantees to have access to legal recourse and to be able to appeal against unfair or discriminatory treatment, which migrants so often lack access to. International human rights law therefore implies significant state obligations towards all migrants. Increasingly, there is recognition that these rights and obligations exist but that existing institutions often fail to ensure that those rights are met.

At the level of international organizations, the mandates of a host of pre-existing UN agencies and non-UN agencies may not explicitly mention migration but indirectly touch upon migration. The cross-cutting and embedded nature of migration means it connects in different ways to the mandates of many international organizations from a variety of different perspectives. Migration is not only the domain of the most obvious organizations—IOM, ILO, and UNHCR—but also intersects with the work of other less obvious agencies. For example, the Office of the High Commissioner for Human Rights is interested in migration because migrants have human rights; United Nations Population Fund works on migration insofar as it touches upon issues relating to demography and fertility; United Nations Programme on HIV/AIDS touches on migration because migrants sometimes have HIV/AIDS; United Nations Institute for Training and Research has developed a role in migration because of the need for state diplomats and UN officials to receive training in an emerging and complex area; the World Bank has developed a concern with migration insofar as there is an empirical link between economic growth and, for example, remittances and circular migration. The existence of so many actors whose work tangentially relates to migration makes inter-agency coordination all the more complicated. It means that a host of agencies participate in the various coordination mechanisms that have emerged for inter-agency dialogue on migration (such as the Global Migration Group or the UNDESA Annual Coordination Meeting on International Migration), rendering coordination particularly challenging.

Given the pre-existing institutional frameworks, there has been a strong and emerging tendency towards not creating new, binding structures but towards working within the existing ones. On a normative level, as states have resisted the creation of new multilateral treaties, there has been a move towards 'soft law' frameworks. In other words, states and non-state actors have generally not sought to create new norms from scratch but have instead interpreted and consolidated the application of existing areas of law in relation to migration. The Guiding Principles on Internal Displacement serve as the archetypal example of this. Rather than seeking a new international treaty on IDPs, non-state actors consolidated existing international human rights law and international humanitarian law standards in a single document, which then became independently influential in influencing states' behaviour towards migration. The creation of IML similarly represents a form of soft law insofar as it is based on the application and consolidation of existing standards in other areas. Discussions of responses to environmental displacement and the proposal for a set of Guiding Principles on the Protection of Vulnerable Irregular Migrants further highlight the scope for developing soft law out of embedded governance. The advantage of the soft law approach is that it is more politically acceptable than the creation of 'hard law', and may nevertheless later acquire the status of hard law either through its incorporation within domestic law or providing a framework for subsequent international agreements. The principal disadvantage is that even though the underlying norms may be binding, the consolidated framework is, by definition, non-binding (Betts 2010a).

Organizationally, this trend in the emergence of creating soft law has been complemented by the development of new coordination mechanisms between international agencies. Rather than working towards the creation of a new UN migration organization, for example, the trend has been to work within the existing tapestry of international organizations and to develop a division of responsibility that can address emerging problems through existing organizations. This has taken place with respect to specific areas of migration. The Guiding Principles on IDPs, for example, has been implemented through a 'cluster' approach that divides responsibility for humanitarian affairs between different agencies. Similarly, in the area of irregular migration, informal partnerships between agencies such as IOM and UNHCR have arisen in specific geographical contexts. Meanwhile, at the overarching level, the Global Migration Group, for example, was created in 2007 in order to offer a space of inter-agency dialogue on migration across the UN system, in the hope of improving coordination.

Trans-regionalism

In the absence of formal multilateral governance and given a lack of clarity over the application of embedded governance, states are increasingly developing a range of migration partnerships to collectively address migration. These types of partnership are arising at the bilateral, regional, and inter-regional levels; some are formal and others based on informal networks. Many of them have a significant North–South dimension, whether because they involve direct inter-regional cooperation, or because South–South cooperation is supported by Northern funding. Collectively the emerging tapestry of bilateral, regional, and inter-regional structures can be described as trans-regional governance.

Trans-regional governance can be defined as 'sets of formal and informal institutions that cut across and connect different geographical regions, constituting or constraining the behaviour of states and non-state actors in a given policy field' (Betts 2010b). It is not reducible to 'inter-regionalism' insofar as it need not necessarily involve an inclusive dialogue between representatives of different regions. Instead, it may involve both inclusive and exclusive structures linking regions through a combination of regional, inter-regional, and bilateral norms and forums. The actors involved in trans-regional governance may be regional, state, or non-state representatives. Trans-regionalism offers a useful concept for capturing the proliferation of cross-cutting institutions that have emerged to regulate relations between migration sending, receiving, and transit regions, in particular. It is a type of governance that is arguably increasingly important in the context of Northern states' attempts to regulate irregular flows within and from the South.

At both the informal and the formal level, global migration governance exists at a number of different levels: regional, inter-regional, bilateral, and even unilateral. The norms and forums that exist at each of these levels are cross-cutting and intersect (Raustiala and Victor 2004; Alter and Meunier 2009; Gehring and Oberthur 2009). The international politics of migration is shaped not only by each of these different levels having an independent effect but also by their interaction. The role of trans-regionalism can be explained by looking in turn at the role of regionalism, informal regional dialogues, and bilateral cooperation.

The region is an increasingly important political unit in relation to migration. Regional Economic Communities (RECs) have emerged around the world. As they have developed regional integration in relation to the movement of goods, services, and capital, so too many have worked to facilitate the movement of labour. This shift towards free movement within regional communities has in turn also led to increasing attempts to develop a common external migration policy. Indeed, this model has been most notably pursued by the European Union (EU), which, as well as liberalizing movement within the EU, has developed a strong common external border (Geddes 2003; Koslowski 2004; Lahav 2004). Unlike most other regions, the EU has also sought to develop an external dimension to its migration and asylum policy, as a means to develop greater extra-territorial authority over the movement of people to its territory (Haddad 2008; Levy 2010; Kunz et al. 2011).

As well as formal regionalism, informal regional dialogues—called Regional Consultative Processes (RCPs)—have become one of the main features of global migration governance. The first RCP is widely regarded to have been the Inter-Governmental Consultations on Asylum, Refugees and Migration (IGC), created in 1985 by sixteen destination countries in the industrialized world, with a permanent secretariat, in order to facilitate information-sharing initially in relation to asylum and now, increasingly, in relation to migration in general. The RCP 'model' is based on a group of states—which may not necessarily be part of the same geographical region—engaging in regular, informal, behind-closed-doors dialogue on migration. The purpose is not to develop formal or binding agreements but to facilitate the development of 'best practices', information-sharing, and the adoption of common standards. During the last twenty years, the RCP model has spread to nearly every region in the world, with the development of, for example, the Regional Consultative Mechanism (RCM) for Central America, Mexico, and the United States; the Budapest Process for Eastern Europe; the Bali Process for Australia and South-East Asian states; the Colombo Process; the Abu Dhabi Process; the Mediterranean '5 plus 5' Process; the International Dialogue on Migration in West Africa (MIDWA); and the International Dialogue on Migration in Southern African (MIDSA) (Nielsen 2007; Hansen 2010; Koehler 2011).

Many of the early RCPs such as the IGC, the Budapest Process, and the RCM emerged *sui generis*, being the initiative of the participating states. However, an increasing number have been 'externally driven', with funding, training, and secretariats being provided by states from outside the RCP region. For example, for regional dialogues in Sub-Saharan African RCPs such as in the Southern African Development Community, Intergovernmental Authority on Development, and East African Community regions, much of the funding and agenda-setting have come from European states and been channelled through IOM (Betts 2010*b*). Indeed, IOM has played a significant role as an intermediary in disseminating the RCP model to many parts of the world. Rather than simply being a forum for dialogue, the RCP model has also served as a means through which models of 'best practice' and capacity-building—especially in relation to irregular migration management—have been disseminated from North to South.

In addition to these structures of regional cooperation, a host of cross-cutting bilateral relationships have emerged, often connecting states across regions. To take the example of Europe and Africa, the EU, for example, has developed a so-called Global Approach, within which it has initiated partnership agreements with third countries that cut across three areas of migration: circular migration, migration and development, and irregular migration (Kunz et al. 2011; Nellen-Stucky 2011). Meanwhile, most individual EU member states have developed bilateral partnerships with preferred African state partners in areas ranging from readmission to circular migration. Notable examples include strong bilateral partnerships on migration between Denmark and Kenya, France and Mali, the United Kingdom and Tanzania, the United Kingdom and Ethiopia, Italy and Libya, Spain and Senegal, France and Senegal, Switzerland and Nigeria, Portugal and Cape Verde, Spain and Morocco, and the EU and South Africa.

The politics of global migration governance

Aside from identifying the institutions that regulate states' responses to migration, the book also tries to characterize the politics of international migration. It asks what configuration of interests, power, and ideas explains the existing institutional framework and determines the international politics of each area of migration. In particular, the book asks why migration is regulated as it is? What have been the historical and political circumstances that have led each area of migration to be regulated in the way that it is? What have been the barriers and impetuses to greater international cooperation? Understanding the politics of each area of migration is important in order to identify the 'boundaries of the possible' for change, and the nature of the cooperation problems that need to be overcome.

In order to explore what drives the politics of international migration, and the prospects for inter-state cooperation, a number of concepts can be drawn from international relations. In particular, one could expect to find an explanation for the types of international cooperation that exist, and their consequences, by looking at interests, power, and ideas. However, these core international relations concepts have rarely been applied to migration. Consequently, the meaning of the concepts of 'interests', 'power', and 'ideas' in relation to the international politics of migration needs to be unpacked to develop a set of concepts to explain why global migration governance is structured in the way that it is.

Interests

International relations attempts to explore where states' preferences come from and how the so-called 'national interest' emerges. It is an important question for global governance because it defines the prospects for mutually beneficial international cooperation. However, identifying and explaining how states define their interests in relation to the international politics of migration is complicated and challenging. Rationalist approaches to international relations tend to assume that the nation-state can be conceived as a 'black box' which can be assumed to be interested in maximizing its own interests (Waltz 1979; Keohane 1984).

This type of approach offers some analytical utility in relation to international migration. States might be assumed to formulate their migration policies on the basis of attempting to maximize their economic and security interests. They attempt to attract 'desirable migrants' who meet the economy's labour market needs, while deterring 'undesirable migrants' who offer little economic benefit and who are perceived to be a threat to that society's security (conceived in the broadest sense). A heuristic starting point might then be to regard states' interests in international politics as being based on maximizing their economic and security interests. Where these interests are best met through international cooperation, one might expect a state to have a preference for cooperation; where they are best met through competition, one might expect as preference for competition.

However, in the area of international migration, it is also clear that states' interests are significantly determined by intra-state politics and there is a need to look within the state. Lobbying and interest group formation within the state play an important role in determining states' positions within the international politics of migration (Moravcsik 1997). Indeed, a political economy approach to the international politics of migration would recognize the need to disaggregate the state and explore the different interests emerging within domestic politics and through the role of the private sector (Drezner 2007). This poses a challenge that if one is to understand the international politics of migration, there is a need to identify the sub-state actors that define the positions of the powerful migration states. It is also important to be aware that in the area of international migration, states' interests may also be strongly influenced by the politics of other issue-areas. Indeed, migration policy may be closely intertwined with interests relating to security, development, and human rights (Betts 2008). Similarly, interests in relation to one area of migration may shape the politics of another area of migration. For example, the politics of asylum and refugee protection has been increasingly shaped by states' interests in relation to irregular migration.

There is also a need to take into account the interests of international organizations themselves. UNHCR, IOM, and ILO have their own institutional interests, which have helped to shape global migration governance. As bureaucracies, they have not simply implemented the preferences of states but have also had their own institutional strategies (Barnett and Finnemore 2004). For example, at different times they have attempted to expand their organizational size and the scope of their work, sometimes competing with one another for authority in relation to different areas of migration. The interests that matter for global migration governance will vary in different areas of migration. However, what is clear is that, in most areas, they involve a complex range of actors and different sets of interests. To understand which interests become relevant and influential, there is a need to explore the role of power.

Power

Power is central to understanding the international politics of migration. As with other areas of world politics, the international politics of migration can be conceived to be 'anarchical', in the sense that there is no overarching global authority. Consequently, states can engage in self-help and attempt to maximize their own interests subject to the constraints created by the behaviour of other states. In many other issue-areas, coherent multilateral institutions serve as an additional constraint on the self-interested behaviour of states.

In the case of the international politics of migration, the absence of a coherent and comprehensive multilateral governance framework means that states can competitively act in their own self-interest. Rather than being constrained by any clear institutional framework, powerful states are able to define their migration policies in accordance with their interests. They can admit the migrants they regard as 'good migrants' and reject the migrants they regard as 'bad migrants'. They will determine their migration policies on the basis of reconciling their economic and security interests.

Within this context, 'power' in the international politics of migration is closely related to states' structural position on a predominantly migrant 'receiving' or 'sending' states. Migrant-receiving states are generally able to determine their own migration policies in accordance with their own interests. Migrant-sending states are generally unable to influence the policy choices of receiving states. In that sense, in the absence of formal regulation, receiving states are the implicit 'makers' of migration governance and sending states are 'takers' of migration governance. This fundamental power asymmetry plays out in both North–South relations on migration as well as in the dynamics within regions, in which regional hegemons are often able to shape regional migration governance on their own terms if they are the preponderant 'receiving state'.

This conception of 'migration power' as based on the sending–receiving dichotomy offers a useful heuristic framework for understanding why many receiving states are opposed to formal multilateral norms on migration, while many sending states are supportive of multilateral institutions. However, it is also important to be aware that the sending–receiving distinction is a false dichotomy, and that in practice, many states are sending, receiving, and transit countries. Furthermore, it is not necessarily the case that migrant-sending states are powerless to influence receiving states. Indeed, strategies such as using transnational actors such as the diaspora (Court 2009) or engaging in issue-linkage within inter-state bargaining (Betts 2009) may partly mitigate stark sending–receiving power asymmetries.

Ideas

It is also important to be aware that ideas also shape the international politics of migration. States' (and other actors') interests are not fixed but change in accordance with the ideas they hold about the world. Rather than assuming ideas and hence interests are fixed and immutable, it is worth understanding ideas as malleable and constitutive of states' interests because it opens up analytical space for understanding why governance is structured as it is and the conditions under which it might be conceived differently.

The way in which states understand the nature of the migration 'problem' is influential in terms of how they approach the international politics of migration. 'Cost' and 'benefit' are ultimately socially constructed, and this is especially the case in the area of migration. Media, public information, advocacy, and political campaigns, for example, all shape the underlying basis of how states understand 'interests' in the area of migration. Recognizing this is especially important in the context of global migration governance, in which the core aims of governance and the 'boundaries of the possible' are significantly shaped by the ideas held by electorates in migrant-receiving states. It opens up the possibility that a core aspect of actors such as international organizations can be to play an epistemic role in shaping dominant ideas.

Furthermore, the way in which migration is understood is commonly in terms of assumed ideas about its relationship to other issue-areas. Migration governance is frequently debated in the context of 'migration and . . . ' debates. The 'migration and development', 'environmental migration', and 'mixed migration' debates, for example, represent the main 'nexuses' or 'nexi' in which migration is discussed. In most cases, the relationships between migration and these other issue-areas (development, environment, and security) are not objective causal relationships but are based on dominant sets of ideas that are influential in shaping and framing academic and policy debates (de Haas 2007; Betts 2010c; Nicholson 2010).

Moreover, it is also important to recognize that different ideas may be subjectively held by different states on migration. What 'migration' means for China, India, Europe, or the United States is not identical and hence the absence of a common understanding of the issue represents a barrier to multilateral cooperation. To take an example, in the context of the Abu Dhabi Process, it became apparent that there is no word in Arabic for 'migration' other than with connotations of permanence and citizenship. In debates on temporary labour migration, it was therefore necessary for IOM to adjust its conceptual language and use the term 'mobility' instead. These types of regional variation in perception have important implications for international cooperation that have often been neglected by Western academic approaches to international politics (Acharya 1997; Acharya and Buzan 2009; Tickner and Waever 2009).

The normative implications of global migration governance

So what would be the case for developing alternative forms of global migration governance? How would this case for a multilateral regime differ from the normative case for the flexible, fragmented, and multi-level status quo? In order to make normative judgements about competing claims about the value of competition versus institutionalization at the international level, international relations has traditionally drawn upon economics to make the 'efficiency' case for international institutions. However, over time it has recognized that other alternative normative criteria can be used to evaluate global governance. Four types of criteria offer a useful starting point for making normative claims about global migration governance: efficiency, equity, legitimacy, or rights-based grounds. The real challenge in applying these types of criteria is not only to identify the case for 'more' or 'less' global governance but also to identify *what kind* of institutionalized cooperation is normatively most desirable.

Efficiency

In international relations, the case for institutionalized international cooperation is generally based on efficiency (Keohane 1984). The efficiency case for global governance is analogous to the case for government intervention at the domestic level. At the domestic level, economists assume that the free market will maximize collective welfare by ensuring that all resources are efficiently allocated through the market mechanism. However, they also recognize that 'market failure' can arise when a society is not at its most efficient point (Pareto Optimality) in the absence of a regulatory framework.

Market failure most commonly occurs when the full costs and benefits of a given actor's choices do not accrue to that actor but are passed on, as positive or negative externalities, to other actors that are not included in the decision-making. The problem with negative externalities is that, in the absence of a regulatory framework, an actor will have little incentive to take into account the negative impact of their choices on other actors, even if the gain to the decision-maker is small and the cost to the other actors is large. The potential problem with positive externalities is that if the benefits of a given choice accrue to a range of actors, while the costs are exclusively borne by the decision-maker, there will be little incentive for actors to individually provide the good in question. An individual actor would be better off free-riding on another actor's choices.

In the case of both positive and negative externalities, society will be collectively worse off if the actors make their choices in isolation, or within a competitive environment, than they would be if they cooperated through the creation of a common regulatory framework. The domestic analogy of market failure has been applied to the realm of international politics to analyse situations in which states are collectively worse off acting in isolation than they would be if they developed institutionalized forms of cooperation.

The most common case of a need for global governance based on externalities arises when there are *global public goods*. A global public good, like street lighting at the domestic level, is one that, once provided, its benefits are non-excludable and non-rival between actors. Non-excludability refers to the notion that the benefits extend to all states irrespective of whether they contribute to its provision; non-rivalry refers to the notion that one state's consumption does not diminish that of another state. Because of the non-excludable nature of the benefits, in the absence of a strong institutional framework, states will have an incentive to free-ride on the contribution of other states and the good will be under-provided. This applies to, for example, climate change mitigation, creating a vaccine for polio, or the international monetary system. In these instances, even though all states value their provision, they will have little incentive to actually contribute to providing those goods. In the absence of an institutional framework to ensure reciprocity, the goods will be under-provided and states will be collectively worse off than they would have been had they cooperated to share the costs of providing the global public good (Kaul et al. 2003; Barrett 2007).

Some authors have tried to make the case that international migration—or the global governance of migration—represents a global public good (Hollifield 2008). This is not true. While the provision of refugee protection might be considered to be a global public good (albeit with asymmetrically distributed costs and benefits) insofar as states collectively value its provision but have little incentive to be the provider because of the partly non-excludable nature of the humanitarian and security benefits of protection, the same logic does not apply to labour migration, for example (Suhrke 1998; Betts 2003). This is because the costs and benefits of labour migration are at least partly excludable because they accrue almost exclusively to the admitting state, the country of origin, or both, but rarely to a wider group of states. Furthermore, there is little that is non-rival about international migration given that one state's decision to admit a given migrant generally prevents that migrant from simultaneously being admitted to another state at the same time.

However, this is not to say that there is no efficiency case for global migration governance based on externalities. There is a case; it is simply not based on global public goods theory per se. Rather, with the efficiency case comes the broader argument that states' migration policy decisions create *externalities*, albeit externalities that, unlike global public goods, do not accrue to all states simultaneously, but are more likely to be dyadic or have effects on small groups of states.

In the case of individual states' migration policy decisions, these inherently confer positive or negative externalities on other states. Because a decision by one state to admit a migrant is a decision that removes an individual from another state, and a decision to reject a migrant is a decision for that migrant to be in another state, migration policy decisions confer externalities. In other words, there is policy interdependence (Moravcsik 1997). For example, when individual migrant-receiving states make policy decisions about skilled labour immigration or the regulation of remittance, these choices have external consequences for the relevant migrant-sending state. Equally, when migrant-sending states make decisions about their policies towards their diaspora, these choices have implications for migrant-sending states.

The existence of policy interdependence and externalities resulting from policy decisions represents a normative basis for developing institutionalized cooperation insofar as it results in the choices that are made leading to outcomes that are sub-optimal in comparison to those that would have maximized the aggregate welfare of the society of states. Put simply, when states make decisions on migration in isolation, they impose externalities on one another and so increase their collective costs and reduce their collective benefits. Acting in isolation, states have little incentive to be concerned with the external costs they impose, while deriving external benefits is likely to make them free-ride on cooperation from other states. In contrast, if they were to cooperate rather than compete, they might be able to maximize the benefits of international migration and then redistribute these benefits in ways that made everyone better off.

However, this efficiency argument does not necessarily justify a formal, multilateral institutional framework. Rather it implies that the 'efficient' type of migration governance will depend on the nature and scope of the externalities involved. Where they are confined to just the sending state, the receiving state, and the migrant, for example, 'efficient' outcomes may result from bilateral cooperation. Where they are confined to a small group of states, 'efficient' outcomes may result from small groups of states engaging in cooperation—for example, on a regional basis.

Equity

Beyond efficiency, one might also build a case for different types of global migration governance based on equity. It is not only the case that states may be *collectively* worse off in a competitive environment, but it is also the case that the costs of inter-state competition are not distributed equitably. In the absence of formal multilateral governance, it is the relatively powerful states that are able to determine the basis of global migration governance. Powerful migrant-receiving states are able to take the migrants they want and leave the migrants they do not want. This essentially means that migrant 'receiving states' end up being the 'makers' of migration governance while migrant 'sending states' are the 'takers' of governance on the terms of the receiving states.

This inequity is especially acute in North–South relations on different aspects of migration. In the refugee regime, the majority of the world's refugees are hosted by Southern states, and there are no formal obligations on Northern states to contribute to 'burden-sharing' through resettlement or financial support. In the area of high-skilled labour migration, most movement is South–North rather than vice versa. In the area of low-skilled labour migration, Northern states can selectively include or exclude people from the South on their own terms. In the absence of formal institutional mechanisms to regulate the way in which powerful Northern states engage with migration in the South, the distributive outcomes of the status quo are arguably inequitable by most normative standards of global justice (Rawls 1972; Beitz 1979; Singer 2002; Pogge 2008).

Consequently, equity-based arguments relating to global migration governance are likely to offer different conclusions than efficiency-based arguments. Where, for example, an efficiency-based argument would identify limited value in creating binding multilateral norms in the absence of global public goods or global public bads, equity-based arguments are likely to favour more inclusive and multilateral forms of institutional arrangement, grounded in claims to distributive justice. Indeed, it is unsurprising that many claims by Southern states in discussions on the need for an inclusive, UN-based multilateral framework at, for example, the GFMD are based in appeals to equity.

Legitimacy

Buchanan and Keohane (2006) analyse the challenges of defining legitimacy in relation to global governance. For them, legitimacy can be seen in two ways. It has a *normative sense*—in terms of having 'the right to rule'—and a *sociological sense*—in terms of being 'widely believed to have the right to rule'. Both of these rely on criteria—the former on objective standards and the latter upon the judgement of an audience. At the national level, legitimacy is generally understood to rely upon public consent, the principal manifestation of which is democratic institutions. In global governance, democracy does not exist in the same way and it is less obvious who the polity is and who the audience should be. Legitimacy is therefore more challenging to define.

For Buchanan and Keohane, three basic options stand out as possible sources of legitimacy: state consent, democratic state consent, and global democracy. The important thing, though, they argue (2006: 417) is that global governance fulfils six basic minimum standards: (*a*) its existence must have a reasonable public basis, (*b*) it must not allow that extremely unjust institutions are legitimate, (*c*) it must be based on the ongoing consent of democratic states, (*d*) it should promote the values that underlie democracy, (*e*) it should reflect the dynamic character of global governance by allowing for change and renegotiation, (*f*) it must overcome two key problems: (i) the problem of bureaucratic discretion and (ii) the tendency that democracies have to disregard the legitimate interests of outsiders, which is all the more problematic at the global level.

Indeed, legitimacy is a particularly important concept in the context of global migration governance. In order to be effective, structures of migration governance need to be procedurally recognized as 'having the right to rule'. The criteria set out by Buchanan and Keohane are particularly applicable in this regard and highlight a core trade-off within migration governance: on the one hand, legitimacy requires carrying public support but on the other hand, it requires that those institutions also promote just outcomes and safeguard the rights of 'outsiders' such as migrants who may not have access to forms of procedural or legal recourse.

Rights

Migration is not just about states. It is also about people, both citizens and migrants. An important normative criterion by which to judge migration governance is the extent to which it respects the rights of individuals.

Few migration policies represent a serious threat to the most fundamental rights of citizens, unless they compromise security or lead to very extreme levels of economic, social, and cultural change. However, many migration policies have implications for the human rights of migrants. At the most extreme end of the spectrum, refugees flee conflict or political persecution and the willingness of states to allow them access to territory can be justified on the grounds that it is the only means by which to ensure they have access to a set of fundamental human rights.

However, rights-based justifications for different types of migration governance are not confined to refugees and other groups of forced migrants. Rather, they apply to some degree across the spectrum of migration. Even though it is not always recognized by states, all migrants—as human beings—have human rights. Above a certain threshold of rights violation in an individual's country of origin, this might create a strong normative claim to international protection and sanctuary, whether for refugees or other groups fleeing desperate situations. Even if the situation in the country of origin does not reach this threshold, all migrants nevertheless have an entitlement to be treated in a way that meets states' obligations under international human rights law.

One of the great challenges for global migration governance is to develop structures that are compatible with and reinforce the human rights of migrants. States have signed up to international human rights law obligations but operationalizing these in the context of migration creates a specific set of challenges. Many migrants do not have access to the treaty body mechanisms that are designed to ensure implementation of the human rights regime, and no alternative institutional mechanism has been created to ensure migrants' access to human rights, especially where they may be vulnerable but fall outside the framework of the refugee regime (Betts 2010*a*, 2010*d*). Rights-based arguments therefore offer significant support for the development of institutions that can address gaps in migrants' access to rights, whether at the national, regional, or multilateral level.

The chapters

Each of the chapters in the book addresses the global governance of a given area of international migration. Each of the authors has been chosen for his/her expertise in that particular area of migration. In order to divide international migration into analytically meaningful areas, the chapters address different 'policy categories' of migration: low-skilled labour migration, high-skilled labour migration, irregular migration, international travel, lifestyle migration, environmental migration, human trafficking and smuggling, asylum and refugee protection, internally displaced people, diaspora, remittances, and root causes. Although in reality migration does not neatly fit into these categories, taking policy categories offers a useful division of analytical labour. This is because, firstly, the different policy categories broadly reflect the different structures of global migration governance and, secondly, they partly reflect the division of academic expertise.

The chapters each address the same three broad areas outlined in this introduction, reflecting upon the institutional, political, and normative dimensions of the global governance of the different areas of international migration. The chapters are intended to offer a stand-alone introduction to the global governance and international politics of different aspects of international migration. However, they are also intended to represent a starting point for developing new analytical and conceptual tools for understanding global migration governance. The first set of chapters analyse different areas of labour migration (skilled and unskilled). The second considers other categories of 'voluntary' mobility (irregular migration and lifestyle migration). The third set examines categories of 'forced' migration (asylum and refugee protection, human smuggling and trafficking, and internal displacement). The fourth group reflects upon a range of new and emerging areas of global migration governance (environmental migration, remittances and the diaspora, and root causes). Finally, the book concludes by attempting to integrate the insights of the different empirical chapters. On an academic level, it attempts to unpack the insights of the book for understanding international politics and global governance of migration. On a policy level, it reflects upon what a normatively desirable and politically feasible global migration governance might look like.

References

Abbott, K. and Snidal, D. (2009) The Governance Triangle: Regulatory Standards Institutions and The Shadow of the State, in W. Mattli and N. Woods (eds), *The Politics of Global Regulation*, Princeton, NJ: Princeton University Press.

Acharya, A. (1997) Ideas, Identity, and Institution-Building: From the ASEAN Way to the Asia-Pacific Way? *The Pacific Review*, 10(3), 319–46.

——and Buzan, B. (2009) *Non-Western International Relations Theory: Perspectives on and Beyond Asia*, London: Routledge.

Aleinikoff, S. and Chetail, V. (eds) (2003) *Migration and International Legal Norms*, The Hague: T.M.C. Asser.

Aleinikoff, A. (2007) International Legal Norms on Migration: Substance without Architecture, in R. Cholewinski, R. Perruchoud, and E. MacDonald (eds), *International Migration Law: Developing Paradigms and Key Challenges*, The Hague: TMC Asser Press.

Alter, K. and Meunier, S. (2009) The Politics of Regime Complexity Symposium, *Perspectives on Politics*, 7(1), 13–24.

Appadurai, A. (ed.) (1986) *The Social Life of Things: Commodities in Cultural Perspective*, Cambridge: Cambridge University Press.

Axelrod, R. (1984) *The Evolution of Cooperation*, New York: Basic Books.

Barnett, M. and Finnemore, M. (2004) *Rules for the World*, Ithaca, NY: Cornell University Press.

Barrett, S. (2007) *Why Cooperate? The Incentive to Supply Global Public Goods*, Oxford: Oxford University Press.

Beitz, C. (1979) *Political Theory and International Relations*, Princeton, NJ: Princeton University Press.

Betts, A. (2003) Public Good Theory and the Provision of Refugee Protection: The Role of the Joint Product Model in Burden-Sharing Theory, *Journal of Refugee Studies*, 16(3), 274–96.

——(2008) North–South Cooperation in the Refugee Regime: The Role of Linkages, *Global Governance*, 14(2), 157–78.

——(2009) *Protection by Persuasion: International Cooperation in the Refugee Regime*, Ithaca, NY: Cornell University Press.

——(2010a) Towards a Soft Law Framework on the Protection of Vulnerable Irregular Migrants, *International Journal of Refugee Law*, 22(2), 209–36.

——(2010b) The Global Governance of Migration and the Role of Transregionalism, in R. Kunz, S. Lavenex and M. Panizzon (eds), *Multi-Layered Migration Governance: The Promise of Partnership*, London: Routledge.

——(2010c) Substantive Issue Linkage and the Politics of Migration, in C. Bjola and M. Kornprobst (eds), *Arguing Global Governance*, London: Routledge.

——(2010d) Survival Migration: A New Protection Framework, *Global Governance*, 16(3), 361–82.

Bhagwati, J. (2003) Borders Beyond Control, *Foreign Affairs*, 82(1), 98–104.

Biersteker, T. and Weber, C. (1996) *The Social Construction of Sovereignty*, Cambridge: Cambridge University Press.

Biersteker, T. and Hall, R. (eds) (2002) *The Emergence of Private Authority in Global Governance*, Cambridge: Cambridge University Press.

Buchanan, A. and Keohane, R. (2006) The Legitimacy of Global Governance Institutions, *Ethics and International Affairs*, 20(4), 405–37.

Busch, M. (2007) Overlapping Institutions, Forum Shopping, and Dispute Settlement in International Trade, *International Organization*, 61(4), 735–61.

Chayes, B. (1998) *The New Sovereignty: Compliance with International Regulatory Agreements*, Boston, MA: Harvard University Press.

Cholewinski, R., Perruchouf, R., and MacDonald, E. (eds) (2007) *International Migration Law: Developing Paradigms and Key Challenges*, The Hague: T.M.C. Asser.

Court, E. (2009) India as 'Rule-Taker' and 'Rule-Maker' in the Politics of International High Skilled Migration: Methodological Challenges Integrating What Happens Between, Within and Across States, Paper presented at the Graduate Research in Progress Seminars for the Social Sciences, May, Nuffield College, Oxford.

Drezner, D. (2007) *All Politics is Global*, Princeton, NJ: Princeton University Press.

Falkner, R. (2008) *Business Power and Conflict in International Environmental Politics*, Basingstoke: Palgrave Macmillan.

Fawcett, L. and Hurrell, A. (1996) *Regionalism in World Politics Regional Organization and International Order*, Oxford: Oxford University Press.

GCIM (2005) *Migration in an Interconnected World: New Directions for Action*, Geneva: GCIM.

Geddes, A. (2003) *The Politics of Migration and Immigration in Europe*, London: Sage.

Gehring, T. and Oberthur, S. (2009) The Causal Mechanisms of Interaction between International Institutions, *European Journal of International Relation*, 15(1), 125–56.

Ghosh, B. (2000) *Managing Migration: Time for a New International Regime?* Oxford: Oxford University Press.

Goldstein, J. et al. (2001) *Legalization and World Politics*, Cambridge: Cambridge University Press.

de Haas, H. (2007) Turning the Tide? Why Development Will Not Stop Migration, *Development and Change*, 38(5), 819–41.

Haddad, E. (2008) *The Refugee in International Society: Between Sovereigns*, Cambridge: Cambridge University Press.

Hansen, R. (2010) *An Assessment of Principal Regional Consultative Processes on Migration (RCPs)*, Geneva: IOM.

Hansen, R., Koehler, J., and Money, J. (eds) (2011) *Migration, Nation-States, and International Cooperation*, London: Routledge.

Hasenclever, A., Mayer, P., and Rittberger, V. (1997) *Theories of International Regimes*, Cambridge: Cambridge University Press.

Held, D. and McGrew, A. (eds) (2002) *Governing Globalization: Power, Authority and Global Governance*. London: Wiley-Blackwell.

Hollifield, J. (2004) The Emerging Migration State. *International Migration Review*, 38(3): 885–912.

Hollifield, J. (forthcoming) Migration as a Global Public Good, in R. Koslowski (ed.), *Global Mobility Regimes*.

Hurrell, A. (2007) *On Global Order*, Oxford: Oxford University Press.

Kaul, I. et al. (2003) *Providing Global Public Goods; Managing Globalization*, Oxford: Oxford University Press.

Keohane, R. (1984) *After Hegemony*, Princeton, NJ: Princeton University Press.

Kingsbury, B. (2009) The Concept of 'Law' in Global Administrative Law, *European Journal of International Law*, 20(1), 23–57.

Koehler, J. (2011) Regional Consultation Processes and Global Migration Management, in R. Kunz, S. Lavenex, and M. Panizzon (eds), *Multi-Layered Migration Governance: The Promise of Partnership*. London: Routledge.

Koremenos, B. et al. (eds) (2003) *The Rational Design of International Institutions*, Cambridge: Cambridge University Press.

Koser, K. (2010) International Migration and Global Governance, *Global Governance*, 16(3), 301–16.

Koslowski, R. (2000) *Migrants and Citizens: Demographic Change in the European State System*, Ithaca, NY: Cornell University Press.

Koslowski, R. (2004) *International Migration and the Globalisation of Domestic Politics*, London: Routledge.

Koslowski, R. (ed.) (forthcoming) *Global Mobility Regimes*.

Krasner, S. (1983) Structural Causes and Regime Consequences: Regimes as Intervening Variables, in S. Krasner (ed.), *International Regimes*, Ithaca, NY: Cornell University Press.

Kunz, R., Lavenex, S., and Panizzon, M. (eds) (2011) *Multi-Layered Migration Governance: The Promise of Partnership*. London: Routledge.

Lahav, G. (2004) *Immigration and Politics in the New Europe: Reinventing Borders*, Cambridge: Cambridge University Press.

Lavenex, S. (2003) Globalization, Trade and Migration: Towards the Dissociation of Immigration Politics? UCLA Ronald Burkle Center for International Relations Working Paper.

Levy, C. (2010) Refugees, Europe, Camps/State of Exception: 'Into The Zone', the European Union and Extraterritorial Processing of Migrants, Refugees, and Asylum-Seekers (Theories and Practice), *Refugee Survey Quarterly*, 29(1), 92–119

Loescher, G., Betts, A., and Milner, J. (2008) *UNHCR: The Politics and Practice of Refugee Protection into the 21st Century*, London: Routledge.

Loescher, G. (2001) *UNHCR in World Politics: The Perilous Path*, Oxford: Oxford University Press.

Martin (2003) Highly Skilled Labour Migration: Sharing the Benefits, ILO Working Paper, http://www.oit.org/public/english/bureau/inst/download/migration2.pdf.

Mattli, W. (1999) *The Logic of Regional Integration*, Cambridge: Cambridge University Press.

——(2003) Public and Private Governance in Setting International Standards, in M. Kahler and D. Lake (eds), *Governance in a Global Economy*, Princeton, NJ: Princeton University Press.

Moravcsik, A. (1997) Taking Preferences Seriously: A Liberal Theory of International Politics, *International Organization*, 51, 513–53.

Morgenthau, H. (1948) *Politics Among Nations*, New York: Knopf.

Nellen-Stucky, R. (2011) EU Mobility Partnerships as a New Tool to Manage Migration?, in R. Kunz, S. Lavenex, and M. Panizzon (eds), *Multi-Layered Migration Governance: The Promise of Partnership*. London: Routledge.

Newland, K. (2010) The Governance of International Migration: Mechanisms, Processes and Institutions, *Global Governance*, 16(3), 331–44.

Nicholson, C. (2010) A Critical Review of the Genesis, Context, Career, Impact and Validity of 'Environmental Migration' as a Policy-Relevant Concept, MPhil Thesis, Oxford University.

Nielsen, A.-G. (2007) Cooperation Mechanisms, in R. Cholewinski, R. Perruchoud and E. Macdonald (eds), *International Migration Law: Developing Paradigms and Key Challenges*, Cambridge: Cambridge University Press.

Olson, M. (1965) *The Logic of Collective Action*, Harvard: Cambridge.

Phuong, C. (2004) *The International Protection of Internally Displaced Persons*, Cambridge: Cambridge University Press.

Pogge, T. (2008) *World Poverty and Human Rights*, Cambridge: Polity.

Raustiala, K. and Slaughter, A.-M. (2002) International Law and Compliance, in W. Carlsnaes, T. Risse, and B. Simmons (eds), *Handbook of International Relations*, London: Sage.

Rawls, J. (1972) *Theory of Justice*, Oxford: Oxford University Press.

Rudolph, C. (2006) *National Security and Immigration: Policy Development in the United States and Western Europe Since 1945*, Stanford, CA: Stanford University Press.

Ruggie, J. (ed.) (1993) *Multilateralism Matters*, New York: Columbia University Press.

Ruggie, J. (2003) Taking Embedded Liberalism Global: The Corporate Connection, in D. Held and M. Koenig-Archibugi (eds), *Taming Globalization: Frontiers of Governance*, Cambridge: Polity Press.

Sadiq, K. (2008) *Paper Citizens: How Illegal Immigrants Acquire Citizenship in Developing Countries*, Oxford: Oxford University Press.

Sahlins, M. (1974) *Stone Age Economics*, London: Tavistock Publications.

Salter, M. (forthcoming) International Cooperation on Travel Document Security in the Developed World, in R. Koslowski (ed.), *Global Mobility Regimes*.

Scholte, J.-A. (2000) *Globalization: A Critical Introduction*, London: Palgrave.

Sell, S. (2003) *Private Power, Public Law*, Cambridge: Cambridge University Press.

Singer, P. (2002) *One World: The Ethics of Globalization*, New Haven: Yale University Press.

Suhrke, A. (1998) Burden-Sharing During Refugee Emergencies: The Logic of Collective Action versus National Action, *Journal of Refugee Studies*, 11(4), 396–415.

Tickner, A. and Waever, O. (2009) *International Relations Scholarship Around the World*, London: Routledge.

Waltz, K. (1979) *Theory of International Politics*, London: Prentice-Hall.

Walzer, M. (1983) *Spheres of Justice*, Oxford: Blackwell.

Weiner, M. (1995) *The Global Migration Crisis: Challenges to States and to Human Rights*, New York: Harper Collins Publishers.

Weiss, T. and Korn, D. (2007) *Internal Displacement*, London: Routledge.

Wilk, R. (1996) *Economies and Cultures: Foundations of Economic Anthropology*, Boulder, CO: Westview Press.

Woods, N. (2002) Global Governance and the Role of Institutions, in D. Held and A. McGrew (eds), *Governing Globalization: Power, Authority and Global Governance*, London: Wiley-Blackwell.

Zetter, R. (1991) Labelling Refugees: Forming and Transforming a Bureaucratic Identity, *Journal of Refugee Studies*, 4(1), 39–62.

Zolberg, A. R. (1989) The Next Waves: Migration Theory for a Changing World, *International Migration Review*, 23(3), 403–30.

1

Low-Skilled Labour Migration

Christiane Kuptsch and Philip Martin

Introduction

International labour migration moves about 100 million workers, 3 per cent of the global labour force, over national borders. There are three major groups of migrant workers: migrants from developing countries in industrial countries, 31 million; migrants from one developing country in another, 30 million; and migrants from one industrial country in another, 28 million.

Receiving countries normally determine who can enter and work for wages. The general policy in both industrial and developing countries that receive migrants is simple—the higher the worker's level of education and skill, the easier it is for the worker to enter and settle. Policies towards less-skilled workers are more diffuse, with traditional immigration countries welcoming some less-skilled workers as immigrants and others as guest workers, reluctant countries of immigration in Europe aiming to integrate low-skilled immigrants who have settled, and Asian countries such as Singapore with high shares of foreign workers in their labour force explicitly implementing 'welcome-the-skilled and rotate-the-unskilled' policies.

This chapter will first provide some background information about international migration and the scope of low-skilled labour migration. It will then examine what institutions and regulations govern low-skilled labour migration today before exploring the politics in this area. Certain institutions and actors call for more low-skilled international migration and see their role in increasing numbers while others emphasize that the most important goal is the protection of migrant workers.[1] This chapter will attempt to elucidate where these competing discourses and visions stem from. It will also examine the prospects for top-down global governance, for example, via a World Migration Organization (WMO), in the last section that reflects upon what is normatively desirable and might be politically feasible as an approach to low-skilled labour migration.

Background: low-skilled labour migration[2]

The number of international migrants is at an all time high. There were 191 million migrants in 2005, according to the United Nations (UN), meaning that 3 per cent of the world's people left their country of birth or citizenship for a year or more.[3] The largest flow of migrants is from less to more developed countries—the more developed countries have about 18 per cent of the world's population and 60 per cent of the world's migrants.

The less developed countries include major migration destinations, such as the Gulf oil exporters. There were 62 million developing country migrants in industrial countries in 2005, but almost as many migrants, 61 million, had moved from one developing country to another, as from Indonesia to Malaysia. There are also large flows of people from one industrial country to another, as from Canada to the United States, and much smaller flows from industrial to developing countries, as with Japanese who work or retire in Thailand (Table 1.1).

UN migrant stock data are based largely on national censuses, and the more developed and less developed categories are not the same as the World Bank's list of high- and low-income countries. Nonetheless, the UN data make clear that the migrant stock is rising fastest in more developed countries and that the decade between 1980 and 1990 saw the most rapid increase, as the number of migrants in more developed countries almost doubled. The apparent slow growth in the migrant stock of more developed countries between 2000 and 2005 may reflect lags in data reporting, since the US migrant stock alone increased by more than 5 million attributed to all more developed countries in this period (Table 1.2).

Most of the world's workers are less skilled. The world's labour force of 3.1 billion in 2005 included 600 million workers in the high-income countries and 2.5 billion in the lower income countries. Almost all labour force growth is projected to be in lower income countries: their labour force is projected to increase by about 825 million between 2000 and 2020, while the labour force in high-income countries is projected to remain stable at just over 600 million. The fact that the growth of the labour force in lower income countries exceeds the current size of the labour force in high-income countries makes clear that most of the world's workers are not likely to migrate to high-income

Table 1.1. International migrants in 2005 (millions)

Origin/destination	More developed	Less developed
More developed	53	14
Less developed	62	61

Source: UN Population Division (2006).
International Migration Report (2005). ST/ESA/SER.A/220.

Table 1.2. International migrants: 1960–2005 (millions)

	1960	1970	1980	1990	2000	2005	1980–2000
World	76	82	100	154	175	191	75%
More developed	32	38	48	90	110	115	131%
Less developed	44	43	52	64	65	75	24%
Changes		1960–70	1970–80	1980–90	1990–2000	2000–5	
World (%)		7	22	54	14	9	
More developed (%)		19	25	88	23	5	
Less developed (%)		-1	20	24	0	16	

Source: UN Population Division (2006).
More developed countries are in Europe and North America plus Australia, Japan, New Zealand, and the ex-USSR.

Table 1.3. World, Developed Country, Less Developed Country Economically Active Population (EAP) 1980–2020 ('000)

	1980	1985	1990	1995	2000
World EAP	1,929,556	2,160,150	2,405,619	2,604,941	2,818,456
More developed EAP	522,683	544,271	568,832	573,626	589,151
Less developed EAP	1,406,873	1,615,879	1,836,787	2,031,315	2,229,305
	2005	2010	2015	2020	
World EAP	3,050,420	3,279,373	3,481,270	3,651,283	
More developed EAP	604,521	613,388	611,392	602,977	
Less developed EAP	2,445,899	2,665,986	2,869,878	3,048,307	
Decade change	1980–90	1990–2000	2000–10	2010–20	
World EAP (%)	25	21	17	17	
More developed EAP (%)	9	5	4	5	
Less developed EAP (%)	31	26	21	20	

Source: ILO Laborsta, http://laborsta.ilo.org/.

countries, although some low-income countries may move into the ranks of the high-income (Table 1.3).

Institutions and regulations

This section lays out the institutions and regulations that govern low-skilled labour migration today.

ILO and UN: setting standards

The International Labour Organization (ILO), a tripartite body that includes representatives of employers, workers, and governments, is mandated to protect migrant workers. The ILO has been dealing with labour migration since its inception in 1919, and its constitutional mandate to protect migrant workers has been re-affirmed by the 1944 Declaration of Philadelphia and the 1998 ILO Declaration on Fundamental Principles and Rights at Work.[4]

The ILO is the organization most active in negotiating, implementing, and monitoring the enforcement of international norms that regulate the employment of low-skilled migrants. Most of the ILO's Conventions, such as the Freedom of Association and Protection of the Right to Organize Convention, 1948 (No. 87), do not distinguish between migrant and local workers, and thus protect migrant as well as local workers. The ILO considers eight of its Conventions to embrace core labour standards. The principles and rights that underlie these Conventions were reiterated in the Declaration on Fundamental Principles and Rights at Work in 1998.[5] Most member states of the ILO have ratified the core labour Conventions, which are in any event binding on ILO members.

The ILO approved two Conventions dealing with migrant workers that reflected the special circumstances of the times in which they were approved. ILO Convention 97 (1949), enacted after the Second World War and anticipating the uneven economic recovery of post-war Europe, sought to protect workers crossing national borders. Convention 97 defines a 'migrant for employment' as 'a person who migrates from one country to another with a view to being employed otherwise than on his own account', that is, the Convention excludes the self-employed.

The bedrock principle of Convention 97 is equality of treatment—migrant wage and salary workers should be treated like other workers in the countries in which they work.[6] Convention 97 aims to protect migrants and ensure equal treatment for them by encouraging countries to sign bilateral agreements[7] that spell out the terms under which workers can cross national borders for employment. These bilateral agreements are envisioned to be relatively detailed, spelling out procedures for private and public recruitment, having labour-sending and labour-receiving governments exchange information on migration policies and regulations, and foster cooperation between public and private agencies in both countries so that employers have accurate information on the migrant workers they hire and migrants have complete information on wages and working conditions abroad.

The second ILO migrant-specific Convention is No. 143 (1975), enacted after oil-price hikes led to recessions in the European countries that had been importing large numbers of guest workers. Convention 143 deals with migration that occurs in abusive conditions on the one hand (Part I) and with equality of opportunity and treatment and the integration of settled migrants on the other (Part II). Convention 143 emphasizes the steps ratifying governments must take to suppress clandestine movements of labour migrants and illegal employment of migrants. For example, it calls for sanctions on employers who hire unauthorized migrants and encourages international cooperation to reduce the smuggling of migrants, including the prosecution of smugglers in both source and destination countries. Convention 143 also calls for 'equality of treatment' in wages and other benefits for employed migrants.[8]

Convention 97 has been ratified by forty-eight states, and twenty-three states ratified Convention 143. There are several reasons why especially migrant-receiving member states seem reluctant to ratify these ILO Conventions, including the fact that some of their provisions may conflict with national legislation. For example, Article 14(a) of Convention 143 asserts that migrant workers should have the right to occupational mobility; most countries tie migrants to particular employers. ILO member states that ratify Conventions 97 and 143 often make exceptions for jobs dominated by migrants, such as farm workers and maids, so that these are excluded from national labour laws establishing minimum wages and other labour protections.

Even if migrant workers are protected by national labour laws that conform to ILO Conventions, they may be denied effective remedies if their rights are violated. For example, US labour law gives practically all private sector workers the right to form or join unions without employer interference. However, if an employer unlawfully fires an unauthorized worker in retaliation for union activities, the worker can be denied the normal remedy of reinstatement with back pay. The US Supreme Court in a 5-4 decision in the Hoffman Plastics case (2002) concluded that requiring employers to provide back pay to unlawfully fired unauthorized migrants would 'encourage the successful evasion of apprehension by immigration authorities, condone prior violations of the immigration laws, and encourage future violations'. In effect, the Court ruled that a worker's violation of immigration laws was more serious than an employer's violation of labour laws (www.supremecourtus.gov/opinions/01pdf/00-1595.pdf).

On 18 December 1990, the United Nations General Assembly approved the International Convention on the Protection of the Rights of all Migrant Workers and Members of Their Families. This eight-part, 93 Article UN Convention,[9] which came into force in July 2003, aims to 'contribute to the harmonization of the attitudes of States through the acceptance of basic principles concerning the treatment of migrant workers and members of their families' (Preamble). The UN Convention, so far ratified by forty net emigration countries, includes most of the protections the ILO Conventions establish for migrant workers, as it was largely inspired by the ILO standards. Yet, it goes beyond them to cover all migrants, including seafarers and the self-employed. It calls on states to adhere to basic human rights standards in their dealings with authorized and unauthorized migrants, including guaranteeing migrants freedom of religion and freedom from arbitrary arrest or imprisonment.

The major employment-related protections are in Part III of the UN Convention, particularly Articles 25–27, which prescribe equality in wages and working conditions for authorized and unauthorized migrants and national workers, assert that migrants should be allowed to join unions, and call for migrant workers to receive benefits under social security systems to which they contribute, or to receive refunds of their social security contributions as they leave countries in which they have made contributions. Authorized migrants should have additional rights set out in Part IV, including the right to information about jobs abroad and a list of 'equal treatments', for example, as regards freedom of movement within the host country, freedom to form unions and participate in the political life of the host country, and equal access to employment services, public housing, and educational institutions.

Part IV, Article 44 of the UN Convention, was among the most contentious: 'recognizing that the family is the natural and fundamental group unit of society', it obligates signatory states to 'take appropriate measures to ensure the protection of the unity of the families of migrant workers . . . to facilitate the reunification of migrant workers with their spouses . . . as well as with their minor dependent unmarried children'. Migrant family members are to have 'equality of treatment with nationals' in access to education, social and health services, and 'states of employment shall endeavour to facilitate for the children of migrant workers the teaching of their mother tongue and culture'. Few migrant-receiving countries adhere to this part of the UN Convention, especially in their treatment of unskilled workers.

The ILO discussed labour migration at its June 2004 International Labour Conference, concluding with a call for a rights-based multilateral framework to improve migration management (www.ilo.org/public/english/protection/migrant). The introduction to the ILO Multilateral Framework on Labour Migration adopted subsequently acknowledges that labour migration is a response to labour surpluses in some countries and shortages in others, and that allowing workers to flow across borders under principles that deal with decent work, cooperation, and dialogue can ensure that labour migration is mutually beneficial. The framework covers nine topics, from promoting decent work to ensuring that migration hastens development in sending countries. Governments are called upon to develop transparent bilateral and multilateral agreements to regulate labour migration, including tripartite consultations that are sensitive to the needs of female migrants and sending nations.

Labour migration has generally been considered a transitional phenomenon, as countries import workers during economic booms and countries stop sending workers abroad as they develop. The framework calls for expanding avenues for regular migration, suggesting that labour migration will not be transitional, and asks governments to assess their need for foreign workers by sector and occupation in order to introduce temporary worker schemes to 'fill shortages in specific sectors'. In developing new migrant worker programmes, the framework calls for consultation with employers and unions as well as non-governmental organizations and migrant organizations, and for respecting the human rights of all migrants, regular and irregular, including the right to form and join unions, to avoid forced and child labour, and to eliminate discrimination against migrants. Governments should ensure equality of treatment between regular migrants and national workers and ensure minimum standards of protection by ratifying Conventions 97 and 143 and the 1990 UN Convention.

Certain guidelines based on these Conventions partially conflict with national laws as implemented today, especially in many receiving countries, such as the call to allow laid-off migrants to remain in the country and seek another job (guideline 9.4), to allow irregular migrants to stay until they recoup unpaid wages (9.5), and to extend labour protections to all sectors with migrants, including domestic helpers and farm workers (9.8). Many of the eleven guidelines cited as a way of using national laws to protect the rights of migrants are hortatory, such as calling for more labour inspectors. The guidelines call for tripartite efforts to curb irregular migration and smuggling and trafficking, including laws that prevent the employment of irregular workers, taking special care to protect foreign domestic helpers, and developing policies to provide effective remedies for migrants whose rights have been abused regardless of their legal status. Some of these guidelines are very general, such as calling on governments and international organizations to deal with the root causes of trafficking, while others are far more specific, such as the call to prohibit employers or agents from holding the identity documents of migrants.

The guidelines call for an orderly and equitable process of labour migration, with legal workers moving over borders via regular channels and with full information. The eleven guidelines on how to move migrants over borders call for migrants to receive information in their own language, reductions in the costs of going abroad to work, and coordination of union efforts to protect migrants in sending and receiving countries. Receiving countries should recognize migrant credentials and eliminate medical tests for migrants that are unrelated to their employment. Sending countries, according to the guidelines, should establish consular services that protect their nationals employed abroad and welfare funds for those in need.

The eight guidelines dealing with labour recruiters and brokers call for a licensing system, contracts that offer them legitimate jobs abroad, and the posting of bonds. There ought to be no migrant-paid fees unless governments, employers, and unions agree that migrant-paid fees are appropriate. Recruiters who violate these guidelines should be punished, and good recruiters should be recognized.

The thirteen guidelines dealing with migrant integration range from calls to enact and enforce anti-discrimination and anti-racism laws to taking positive steps to help migrants, including giving them access to legal status and providing migrants and their families with educational opportunities, including language and cultural courses. Governments should highlight the contributions of migrants to host societies to facilitate their acceptance and integration, and children born to migrants abroad should have the right to birth registration and a nationality and be able to go to local schools. Finally, the guidelines call on governments to 'consider allowing migrant workers to participate in political activities after a period of legal residence in the country'.

The ten migration and development guidelines include a call for more analysis of the economic contributions of migrants to receiving countries, reducing the cost of remittance transfers and increasing their economic impacts in sending countries, and developing ethical worker recruitment guidelines to avoid the loss of workers with critical skills, such as health-care workers. However, in what could be a contradiction to the call for help to integrate abroad, the migration and development guidelines call for encouraging circular and return migration and reintegration into countries of origin.

The ILO Conventions and the Multilateral Framework, as well as the UN Convention and other international agreements that call for equal treatment for migrants,[10] erect a set of obligations on governments that should protect low-skilled migrant workers. The Conventions and framework do have effects, especially in middle-income developing countries that are in the process of establishing systems to regulate and protect migrants, as in Costa Rica, South Africa, and Thailand.

However, the institutional framework embodied in ILO and UN Conventions offers much less than what proponents of a WMO believe is needed to move more workers legally over national borders. In some variations of the call for a WMO, a UN body would publish 'migration targets' for countries and assist governments to establish mechanisms to move workers from one country to another (Ghosh 1999; Bhagwati 2003).

This is not to say that the ILO's and UN's role is limited to standard setting and monitoring. Standard setting simply distinguishes these organizations from others which, similar to the ILO and UN, are involved—and increasingly so—in operational activities as well as policy advice and research about low-skilled labour migration.

IOM and UNDP: operational activities

The International Organization for Migration (IOM) calls itself

> The migration agency, [making] IOM the leading inter-governmental organization in the field of migration [that] works closely with governmental, intergovernmental and non-governmental partners.... IOM works to help ensure the orderly and humane management of migration, to promote international cooperation on migration issues, to assist in the search for practical solutions to migration problems and to provide humanitarian assistance to migrants in need, including refugees and internally displaced people. The IOM Constitution recognizes the link between migration and economic, social and cultural development, as well as to the right of freedom of movement. IOM works in the four broad areas of migration management:

41

> Migration and development; facilitating migration; regulating migration; forced migration. (see www.iom/int)

IOM began as a logistics agency. Its predecessor established in 1951, the Provisional Intergovernmental Committee for the Movement of Migrants from Europe (PICMME), which became the Intergovernmental Committee for European Migration (ICEM) in 1952, was mandated with reducing population pressures that threatened economic and political stability in Europe after the Second World War. The Constitution of ICEM stated that it was to 'promote the increase of the volume of migration from Europe by providing, at the request of and in agreement with the Governments concerned, services in the processing, reception, first placement and settlement of migrants which other international organizations are not in a position to supply'. Over the years, the Committee expanded its activities to other regions and this was acknowledged by its becoming the IOM with a new constitution in 1989. Special emphasis was now placed on an increased range of movements where assistance might be required, including voluntary return; the list of services was expanded; and the link between migration and development stressed. Importantly, the organization's temporary character and its subsidiary status (where it supplied services only when other organizations could not do so) were abolished (for more details, see Ducasse-Rogier 2001).

IOM has experienced rapid growth since, especially over the past ten years. Membership increased from 67 states in 1998 to 125 states in 2008; total expenditures increased from US$242.2 million in 1998 to US$783.8 million in 2007, with a high point of US$952 million spent in 2005; field locations increased from 119 in 1998 to more than 420; IOM had more than 1,770 active projects in 2008 as compared to 686 ten years earlier; and operational staff increased from some 1,100 in 1998 to approximately 5,600 in 2008 (see www.iom/int).

IOM deals increasingly with labour migration, including migration for jobs that require low skills. The World Migration Report 2008 has the theme 'Managing Labour Mobility in the Evolving Global Economy'. IOM helps governments to negotiate bilateral agreements on temporary labour migration, sometimes co-signing memorandums of understanding (MOUs) that lay out the terms on which low-skilled migrants move from one country to another, as between Guatemala and Canada, and sometimes helping with the selection of migrants under temporary programmes (see Compendium of Good Practice Policy Elements in Bilateral Temporary Labour Arrangements, GFMD 2008).

The United Nations Development Programme (UNDP) has only recently started to launch operational activities in the area of labour migration and get involved in global migration governance. It is the lead agency in an initiative on migration and development sponsored by the European Commission and implemented jointly by UNDP, United Nations High Commissioner for

Refugees, United Nations Population Fund, and ILO under the 'Delivering as One' approach of the United Nations, including also IOM as a partner. This initiative, launched in December 2008, will provide some 10 million Euros to support civil society organizations and local authorities seeking to contribute to linking migration and development (see www.migration4development.org).

In addition, in 2009 UNDP's flagship publication, the *Human Development Report*, will be about migration, taking as its starting point that the global distribution of capabilities is extraordinarily unequal, that this is a major driver for the movement of people, and that migration can expand the choices of people (see http://hdr.undp.org/en/reports/global/hdr2009/). It is too early to say what take the report will have on the desirable international migration architecture but clearly it will influence the thinking on this matter—as World Bank and Organisation for Economic Co-peration and Development (OECD) research and publications have done in the past.

World Bank and OECD: research shaping the global agenda

The World Bank's 2006 Global Economic Prospects report on *Economic Implications of Remittances and Migration* as well as related publications (e.g. *The International Migration Agenda and the World Bank: Managing Risks, Enhancing Benefits*, World Bank 2006b) were influential in articulating the idea that more migration of low-skilled emigrants from developing to industrialized countries could make a significant contribution to poverty reduction via increased remittances. The report suggested that a good way of 'increasing such emigration would be to promote managed migration programs between origin and destination countries that combine temporary migration of low-skilled workers with incentives to return'. Overall, according to the World Bank, such programmes represent a 'feasible approach' to capture efficiency gains from labour migration (World Bank 2006a: p. xv).

The 2005 final report of the Global Commission on International Migration *Migration in an Interconnected World: New Directions for Actions* had already recommended that states and the private sector should consider introducing 'carefully designed temporary migration programmes as a means of addressing the economic needs of both countries of origin and destination', however highlighting less the global efficiency gains from additional low-skilled migration and more the need for a 'well regulated liberalization of the global labour market' (GCIM 2005: 16–17).

Similarly, the OECD, another important actor in the diffusion of ideas about migration, in its *International Migration Outlook 2008* concluded that more migration of low-skilled workers is good. However, temporary migration should be for temporary jobs. The report found that about 2.5 million temporary migrant workers entered OECD countries in 2006, roughly three times the number of workers who entered on a permanent basis; and the majority of the temporary labour entries concerned low-skilled occupations. In a press release accompanying the launch of the report, OECD Secretary General Angel Gurría said:

> Some temporary programmes, notably those that involve seasonal jobs during harvest periods or peak tourist seasons, work well.... Cycling repeated waves of temporary migrants in and out of the country to occupy the same jobs is inefficient. Employers have to retrain workers every time rather than retain experienced staff. Enforcing such a scheme on employers entails substantial economic and political cost. More likely, economic rationality would win out over artificial or badly-designed regulations, with the risk that employers cheat the system. (OECD 2008)

The role of trade unions

Trade unions are among the institutions with an interest in low-skilled labour migration. While highly skilled migrants are often not organized and difficult to convince to join unions, and while competition for highly skilled migrants helps to protect them, the case is different for low-skilled migrant workers.

In a number of countries, trade unions are represented in tripartite commissions that manage migration, which gives them a direct voice in the governance of migration at a domestic level. But the trade unions' strategy is also to work across borders to protect migrant workers. In temporary foreign worker schemes, they take part in recruitment processes for example. Or they devise mechanisms whereby membership in a trade union of the country of origin gives automatic membership to that in the country of destination, as with the Union Network International (UNI) Passport. The Global Union Federation UNI organizes craft and service workers (postal, tourism, electricity, telecom, social security, commerce, finance, media, cleaning, and security) and launched its passport scheme in 2000. The passport allows a unionized migrant to be 'hosted' by a UNI-affiliated union in the destination country. With the passport comes a considerable list of benefits: from information on working conditions, the banking system, tax regulations, opportunities to participate in local union activities and training courses, to advice on labour issues and legal support (Schmidt 2006).

Bilateral cooperation between German and Polish trade unions in the construction sector has led to the foundation of a European migrants union. In 2004 the German IG BAU founded the European Migrant Workers' Union (EMWU) to organize migrant workers of all nationalities who work for a limited period of time in one or several member states of the European Union (other than their own), especially in the construction or agricultural sector. The EMWU was a response to abuses such as wage payments far below collective bargaining agreements or employment without social protection coverage, mainly of Polish workers on construction sites of the Postdamer Platz in Berlin, Europe's biggest building area in the 1990s (Schmidt 2006).

Especially in Europe, but also elsewhere, for example between India and Nepal or in the Caribbean, trade unions have become an important player in the defence and protection of migrant workers in low-skilled jobs.[11]

Politics: numbers vs. rights, neo-liberal vs. liberal approaches

Competing discourses and visions

There are competing discourses and visions about low-skilled labour migration and its governance. The ILO and UN Conventions do not discuss how much low-skilled labour migration there should be. Instead, they say that if there is labour migration, migrant workers should be treated like local workers. The Conventions and the organizations where these Conventions were adopted emphasize the importance of migrant rights and equal treatment and non-discrimination norms. A 'rights-based approach' befits organizations mandated to social justice and social and political rights.

The IOM and the World Bank, on the other hand, call for more low-skilled migration. Traditionally, the IOM had the mandate to 'increase the volume of migration' (see above), while the World Bank has evolved from a facilitator of post-war reconstruction to today's goal of reducing poverty. In comparison to the ILO and UN, the World Bank is dominated more by a quest for economic efficiency and puts less emphasis on individuals and their rights.

Indeed, economic theory posits a trade-off between migrant numbers and rights. If the demand for labour is negatively sloped, then higher wages are associated with less employment—there is a trade-off between employment and wages in the sense that, as wages rise, employers substitute capital for labour or take other steps to reduce employment. If rights for low-skilled migrants cost money, as when migrants are paid the same wages and have access to the same benefits as local workers, their costs rise, and there may be less demand for them (Ruhs and Martin 2008). For this reason, a negatively sloped demand for labour can lead to a trade-off between the number of low-skilled migrants employed and the rights accorded to them. The World Bank recognizes this, and focuses on the benefits of more migrant workers and increasing remittances for alleviating poverty rather than examining the costs; that is, how much worker rights may have to be curbed in order to expand the number of low-skilled migrants and what such a move might imply for the migrants and the host country labour markets and societies in general.

The rights discourse which has been predominant for a long time in the area of low-skilled migration has become challenged by this approach, and in addition has been defied very explicitly during negotiations in the World Trade Organization (WTO) concerning the General Agreement on Trade in Services (GATS).

Challenges to the rights regime

GATS MODE 4: NUMBERS VS. RIGHTS

There are four major modes or ways to provide services across national borders: cross-border supply, consumption abroad, foreign direct investment (FDI) or commercial presence, and Mode 4 migration, which the GATS refers to as the temporary movement of 'natural persons'.[12]

Developing countries led by India advocate liberalization of Mode 4 movements of service providers with reforms in four major areas:[13] eliminating the economic needs tests receiving countries use to determine if foreign workers are necessary, expediting visa and work permit issuance, facilitating credentials recognition and obtaining needed licenses, and exempting foreign service providers from participating in work-related benefit programmes and the payroll taxes that finance them.

Economic needs tests require employers seeking permission to hire migrant workers to satisfy their governments that local workers are not available. There are two major types of tests: pre-admission and post-admission. Pre-admission tests, sometimes called labour certification, require employers to demonstrate to labour agencies that they tried to find local workers while offering at least prevailing or government-set wages—if they fail to find local workers, they are 'certified' to employ foreign workers. To obtain certification, employers place advertisements seeking local workers for a specified period of time and keep logs that record why local applicants were not hired. This has the effect of keeping the border gate closed until the government certifies or agrees that foreign service providers are truly needed.

The alternative is a post-admission test or employer attestation. Under this trust-the-employer approach, the employer seeking to hire foreign workers attests or certifies that the foreigner is needed to fill the job and makes other assurances, such as promising to pay foreigners the higher of the minimum or prevailing wage and guaranteeing that the job is not vacant because of a lawful labour dispute. Government approval of employer attestations in countries such as the United States is virtually automatic, and there are generally no inspections unless the labour department receives complaints. Post-admissions tests allow employers to open border gates, often within days of applying for visas for foreign service providers.[14]

Developing countries and most employers prefer few or no economic needs tests, post-admission rather than pre-admission tests, and more transparency in procedures used by government agencies to determine prevailing wages and other factors that are used in both pre-admission and post-admission systems.[15] Labour departments usually consider protecting low-skilled workers a top priority, so the demand to end economic needs tests seeks to minimize the role of labour departments in admissions decisions.

Wages lie at the core of economic needs tests, and the wage equality that is a bedrock principle of ILO and UN Conventions is often seen by those who want to liberalize Mode 4 migration as protectionism. Chaudhuri et al. (2004) assert that 'Wage-parity... is intended to provide a nondiscriminatory environment, [but] tends to erode the cost advantage of hiring foreigners and works like a de facto quota.' Chanda says that wage parity 'negates the very basis of cross-country labor flows which stems from endowment-based cost differentials between countries' (Chanda 2001: 635).

Instead of wage parity between local and foreign workers, Chanda argues that the wages of foreign service providers can be below host country wages but 'within a fair margin'. She argues that foreign service provider wages could be 'decided mutually by the concerned countries under bilateral wage agreements and discussions between professional or industry associations in these countries' (Chanda 2001: 650). In a bid to admit more low-skilled migrants, Chanda advocates a tax on less-skilled migrant service providers to generate funds to compensate local workers whose wages may be depressed or who may lose their jobs because of the presence of Mode 4 service providers (Chanda 2001: 650).

Visa and work permit procedures determine if a particular individual can actually enter the country. After an employer receives permission to hire a foreign service provider, the foreigner must normally be interviewed by a government agency, such as consular staff in the migrant's country of origin, to determine if she is eligible for entry and work visas. These procedures can be simple and handled by mail or require in-person interviews that must be scheduled and may involve travel from the migrant's residence to a consular office. There may also be fees involved in obtaining required visas. This multi-layered system may limit migration, prompting calls for 'one-stop GATS visa shops' to issue multiple entry visas and work permits.

Another demand is faster recognition of qualifications earned in the migrant's country of origin, a factor that affects professionals more than low-skilled migrants. There are few national and fewer international bodies vetting individuals who earned their qualifications abroad. Instead, the usual way to facilitate the recognition of an individual's credentials is via mutual recognition agreements (MRAs), for example within the European Union (EU) and between previous mother countries and colonies, as in the British Commonwealth. The basic principle of an MRA is that, if one government issues or recognizes a credential or licence, others will do so on a reciprocal basis.

The fourth demand centres on social security and related tax issues. Payroll taxes add 20–40 per cent to wages in most industrial countries. If migrant service providers were exempt from work-related taxes, they would be 20–40 per cent cheaper. However, exempting migrant service providers from work-related taxes and benefit programmes may violate the WTO norm of 'national treatment' as well as ILO Conventions calling for equality between migrants and local workers.

Although the terminology used in the GATS Mode 4 negotiations is 'service provision' rather than 'labour migration', the message that stems from these negotiations for low-skilled labour migration is clear: developing countries point to the trade-off between numbers and rights, and many of those advising their governments urge an expansion of migrant numbers by restrictions on rights. Economic language is usually used: migrants are 'labour' or 'migrant labour', that is, a factor of production; they are not usually referred to as 'migrant workers', that is, as individual human beings with rights.

MIGRANTS' SELF-EXPLOITATION AS DRIVING NUMBERS

The Gulf Cooperation Council (GCC) states have some of the highest shares of migrants in private sector work forces and among the lowest levels of migrant worker rights. Over 90 per cent of private sector workers in most GCC countries are migrants, and they are generally prohibited from forming or joining unions or taking other steps to pressure employers to raise wages. Labour law coverage is incomplete, so that many workers, including those employed in private households, are often not covered by labour laws.

Israeli–Lebanon fighting in summer 2006 resulted in the return of Filipina domestic helpers who complained of mistreatment. Between 1990 and 2005, the Philippines had banned migration to Lebanon because of frequent mistreatment of domestic helpers. That ban was lifted in 2005, and then reimposed in 2006. The government responded with the 'Supermaid' programme that, beginning in 2007, requires Filipina domestic helpers abroad to be paid at least US$400 a month. The number of Filipinas deployed as domestic helpers fell sharply—there were 91,000 newly hired household service workers in 2006 and 40,000 in 2007. The Philippines Overseas Employment Agency (POEA) suspects that some began to leave as gardeners or other types of workers not covered by the US$400 a month minimum wage. In other words, establishing a minimum wage for one type of worker, domestic helper, may have led to domestic helpers going abroad to fill jobs not covered by the minimum wage, such as gardeners.

The fact that many migrants are employed in countries that offer relatively low wages and few rights suggests that they are willing to accept unfavourable conditions in exchange for same job opportunity at all. Making a decision to go abroad as a gardener for US$200 a month knowing that the job is a domestic helper and should pay US$400 a month may not be in the migrant's best interest, as defined by the migrants' government. However, one should not underestimate the migrants' agency, their capacity to make independent decisions. It is a simple fact that migrants oftentimes forego their rights because they have no better options.

A DOMESTIC DRIVER OF NUMBERS: THE ROLE
OF SPECIAL INTEREST GROUPS

Most formal agreements dealing with low-skilled migrants are bilateral or regional. Most of the bilateral agreements are signed by labour-receiving governments at the behest of some of their employers who want legal access to low-skilled migrants, while the regional agreements that permit freedom of movement are usually signed by governments that expect relatively few workers to cross national borders.

One of the best known bilateral agreements admitting low-skilled migrants was the series of Mexico–US agreements known as the Bracero Program. It illustrates how one group of influential employers, farmers with large acreages of mostly irrigated crop land in the Western states, were able to persuade the US government to negotiate an agreement with Mexico to import low-skilled workers during the Second World War, and then expand the programme during peacetime in the 1950s. The major economic effect of the 1942–64 Bracero Program was to hold down farm wages, which increased the value of farm land (Martin 2009: ch. 2).

The 1930s were considered the 'Grapes of Wrath' decade in Western US agriculture, as millions of small farmers and their families moved west when drought caused many to lose their farms. Most expected to become hired hands on Western farms, learning how to grow fruits and vegetables and then becoming family farmers in their own right. However, Western agriculture was a capital-intensive business of large units that depended on armies of seasonal workers, inspiring John Steinbeck's novel documenting the treatment of white small farmers at the hands of employers accustomed to immigrants with no other US job options. Reformers agreed that fundamental changes were needed, but they disagreed on whether hired farm workers should be turned into small farmers or treated as factory workers and protected by labour laws.

Instead of reforms, the Second World War allowed farm employers to persuade the US government to negotiate a programme that brought Mexicans to work in US agriculture and railroads. At the time, US farm workers were not protected by the minimum wage, but Mexico insisted that Braceros receive at least US$0.30 an hour, so many US farmers initially refused to hire Braceros, fearing that they would have to pay their US workers at least US$0.30 a hour as well (CRS 1980: 22).[16] Foreign farm workers were about 2 per cent of US farm workers during the Second World War and half were in California.

The Bracero Program grew larger and lasted longer than anticipated. Wartime admissions peaked at 62,000 in 1944, and reached 450,000 a decade later. Illegal immigration increased as well, especially in the late 1940s and early 1950s. Braceros often had to pay bribes in Mexico to get on recruitment lists, and they soon learned that US employers preferred to hire workers in illegal situations to avoid paying transportation costs and the minimum wage. In 1954, there were 3.5 Mexicans apprehended for every Bracero admitted (both tallies record events, since the same individual is counted each time he is admitted as a Bracero or apprehended). Between 1942 and 1964, more Mexicans were apprehended than were admitted legally as workers.

The availability of Braceros held down farm wages during the 1950s, allowing labour-intensive agriculture to expand.[17] Hiring Braceros, in the words of Ernesto Galarza, was 'like the sprinkling systems of mechanized irrigation, Braceros could be turned on and off' and paid only when there was work for them to do (Galarza 1977: 265). Numerous commissions and reports criticized farmers for mistreating and underpaying Braceros and US farm workers. The CBS documentary *Harvest of Shame*, which aired on Thanksgiving Day in November 1960, featured Edward R. Murrow challenging the US government to improve conditions for farm workers. In response, the US Department of Labor began to enforce Bracero regulations, which raised their cost and prompted labour-saving mechanization.

The Bracero Program began as an effort to avoid raising farm wages when the Second World War shrank the pool of workers willing to be available seasonally. It expanded during the 1950s, helping to bolster land prices, and was ended in the midst of the civil rights movement, when the US government made dealing with 'people left behind' a priority. There was a 'golden age' for US farm workers between the end of the Bracero Program in the mid-1960s and the upsurge in unauthorized Mexico–US migration in the early 1980s, when unions signed contracts that in some cases raised entry-level wages to twice the minimum wage.

The lesson of the Bracero Program is that special interests were able to manipulate low-skilled migration policy to benefit themselves. In US policy-making on low-skilled migration, it has more often been the case that special interests obtained access to migrant workers—other political factors such as power, ideas, and efficiency played minor roles. Indeed, in some cases, importing low-skilled migrant workers was economically inefficient, as exemplified by the US policy of protecting the sugar industry from free trade and importing migrant workers to hand cut US sugar cane.

Neo-liberalism vs. liberalism

The GATS Mode 4 negotiations demonstrate that there is lack of agreement in the international arena whether more migration is desirable or whether migrant rights should be preserved at all costs. This trade-off between numbers and rights can also be coined as a struggle of ideas between neo-liberal vs. liberal approaches to labour migration.

Neo-liberalism is very much a theory about economic arrangements, for example, against state interference with private property and in market exchanges. The focus is on free markets. 'Classical' liberalism in contrast is primarily about human freedoms, protecting individuals from unacceptable state incursions on their liberty, and ensuring that all individuals within the polity are able to enjoy these rights. Liberalism is also the theory that highlights the equal treatment of all individuals irrespective of their particular character-istics, the universal applicability of liberal rights, and the need to limit state power over the individual (Hansen forthcoming).

Glivanos (2008) points out that current neo-liberal thought combines two strands of classical theory, especially to explain the function of private property. The Austrian tradition views market individualism as maintaining individual freedoms (Hayek, Ludwig von Mises, Schumpeter) while neoclassical econ-omists emphasize the importance of markets to achieve efficiency (Chicago School of Economics). Ha-Joon Chang (2002) views this combination as an 'unholy alliance' that results in an unfavourable perception of the state and its role. The state is no longer seen in its benevolent function, as under Keynesian-ism; it has lost its role as impartial arbiter and social guardian. Instead, the state is perceived as an organization catering to self-interested bureaucrats and polit-icians who work for their client groups and not in the general interest.

Neo-liberal (market-based) approaches to labour migration tend to look at overall (global) gains from migration and less at distributional effects. They see migrants as rational actors who may be willing to accept unfavourable labour conditions in host countries because these may still be better than what they would find at home or because they are simply faced with extremely limited options (see above on migrants who go to the GCC states).

Liberal (rights-based) approaches, on the other hand, include the notion that the state has a protective function, including also protecting people from themselves and their own decisions, for example, to submit themselves to abuse, which explains the insistence on not giving up migrants' rights in favour of increased numbers.

The dominance of neo-liberal thought since approximately the 1980s (the Reagan–Thatcher years) would be one explanation for the reticence to ratify the 1990 UN Convention on Migrant Workers: this Convention is very much about individual human rights, political rights, and so forth. This dominance also explains the interest in actions of individual migrants as heralds of develop-ment in their countries of origin—remittances, the role of diasporas—vs. state-led development (aid), the latter being suspect in neo-liberal thinking.

Normative dimensions

Prospects for top-down global governance

What are the prospects for top-down global governance in the area of low-skilled labour migration, including the setting of migration targets, suggested by and implemented via a WMO? Such prospects are slim. The tensions be-tween proponents of 'rights' and those of 'numbers', or in other words between liberal and neo-liberal approaches to low-skilled labour migration, do more to impede than establish a global mechanism. But apart from these competing discourses and underlying ideologies, there are also interests at stake.

Major migrant-receiving states have no overwhelming interests in more low-skilled labour migration. There are no compelling economic arguments for more such migration, and most states would be reluctant to yield sovereignty to a WMO.

How much low-skill migration is optimal? There is no obvious answer, which is why low-skill migration is often controversial. Adding more workers without increasing unemployment raises economic output or gross domestic product (GDP), but may not raise per capita GDP, which is the most commonly used measure of economic welfare.

Most of the research on the economic effects of admitting low-skilled migrants into industrial countries concludes that they have few negative effects on the wages or unemployment rates of similar native workers. If low-skilled migrants benefit from higher wages, their employers benefit by getting jobs filled at low cost, and sending countries benefit from remittances while receiving countries have a larger GDP, the result is a win-win-win-win outcome that suggests there should be more low-skilled migration from poorer to richer countries, as the World Bank (2006a) urges.

The labour market effects of immigrants have been summarized as follows:

> Although immigrant workers increase output, their addition to the supply of labor... [causes] wage rates in the immediately affected market [to be] bid down... Thus, native-born workers who compete with immigrants for jobs may experience reduced earnings or reduced employment. (CEA 1986: 221)

Economists and other social scientists have used three kinds of studies to estimate the labour market effects of migrants: case studies, city comparisons, and economic mobility studies. Most of these studies have been done in the United States. Case studies examine the impacts of immigrants in a particular industry or occupation. For example, when unionized farm workers in Southern California went on strike for a wage increase in 1982, many were replaced by unauthorized newcomers recruited to break the strike by labour contractors. Displacement in this case was a result of a competition between employers—the unionized harvesting association lost business and eventually closed as labour contractors hiring unauthorized newcomers expanded (Mines and Martin 1984). Migrants are often hired via networks, so that once a network is established in a particular workplace, migrants can fill vacancies via word of mouth, as occurred in Southern California janitorial services (GAO 1988: 39–41).

City comparisons examine labour market trends in cities with higher and lower shares of immigrant workers. These studies begin with the assumption that, if the presence of immigrants depresses wages or displaces workers, cities with a higher share of immigrants in their labour forces should have lower wages or higher unemployment rates for local workers similar to the migrants. However, in the United States during the 1980s, city comparisons found few of the wage and displacement effects they expected to find, prompting George Borjas (1990: 81) to conclude that:

> modern econometrics cannot detect a single shred of evidence that immigrants have a sizable adverse impact on the earnings and employment opportunities of natives in the United States.

As more data became available, researchers realized that, instead of staying in 'immigrant cities', local workers who competed most directly with migrants moved away from immigrant cities, or did not move to them, so that the effects of immigration on wages or unemployment were quickly diffused throughout the labour market rather than being measurable in an immigrant city. The local workers who remained in immigrant cities were often employed by government or in firms that negotiated national contracts, so their wages did not respond immediately to an influx of migrant workers. Such internal migration can make it hard to estimate the effects of migrants in any city (Borjas 1994).

The third type of economic study that could provide normative guidance for migration policy deals with integration, asking whether migrants pay more in taxes than they consume in tax-supported services. Migrants should be expected to be net tax contributors because most are of working age, and most tax-supported services are consumed by the young and old. However, migrants also age, and they may have children abroad, so a comprehensive assessment requires estimates of taxes paid and services consumed over the lifetime of the migrant and his/her children.

The most definitive such assessment was done in the United States in 1997 (Smith and Edmonston 1997). It concluded that the 'taxes paid–benefits received' balance depended primarily on earnings, which rise over time. Using data on migrants who arrived at different times, researchers attempted to develop a motion picture of migrants and their children, projecting earnings, taxes paid and government services received, and the earnings and tax–benefit ratios of the children and grandchildren of migrants. The result was that the average migrant had a positive present value of US$80,000 in 1996, meaning he/she would pay this much more in taxes than he/she received in tax-supported benefits. However, the balance was negative for the newly arrived migrant, US$3,000, and this was offset by a positive present value of US$83,000 for the migrants' children.

The present 'values' of low-skilled migrants do not make a strong normative case for more such migration. Migrants with more than secondary school education had a present value of US$105,000, and this rose to US$198,000 with the excess of taxes paid over benefits received for their children and grandchildren. However, migrants with less than secondary school education impose a lifetime cost of US$89,000—even with a positive balance of US$76,000 from their children and grandchildren, their net present value is −US$13,000, leading to this conclusion:

> If the policy goal were to maximize the positive contribution of immigration to public sector budgets, that could be achieved by policies favoring highly educated immigrants and not admitting immigrants over age 50. (Smith and Edmonston 1997, table 6.3)

Perhaps an even stronger argument against a WMO is sovereignty, as illustrated by the history of IOM (and its predecessor PICMME). The establishment of PICMME was linked to two contrasting visions of migration (both forced and economic), with the ILO–UN on one side and the US government on the other. Cold War politics and a reluctance to accept a large influx of migrants for solely humanitarian reasons spurred differences between the United States and the ILO–UN, with the United States calling for an institution that fostered inter-governmental negotiations, while the ILO–UN plan called for international cooperation under the leadership of a single international organization (Karatani 2002: 519).

While initially the United States and the United Kingdom, to a certain extent, supported ILO initiatives to coordinate the actions of international organizations, both countries were concerned that international cooperation would interfere with their migration policies and their ability to select migrants based on national policies. The ILO's attempt to organize support for its migration proposals in a conference held in Naples in October 1951 failed because it lacked US and to a certain extent British and Australian support. Instead, the US vision of an inter-governmental agency outside of the UN system, concerned primarily with the transport of migrants and refugees, was realized in the December 1951 Brussels conference, which established PICMME.[18]

States today, and in particular important migrant-receiving states, continue to be keen on keeping their sovereign right over who might enter their country, when, and under what circumstances. The reference to this right has made it into almost every recent international policy document on migration, including also the ILO's Multilateral Framework on Labour Migration.

Perhaps increased cooperation among the existing international organizations that deal with migration in some form or other can be taken as another indicator for continuing the fragmented global governance of low-skilled migration, albeit with the will to better coordinate action than in the past. The UNDP-led Migration and Development Initiative as well as consultations among international organizations that took place in Geneva in December 2008 in preparation for the 2009 Human Development Report can serve as examples.

Basic principles for future governance of low-skilled labour migration or why uphold a rights-based approach?

There are good reasons to uphold the rights-based (liberal) approach to labour migration. First, there is a domestic argument. Labour laws exist primarily to protect less-skilled native workers by setting minimum wages and other standards; less-skilled migrant workers need protection as much or more than similar local workers. The normative case for treating low-skilled migrants the same as local workers is straightforward—protecting migrants protects local workers by discouraging employers from hiring migrants because they have fewer protections.

Second, it is not clear by how much rights would have to be reduced to bring about more numbers, and there is the question whether reduced rights will actually lead to more development in countries of origin. The extreme case of right-less workers in irregular situations is a case in point. If such workers are deported shortly before their wage payment is due, there is *nothing* to remit back home; there are probably family members who have paid for the travel of the migrant in the first place and 'lost' their investment. Moreover, large numbers of migrants alone will not necessarily lead to development. Mexico and the Philippines are both countries that have based their development model on emigration in large numbers, and they are not among the most successful economics.

Third, if low-skilled labour migration were to be 'negotiated' in the same way as trade agreements, there is the risk that increased numbers might come at the price of stratified labour markets, that is, we might witness migrants' assignment to particular jobs in the international division of labour and ensuing social conflicts.

Perhaps the strongest argument for upholding a rights-based approach is that a differentiated treatment of migrant and local workers undermines the basis of societies that are constructed around non-discrimination and human rights, and especially multi-cultural and multi-ethnic societies.

Conclusions and outlook

Global governance can be direct, as with the WTO encouraging free trade and investment and establishing rules to govern trade in goods and capital flows, or indirect with norms adopted in certain organizations but these not having the 'monopoly' of dealing with the issue-area, as when ILO and UN Conventions call for governments to ensure that low-skilled migrants are treated equally in the labour market. This rights-based approach to governing labour migration does not encourage low-skilled migration—it merely says that if countries decide to send workers abroad or receive them, the migrants should be treated the same as local workers.

Our review of institutions, politics, and normative dimensions of low-skilled migration has shown that the rights-based approach is being challenged by institutions and actors that push for larger numbers of low-skilled migrants, for the most part under new temporary foreign worker schemes. The challenge operates through organizations whose mandate is to increase migration in an orderly fashion (IOM) and to look out for global efficiencies in an attempt to reduce poverty (World Bank) as well as via WTO discussions on liberalizations under GATS Mode 4 which are officially about service provision, not labour migration, but where the call to reduce the rights of migrant workers in the low-skill category is especially open. This is not to say that positions are completely one-sided. On the ILO–UN side there is no denial that migration can contribute to development, and on the IOM–World Bank side there are frequent references to migrants' rights, yet the emphasis is very different.

The drive for larger migrant numbers and if needed at the expense of their rights also comes from the migrants themselves. Migration may be their best option, even when they are being exploited. Special interests, such as employers in particular economic sectors, can also be counted among the drivers for more migration whereas trade unions have started to work cross-border to defend migrants' rights and vehemently oppose any increase in the number of low-skilled migrants if this is associated with reductions in migrants' rights.

We believe it will be difficult to develop a system of top-down global governance that sets targets of migrants to fill jobs requiring low skills. There are many reasons, including the different visions and interests above and also the fact that most countries do not want to exchange low-skilled migrants, so the reciprocity that lies at the heart of WTO trade and capital negotiations is missing. Furthermore, low-skilled migrants are normally confined to certain subsectors of the economy, so that their presence can be viewed more as a benefit to a special interest group than a broad-based benefit for the economy. Highly skilled migrants, by contrast, may benefit from both reciprocity and the fact that they are more likely to generate positive externalities for the host country.

Notes

1. The issue of temporary foreign worker schemes is particularly relevant in this context because most states today prefer to offer low-skilled jobs to foreign workers only on a temporary basis.
2. A note on terminology: if we speak of 'low-skilled migrants', this can also include migrants with a high level of education who apply for or work in jobs much below their qualifications.
3. United Nations (2006) Report of the Secretary General on International Migration (A/60/871) (May). www.unmigration.org. Table available at: www.un.org/esa/population/publications/2006Migration_Chart/2006IttMig_chart.htm.
4. For the origin of the ILO's migration mandate and ILO's involvement in international labour migration over the years, see Böhning (2009).
5. Freedom of Association and Protection of the Right to Organize Convention, 1948 (No. 87), and Right to Organize and Collective Bargaining Convention, 1949 (No. 98); Forced Labour Convention 1930 (No. 29), and Abolition of Forced Labour Convention,

1957 (No. 105); Equal Remuneration Convention, 1951 (No. 100); Discrimination (Employment and Occupation) Convention, 1958 (No. 111); Minimum Age Convention, 1973 (No. 138); Worst Forms of Child Labour Convention, 1999 (No. 182). Conventions that cover issues such as minimum wages and safety and health at work did not come under the 1998 Declaration.

6. Convention 97 excludes border-crossing commuters (frontier workers), seamen (covered by other ILO Conventions), and artists and similar professionals abroad for a short time.

7. ILO Recommendation No. 86 includes a model bilateral agreement for migrant workers, and has been used as a model for many of the bilateral agreements that were established.

8. Conventions Nos. 97 and 143 exempt seafarers, frontier workers, the self-employed, artists, and trainees.

9. ILO Convention 97 is about 5,600 words, Convention 143 is 3,000 words, and the UN Convention is over 14,000 words.

10. The Vienna Declaration and Programme of Action on Human Rights (1993) and the Cairo Programme of Action of the International Conference on Population and Development (1994) affirmed the importance of promoting and protecting the human rights of migrant workers and their families, while the Beijing Platform of Action of the Fourth World Conference on Women (1995) paid special attention to the rights of women migrants and urged that migrants be protected from violence and exploitation. The United Nations Commission on Human Rights in 1999 appointed a Special Rapporteur to investigate violations of the human rights of migrants, and the World Conference on Racism, Racial Discrimination, Xenophobia, and Related Intolerance in 2001 issued the Durban Declaration and Programme of Action, including a call for governments to allow migrants to unify families abroad and take steps to reduce the discriminatory treatment of migrant workers. The UN General Assembly in 2000 adopted the Convention Against Transnational Organized Crime, which has two additional protocols: the UN Protocol to Prevent, Suppress, and Punish Trafficking in Persons, especially Women and Children, and the Protocol Against the Smuggling of Migrants by Land, Sea, and Air.

11. For more examples of trade union action, see Schmidt (2006).

12. Temporary is not defined in the GATS, but GATS explicitly does not apply to immigration or settlement. Most WTO members limit service providers to less than five years in their country.

13. Chanda (2004: 634) calls these four categories restrictions on entry and stay, recognition of credentials, differential treatment, and regulations on commercial presence, a taxonomy that groups economic needs test and visa/work permit issuance.

14. There are also in-between labour market checks. One strategy, 'blanket certification', involves the government specifying labour-shortage occupations such as nursing and approving employer requests for foreign nurses if the employer makes wage and other assurances. Employers who are requesting workers to fill jobs for which there is no blanket certification must go through the normal certification steps of searching for local workers.

15. In some countries, there is no appeal if a labour agency rejects an employer's application for a foreign service provider visa.

16. East coast farmers recruited workers from the British West Indies (BWI) under separate MOUs made between the War Food Administration and the Bahamas (16 March 1943), Jamaica (2 April 1943), and Barbados (24 May 1944). Some 4,698 Bahama Islanders and 8,828 Jamaicans were admitted in 1943. Florida was the peak Second World War employer of BWI nationals, employing 4,688 Bahamians on 26 May 1945.

17. Average hourly earnings of farm workers in California, as measured by a USDA survey of farm employers, rose 41 per cent, from US$0.85 in 1950 to US$1.20 in 1960. Average hourly earnings of factory workers rose 63 per cent from US$1.60 in 1950 to US$2.60 in 1960 (both are in nominal dollars).

18. For more information, see Böhning (2009), Ducasse-Rogier (2001), and Karatani (2002).

References

Amin, M. and Mattoo, A. (2005) Does Temporary Migration Have to be Permanent? World Bank Policy Research Working Paper No. 3582, Washington, DC: World Bank.

Bhagwati, J. (2003) Borders Beyond Control, *Foreign Affairs*, January/February.

Böhning, W.R. (2009) A Brief Account of the ILO and Policies on International Migration, ILO Century Project—Ideas, Policies and Progress. ILO 90th anniversary publication, http://www.ilo.org/public/english/century/information_resources/papers_and_publications. htm.

Borjas, G.J. (1990) *Friends or Strangers: The Impact of Immigrants on the U.S. Economy*, New York: Basic Books.

——(1994) The Economics of Immigration, *Journal of Economic Literature*, XXXII, 1667–717.

Chanda, R. (2001) Movement of Natural Persons and the GATS, *World Economy*, 24(5) 631–54.

Chanda, R. (2004) Movement and Presence of Natural Persons and Developing Countries: Issues and Proposals for the GATS Negotiations, South Centre Working Paper 19, http://www.southcentre.org.

Chang, H.-J. (2002) Breaking the Mould: An Institutionalist Political Economy Alternative to the Neoliberal Theory of the Market and the State, *Cambridge Journal of Economics*, 26, 540.

Chaudhuri, S., Mattoo, A., and Self, R. (2004) Moving People to Deliver Services: How Can the WTO help? *Journal of World Trade*, 38(3), 363–94.

Congressional Research Service (CRS) (1980) Temporary Worker Programs: Background and Issues, Prepared for the Senate Committee on the Judiciary, February.

Council of Economic Advisors (CEA) (1986) *The Economic Effects of Immigration*, Washington, DC: Council of Economic Advisors.

Ducasse-Rogier, M. (2001) *The International Organization for Migration, 1951–2001*, Geneva: IOM.

Galarza, E. (1977) *Farm Workers and Agribusiness in California, 1947–1960*, Notre Dame, IN: University of Notre Dame Press.

General Accounting Office (GAO) (1988) *Illegal Aliens. Influence of Illegal Workers on the Wages and Working Conditions of Legal Workers*, Washington, DC: General Accounting Office, PEMD-88-13BR.

Ghosh, B. (1999) *Managing Migration: Time for a New International Regime?* Oxford: Oxford University Press.

Glivanos, I. (2008) Neoliberal Law: Unintended Consequences of Market-Friendly Law Reforms, *Third World Quarterly*, 29(6), 1087–99.

Global Commission on International Migration (GCIM) (2005) Migration in an Interconnected World: New Directions for Action, Also available electronically: www. gcim.org (October).

Global Forum on Migration and Development (GFMD) (2008) Available at http://www. gfmd.org/en/gfmd-documents-library/manila-gfmd-2008/cat_view/933-manila-gfmd-2008/945-contributions-to-roundtable-preparations.html.

Hansen, R. (forthcoming) The Two Faces of Liberalism.

International Labour Organisation (ILO) (2005) *ILO Multilateral Framework on Labour Migration. Non-Binding Principles and Guidelines for a Rights-Based Approach to Labor Migration*, Geneva: ILO.

Karatani, R. (2002) *How History Separated Refugee and Migrant Regimes: In Search of Their Institutional Origins*, New York: Oxford University Press.

Kategekwa, J. (2008) Liberalization of Trade in Health Services, South Centre Research Paper 16, http://www.southcentre.org.

Martin, P. (2009) *Importing Poverty? Immigration and the Changing Face of Rural America*, New Haven, CT: Yale University Press.

Mines, R. and Martin, P. (1984) Immigrant Workers and the California Citrus Industry, *Industrial Relations*, 23(1), 139–49.

OECD (2008) Tailor Immigration Policies to Future Needs, Says OECD, Press release, 10 September 2008.

Ruhs, M. and Martin, P.L. (2008) Numbers vs. Rights: Trade-Offs and Guest Worker Programs, *International Migration Review*, 42(1): 249–65.

Schmidt, V. (2006) Temporary Migrant Workers: Organizing and Protection Strategies by Trade Unions, in C. Kuptsch (ed.), *Merchants of Labour*, Geneva: ILO/IILS.

Smith, J. and Edmonston, B. (eds) (1997) *The New Americans: Economic, Demographic, and Fiscal Effects of Immigration*, Washington, DC: National Research Council.

Tamas, K. and Münz, R. (2006) *Labor Migrants Unbound? EU Enlargement, Transitional Measures and Labor Market Effects*, Stockholm: Institute for Futures Studies.

UN Population Division (2006) *International Migration Report 2005*, ST/ESA/SER.A/220.

World Bank (2006a) *Global Economic Prospects 2006: Economic Implications of Remittances and Migration*, Washington, DC: World Bank.

——(2006b) *The International Migration Agenda and the World Bank: Managing Risks, Enhancing Benefits*, Washington, DC: World Bank (September).

World Trade Organization (WTO) (2004) *World Trade Report, The Liberalization of Services Trade through the Movement of Natural Persons*, http://www.wto.org/english/res_e/book-sp_e/anrep_e/world_trade_report04_e.pdf.

Wurcelm, G. (2004) Movement of Workers in the WTO Negotiations: A Development Perspective, CGIM Global Migration Perspectives No. 15, http://www.gcim.org/en/ir_gmp.html.

2

High-Skilled Labour Migration

Alexander Betts and Lucie Cerna

Introduction

There is no easy distinction between 'high-skilled' and 'low-skilled' labour migration. However, highly skilled labour migration (henceforth HSLM) can be broadly understood to relate to migrants with a university degree or equivalent skills and training (Salt 1997). Martin (2003) identifies HSLM as comprising migrants who fall within the part of the workforce often described as 'professional, technical, kindred and related workers' (PTKs workers)—who have education or specialized knowledge that takes time to acquire, usually equivalent to a four-year post-secondary education. It commonly relates to the movement of nurses and health-care professionals, engineers, IT specialists, and teachers, for example. Although there are no authoritative estimates of HSLM numbers, Martin (2003) argues that the larger proportion of migration is HSLM, the harder it is to immigrate into that country such that HSLM is more prevalent in the industrialized world than the developing world. Based on extrapolation, he suggests that 75 per cent of migrants in the industrialized world are from the developing world, and of these, around 20 per cent—or 8 million—have PTK characteristics, with immigrants thereby comprising around 9 per cent of all PTKs in the industrialized world.

HSLM is controversial because of its distributive consequences, producing 'winners and losers'. It is conventionally seen as yielding benefits to receiving states and imposing costs upon sending states, not least through the so-called 'brain drain' effect and the implications that HSLM has for the domestic labour force. However, the role of remittances and of possibilities for circular migration to enable sending country nationals to return to their country of origin with new skills and resources has led to recognition that HSLM may, under certain conditions, lead to 'win-win' outcomes (GCIM 2005). These issues surrounding HSLM in a North–South context have contributed to the emergence of the so-called

'Migration and Development' debates that have come to dominate inter-state discussion on international cooperation and migration (Martin et al. 2007).

In contrast to many other areas of migration, HSLM is generally considered to be desirable by receiving countries. Consequently, depending on their economic situation, states are likely to have a preference for attracting, rather than excluding, the highly skilled. Yet, most migrant-sending states have little ability to control the exit of the highly skilled for their territory. Increasingly, this means that the international politics of migration is characterized by inter-state competition to attract the most desirable and skilled immigrants. As we enter an increasingly internationalized or global labour market for the highly skilled (Chiswick 2005: 7), so competition for labour is becoming an emerging feature of big power politics (Hollifield 2009). Where once states competed primarily at the level of military power, today great powers compete primarily in terms of their relative economic power and high-skilled labour.

In the context of this competitive environment, most states retain sovereign authority over their HSLM policies, unilaterally identifying the (*a*) economic sectors and (*b*) quotas for which they wish to liberalize their labour markets and make immigration visas available. They also adjust these policies in accordance with the evolving needs of their domestic economies. In some cases, this type of labour market liberalization will take place through limited forms of reciprocity—whether at the bilateral, regional, or global level—but on the whole the governance of HSLM remains at the unilateral level with individual states reluctant to delegate authority.

In many ways, this predominantly unilateral feature of the global governance of HSLM is unsurprising. Unlike refugee protection—which may be considered to be to some extent a global public good (the benefits of governance are non-excludable and non-rival between states)—or irregular migration and low-skilled labour migration—which may be considered to be a club good (the benefits of governance are excludable but non-rival between states), HSLM is generally a private good (for which the benefits of governance may be both excludable and rival between states). If liberalization takes place in relation to HSLM, for example, the benefits and costs will be confined to the sending states, the receiving state, and the migrant. Furthermore, given that—unlike low-skilled labour migration—the supply of HSLM is finite, it is characterized by rivalry between states. The private good character of HSLM means that one would expect global governance to be predominantly characterized by unilateralism and bilateralism, rather than multilateralism or regionalism.

However, one would nevertheless expect forms of bilateral cooperation to arise as a result of interdependence. Keohane and Nye (2001) define interdependence between actors A and B as occurring when costly effects are experienced in their bilateral interactions. The source of influence between interdependent actors is an asymmetry in the costly effects of these externalities, where the more powerful actor (A) is defined as the one that experiences fewer costly effects. By definition, HSLM creates a bilateral relationship between a sending state and a receiving state. The resulting interdependence may be symmetrical or asymmetrical.

Symmetrical interdependence can be defined as occurring when the costs and benefits of interaction are relatively evenly shared. Where it exists, cooperation may be more likely as a means to share the benefits and address the costs. For example, in the case of HSLM, regional cooperation becomes possible because of symmetrical interdependence. Asymmetrical interdependence can be defined as occurring when the costs and benefits of interaction are relatively unevenly shared. Where is exists, cooperation is less likely. In the case of HSLM, there will be little incentive for Northern states to be concerned with the costs of 'brain drain' in the South.

Consequently, bilateralism is more likely to be seen when there is symmetrical interdependence. However, unilateralism is more likely to take place when there is asymmetrical interdependence. Nevertheless, in situations in which there is asymmetrical interdependence, one may nevertheless see bilateral agreements. In the case of HSLM, for example, such situations may arise when issue-linkages incentivize bilateral cooperation involving HSLM and another migration issue such as low-skilled labour migration or another issue-area such as development.

A thin layer of multilateralism has emerged that has some relevance to HSLM, most notably around World Trade Organization (WTO) General Agreement on Trade in Services (GATS) Mode 4 and the Global Forum on Migration and Development (GFMD). However, it would be wrong to characterize HSLM governance as multilateral on this basis. Rather, Mode 4 is very limited in scope, implying very little constraint on state sovereignty, and is largely a reflection of declarations of unilateral liberalization that would have taken place anyway. Meanwhile, the GFMD is a dialogue and its role is more in facilitating subsequent bilateral deals than in attempting to create binding multilateral cooperation. The GFMD is nevertheless relevant to HSLM insofar as it plays a growing role in providing information, encouraging issue-linkage, and reducing transaction costs of bilateral cooperation (Abbott and Snidal 2001).

This chapter explores three areas. Firstly, it offers a characterization of the global governance of HSLM, suggesting that it is predominantly characterized by unilateral liberalization and bilateralism. Secondly, it offers an explanation for this type of governance, drawing upon global public goods theory and the literature on interdependence. Thirdly, it sets out the normative case for collective action on HSLM, based on efficiency and equity arguments. The chapter's core argument is that the absence of formal multilateral cooperation on HSLM is unsurprising given the confined distribution of externalities involved in HSLM. Nevertheless, opportunities exist for the development of mutually beneficial forms of collective action based primarily on bilateral partnership agreements, and there are strong efficiency and equity arguments supporting the role of a multilateral dialogue in the gradual emergence of the partnerships.

Characterizing the global governance of HSLM

In the context of HSLM, the most relevant governance cannot be considered to be 'global' in the sense of implying formal or multilateral rules and regulations. Authority over HSLM lies predominantly with states and in particular migrant-receiving states to determine which categories of HSLM they wish to attract and admit in accordance with their own economic interests (Siddique and Appleyard 2001). Nevertheless, HSLM is increasingly subject to a growing and complex array of bilateral agreements that facilitate forms of reciprocity for mutual gain while, moreover, two emerging multilateral forums serve to facilitate gradual liberalization in HSLM and the development of partnerships for mutual gain: notably GATS Mode 4 within the WTO context and the GFMD. This section briefly describes the global governance of HSLM, characterizing it as predominantly unilateral and bilateral, with an emerging layer of facilitative multilateralism.

Unilateralism

The governance of HSLM is predominantly characterized by unilateralism. States retain full sovereignty over who they admit into their territory and to whom they accord the right to work. Based on the preferences of domestic interests groups, states can define their labour immigration policies in accordance with their own economic needs. They will generally determine labour immigration strategies based on an analysis of their structural and cyclical economic circumstances, identifying the economic sectors and quotas within which visas will be available to high-skilled foreign workers. For example, the United States establishes how many H-1B visas it will make available and for which skill sectors, adapting this according to its own changing interests. Meanwhile, Europe, Canada, and Australia, for example, follow a similar approach.

On the other hand, predominantly HSLM-sending states generally have very little choice about the emigration of their trained workers. The internationally accepted norm against preventing exit from the territory means that most developing countries have limited ability to stop doctors, nurses, IT specialists, and engineers, for example, from attempting to pursue their careers abroad. The only limited means that most sending states have of influencing their highly skilled emigrant population is through policies directed towards diaspora engagement. India and the Philippines, for example, have developed concerted transnational strategies to engage their skilled diaspora abroad, maintaining their sense of national identity and financial engagement with the homeland.

In this context, most HSLM receiving countries have very little incentive to bind themselves to formal multilateral rules on HSLM. They are able to pick and choose between the sectors and provenance of their immigrants, and retain the flexibility to adapt their requirements with structural and cyclical economic change or shifting private sector priorities. The only structural constraint on industrialized receiving states comes from the emerging inter-state competition for talent that is gradually developing between receiving states. Beyond this, though, their interests are served more by a liberal global market based on inter-state competition than one which regulates or binds them in their immigration policies. Unilateral liberalization can therefore be seen to be the dominant characteristic of HSLM governance.

Bilateralism

The main exception to this dominant unilateralism is the emergence of bilateralism. In 2004, for example, it was estimated that there were around 176 bilateral agreements relating to labour recruitment (OECD 2004). Hatton (2007: 372) argues that the number of bilateral agreements in this area has increased significantly over time, in many cases being tailored to meet the needs of specific economic sectors in the receiving countries. The process of developing bilateral agreements is not limited to governmental authorities but often involves private and non-governmental organizations such as recruitment agencies, labour unions, professional associations, and employers (Hatton 2007).

A significant proportion of these bilateral agreements are conceived along North–South lines based on the recognition of mutual gain. Hatton (2007) highlights how receiving countries stand to benefit from improved access to high-skilled workers, while sending countries benefit from sharing in the benefits of their labour having access to developed country labour markets—through, for example, training and cultural exchange programmes. From a sending country perspective, bilateral cooperation may enable 'brain drain' to turn into 'brain gain' or to have other subsidiary benefits. In this context, HSLM is increasingly addressed in the context of debates on 'migration and development' and through the concept of 'circular migration', where the nationals of Southern states may be allowed to move temporarily to work in Northern states, returning with skills and other resources.

An important illustration of these types of bilateral agreements is in the context of health workers. The GFMD, for example, outlined a range of cases in which European states have fostered bilateral cooperation in relation to health workers. For instance, the UK government, in cooperation with other actors such as the Global Fund to Fight AIDS, TB, and Malaria, has been working with the government of Malawi to establish a six-year reform programme in the Malawian health sector in order to increase the salaries for health workers, create incentives to work in rural areas, return professionals from abroad, and strengthen local training capacity. Meanwhile, Belgium, Canada, the Netherlands, the United States, and others are funding programmes in the education and health sectors in the Caribbean countries, Democratic Republic of Congo, and Ghana (GFMD 2007: 10). Here, countries in the North offer support to countries in the South with the training of health workers, the creation of incentives for retention, and return of workers.

Occasionally, this type of bilateral cooperation takes place on a South–South basis. For example, Cuba has sent more than 67,000 health professionals to ninety-four countries since 1960, even though these 'medical brigades' exemplify a special form of South–South technical cooperation, which is based on the Cuban government's great investment in quality health education and surplus production of migrant labour as aid support. In addition, movements between developed and developing countries are assisted by non-governmenal organizations, such as Médecins sans Frontières, which currently supplies more than 3,400 medical missions every year to almost seventy countries. The movements of health-care workers are often short-term or circular (GFMD 2007: 10). Receiving countries gain through the high-skilled doctors and nurses, whereas sending countries receive an increase in human capital of their workers, who return to their home country.

An important feature of these 'migration and development' partnerships is that regional actors—notably the European Union (EU)—sometimes act as coherent political actors in establishing bilateral relationships. For example, due to labour market shortages in particular sectors, the European Commission (EC) has passed a directive on the admission of high-skilled immigrants for third-country nationals (i.e. EU Blue Card). The EU Blue Card is meant to create a single application procedure for non-EU workers to reside and work within the EU, and to establish a common set of rights for workers in member states. Each member state will maintain the right to determine the number of immigrant workers that can be admitted into the domestic labour market through the Blue Card, which raises the question whether the directive will provide any added value or only be based on a lowest-common denominator (Cerna 2008).

Even though measures to foster circular migration were not specifically introduced in the EU Blue Card proposal, the promotion of ethical recruitment standards to limit—if not ban—active recruitments by member states in developing countries already suffering from serious brain drain (especially in Africa) was included (EC 2007b). The EC supports the idea of circular migration, as mentioned in the EC Communication on Circular Migration released on 16 May 2007 ('On circular migration and mobility partnerships between the European Union and third countries'). The EU would like to focus on labour migration in general, but is willing to put in place 'mobility partnership that could include, at the request of the third country in question, measures to help address the risk of brain drain. They could also include mechanisms to facilitate circular migration, which by nature can help mitigate brain drain' (EC 2007a). Cooperation efforts are visible between the EU and developing countries. The EU has become more interested in third-country nationals from the North and the South to fill labour market shortages, without depleting the countries of their high-skilled workers. This also has to do with (self-interested) development efforts, mentioned above.

Within this emerging tapestry of bilateral relationships, many Southern states are becoming increasingly active in pursuing partnerships with Northern states. India offers a case in point. The Ministry of Overseas Indian Affairs (MOIA) specializes in trying to maximize opportunities that come from the presence of non-resident Indians (NRIs). For example, it has actively pursued bilateral agreements with Poland, Belgium, France, Sweden, the EU, and the United States, with varying degrees of success (NRIOL 2007). One of its main focuses has been to secure access to Northern labour markets for high-skilled migrants, especially those from its emerging IT sector. The underlying logic is that such partnerships can be win-win: receiving countries receive needed high-skilled workers; in return they offer certain benefits and privileged market access to these Indian workers (Kirkegaard 2008).

An emerging layer of multilateral facilitation

There is very little formal multilateral regulation of states' HSLM policies. However, two institutions nevertheless play some role—albeit in different ways—as facilitators of bilateral cooperation: the WTO and the GFMD. It would be wrong to see them as a manifestation of strong, binding, multilateral governance in the area of HSLM but it would also be incorrect to suggest that they have no relevance in the global governance of HSLM. Their role as 'facilitators of bilateralism' can be explained in turn.

Within the framework of the WTO, GATS covers four major groups of services. Mode 1 focuses on cross-border supply—services but not consumers cross borders (e.g. telephone services). Mode 2 focuses on consumption abroad—the consumer travels abroad to receive the service (e.g. tourism). Mode 3 focuses on foreign direct investment or commercial presence—services are provided abroad via a subsidiary of a firm located in the country where the service is provided (e.g. banking). Mode 4 focuses on the temporary movement of natural persons—services are provided by individuals abroad (e.g. consultants travelling across borders) (Martin 2003).

WTO GATS Mode 4 is unique in that it relates to the movement of individual service providers across borders and so implies a potentially binding obligation on states to admit non-nationals into their territory (Lavenex 2003). Lavenex (2006: 47) argues that Mode 4 has potentially profound implications for migration:

> GATS is the first multilateral treaty to include binding multilateral rules on migration. Although the treaty allows for a great degree of flexibility and does not in practice exceed existing national commitments of the participating countries, it does have direct implications for national immigration systems and labour market regulations, especially since once

adopted, these commitments cannot be unilaterally reversed. In addition, the WTO's dispute settlement system provides for a supranational enforcement mechanism to ensure compliance.

However, in practice Mode 4 is so far very limited in scope, applying only to a narrow group of people. Firstly, it is not 'a high-skilled migration clause' but is confined to temporary, skilled, contractual service providers engaged in intra-firm movement. As point two in the GATS Annex states: 'The Agreement shall not apply to measures affecting natural persons seeking access to the employment market of a Member, nor shall it apply to measures regarding citizenship, residence or employment on a permanent basis' (cited in Martin 2006).

Secondly, it is limited to the specific visa commitments that individual states are prepared to make in the context of broader WTO negotiations.[1] Indeed up to now, these commitments have been extremely limited. Crucially, GATS negotiations are often not reciprocal (Hatton 2007). Rather, they involve individual states making commitments to liberalize in relation to (a) a given employment category, (b) a given country or countries, and (c) a given quota. Only once a liberalization commitment is made do the rules become binding.

At the moment, these commitments are relatively limited, and have been subject to polarization, most notably between India and the United States. The GATS states explicitly that countries may cite national immigration policies as a reason not to open a particular sector to the temporary movement of natural persons or to deny entry to certain individuals. This clause has been a source of divisiveness within US domestic politics in which the US Trade Representative has viewed Mode 4 as a trade issue while other actors have seen Mode 4 as an immigration issue for which Congress approval is required in order to make concessions.[2] India in turn has sought concessions from the United States in the area of GATS Mode 4 and attempted to implicitly link a demand for such concessions to its willingness to liberalize in other areas of the trade negotiations as part of the Doha Round of trade talks (Beattie 2008).

In summary, then, GATS Mode 4 has, until now, been extremely limited in the scope of its implications for creating binding obligations in the area of HSLM policy. Rather than creating significant or reciprocally negotiated obligations, it has simply served as a forum within which states have declared existing commitments to liberalize their high-skilled labour markets, which they would probably have made unilaterally in any case. However, insofar as the Mode 4 framework institutionalizes these unilateral commitments and makes them binding over time, it may eventually become a more significant regulatory framework.

The creation of a GFMD was proposed by the UN Secretary General at the United Nations (UN) High-Level Dialogue on Migration and Development in September 2006. It was established outside the UN system as a state-driven process, with the role of the UN Special Representative on Migration and Development providing a link to the UN system. The objectives of the GFMD are to improve dialogue and cooperation between states and to promote practical outcomes on international migration and development issues. The first meeting took place in Brussels in 2007, the second in Manila in 2008, the third in Athens in 2009, and the fourth in Mexico City in 2010. Subsequent forums are planned for Madrid and Buenos Aires, for example. Civil society stakeholders were not directly involved, although provisions for separate deliberations were provided. At the request of migrant-receiving states predominantly in the North, the GFMD is conceived as an informal consultative nature. Its approach is to be non-binding, state-led, voluntary, and informal (Wickramasekara 2008). Its thematic focus is not intended to address international migration in general but the narrow set of issues that can be subsumed under the category of 'migration and development'.

Although the GFMD was conceived as an informal dialogue, it is not without significance for international cooperation. As a model, it offers the possibility that like-minded states may choose to pursue issues raised and discussed in the Forum on a bilateral basis. Indeed, there is evidence to suggest that the discussions of circular migration initiated at the first Forum in 2007 contributed to the development of an agreement for a pilot project on circular migration between the EU and Mauritius. In that sense, the GFMD's relevance can be understood to be as a facilitator of bilateral partnerships rather than as a vehicle for the development of binding multilateral governance. It increasingly plays that role in relation to HSLM by bringing together states in a forum in which information is provided, playing an epistemic role in the development of new knowledge on the relationship between migration and development, reducing some of the transaction costs of bilateral cooperation, and enabling issue-linkage across migration and development issues.

Explaining the global governance of HSLM

The previous section has characterized the governance of HSLM as primarily existing at the unilateral and bilateral levels. The question then is to explain why this is the case. A number of authors have argued for greater formal multilateralism in the area of labour migration (Bhagwati 2003; Ghosh 2005; Hollifield 2009), regarding the status quo to be sub-optimal and somehow surprising. This section, however, suggests that the characterization outlined above is not as counter-intuitive as many of these accounts imply. It uses global public goods theory to explain why HSLM governance is predominantly unilateral and bilateral rather than multilateral, and interdependence theory to explain when and why bilateral agreements emerge.

HSLM governance as a private good

In international politics, as in domestic politics, the most common justification for the creation of binding, formal institutions is the existence of externalities

(Kahler and Lake 2003). If a state is positively or negatively affected as a result of the choices of another state, and has no influence over that choice, there may be a strong case that those states would be collectively better off creating common institutions to facilitate collective action. This is because if one state acts in isolation, it will not have any incentive to take into account the external costs and benefits of its decision-making, and hence may over-produce negative externalities and under-produce positive externalities. If all states have little incentive to take into account the externalities of their choices, the likelihood is that all states will be worse off than they would have been had they collaborated.

International Relations has long recognized that the nature of the externalities involved in a given issue-area is important for considering the types of collective action that will return states to a collectively optimal position. In particular, global public goods theory has been developed to explore the types of institutional framework that are required to address different global problems, based on an understanding of the types of externalities involved. A global public good—as with a domestic public good like street lighting—has two main characteristics: its benefits are non-excludable between states (i.e. all actors benefit once a good has been provided irrespective of whether they themselves contribute) and its benefits are non-rival between states (i.e. the enjoyment of the benefits by one actor does not diminish the enjoyment of the good by other actors). For global public goods, it has been argued that multilateral collective action is required in order to avoid states free-riding on the contributions of other states and this in turn leading to a collectively suboptimal outcome in which all states are worse off that they would have been had they collaborated (Olson 1965).

Some authors have argued that it is counter-intuitive that there is no global migration regime because such a regime would represent a global public good (Ghosh 2005; Hollifield 2009). This is a misleading argument. The governance of refugee protection may be to some extent a global public good, given that if one state provides protection all other states benefit to some degree from the human rights and security benefits. One would therefore expect the type of multilateral regime that already exists for refugees. However, the same logic does not apply so easily to other areas of international migration. The governance of irregular and low-skilled migration, for example, are better conceived as club goods, given that although the benefits may be non-rival, institutional structures can be conceived that make the benefits of governance excludable. One might therefore expect regional, inter-regional, or 'club' structures of governance to emerge to regulate irregular and low-skilled labour migration. For HSLM, though, the logic is different. The governance of HSLM is not only excludable—given that the costs and benefits can be restricted to the sending and receiving state and the migrant—but it is also characterized by rivalry— given that, unlike for unskilled labour migration, the supply of the highly skilled is finite. The governance of HSLM is therefore more appropriately conceived as a private good, for which one would anticipate unilateral or bilateral governance.

Hollifield (2009) argues that migration governance—if it were to exist—would represent a global public good, because the benefits of orderliness and predictability of movement that it would bring would be available to all states and make them collectively better off than they currently are. To some extent the logic behind that argument has validity. As with international trade, if all protectionist barriers were lifted and liberalization took place to allow labour to move in the same way as goods, services, and capital, then the likelihood is that aggregate global welfare would increase (Holzinger 2003). It would enable labour to be employed where it was most efficient. Indeed, this is part of the logic that has led the EU to facilitate the free movement of labour on a regional basis (Hatton 2007). However, making this argument—that full liberalization, if it were to happen, would lead to a Pareto Optimal outcome—is not the same thing as arguing that the governance of migration is inherently a global public good.

From the starting point of a world in which there are barriers to the mobility of high-skilled labour migrants and a shift towards the full liberalization of labour mobility is remote, the creation of inter-state rules relating to the regulation and liberalization of HSLM cannot be seen to have the properties of non-excludability or non-rivalry. On the contrary, if a state or group of states agree to liberalize in the area of HSLM, the benefits and costs of that liberalization are confined to the receiving state, the sending state, and the migrant. There is nothing inherent about HSLM that makes those costs and benefits of a change in regulation or liberalization significantly diffuse beyond the two states involved. Moreover, the governance of HSLM also exhibits the characteristic of rivalry insofar as the supply of talent is finite and so one state's decision to take in a highly skilled migrant, by definition, means that the benefits of that worker are unavailable to another state.

These inherent characteristics of excludability and rivalry mean that the governance of HSLM is more appropriately conceived to be a private good than a global public good. Its benefits are confined and finite. As with private goods in domestic politics, one would therefore not anticipate the emergence of binding, formal multilateral institutions. Rather, the type of governance one would anticipate would be based predominantly on unilateralism and bilateralism rather than the type of formalized multilateralism that exists in the case of refugee protection. In other words, it is an area in which states can and do compete over costs and benefits rather than those costs and benefits being inherently open to all.

The role of interdependence

Given this private goods logic, the default form of governance would be unilateralism. However, in practice, HSLM is increasingly characterized by an emerging tapestry of bilateral agreements. Interdependence theory offers an explanation for when and why these bilateral agreements emerge. Keohane and Nye (2001) describe interdependence between actors A and B as occurring when costly effects are experienced in their bilateral interactions. They describe two types of interdependence—sensitivity and vulnerability interdependence. Sensitivity interdependence refers to how quickly changes in one country bring about changes in the other country, and the significance of the costly effects. Vulnerability interdependence is premised on the ability of the affected country to offset the costly effects through policy change.

It is easy to see how this logic plays out in the context of HSLM. Sending countries are sensitivity interdependent to the unilateral migration governance exercised by receiving states. The decision of a receiving state A to admit or not admit a high-skilled migrant from sending state B has costly implications for B in terms of loss of human capital ('brain drain').[3] However, it may also have positive implications in terms of remittances or the return of that individual with new skills. Indeed B's vulnerability interdependence will be related to its ability to offset costs or to attain benefits that stem from movement by, for example, securing the benefits of remittances or training.

Keohane and Nye (2001) judge power according to the uneven distribution of costly effects across interdependent actors. Indeed this highlights how in some cases interdependence may be relatively more symmetrical and in other cases it may be more asymmetrical in terms of the distribution of costs and benefits. In the case of HSLM, for example, there may be situations in which the costs and benefits are highly asymmetrical—with receiving state A benefiting from 'taking' the migrants it wants, and B unequivocally losing as a result of the 'brain drain' effect. On the other hand, though, the effects may be more symmetrical and potentially mutually beneficial. This may be the case if B shares in the benefits of movement or if B's own policies—in areas such as education and training—exert influence on the costs and benefits available to A.

Where interdependence is highly asymmetrical, one would anticipate that bilateral collective action would be less likely. The receiving state A would be in a position to unilaterally determine its own immigration policies without being concerned by the policies of sending state B. On the other hand, though, where interdependence is more symmetrical and A is dependent upon B in order to maximize the benefits and minimize the costs of HSLM, a bilateral agreement would be more likely since it could lead to mutually beneficial outcomes.

In the context of North–South partnerships on HSLM, issue-linkage represents one means by which interdependence may be made more symmetrical by adding migration or non-migration issues to the bargain in areas in which the North may have sensitivity interdependence. Indeed, the 'migration and development' context has allowed issue-linkage across different areas of migration in ways that have created a basis for reciprocity that can lead to mutual gain. In many of the agreements, Northern partners have benefited from privileged access to skilled migrants or guarantees of readmission, while Southern states have benefited from a Northern commitment to facilitate remittance flows or to provide training and education. In other words, issue-linkage has contributed to making interdependence more symmetrical, enhancing the prospects for mutually beneficial bilateral agreements.

The multilateral structures that have emerged in relation to HSLM have helped to facilitate states' recognition of bilateral opportunities. In particular, the GFMD has served as a 'clearing house' for prospective bilateral partnerships. By providing information, a space for dialogue, and enabling the participation of epistemic communities, it has enabled states to recognize possibilities for managing interdependence through mutually beneficial bilateral partnerships. To a lesser extent, GATS Mode 4 has also served a role in facilitating reciprocal liberalization. However, the logic has been slightly different insofar as that the concessions have been largely based on unilateral commitments by receiving states implicitly connected to more diffuse reciprocity across the entire framework of trade negotiations.

The normative case for collective action on HSLM

So having outlined what the global governance of HSLM is, and offered an explanation for why it is as it is, the question that remains is: how *should* it look? In many ways analysis of this question follows logically from what has been outlined and argued above. The nature of HSLM governance as a private good undermines the efficiency case for formal, binding multilateral governance in this area to a large extent but it does not foreclose an efficiency case for facilitative multilateralism that works to enable mutually beneficial bilateral partnerships. In contrast, however, there may be a stronger equity case for multilateralism to have more 'teeth' but the practical constraints on achieving this mean that equity concerns may be more feasibly met through forms of 'facilitative multilateralism'.

Efficiency

In theory, a fully globalized labour market would be Pareto Optimal for all states. Just as the argument is often made that economic liberalization for goods, services, and capital is more efficient than protectionism, so the same claim could be made with regard to HSLM; aggregate welfare would be better off with full liberalization. However, full liberalization is not going to happen any time soon because of power. Beginning with the status quo, the challenge is that liberalization creates 'winners and losers'. Receiving states are reluctant to concede sovereignty over liberalization because, firstly, they benefit more from having the authority to choose when and how they liberalize; secondly, in the context of competition for economic power, they are concerned with their relative economic gains vis-à-vis other HSLM receiving states, and hence they compete for the best talent. This means that the efficiency case in relation to collective action on HSLM cannot begin from this level of arguing for or against full liberalization. Rather, it is more sensibly developed on the basis of making the case for specific win-win partnerships.

Furthermore, the fact that HSLM cannot be conceived to be a global public good but is rather a private good changes the argument in favour of formal multilateral governance. It means that there is nothing inherent about the nature of the externalities and types of interdependence involved that means there is a strong efficiency case for governing HSLM at a formal, multilateral level. Nevertheless, there may be a strong efficiency case for some forms of collective action. In many situations, policies can be developed for mutual gains, especially on a bilateral level. Where South–North HSLM, for example, takes place, there is a strong case that both the sending and the receiving state may be collectively better off with cooperation than they would be acting in isolation. Northern states may be better equipped to identify and recruit high-skilled workers given collaboration, and Southern states may be better equipped to secure benefits relating to remittances, training and education, and eventual return.

Even though the efficiency case for formal, binding multilateral regulation is weak given the private goods nature of HSLM governance, there is a normative case for multilateral structures that work to facilitate 'win-win' partnerships between sending and receiving states. For example, the GFMD could have a strong role to play in information provision, reducing transaction costs, and creating opportunities for issue-linkage (Keohane 1982). In that sense the normative case for multilateralism on HSLM would not support a GFMD (or similar structure) as a facilitator of 'global governance' per se or a multilateral, UN-based normative framework but rather a GFMD that facilitated the creation of mutually beneficial bilateral partnerships.

Equity

As with many areas of migration, HSLM potentially creates winners and losers. This is most likely to be the case when it involves high-skilled labour mobility from South to North, possibly leading to 'brain drain'. Much of the so-called 'migration and development' debate has been about trying to identify the conditions under which Southern states may share in the benefits of this type of migration, through, for example, remittances and training (Olesen 2002; Winters et al. 2003; UN 2006). Nevertheless, the benefits and costs are often asymmetrically distributed. Given that Northern states can attract the highly skilled from the South and few Southern states are able to prevent or incentivize people not to move, Northern states end up being implicit 'rule-makers' and Southern states 'rule-takers'. Even when bilateral partnerships emerge, they are often skewed in favour of the migrant-receiving state's interests.

This creates a potentially strong equity case for developing more binding forms of multilateral governance in the area of HSLM. Indeed, some Southern states have called for binding, rule-based frameworks to limit the 'brain drain', while other Southern states such as India have, in contrast, called for binding, rule-based frameworks to force Northern states to open up their labour markets to the Southern highly skilled (Martin 2006). Indeed, it is fairly clear that in relation to HSLM, Southern migrant-sending states have a weaker bargaining position than Northern migrant-receiving states. This creates a power asymmetry in bilateral negotiations in which Southern states effectively have to 'take what is on offer' or be faced with Northern states acting unilaterally on HSLM.

From this, one could make a strong equity case for binding multilateralism. However, in the short to medium term it is clear that such structures are not going to come into existence and the more realistic option to ensure greater equity than exists under the status quo is likely to be the development of the type of 'facilitative multilateralism' outlined above. Rather than seeking binding rules, a dialogue such as the GFMD at least has the potential, over time, to socialize states into thinking about migration partnerships in ways that take into account equity considerations and make them more aware of the implications of interdependence. Dialogue will not dismantle inter-state power asymmetries but it may gradually sensitize states to the need to cooperate and the value of ensuring that those partnerships are equitable and just.

Conclusion

The governance of HSLM is predominantly based on unilateralism. Migrant-receiving states retain sovereign authority to determine who they admit into their territory and to whom they accord the right to work. When they open up their labour market, it is based on unilateral liberalization. In some cases, though, states do engage in bilateral agreements on HSLM or that link HSLM to other sets of issues. For example, a range of North–South partnerships are increasingly based on Northern states getting privileged access to highly skilled workers in exchange for helping to create the conditions under which Southern states can share in the benefits of HSLM. Although there is a thin layer of multilateralism relevant to HSLM—notably through the WTO and the GFMD—this does not imply that HSLM governance can or should be characterized as 'multilateral'. Rather, these structures are best understood as institutions that reflect the dominance of unilateralism and work to facilitate bilateralism.

The explanation for the status quo is relatively simple: externalities. Unlike the global governance of refugees which can be broadly characterized as a global public good or the global governance of irregular and low-skilled migration which can be understood as a club good, the governance of HSLM represents a private good. The costs and benefits of HSLM are confined to the sending country, the receiving country, and the migrant. The costs and benefits of a given form of liberalization or regulation are characterized by excludability rivalry. This means that states can effectively regulate this issue through unilateralism or bilateral partnerships.

One would expect unilateral behaviour to dominate where there is asymmetrical interdependence. When the sending state bears the costs of interdependence, the powerful receiving state will have little incentive to act in any way other than unilateralism. In contrast, bilateralism will be more likely where there is more symmetrical interdependence, and hence there are mutual benefits from cooperation or when issue-linkage connects HSLM to areas in which the receiving state has a higher degree of sensitivity interdependence and hence an interest in cooperation.

Given the type of externalities that exist, the dominant type of cooperation that one would expect to see in the area of HSLM is collective action based on bilateral partnerships. Yet this is not to say that multilateral institutions have no role to play. It just means that their role is likely to be most appropriately targeted at the facilitation of bilateral partnerships than the development of binding multilateral norms. In particular, there is a strong efficiency and equity case for a multilateral dialogue to facilitate bilateral agreements, along the lines of the GFMD. The value-added of an entity like the GFMD is that it can be the facilitator of mutually beneficial bilateral partnerships on HSLM through, for example, reducing transaction costs, providing information, and identifying possible issue-linkages across migration and development.

Notes

1. Interview with Alejandro Jara, Deputy Director of the WTO, July 2008; interview with Antonia Carzaniga, WTO employee responsible for GATS Mode 4 negotiations, July 2008.
2. Interview with Paul Malar, Economic Counsellor of the Australian Permanent Mission to the WTO, July 2008. For an analysis of the US domestic interest groups affected by Mode 4, see, for example, Sarah Anderson, 'U.S. Immigration Policy on the Table at the WTO', *Global Politician*, http://www.globalpolitician.com/21446-immigration.
3. The term 'brain drain' is used as a synonym for the movement of human capital, where the net flow of expertise is heavily in one direction (Salt 1997).

References

Abbott, K. and Snidal, D. (2001) International 'Standards' and International Governance, *Journal of European Public Policy*, 8(3), 345–70.

Beattie, A. (2008) Visa Offer Adds to Doha Momentum, *Financial Times*, 27 July.

Bhagwati, J. (2003) Borders Beyond Control, *Foreign Affairs*, 82(1), 98–104.

Cerna, L. (2008) Towards an EU Blue Card? Delegation of National High-Skilled Immigration Politics to the EU Level, COMPAS Working Paper WP-08-65.

Chiswick, B. (2005) High-Skilled Immigration in the International Arena, IZA Discussion Paper 1782, http://ftp.iza.org/dp1782.pdf.

European Commission (EC) (2007a) Circular Migration and Mobility Partnerships Between the European Union and Third-Countries, EC Memo 197 (16 May), http://europa.eu/rapid/pressReleasesAction.do?reference=MEMO/07/197.

——(2007b) Attractive Conditions for the Admission and Residence of Highly Qualified Workers, EC Memo 423 (23 October), http://europa.eu/rapid/pressReleasesAction.do?reference=MEMO/07/423.

Ghosh, B. (2005) Managing Migration: Whither the Missing Regime?, Draft Article of The Migration Without Borders Series, UNESCO, http://unesdoc.unesco.org/images/0013/001391/139149e.pdf.

Global Commission on Migration (GCIM) (2005) *Migration in an Interconnected World: New Directions for Action*, Geneva: GCIM.

Global Forum on Migration and Development (GFMD) (2007) Session 1.1: Highly Skilled Migration: Balancing Interests and Responsibilities, GFMD Background Paper, Brussels, 9–11 July, http://www.gfmd-fmmd.org/en/system/files/RT+1+1+Background+paper+en.pdf.

Global Forum on Migration and Development (GFMD) (2008) Available at http://www.gfmd.org/en/gfmd-documents-library/manila-gfmd-2008/cat_view/933-manila-gfmd-2008/945-contributions-to-roundtable-preparations.html.

Hatton, T. (2007) Should We Have a WTO for International Migration? *Economic Policy*, 22(50), 339–83.

Hollifield, J. (2009) A Public Goods Approach to Managing Migration, Paper prepared for United Nations Conference, New York.

Holzinger, K. (2003) The Problems of Collective Action: A New Approach, Max-Planck Institute Papers.

Kahler, M. and Lake, D. (eds) (2003) *Governance in a Global Economy: Political Authority in Transition*, Princeton, NJ: Princeton University Press.

Keohane, R. (1982) Demand for International Regimes? *International Organization*, 36(2): 325–55.

——and Nye, J. (2001) *Power and Interdependence*, 3rd edn, New York: Longman.

Kirkegaard, J.F. (2008) Demand the Supply, Peterson Institute of International Economics (27 March), http://www.petersoninstitute.org/publications/opeds/oped.cfm?ResearchID=901.

Lavenex, S. (2003) Globalization, Trade and Migration: Towards the Dissociation of Immigration Politics? UCLA Ronald Burkle Center for International Relations Working Paper.

——(2006) The Competition State, in M.P. Smith and A. Favell (eds), *The Human Face of Global Mobility: International Highly Skilled Migration in Europe, North America and the Asia-Pacific*, New Brunswick: Transaction Publishers.

Martin, P. (2003) Highly Skilled Labour Migration: Sharing the Benefits, ILO Working Paper, http://www.oit.org/public/english/bureau/inst/download/migration2.pdf.

——(2006) GATS, Migration and Labour Standards, International Institute for Labour Studies Discussion Paper 165, Geneva: ILO.

——Martin, S., and Cross, S. (2007) High-Level Dialogue on Migration and Development, *International Migration*, 45(1), 7–25.

Non-Resident Indians Online (NRIOL) (2007) Manpower from India Needed to Support Ageing Population There, (27 August), http://www.nriol.com/content/snippets/snippet1168.asp.

Olesen, H. (2002) Migration, Return and Development: An Institutional Perspective, *International Migration*, 40(5), 125–50.

Olson, M. (1965) *The Logic of Collective Action*, Cambridge, MA: Harvard University Press.

Organisation for Economic Co-operation and Development (OECD) (2004) *Migration for Employment: Bilateral Agreements at a Crossroads*, Paris: OECD.

Ruhs, M. and Martin, P.L. (2008) Numbers vs. Rights: Trade-Offs and Guest Worker Programs, *International Migration Review*, 42(1), 249–65.

Salt, J. (1997) International Movements of the Highly Skilled, OECD Occasional Papers 3.

Siddique, M. and Appleyard, R. (2001) International Migration into the 21st Century: Selected Issues, in M. Siddique (ed.), *International Migration into the 21st Century*, Northampton, MA: Edgar Elgar.

UN Population Division (2006) *International Migration Report 2005*, ST/ESA/SER.A/220.

United Nations (UN) (2006) International Migration and Development, Report of the Secretary-General (18 May), UN Doc. A/60/871.

Wickramasekara, P. (2008) Globalisation, International Labour Migration and the Rights of Migrant Workers, *Third World Quarterly*, 29(7), 1247–64.

Winters, A. et al. (2003) Liberalising Temporary Movement of Natural Persons: An Agenda for the Development Round, *The World Economy*, 26(8), 1137–61.

3

Irregular Migration

Franck Düvell

Introduction

Large-scale irregular migration is a relatively new social phenomenon. Whilst it has been reported as early as the 1930s, such as in Palestine, the Netherlands, and in the United States, and again in the United States during the 1950s, it only became a large-scale and global phenomenon from the 1980s. Meanwhile, irregular migration is reported from almost every country across the globe, such as Russia and the United Kingdom, South Korea and Malaysia, Venezuela and Chile, South Africa and even Botswana. It is equally recorded from high-, medium-, and low-income countries. The United Nations' population division (1997: 27) states that undocumented migration is 'one of the fastest growing forms of migration in the world today'. Estimates on irregular immigrants suggest that there could be between 2–4 million in the European Union (EU) (Vogel 2009), 8–12 million in the United States (Cornelius 2006), and over 6 million in Russia. Worldwide there might be 40 million or more migrants who are irregular (Düvell 2006). This amounts to about a fifth of all global migrants.[1]

Over the past ten to fifteen years, irregular migration[2] has become a top policy concern. In 1986, the international reporting system on migration of the Organisation for Economic Co-operation and Development (OECD) began to regularly report on irregular migration. Meanwhile, a plethora of bilateral and multilateral European, American, and other regional actors, as well as intergovernmental and international policies and institutions, including non-governmental organizations (NGOs) are devoted to or play a role in tackling this phenomenon. Whilst many policies and politics explicitly address irregular migration, even more are embedded in politics that address other policy fields, such as economic cooperation or development. This chapter will illustrate that the governance of irregular migration is a driving force in the globalization of migration policy as a whole.

So far, the governance of irregular migration is not guided by an international normative or institutional framework, hence it is not yet global; instead it is of a mostly regional nature as expressed by several regional consultation processes (RCPs). However, a trend can be observed towards an expansion of regional regimes that as a consequence become increasingly inter- and trans-regional and suggest more global approaches. Initially, the governance of irregular migration has been mostly driven by security concerns and aims at repressing this type of migration. In the meantime, the human rights aspects of irregular migration have also gained importance though it still plays only a minor role (Koser 2005).

This chapter considers any policy initiative addressing irregular migration that goes beyond the scope of the national, such as bilateral, multilateral, and regional arrangements. Most of these are not global by definition though this contribution argues that they represent either a step towards the emergence of a global approach or a facet of more or less coordinated global policies. First, it sketches the emergence of irregular migration as an issue for regional and global governance. Second, it analyses two cases of regional, inter-regional, and trans-regional approaches to irregular migration: Europe and the Americas. Third, building upon these cases, it explains the emerging trends in actors and institutions at the global level, highlighting the growing role of RCPs as a model for governance in this area, and the relatively limited protection regime for vulnerable irregular migrants.

The emergence of irregular migration as an issue for regional and global governance

Nowadays, the concept of 'illegal immigration' is so frequently used in public and policy discourses, and has become so common, that it tends to be forgotten that this has not always been the case. Indeed, it has only gained such prominence in recent decades. Therefore, it must be treated as a rather new, late-modern feature.

> It was only when states were in a position to formulate rules governing the entry and residence of foreigners and to enforce them that contravention of those rules—and consequently the concept of illegal immigration—became possible. (House of Lords 2002, part 2, paragraph 17)

Whilst immigration restrictions that addressed unwelcomed immigrants as 'undesirable aliens', 'fugitive offenders', or 'continental agitators' were introduced from the late nineteenth century,[3] the concepts of 'aliens illegally present in the country' (US 1920s, see Ngai 2004) or 'clandestine entrance' (Netherlands) were first applied during the 1920s and 1930s. The first systematic use of the concept of 'illegal migration' seems to date back to British foreign policies and refers to unwanted Jewish immigration to Palestine prior to the founding of the state of Israel (1920–47) (Bauer 1971). After the Second World War however, under conditions of economic growth and a demand for workers, aliens who entered European countries were rather conceptualized as 'spontaneous migrants' and could easily regularize their position (Siméant 1998: 130; Engbersen 2001). Only in the United States during the 1950s, for about a decade under President Eisenhower, serious efforts were made to reduce irregular migration from Mexico (Dillin 2006). European practices began to change only with the economic crisis of the late 1960s and 1970s, which resulted in protectionist migration policies and the implementation of immigration restrictions in all European countries.[4] And in the United States, after 1990, efforts were stepped up again to tackle irregular immigration (Hanson 2007: 10). Once it became clear that regulations and enforcement actions did not produce the intended results, successive legislation was introduced that penalized irregular migrants and increasingly also those who facilitate irregular immigration and employers.[5] Finally, throughout the 1980s and 1990s, visa regulations were imposed by all OECD countries onto an increasing number of countries. This 'reduced freedom of movement' (OECD 1990: 84) for refugees, labour migrants, family members, and tourists alike led to an increase of irregular migration. As a consequence, unwanted migrants were 'criminalized' and their entry discouraged (Luciani 1993; Guiraudon 2002).

In the United States, large-scale irregular migration was recorded during the 1940s (Dillin 2006) and again from the 1970s (Martin 1986). In Europe, irregular migration was initially only occasionally recorded as in France during the late 1960s (Holm 2004), the United Kingdom and Germany during the early 1970s (Diamant 1973), and Italy as late as during the early 1990s (see Sciortino and Colombo 2004). Only from the 1980s and 1990s was large-scale irregular immigration recorded across almost all OECD countries. Two processes explain this phenomenon (Düvell 2006). First, economic transformation in industrialized countries generated a demand for flexible, low-skilled, and low-paid workers, notably in the service sector. But neither were indigenous workers available or prepared for such jobs nor was supplementary labour migration wanted politically. Hence, a tension was created between economics and politics which triggered irregular immigration. Second, in the wake of the collapse of the communist bloc and a series of conflicts across the globe, an 'asylum crisis' unfolded. Subsequently, large numbers of refugees and migrants often irregularly entered OECD countries and turned to the asylum system. Some irregular migration is permanent immigration, some is temporary immigration, and some is purely for transit purposes; the motives of the individuals range from seeking refuge, finding employment, joining family members, and gaining experience to pursuing certain lifestyles.

At the level of discourse, irregular migration—or 'illegal migration' as it is often referred to[6]—is as blurred as it is politically loaded. 'Illegal migration' can refer to clandestine entry, overstaying, or irregular employment. It covers serious offences such as falsifying documents and comparably minor deviations from the rules, such as working a few more hours than permitted. Frequently, irregular migration is conflated with refugees and asylum seekers and with human smuggling and trafficking; and sometimes it is related to organized crime. Often, unwanted migrants are scapegoated, stereotyped, and criminalized and held responsible for an array of social problems, such as unfair competition over jobs, under-cutting wages, or welfare fraud. The purpose usually is to alert the public, dramatize the discussion over migration, or to call for tougher policies (Bigo 2001; for the EU also see Vollmer 2009). Thus, as shown below, 'illegal migration' has almost become a kind of war cry.

Alternatively, some economists are less critical about the effects of irregular migration. For instance, Hanson (2007: 5) concludes 'that there is little evidence that legal immigration is economically preferable to illegal immigration. In fact, illegal immigration responds to market forces in ways that legal immigration does not.... It provides US businesses with the types of workers they want, when they want them, and where they want them.' Equally, Boswell and Straubhaar (2003: 1) suggest there can be an 'economically optimal level of illegal migration'. Finally, certain industries and employers reject and criticize enforcement actions that are too tough. Thus, law and policy makers receive contrasting messages and must find the right balance.

As it is shown, the general conditions for irregular migration are set by economic and political parameters. But migration became irregular only by the introduction of protectionist immigration policies, according restrictions, and the criminalization of unwanted migrants. People who nevertheless wish to migrate for the sake of realizing their aspirations sometimes ignore or violate the law. Ultimately, irregular migration is an expression of a confrontation between self-selected or autonomous agents and the state (Düvell 2005; also see Shrestha 1987) and can be interpreted as a social conflict (Jordan and Düvell 2002). Thus, irregular migration is a product of specific political–economic conditions and a legal, political, and social construct of the late twentieth century.

Initially, irregular migration was discussed and dealt with on the national level only and states only dealt with irregular migrants at their borders or on their territory. But from the late 1970s, irregular migration was reported regularly to international bodies, notably the OECD's reporting system on migration (SOPEMI), and thereby entered the international stage. For instance, references to 'uncontrolled flows' were made in 1976 (OECD 1977: 38) and to 'clandestine immigration' in 1977 (OECD 1978: 5). In 1980, the first referral to 'illegal immigration' was found (OECD 1981: 16), made it to the headlines in 1986 (OECD 1986: 15), and in 1998, finally became a permanent column of the SOPEMI reports. From the mid-1980s, efforts were made by the EU to first develop a supranational policy response and second, from the early and mid-1990s, to promote regional processes involving non-EU countries. And in

North America, from the late 1980s, a tripartite response by the United States, Canada, and Mexico began to take shape. This was subsequently accompanied by increasing and often security-led transatlantic cooperation. Finally, regional processes almost became a model for tackling irregular migration and were promoted worldwide in particular by the International Organization for Migration (IOM).

The case of Europe: from supranational to regional governance

Internal dimension—the emergence of a focus on control

One of the core values of the EU concerns migration. From 1951, all member states agreed on the right of all regular citizens and residents of the EU to free movement within the Union for the purpose of leisure, employment, and residence. From the mid-1980s, this was supplemented by increasingly restricting the rights of citizens of non-member states to enter the EU. In 1985, the Commission of the European Community in its first ever 'guidelines for a community migration policy' declared 'illegal immigration' a topic on the European level. First, irregular migration was covered by the Trevi working group (Bunyan 1993*a*). This was set up in 1976 to deal with political radicalism and terrorism but from 1985 its mandate was expanded to cover irregular immigration, external borders, and expulsions (see Commission of the European Union 1993). From that period, irregular migration was considered a security issue and dealt with by ministries of interior. This common European approach was reaffirmed by the Council of the European Community's crucial Palma document (1989) setting out 'areas of essential action' such as 'a system of surveillance at external frontiers', 'combating illegal immigration networks', and a 'system to exchange information on people who are "inadmissible" to the EC'. The Palma document also introduced the principle doctrine of EU migration policies which is still valid today: internal free movements require tough immigration and external border controls. However, neither of these were particularly efficient and produced little results. Accordingly, in 1986, the ministerial conference set up a new body, the Ad Hoc Group Asylum, Visa, External Borders, and Deportations. Amongst its first policies was the introduction of carrier sanctions which shifted the burden of responsibility for irregular migration to transportation businesses and effectively integrated them into the fight against irregular immigration. Much more important, however, was that from 1985 the more committed governments, notably Germany, France, Belgium, the Netherlands, and Luxembourg, set up a parallel process, the Schengen agreement, to act as a pacemaker. In 1991, the Maastricht Treaty merged the previously fragmented internal, legal, and migration matters into a comprehensive policy pillar of 'Justice and Home Affairs' (JHA). Simultaneously, the EU's principle body, the ministerial conference, acknowledged that 'illegal migration' was a major political topic which should be addressed (*a*) through joint efforts which should (*b*) go beyond the EU's boundaries. Further agencies, such as the Centre for Information, Discussion and Exchange on the Crossing of Borders and Immigration (CIREFI) were established 'for the purpose of fighting illegal immigration' and 'to collect information on legitimate and illegitimate migration flows, illegitimate immigration methods, genuine and false travel documents, refused asylum seekers and illegal immigrants, deportations and carriers' (Ad Hoc Group Immigration 1992). Finally, in 1998, a High Level Working Group Asylum and Migration (HLWG) of senior civil servants was set up and mandated to (*a*) 'develop a strategic approach and a coherent and integrated policy... for the most important countries and regions of origin and transit of asylum seekers and migrants, without geographical limitations' (Council of the European Union 1999*a*) and (*b*) to produce 'horizontal analyses of a limited number of countries of origin of asylum seekers and illegal immigrants and... to provide concrete suggestions for measures for managing and containing migration' (Council of the European Union 1998).[7] The HLWG has considerable discretion in performing its tasks including collaboration with non-EU authorities (see next section); some of its initiatives are rather secretive, enforcement agency driven, proactive and autonomous from EU governance, and lack legal regulation (Council of the European Union 1999*b*). So far, however, this had rarely left the realm of declarations and intentions and had led to little joint or common structure or action.

This only changed in 1999 when the Amsterdam Treaty came into force, notably Article IV, paragraphs 61–69 on 'visa, asylum, immigration and other politics regarding the free movement of persons' set as a target to harmonize and improve cooperation on police, customs, and justice in migration and asylum matters within five years. EU commissioner Vitorino in his seminal draft of a 'community immigration policy' (Commission of the European Union 2000*a*) first sketched a coherent policy on irregular migration. He relates 'the fight against illegal immigration' to 'relations with countries of origin and transit' (Ibid.: 6) and 'work in close partnership with' these (Ibid.: 14), suggests 'police co-operation to pool knowledge of trafficking operations which by their nature are international, action at the point of entry including border controls and visa policies, legislation against traffickers' (Ibid.: 12), believes that 'many economic migrants have been driven either to seek entry through asylum procedures or to enter illegally' (Ibid.: 13), and proposes 'information campaigns... about legal possibilities... and the dangers of illegal migration and trafficking' (Ibid.: 12). Further to this, Vitorino suggests combining enforcement measures with 'opening up legal admission policies for labour migration' (Ibid.: 14). This was reinforced and sped up by the Tampere presidency conclusions which agreed in a 'coherent approach' (Commission of the European Union 2000*a*) including (*a*) to 'tackle at its source illegal immigration', (*b*) 'consistent control of external borders to stop illegal immigration', (c) 'combating those who engage in trafficking in human beings and economic exploitation of migrants', and (d) 'efforts to detecting and dismantling the criminal networks involved' (also see Commission of the European Union 2001). Thus, governing irregular migration has been related to governing refugees and regular labour migrants (see Commission of the European Union 2001). The trade-off is that adequate protection of refugees and orderly flows of migrant workers require tough measures on irregular migrants.

There are two more aspects to the Amsterdam programme: first, the northern member states sometimes blamed their southern and eastern neighbours for their 'soft touch' in border and illegal immigration matters and perceived them as the 'soft underbelly' of the EU (see e.g. Hollifield 1994). Through common policies, they hoped to increase their influence on their neighbours and pushed for more restrictive measures. Finally, preparations were made for a common external border control policy and a common border police force (Commission of the European Union 2002). Second, visa and more specifically bought or falsified identity and/or travel documents were identified as crucial aspects of preventing unwanted migration (HLWG 1999) and the Schengen Information System (SIS) was introduced to collect data on visa applicants including those who were rejected, refused entry, or previously deported. Common visa procedures were introduced to prevent abuse of visas and a common list of visa countries agreed, in particular of countries known for sending irregular immigrants (Commission of the European Union 2000b). Vice versa, in order to qualify as a non-visa 'white list' country, these had to demonstrate that they satisfied EU conditions and 'reorganized their border control to better combat illegal migration' (Düvell and Vollmer 2009).

On the institutional side, various new agencies were introduced, notably the Strategic Committee for Immigration, Border and Asylum (SCIBA), which like HLWG and CIREFI, lie beyond the scope of parliamentary control (Bunyan 1993b): on the executive level, EURODAC, a fingerprint database; FADO, a databank for False and Authentic Documents; Europol, the European Police; and since 2005 Frontex, the EU's agency for coordinating controls of the external border, play important roles. All these agencies were meant to represent an 'early warning system illegal migration' (Council of the European Union 1999a). They focus on the security and repressive side and not specifically on the human rights side.

The external dimension: expanding the European regime

From the mid-1990s and parallel to establishing a coherent supranational EU migration control system, efforts were made to expand this regime to other regions and countries. On the one hand, all EU candidate countries were targeted (Poland, Hungary, Czech Republic, Slovakia, Lithuania, Estonia,

Latvia, Cyprus, Malta, Romania, and Bulgaria). Thirteen years before these countries finally joined the EU they had to begin implementing EU migration control standards and complying with EU migration policies. On the other hand, non-EU candidate countries in particular in the neighbourhood of the EU were also targeted. Typically, an EU member state, with the support of one body or another, organized an international governmental conference and invited the relevant EU and non-EU governments. For instance in 1991, in the wake of the collapse of the communist states, the JHA ministerial conference initiated by the German government set up an international process to address external border issues; this was to become the Budapest Process. It aimed to improve border controls and to coordinate 'measures for controlling illegal migration' from Central and Eastern Europe. It was institutionalized with a permanent secretariat hosted by the International Centre for Migration Policy Development (ICMPD, see below) which gathered and analysed data from national information centres. For instance, at Budapest Process meetings, governments discussed how to act on migration strategies, routes, and smugglers (Prague 1997), whilst the 1998 conference specifically concentrated on certain routes, notably from Turkey through Albania. Thus, more effort was put on controlling the *hinterland*. From the mid-1990s, concerns were associated with the Mediterranean and in 1995 an agreement was reached between the EU and its non-EU Mediterranean neighbours (Maghreb states, Egypt, Israel, Syria, Lebanon, Palestine, and others), the Barcelona Process, which aimed at containing unwanted migration and readmitting irregular immigrants.[8] *The European* (31 November 1995) interpreted the overarching aim as 'hold[ing] back the millions in North Africa, a flood of illegal migrants waiting to penetrate the borders'. On top of this, the EU, United States, and Canada entered into coordinated efforts and established a 'new transatlantic agenda' to 'jointly address the challenges of international crime, terrorism, drug trafficking and mass migration' (Council of the European Union 1995).[9] Equally, an 'inter-regional framework agreement' with the Mercosur (the common market in South America) countries was established. And in 2002, efforts were made to even integrate Asia into these policies and an Asian–European Meeting (ASEM) was held that involved the EU and fifteen Asian countries.[10] In all cases the governments agreed on the necessity to work together in order to manage migration flows in particular with the view to tackling irregular migration (Council of the European Union 2002*b*).

All this was intensified after the Council of the European Union's Tampere conference which agreed to expand its fight against irregular migration, to integrate all countries of transit and origin into a comprehensive migration control policy, and to globally export its policies (Council of the European Union 1999*e*). According to the 2000 French presidency aspirations, this included (*a*) persecution of carriers, (*b*) facilitation of illegal entry and residence, and (*c*) mutual recognition of deportation orders and improved immigration controls. The French presidency also organized an international seminar 'on illegal immigration networks' attended by senior ministry representatives of all member states, the candidate countries, and the United States, Canada, Mexico, Australia, and Interpol. It was exemplified 'to put the fight against illegal immigration to the front of the community', to enforce 'a closed door policy for those who immigrate illegally and who must be effectively deported', and to develop 'a global approach for combating [illegal migration] networks including all suitable measures, from country of origin to destination' (Council of the European Union 2000*b*).[11] This geo-political strategy was reaffirmed in 2000 by the Council of the European Union (2000*c*) seeking 'cooperation with a large number of states'. These claims reflect a certain aggressive approach and illustrate the intention of the EU to join up with other countries to promote a global approach. Migration concerns were also integrated in the stability pacts for Eastern Europe, South East Europe, and the action plans with Ukraine and Russia. In all cases the EU demanded a 'decisive role' on the issues of 'human trafficking', 'illegal migration', and 'migration and border control'.

This expansionist approach was implemented along various lines. Firstly, the HLWG, a crucial player in these developments, was commissioned to set up 'action plans' on six countries/areas of major concern (Iraq, Morocco, Albania, Somalia, Sri Lanka, Afghanistan, and its neighbouring regions). These aimed at containing and readmitting unwanted (i.e. irregular and refugee) migrants and keeping them close to the country of origin, and training authorities in transit countries (e.g. Commission of the European Union 1998). Thus, all relevant routes of irregular migrants from the countries of origin through the various countries en route to EU neighbouring countries were targeted. First, these aims entered into the 2000 EU-West Balkan summit (Council of the European Union 2001*a*), then the Balkan Stability pact's migration/asylum initiative which was intending 'the development of regional cooperation...in the combat against illegal immigration' (Agence Europe 2001) before they were finally 'extended to the entire Western Balkan region' (Swedish Ministry of Foreign Affairs 2001). This demonstrates how such processes gain momentum, interact with other processes, become self-fed, and extend into other regions.

Second, deportation policies and readmission agreements complemented the EU's relations with countries of transit and origin. For instance, the 1995 EU Mediterranean development conference in Barcelona agreed to contain future unwanted migration and to return undocumented immigrants. In 1999, the (German) presidency of the council stated that 'readmission clauses in association and cooperation agreements with third countries [have] a major role to play' and 'in view of a coherent readmission policy could include all areas,... especially economic, development and foreign policy aspects' (Council of the European Union 1999*c*).[12] The Danish government even suggested that in case countries of origin caused problems, 'continuous consular pressure and visa policies' shall be used and readmission issues linked with 'aid, trade, and investment' policies (Council of the European Union 1999d). This was first applied to the EU's negotiations with the African, Caribbean, and Pacific countries (ACP) over a new cooperation framework.[13] Next, the Seville council meeting (2002) agreed to apply the ACP negotiation principles to all countries. Thus, all countries that had any formal links with the EU—in particular Eastern European and Caucasus countries (see Council of the European Union 2000a)— were forced into a 'joint management of migration flows' and in particular in a 'comprehensive plan to combat illegal migration and human trafficking' (Council of the European Union 2002a). By 2002, the EU had developed a comprehensive and joint return policy (Council of the European Union 2002c). Meanwhile, readmission agreements on the return of illegal immigrants have been implemented with seventeen countries in Europe, Asia, and Africa. By 2000, about 350,000 migrants were deported annually in addition to another 165,000 that were returned under programmes such as the IOM assisted voluntary return schemes.[14]

Third, the EU began to deploy policy advisors and enforcement agents in non-EU countries, thereby national actors had gone international. Following a British suggestion (Council of the European Union 2001c), the council 'adopted . . . the establishment of a network of liaison officers to control migration flows' in the Balkans (Council of the European Union 2001a). Teams of EU 'police and immigration officers' were deployed 'alongside the state border services of Bosnia-Herzegovina and Croatia, . . . both at air and land borders' and 'expert assistance and training' provided to 'combat illegal migration' (Council of the European Union 2001b).[15] The EU also promotes 'border management to combat illegal migration on the Ukrainian-Moldavian border' (Statewatch 2001: 4) and finally set up the EU Border Assistant Mission (EUBAM). Meanwhile, German federal police officers train Ukrainian borders guards.

Finally, the Council of the European Union (2000d) internationally promotes policies targeting the employers of irregular immigrants. Thereby, measures representing internal control practices enter the international stage. Such policies, however, are not particularly popular as they tend to bring governments into conflict with the powerful business, trade, and agricultural associations which may explain why often they are not strictly enforced.

Meanwhile, there are hardly any European development aid, reconstruction, trade, or technical cooperation negotiations or agreements with Eurasian, African, Asian, or South American states that do not also include a paragraph on 'illegal migration' and readmission policies. Immigration concerns, notably over irregular migration are embedded in many other policy fields; they represent a driving force in the development of a common EU migration policy and a potentially global regime (see Garson 2004). In effect, sending and transit countries are held responsible for irregular migration to the EU and forced to comply with certain EU policies.

The case of the Americas: NAFTA, SPP, and the Puebla Process

*The internal dimension: tackling irregular migration
in the United States of America*

In the United States, immigration restrictions date back to 1882 and the Chinese Exclusion act. In the 1950s, the US government launched its first major policy on irregular migration, 'Operation Wetback'; this involved large-scale internal controls and led to the deportation of several hundred thousand irregular immigrants, principally Mexicans (Garcia 1980). Before and after this, however, a 'good old boy system' ensured that those industries and employers with a demand for irregular workers would not be targeted (Dillin 2006). During the 1960s, the United States began to concentrate on controlling its external borders, notably in the South (Stobbe 2004). In 1986, after a decade of controversies (Chiswick 1988), the Immigration Reform and Control Act (IRCA) introduced better border control measures implemented through (*a*) targeted operations ('Operation Blockade', 1986, later renamed 'Operation hold the line' and 'Operation Gatekeeper', 1994) and (*b*) the expansion of the staffing level and authority of the border patrols who could now set up controls on motorways. Finally, IRCA also introduced certain labour market controls and employers sanctions. On the other hand, new legal migration channels were introduced with the aim to provide businesses with the workers they needed (Donato and Carter 1999); in addition, IRCA also introduced large-scale regularization for several million irregular immigrants. Lobby groups such as farmers seemed to have a significant impact on the provisions of this law (Chiswick 1988). On the institutional level, a Law Enforcement Support Centre (LESC) was set up in 1994 to assist federal police forces in determining an arrested individual's immigration status (Vogel 2009). In sum, four policy elements— two exclusive and two inclusive—were developed: border controls and deportations, and legal migration channels and regularizations. Chiswick (1988: 111), however, found the enforcement side of the legislation a 'toothless tiger'. Pressure for tougher measures was then developed on the federal level and some border countries, notably California which in 1994 introduced legislation that denied state benefits to irregular immigrants (Proposition 187).

In 1996, the Illegal Immigration Reform and Immigration Responsibility Act (IIRIRA) aimed at further enhancing the external borders, notably by introducing a short stretch of border fence between the United States and Mexico (Fragomen 1997). Furthermore, it nationally restricted irregular immigrants' access to certain public services, notably social benefits and national health care and expanded police officers' power to arrest under certain conditions. Thus, two new policy elements, border fences and entry bars to social services, were introduced. Until 2001, however, the focus of immigration enforcement remained on controls of the external borders, especially the land border with

Mexico; indeed, in 1996 the national police was advised by the Department of Justice not to detain anyone solely on suspicion of an immigration offence (Vogel 2009). This only changed with the terrorist attacks on 11 September 2001. First, in 2002, the above advice was withdrawn and further to this, local police were successively empowered to enforce immigration law (Migration Policy Centre 2007). Second, greater attention was put on the air borders and on international arrivals. Harsher legislation, notably the 2006 Border Protection, Antiterrorism, and Illegal Immigration Control bill, however, failed to pass the Senate but nevertheless inspired an increase in internal controls and workplace raids (De Genova 2006). Third, the institutional structure was reformed and responsibility was shifted from the Immigration and Naturalization Service (INS) to the new Department of Homeland Security (DHS). And fourthly, the conventional focus on irregular immigrants from Mexico was supplemented by a focus on Arab and Muslim migrants (De Genova 2006).

To conclude, irregular migration was for long considered mainly an economic issue and policy remained relatively relaxed; only when migration became associated with sovereignty and security concerns, were control policies significantly stepped up. During the 1950s–1980s, US policies on irregular migration were based on targeted operations but not so much on routine control and enforcement. First efforts to enhance border controls and expand internal controls in 1986 remained inefficient. Only from 1993 onwards, 'the U.S. Government has been seriously committed to reducing the flow of unauthorized immigration', initially basically targeting migration from Mexico (Cornelius 2006: 2). Whilst internal controls were first introduced nationally in 1996, these only became more prominent after 2001. Also after 2001, the focus on the land borders was supplemented by a stronger focus on international arrivals on the air borders only to shift back to land borders after 2004 (Swarns 2004). These changes are reflected in the US expenditure on border controls, which increased from around US$500 million in 1989 to around US$3.7 billion in 2006 (Cornelius 2006), the expansion of the powers to arrest of various enforcement agencies, and an increase in officers involved in border and immigration controls. So far, these policies seem to have had little or even 'no discernible effect on the overall flow of illegal migrants from Mexico' and probably also from other countries; instead they have significant unintended consequences such as the settlement and constant rise of the irregular immigrant population in the United States (Swarns 2004: 1).

The external dimension: collaboration within the region and beyond

In response to large-scale irregular migration from Mexico to the United States, first, bilateral agreements between Mexico and the United States introduced some level of cooperation such as joint border controls and granting US agents rights to gather intelligence in Mexico. Whilst the United States wished to reduce irregular immigration, the Mexican authorities were concerned about nationals from other countries irregularly transiting the country on their way north (Rohter 1989). Thus, Mexico too began stepping up its efforts to control migration and address smuggling and irregular (transit) migration. This process experienced a push when in 1993 the North American Free Trade Association (NAFTA) was introduced. In a famous statement the Mexican chief negotiator hoped that by raising Mexican living standards and wage levels NAFTA would reduce illegal immigration by up to two-thirds: 'NAFTA is our best hope for reducing illegal migration in the long haul' (Attorney General Janet Reno 1994, quoted in Morris 2006). He proved to be wrong; instead the income gap has risen considerably and only sped up irregular migration (Cornelius 2006; Papademetriou 2006). In 2001, Mexico introduced Plan Sur which targeted the Southern Mexico border with Guatemala and Belize and the transit routes to the Mexican–US border to tackle irregular transit migration from the countries south of Mexico. Some sources say this was mainly to 'woo' the United States (Tuckman 2001). Finally, in 2005, and under the combined impact of continuing irregular migration and considerable security concerns in the wake of 9/11, NAFTA was supplemented by the Security and Prosperity Partnership (SPP) of North America. This is a dialogue outside legislative processes— including coordinated border surveillance technologies, intelligence gathering on foreign nationals, and border liaison mechanisms of cities on both sides of the border (Embassy of the United States 2001)—and criticized for its 'regional border militarization' (Walia and Oka 2008).

The North American integration process, however, lacked the political vision that inspired the unification of Europe. The latter embraces political, economic, and cultural integration including the principle of free movement and choice of employment and residence. This, because internal EU migration became regular, not only effectively reduced irregular migration from Central and Eastern Europe to zero but also resulted in a decrease of the total irregular immigrant population by 1–1.3 million from 2001 to 2008 (Vogel 2009). In contrast, American integration had mostly economic motives and does not provide rights to freedom of movement of people; this results in a situation that from a comparative perspective could be depicted as incomplete integration. The negative effect is a significant increase of irregular migration from 8.4 million in 2000 to 10.7 million or more in 2007 (Camarota 2009).

Since the early 1990s, a plethora of initiatives has emerged in North, Central, and South America (NAFTA, SPP, Plan Sur, Puebla-Panama Plan (PPP), Mesoamerica Project, US–Mexico Border Partnership, Plan Mexico, and Puebla Process) that directly or indirectly target irregular migration. Emphasis was put on technological armament, border controls, joint operations and return, elements also found in European policies. Most of these processes are regional in scope and involve—except the Puebla Process—a very limited number of states, often just two or three (United States, Canada, and Mexico). Its diversity illustrates that there is no comprehensive (regional) policy; instead, processes are conflicting and overlapping. Some believe that most of these processes are inefficient (Bricker 2008), others criticize US domination and 'subordination' of its neighbours (Wise 2003).

From 2001 and in response to Islamist terrorism in the United States, Spain, the United Kingdom, and elsewhere, (irregular) migration was linked with international terrorism. This spurred a new round of policy responses and cooperation in the field of (advance passenger) data exchange, in particular. More recently, in 2008, a group of six EU member states[16] suggested a new 'Euro-Atlantic area of cooperation' to 'integrate much policing, intelligence gathering and policy-making' across the Atlantic to tackle 'terrorism, organised crime, and legal and illegal migration' (*The Guardian*, 7 August 2008*a*). Until August 2008, exchange of passenger data between the EU and United States generated 25,000 alerts which resulted in 2,100 arrests for offences such as 'murder and possession of firearms to tobacco-smuggling' though seemingly none for immigration offences (*The Guardian*, 7 August 2008*b*). So far, the impact of these policies on irregular migration is unclear though it appears as if mostly non-immigration offences were detected.

Emerging global actors, institutions, and normative frameworks

As shown above, international organizations such as IOM and OECD played an important role in declaring irregular migration a policy concern of global relevance and pushing it onto the policy agenda. Five different actors in particular—agencies and processes—with different mandates play a major role in regionally and/or globally promoting and coordinating the governance of irregular migration. These are the International Organization for Migration (IOM), the United Nations (UN) and several of its agencies, the Intergovernmental Consultations on Migration, Asylum and Refugees in Europe, North America and Australia (IGC), and to a lesser extent the International Centre for Migration Policy Development (ICMPD) and the International Labour Organization (ILO) (for others see Newland 2005).

The IOM's aim is 'managing migration for the benefits of all'.[17] However, it is an intergovernmental non-UN organization and only nation-states can be members. Consequently, IOM tends to enforce its member states', policies, and in particular those of the more potent Western countries, who through funding IOM's programmes and operations, have decisive influence over the direction the organization takes. For instance, in implementing the Migration Information Programme, the IOM's field offices are understood as outposts of a global 'migration warning system' that feeds back to the destination countries intelligence about migration movements, patterns, and networks (IOM 1995*a*). Amongst its main focuses is the return of irregular migrants and sometimes they are even involved in detention or detention-like facilities (Nauru and Ukraine) or return centres (as in Libya).[18] IOM frequently intervenes in sending and transit countries, as in the case of Turkey, which was advised to improve its border controls in order to prevent irregular migration (IOM 1995*b*). Notably through its many capacity building programmes, it advises governments on the control of migration, for instance, IOM urged Azerbaijan to 'prevent illegal migration from, through and to' the country and to develop 'modern migration management structures including a border management' (IOM 1998).

ICMPD is another intergovernmental agency with eleven member states, thirty cooperating governments and international organizations[19] though with a European, Mediterranean, and, more recently, also Central Asian but not a global ambition. It is a think tank and research institute which principally 'supports governments' (ICMPD 2008*a*). Through its Mediterranean Transit Migration programme, notably its pillar on 'enhancing operational co-operation to combat irregular migration' (ICMPD 2010) and through intelligence work and collaboration with agencies such as Europol and Frontex, ICMPD (2008*c*) seems to become involved in enforcement matters. Amongst its aims is 'reinforcing migration control co-operation between countries in Central/Eastern and Western Europe' (ICMPD 2002*a*) 'with an emphasis on combating irregular movements' (ICMPD 2002*b*). For instance, in order to deal with 'illegal migrants [that] have crossed Russia en route towards the EU' who are also turning 'Ukraine [into] a major transit country for illegal migrants' ICMPD provides 'comprehensive technical assistance to the Ukrainian authorities in the area of identification of forged and falsified documents' (ICMPD 2008*b*). ICMPD's activities also include 'Mediterranean Transit Migration', 'East Africa Migration Routes', and 'illegal migration in the West Balkan region'. On the Balkans, ICMPD contributes to 'enhance the communication and the information exchange on illegal migratory flows, mainly, but not exclusively, between the border police services of Albania, Croatia, Bosnia and Herzegovina, FYR Macedonia, Montenegro, and Serbia' (ICMPD 2002*b*). ICMPD has expanded its agenda from European and intra- to inter-regional activities.

In 1997, ILO, later than other agencies, decided to pay more attention to labour migration (ILO 1997) including irregular migrants. The general line taken by ILO is in protecting regular and, within limits, also irregular migrant workers; therein its mandate is rather different from that of IOM, IGC, or ICMPD. Actors within ILO (2005: 13) believe that irregular migration should be addressed through more 'opportunities for legal migration and freer circulation of labour, as well as regularization programmes'. But sometimes the line on irregular migration diverts from the protection principle and focuses too on repressing and 'discouraging' such migration (ILO 2001). For instance, in 1999, ILO and IOM jointly with several governments held an 'International Symposium on Migration: Towards Regional Cooperation on Irregular/Undocumented

Migration' in Bangkok, which aimed to tackle undocumented migration on an intergovernmental level. At this event, Horiuchi (1999), regional director of ILO in Asia, demanded that states 'must collaborate to suppress clandestine movements of migrants for employment,... to pool their energies to target the organizers of such movements and the employers of illegal migrants'; she reiterates that the ILO Convention 143 'calls for regular contacts and exchanges of information to make sure that traffickers in manpower can be prosecuted no matter what country they operate in'.

The United Nations established various normative frameworks, such as the Convention against Transnational Organized Crime (2000), the Protocol to Prevent, Suppress, and Punish Trafficking in Persons (2003), and Protocol against the Smuggling of Migrants by Land, Sea, and Air (2004). Some UN agencies, such as the UN Office on Drugs and Crime (UNDOC), the International Maritime Organization (IMO), or the United Nations Public Administrations Network (UNPAN) play a role in irregular migration governance. UNDOC, by its mandate concentrates on the security and crime aspects of irregular migration, investigates routes and practices and engages in promoting repressive national legislation, as in Africa (UNDOC 2006). IMO gathers data from national agencies as well as from shipping businesses and reports on 'boat people' and their smugglers. The 'Transport of Migrants by Sea' protocol authorizes states to intercept vessels in international waters that are suspected of carrying irregularly travelling migrants and refugees. The precedence case was set by the *Tampa* which rescued refugees from a sinking boat but was stopped in 2001 by Australian authorities and redirected to the remote Pacific island Nauru where these migrants and refugees were detained. Meanwhile, interception at sea has become common practice in the Mediterranean, Caribbean, and Indian Ocean.

The emergence of regional and other consultation processes

Since the mid-1980s, governments and international organizations increasingly began to collaborate on a regional level involving receiving, transit, and sending countries with the aim to jointly and comprehensively target the land and sea paths and the support networks of irregular migrants. Meanwhile, a dense schedule of intelligence sharing, consultations, and operations has emerged. Hansen (2010) identifies fourteen RCPs (Table 3.1).

There are more regional policy processes, such as within the Community of Independent States (CIS), the Specialized Migratory Forum of Mercosur, the aforementioned SSP of North America, the Berne Initiative (BI) (2001), and the Manila Process (1996), though the latter two were subsequently abandoned. The organizational structures of these processes vary considerably: certain processes have permanent secretariats; this is the case for the Budapest Process (hosted by ICMPD), Söderköping Process (staffed by IOM and United Nations

Table 3.1. Regional consultation processes

Region	Process	Acronym	Year	Number of governments involved (and partners)
Europe	Intergovernmental Consultations on Migration, Asylum and Refugees	IGC	1985	17 (IOM, UNHCR, EC)
	Budapest Process		1991	49 (ICMPD, IGC, IOM, UNHCR, UNDOC, etc.)
	Cross-border cooperation process	Söderköping Process	2001	10 (EC, IOM, UNHCR)
	Regional ministerial conference on migration in the Western Mediterranean	5+5 Dialogue	2002	10 (IOM, ICMPD, ILO)
	Mediterranean Transit Migration Dialogue	MTM Dialogue	2002–3	7 plus 27 EU member states (Europol, Frontex, Interpol, IOM, UNDOC, UNHCR)
Asia and Middle East	Intergovernmental Asia–Pacific Consultation on refugees, displaced persons, and migrants	APC	1996	35 (IOM, UNHCR)
	Process on people smuggling, trafficking, and related transnational crime	Bali Process	2002	43
	Ministerial Consultations on overseas employment and contractual labour for countries of origin in Asia	Colombo Process	2003	11
	Ministerial Consultations on overseas employment and contractual labour for countries of origin and destinations in Asia	Abu Dhabi Dialogue	2008	20
Africa	Migration Dialogue in West Africa	MIDWA	2000	15 (IOM, ILO, UNHCR, UNDOC, etc.)
	Migration Dialogue in South Africa	MIDSA	2000	16 (IOM)
	Intergovernmental authority on Development/Regional Consultative Process on migration	IGAD-RCP	2008	6 (IOM, 16 EU, and American countries)
Central and South America	Regional Conference on Migration	RCM or Puebla Process	1996	11
	South American Conference on Migration	SACM	1999	12

High Commissioner for Refugees (UNHCR) staff), IGC, ACP, and Puebla Process, for example. In contrast, for the Colombo Process, the Abu Dhabi Dialogue, SACM, and the BI secretarial activities are provided by IOM or in the case of MTM by ICMPD, whilst 5+5 Dialogue, MIDSA, MIDWA, and the Bali Process have no secretariat at all. This demonstrates that IOM and, to a lesser extent, ICMPD play a significant role in setting up and/or supporting RCPs (see RCM 2004: 2; Hansen 2010) and illustrates IOM's effort to promote and export modern and efficient policies and practices to transit and sending countries. Further to these RCPs, 'inter-agency mechanisms' (Newland 2005: 13) were instigated that rather aimed at communication between the major international organizations. These processes were, first, the Geneva Migration Group (IOM 2003b, 2003c), an 'informal, unbureaucratic mechanism of UNHCR, UNHCHR, UNODC, UNCTAD, ILO, and IOM' and second, the UNHCR-IOM Action Group on Migration and Asylum (IOM 2003a). These two processes bring together globally acting agencies and thus have a global scope. Not all such processes deal with irregular migration and only the latter activities shall be analysed.

Most of these consultation processes were set up with the aim to pool resources in order to tackle irregular migration, amongst other issues (see Hansen 2010; Koppenfels 2001). For instance, IGC was set up by the Swedish government as an 'informal forum for information exchange and for the planning of innovative solutions and strategies'.[20] It is a rather small, almost elitist, and secretive agency[21] and little is known about their activities. The IGC seem to play a role in setting the agenda and suggesting certain strategies to national and international bodies. 'Illegals' are only one amongst its many themes, such as asylum, temporary protection, return, and human trafficking. Through consultations on 'country of origin information, ... smuggling, ... illegal migration and many others states have been able to improve their policies and practices' (coordinator of IGC, quoted in Kessel 2004: 2). The Söderköping Process (2010) 'promotes dialogue on asylum and irregular migration' on the eastern borders of the EU whilst the MTM Dialogue

> focuses on enhancing operational co-operation to combat illegal migration or, in other terms, on shorter-term measures to address irregular flows. The second pillar deals with a longer-term perspective by focusing on addressing the root causes of irregular flows through development co-operation and a better joint management of migration. (ICMPD 2010)

The Bern Initiative was an intergovernmental 'consultative process' (Federal Office for Refugees, undated, 1) set up by the Swiss government. It concentrated primarily on irregular migration, criminal and security aspects (Ibid.: 2) and aimed to develop an 'International Agenda for Migration Management'. The Puebla Process 'emerged due to concerns over irregular migration affecting the entire region' (Koppenfels 2001: 34). On the one hand, it takes a humanitarian approach and aims to protect the rights of migrants including those of irregular migrants and thus reflects a balanced influence of both sending and receiving countries. On the other hand, it developed a network of liaison officers in order to 'combat(ing) migrant smuggling' and 'joint training and law enforcement exercises' to 'stem smuggling and other undocumented activities' (Ibid.). In Eurasia, irregular migration is mostly dealt with by (*a*) the CIS agreements on cooperation in fighting irregular migration (1998) and (*b*) the policy framework on counteracting irregular migration (2004), though this has not yet led to a common control regime (Ivakhnyuk 2008: 21).

The dynamics of regionalization processes in the field of irregular migration are complex. At least three patterns can be identified: (*a*) either, a receiving country approaches a transit or sending country arguing that they have an irregular migration problem because the other country does not properly secure its borders and therefore calls for collaboration. (*b*) Alternatively, IOM or another actor explains to a government that they have a problem with irregular or transit migration which previously this government believed they did not have. Next, IOM informs the government that they have got some solutions to this problem and could offer 'capacity building'. (*c*) Or a transit/receiving country believes that it has problems with irregular migration and invites others—governments or intergovernmental organizations—to address the issue. Often, it is the EU in interaction with intergovernmental and international organizations rather than the United States that pushes its irregular migration policies onto an international level. It is plausible to assume that this has to do with the fact that the EU is traditionally more in favour of multilateral approaches than the United States. On the other hand, there are governments that hesitate or refuse to collaborate with others on these matters, such as Russia, China, or until 2007 Libya; but also Mexico, Turkey, and Ukraine, at certain points, were not enthusiastic about accepting EU or US perspectives. This is because such collaboration is perceived as undermining sovereignty or because it is simply not in the national interests of these countries. Notably, preventing irregular transit migrants from entering EU or US territory or returning clandestine third-country nationals to a country means that they remain in the transit country where they then become a problem for that country. Hence the burden is simply shifted from one country to the other, as some argue (e.g. Kirisci 2006).

Most actors share a tough 'combating illegal migration' rhetoric: aim at identifying migration routes, strategies, and networks; promote, export, and expand the destination countries' interests, policies, and technologies.[22] An important course of action is the rise of 'semantic networks' (Bigo 2001: 135) in which doctrines and concepts are developed. On the other hand, it is sometimes criticized that such regional processes are implemented at the expense of refugee and human rights (e.g. Amnesty International and Human Rights Watch 2002).

The vision of some of the consultation processes is to initiate policy processes that have a global scope. In particular, the Secretariat of the Budapest Group (1999: 45) explicitly stated that 'because criminal organisations internationalise their activities this should also apply to law enforcement. International cooperation and harmonisation is the only way to gain sustainable results.... Governments and organisations should be formed into an international machinery'. Following a similar logic, an IGC representative suggests 'that unilateral, bilateral and in some cases regional measures are sometimes insufficient responses to better migration management. It appears logical, therefore, that it is time to pursue broader arrangements' (Kessel 2004: 3).

Towards a global protection regime

Whilst preventing and combating irregular migration are the dominant themes in global governance, 'shocking images of migrants in distress' have also triggered 'growing international concern with the human rights of irregular immigrants' (Betts 2010). Three policy strands can be identified: (*a*) opening up legal migration channels, (*b*) improving the legal and social conditions of irregular immigrants, and (*c*) regularizing irregular immigrants. These themes are found in EU as well as American statements (e.g. Commission of the European Union 2000*a*; RCM 2004).

On the global and normative level, seven UN Conventions address the social and human rights of irregular immigrants in one way or another. Usually, these Conventions clarify that rights shall be enjoyed 'by everybody', 'by all persons' regardless of immigrant or other status. This implies that irregular migrants are principally included in most basic international rights agreements. Four ILO policies and Conventions on migrant workers' rights also address migrants in an irregular position. In particular, the International Convention on the Protection of the Rights of All Migrant Workers and Members of their Families which was adapted in 1990 and finally came into force in 2003 intends a globally accepted protection framework. In particular, the second part spells out the human rights of irregular migrants. So far, it is ratified by only thirty-eight countries, all are non-Western sending countries and no receiving country has yet acknowledged the rights of irregular migrants as specified in this document. On a regional level, three EU Conventions also cover irregular immigrants (Table 3.2).

So far, on the institutional side, GCIM and UNHCR have acknowledged the protection needs of irregular immigrants (GCIM 2005; UNHCR 2007*b*). Whilst UNHCR's main mandate is refugee protection, it also occasionally addresses irregular migration. UNHCR, for example through its 'mixed migration' initiative (UNHCR 2007*a*), criticizes trends of conflating irregular migration and forced migration and exposes politics, such as unlawful deportations ('*refoulement*') that prevent refugees from seeking asylum and undermine the refugee

Table 3.2. Normative framework for the protection of irregular immigrants

Global	International Convention on the Elimination of All Forms of Racial Discrimination	ICERD
	International Covenant on Civil and Political Rights	ICCPR
	International Covenant on Economic, Social and Cultural Rights	ICESCR
	Convention on the Elimination of All Forms of Discrimination Against Women	CEDAW
	Convention against Torture and other cruel, inhuman or degrading treatment or punishment	CAT
	International Convention on the Protection of the Rights of All Migrant Workers and members of their families	ICRMW
	Convention on the Rights of the Child	CRC
	ILO resolution concerning a fair deal for migrant workers in a global economy	
	ILO Convention No. 97 concerning migration for employment	
	ILO Convention No. 143 concerning migrations in abusive conditions	
	ILO promotion of equality of opportunity and treatment of migrant workers	
Regional	Charter of Fundamental Rights of the European Union (Council of Europe)	CHART
	European Convention for the protection of human rights and fundamental freedoms	
	European Social Charter	ESF

protection regime. Further to this, two UN instruments were introduced to monitor and report on the implementation of the above-mentioned Conventions, the UN Special Rapporteur on the Human Rights of Migrants and the UN Special Rapporteur on the Right of Everyone to the Enjoyment of the Highest Attainable Standard of Physical and Mental Health.

Finally, there are various non-governmental efforts to inter-regionally and even globally address the human rights situation of irregular migration and to lobby national, EU, and international events and organizations. For instance, Migrants Rights International (MRI) and December 18 both have a global scope and lobby national governments for signing the ICRMW. The Platform for International Cooperation on Undocumented Migrants (PICUM) is a renowned Brussels-based European umbrella organization with some US and African members bringing together NGOs that in one way or another promote social and human rights of 'undocumented migrants'. The idea is to 'mainstream' irregular migration and to embed the rights of irregular migrants into any policy that affects irregular migrants.

Betts (2010) argues that 'the broad norms [to protect irregular immigrants] already exist' but that states remain 'reluctant to commit to new formal multilateral agreements' and that it lacks the authoritative consensus to apply these instruments. Thus, a 'soft law' approach is envisaged that could overcome the obstacles in introducing a meaningful protection regime.

Conclusion: from regional to global governance of irregular migration

During the 1980s, governments in those countries that were at the receiving end of irregular migration, notably the northern countries of the EU and in North America, came to the conclusion that national unilateral restrictive policies aimed at closing and controlling borders and immigration were insufficient for preventing unwanted and irregular migration. Thus, states began to collaborate with other states in order to address the issue. Often, the governance of irregular migration is interlinked with the governance of other concerns such as (organized) crime, drug trafficking, and terrorism and embedded in other policies such as development, trade, tourism, and international relations. Thus, politics on irregular migration are as much a separate policy field as they are part of broader policy fields. In any case, the desire to tackle irregular migration is so strong that in Europe, states were even prepared to enter into supranational arrangements that would compromise their sovereignty. Indeed, concerns over irregular migration appear to be the strongest motivation behind the emergence of regional and global governance of migration.

So far, most governance is indeed not global in nature but intra- and inter-regional. Certainly, one of the most striking features of the global governance of irregular migration is its regional characteristics. This follows from two logics: first, irregular migration governance unfolds along the paths of irregular migrants; second, it is pragmatic rather than normative. Various regional governance processes in Europe and North America show a trend to expand their scope from intra- to inter-regionalism. In particular from the EU, notably the Schengen states, irregular migration governance spread to transit and sending regions like shock waves. In particular, the Budapest and Söderköping processes in Europe and the SSP in North America are based on very dense agendas of almost weekly meetings, consultations, exchange of data, training, and joint exercises for intelligence and enforcement staff. In fact, this practice of intensive horizontal cooperation of visa, customs, and immigration officers across borders perfectly illustrates what Bigo (2001) describes as 'administrative networks' and which Slaughter (2004) describes as the emergence of government and policy networks.

Nevertheless, it can be concluded that the regional EU's regime is more developed than NAFTA/SPP, the Puebla, or the APC Process. Beyond the regional level, various processes and institutions have broader aspirations: IOM and ILO, by mandate, have a global scope whilst IGC and the Budapest Process at least promote global approaches. It must be noted, however, that all these processes are very volatile and dynamic. Tensions between different states and actors remain high, as between sending and receiving countries or between organizations with different and partly conflicting mandates such as IOM, ILO, and UNHCR.

Regional processes rise and fall, such as the Manila Process or the Bern Initiative, and institutions rise and diminish in relevance, such as the IGC. Newland (2005: 13) suggests not to overestimate consultation processes and dialogues; the real meaning of these is that they play a role in 'knitting together the policy networks' that in Slaughter's conception (2004) are the 'building blocks' of global governance.

Four forms of collaboration can be identified, (a) those of receiving countries, (b) of receiving with transit and sending countries, (c) of mostly sending countries (all three of which usually involve international organizations) whilst (d) that bring together only international organizations. Usually, the initiative is taken by the receiving countries who raise their concerns with the transit and sending countries; thereby a political snowball effect is triggered which leads to subsequent arrangements. Alternatively, the initiative comes from an intergovernmental organization, usually the IOM. Institutions are usually set up by receiving countries either almost exclusively representing receiving countries (OECD, ICMPD, IGC, and Bern Initiative) or bringing together sending, transit, or receiving countries (e.g. IOM, Budapest and Söderköping processes, and SPP). Other arrangements, notably the Puebla and the Colombo Process, instead represent the sending countries' concerns. However, the former two types of institutions must be considered the more powerful and influential and the dominant policy is to keep away irregular migration from the receiving countries.

Irregular migration governance occurs on formal and informal levels and both have their advantages: whilst formal processes are more reliable and accountable, informal processes are very efficient and produce quick results (see Thouez and Channac 2006: 377). These regional interstate collaborations go well beyond policy transfer (circulation of ideas, sharing information) and instead often take the form of joint policy actions (exchange of knowledge, data, technologies, infrastructure, and staff) and even lead to joint operations, more so in Europe, less in North America; in contrast, the global level is rather characterized by policy transfer than policy action. In sum, both forms of collaboration facilitate policy convergence in all areas (ideology, technology, policies, and politics) and on a global scale.

The governance of irregular migration combines four paradigms: exit controls, travel controls, entry controls, and residence and employment controls. These aim at the prevention of irregular migration, at frustrating irregular migrants' journeys or, in case they succeed, their return. Successively, a whole set of politics has been designed ranging from false-proved visa and identity documents, exchange of passenger data, carrier sanctions (which effectively integrates private businesses into control politics), enhanced border controls, militarization of exit and entry controls, intelligence gathering on smugglers, networks and paths, readmission agreements, and employer sanctions to national measures (internal controls of labour markets and social systems) that diminish the opportunities for irregular immigrants.

The governance of irregular migration involves two partly conflicting, partly supplementary fields: (*a*) the control, prevention, and combating of irregular migration and (*b*) the protection of irregular migrants. So far, governance concentrates on the prevention aspect whilst the protection aspect is much less developed. This demonstrates that states' primary concern is the protection of their territory, citizens, and national systems and not the protection of irregular migrants' rights. In particular, the governance of borders and irregular migration sometimes come into conflict with the protection of refugees and other vulnerable migrants. Indeed, policies to prevent irregular migration are often found to be indifferent about the type of people prevented from migrating and therefore affect refugees, economic, and other migrants in similar ways. Notably, return practices sometimes clash with protection policies.

Finally, governance in the field of irregular migration faces a principle paradox of our time: whilst the politics of globalization promote the free flow of goods, capital, and information, the flow of people is subject to myriad restrictions. Considering the impact of regional and global efforts to reduce irregular migration generates mixed results. The achievements of the Puebla Process in preventing irregular migration were considered considerable (Koppenfels 2001). In Europe too, irregular transit migration as well as the stock of irregular immigrants is decreasing (Düvell and Vollmer 2009; Vogel 2009); in contrast, in the United States, irregular migration seems to continue (Cornelius 2006). Newland (2005: 3), in her report to the GCIM, was rather sceptical about the results of such policies, arguing that 'governments have won many battles against unauthorized migration, but they are, by and large, losing the war for control over who enters, leaves, and remains on their territories'. Meanwhile, thousands of migrants have so far lost their lives crossing international borders in increasingly hazardous ways, which raises significant ethical issues for such policies (see Spijkerboer 2007).

Notes

1. Figures of hidden populations are notoriously vague and ought to be treated with care.
2. Here irregular migration is applied as a sample term covering irregular emigration, journeys, immigration, and settlement.
3. E.g. 1849 Netherlands Aliens Act, 1882 Chinese Exclusion Act in the United States, similar anti-Chinese restrictions in Canada (1885), and the 1905 Aliens Restrictions Act in Great Britain.
4. UK 1968 and 1971 Immigration Acts; recruitment stops in Germany, Netherlands, France, Belgium, etc.
5. UK, 1971 Immigration Act (illegal immigration) and 1996 Immigration Act (illegal employment); Germany, 1982 'Law to Combat Illegal Employment'; France, Pasqua Laws 1986 and 1993; Spain, 1985 Organ Law; US 1986 Immigration Reform and Control Act; Italy, emergency ordinances in 1995 and 1996, 2002 Bossi-Fini Law.

6. The expression 'illegal migration' contributes to the stigmatization and criminalization of certain groups and reinforces their exclusion (see Düvell et al., 2010). Therefore, it is considered ethically problematic; instead academics usually use the terms undocumented, unauthorized, or irregular migration.

7. Translated from German version.

8. EU Development Conference, Barcelona, 27–28 November 1995.

9. Also see the New Transatlantic Agenda 1995; EU–Canada Political declaration and action plan 1996; Joint Declaration on JHA cooperation, December 2000; Statewatch (2002).

10. Brunei, Combodia, China, India, Japan, Korea, Laos, Malaysia, Mongolia, Myanmar, Pakistan, the Philippines, Singapore, Thailand, and Vietnam; also see www.europa.eu.int/external_relations/asem/intro.

11. A similar conference in Athens prepared the ground for tackling irregular migration across the Mediterranean in particular targeting Morocco (*Tageszeitung* 5 October 2001).

12. Translated from German version.

13. See the partnership agreement between the members of the group of states of Africa, Caribbean, and Pacific countries, and the European Union and its member states; Cotonou agreement, Article 13, http://europa.eu.int/comm/development/cotonou/agreement_de.htm.

14. Own calculation.

15. The decision process was as follows: (*a*) conclusions of a seminar of immigration liaison officers in November 2000 in Funchal, (*b*) CIREFI call for attention, (*c*) SCIBA discussed the matter and instructed CIREFI to work out a concept, further expert meetings by the Commission, (*d*) the council's Presidency proposes to adopt the plan.

16. Germany, France, Sweden, Portugal, Slovenia, and Czech Republic; the United Kingdom participated as an observer.

17. From its website www.iom.org.

18. 'Voluntary return' because the choice of to be deported or to leave 'voluntarily' would be more appropriately categorized as a form of 'removal', see Düvell 2005.

19. Members: Austria and Switzerland (founding members), Bulgaria, Croatia, Czech Republic, Hungary, Poland, Portugal, Slovakia, Slovenia, and Sweden. Actively supporting governments: Albania, Bosnia and Herzegovina, Canada, Cyprus, Estonia, Georgia, Latvia, Lebanon, Lithuania, FYR Macedonia, Russia, Sri Lanka, Turkey, and Ukraine. Cooperating organizations: IOM.

20. This quote was retrieved in 2002 from www.igc.ch.

21. Since around 2003 or 2004, the IGC website has been password protected and its documents no longer accessible to the public.

22. The role of researchers of research institutions and think tanks contributing or facilitating such processes is another sensitive though non-researched aspect.

References

Ad Hoc Group Immigration (1992) SN 4816/92 WGI 1277, 16 November 1992.

Agence Europe (2001) Launch of Migration/Asylum Initiative in Framework of Stability Pact, 6 April 2001.

Amnesty International and Human Rights Watch (2002) *Statement by Amnesty International & Human Rights Watch to Governing Council*, Geneva: International Organization for Migration, 2–4 December 2002.

Bauer, Y. (1971) Illegal Immigration, in R. Patai (ed.), *Encyclopedia of Zionism and Israel*, 2 vols., New York: Herzl Press/McGraw Hill.

Betts, A. (2010) Towards a 'Soft Law' Framework for the Protection of Vulnerable Irregular Migrants, *International Journal of Refugee Law*, 22(2), 209–36.

Bigo, D. (2001) Migration and Security, in V. Guiraudon and C. Joppke (eds), *Controlling a New Migration World*, London: Routledge, pp. 121–48.

Boswell, C. and Straubhaar, T. (2003) *The Back Door: Temporary Migration and Illegal Employment of Workers*, Geneva: ILO, http://www.ilo.org/public/english/bureau/inst/download/boswell.pdf (accessed 8 March 2004).

Bricker, K. (2008) Mexico Spending Plan Released, *Narcosphere*, 16 September, http://narcosphere.narconews.com/notebook/kristin-bricker/2008/09/plan-mexico-spending-plan-released-0.

Bunyan, T. (1993a) Trevi, Europol and the European State, in T. Bunyan (ed.), *Statewatching the New Europe*, London: Statewatch, pp. 15–36.

——(ed.) (1993b) *Statewatching the New Europe*, London: Statewatch.

Camarota, S. (2009) *Illegal Immigrants and HR 3200: Estimates of Potential Costs to Taxpayers*, Washington, DC: Centre for Immigration Studies.

Chiswick, B. (1988) Illegal Immigration and Immigration Control, *Journal of Economic Perspectives*, 2(3), 101–15.

Commission of the European Community (1985) Guidelines for a Community Migration Policy, BullEC, Supplement 9/85, Luxembourg.

——(2001) On a Common Policy on Illegal Immigration, Communication from the Commission to the Council and the European Parliament, COM(2001) 672 final, Brussels.

——(2001) On a Common Policy on Illegal Immigration—Communication from the Commission to the Council and the European Parliament, COM(2001) 672 Final, Brussels.

Commission of the European Union (1993) Draft List on the 'Acquis' of the Union and of its Member States in the Fields of Justice and Home Affairs (situation as on 1 July 1993), Report from: K.4 Committee dated: 3 November 1993 to Permanent Representatives Committee, 9568/93, 2 November 1993, Confidential CK4 2, No. prev. doc.: CIRC 3678/93.

——(1998) EU Action Plan on Influx of Migrants from Iraq and the Neighbouring Region—Report on Points 29 and 36, Commission Staff Working Paper, SEC(1998) 466, 16 March 1998, Brussels.

——(2000a) On a Community Immigration Policy, Communication from the Commission to the Council and the European Parliament, Communication from Mr Vitorino in agreement with Mrs Diamantopoulou, COM(2000)11, Brussels.

——(2000b) Proposed Regulations on Visa List, COM(2000) 27, 26 January 2000, Brussels.

——(2002) Towards Integrated Management of the External Borders of the Member States of the EU, COM(2002)233 Final, 7 May 2002, Brussels.

Cornelius, W. (2006) *Impacts of Border Enforcement on Unauthorized Mexican Migration to the United States*, New York: Social Science Research Council.

Council of the European Community (1989) 'Palma document'. Free Movement of Persons, A Report to the European Council by the Coordinators' Group, June 1989, Madrid.

Council of the European Union (1995) The Transatlantic Agenda (and Joint Action Plan), K.4 Committee, 3 December 1995, Brussels.

——(1998) Press release, 3 December 1998.

——(1999a) Terms of References of the High Level Working Group on Asylum and Migration, 22 January 1999, 5264/2/99, JAI1, AG1.

——(1999b) Intensification de la Coopération Entre CIREFI et Europol Dans le Domaine de L'immigration Clandestine et des Questions Connexes, 10918/1/99, CIREFI 48, COMIX 231, Europol 40, de la: CIREFI, 22 October 1999, Brussels.

——(1999c) Strategy on Migration and Asylum Policy, Ref: 6097/99, MIGR 18, 12 April 1999, Brussels.

——(1999d) Note from Danish Delegation to: Migration/Expulsion Working Group, Subject: Analysis of the Institute Concerning Readmission Agreements, 7707/99, MIGR 31, 27 April 1999, Brussels.

——(1999e) Presidency Conclusions of the Tampere European Council 15 & 16 October 1999, (SN 2000/99), Brussels.

——(2000a) Note from Presidency to Article 36 Committee and Strategic Committee on Immigration, Frontiers and Asylum, Subject: Programme for External Relations in the Field of Justice and Home Affairs, 5229/00 (LIMITE), ENFOPOL 4, 11 January 2000, Brussels.

——(2000b) Seminar on Illegal Immigration Networks, on 20 and 21 July 2000, Note from French Presidency, 12211/00 LIMITE JAI 109 ASIM 22, 12 October 2000, Brussels.

——(2000c) Programme for External Relations in the Field of Justice and Home Affairs, Note from Presidency to Article 36 Committee and Strategic Committee on Immigration, Frontiers and Asylum, 11 January 2000, 5229/00 (LIMITE) ENFOPOL 4, Brussels.

——(2000d) Collecting Information on Existing Legislation on Preventing and Combating Illegal Immigration Networks, Note from Portuguese Presidency to CIREFI, 21 January 2000, 5579/00, CIREFI 1, Brussels.

——(2001a) Illegal Immigration via the Western Balkan Route, Note from UK Delegation to Strategic Committee on Immigration, Frontiers and Asylum, CIREFI 3, MIGR 3, 5496/01, 52, COMIX, 19 January 2001, Brussels.

——(2001b) Note from United Kingdom Delegation to SCIFA: Illegal Immigration via the Western Balkan Route, 5496/01, CIREFI 3, MIGR 3, Comix 52, 19 January 2001, Brussels.

——(2001c) Creation of a Network of Liaison Officers to Help Control Migration Flows in the Balkans, 6612/01, Limite, CIREFI 14, Comix 172, Brussels.

——(2001d) Liaison Officers—Common Use of Liaison Officers of EU Member States, Note from Presidency to Police Cooperation Working Party, 5406/01, Enfopol 6, 17 January 2001, Brussels.

——(2002a) Presidency Conclusions at the Seville European Council, 21–22 June, Brussels.

——(2002b) Advances Made in Combating Illegal Immigration, 10009/02, JAI 141, MIGR 56, 14 June 2002, Brussels.

——(2002c) Grünbuch: Über eine Gemeinschaftspolitik zur Rückkehr Illegal Aufhältiger Personen, KOM (2002)175 Endgültig, Brussels.

De Genova, N. (2006) *Migrant 'Illegality' and the Metaphysics of Antiterrorism: 'Immigrants' Rights' in the Aftermath of the Homeland Security State*, New York: Social Science Research Council.

Diamant, M. (1973) Die Illegalen, *Der Gewerkschafter*, 12, 474–75.

Dillin, J. (2006) How Eisenhower Solved Illegal Border Crossings from Mexico, *Christian Science Monitor*, July, http://www.csmonitor.com/2006/0706/p09s01-coop.html.

Donato, K. and Carter, R. (1999) Mexico and the US Policy on Illegal Immigration, in D. Haines and K. Rosenblum (eds), *Illegal Immigration in America*, Westport, CT: Greenwood Press, pp. 112–29.

Düvell, F. (2005) Globalisation of Migration Control. A Tug-War between Restrictionists and the Human Agency? in H. Henke (ed.), *Crossing Over: Comparing Recent Migration in Europe and the United States*, New York, Oxford, MA: Lexington Books, pp. 23–46.

——(2006) *Illegal Immigration in Europe*, Houndmills: Palgrave/Macmillan.

——Triandafyllidou, A., and Vollmer, B. (2010) The Ethics of Researching Irregular Migration, *Population, Space and Place*, 16(3), 195–211.

Düvell, F. and Vollmer, B. (2009) *Irregular Migration in and from the Neighbourhood of the EU. A Comparison of Morocco, Turkey and Ukraine*, Athens: ELIAMEP.

Embassy of the United States (undated, probably 2001) Borders and Law Enforcement. A Border Community United. The U.S.–Mexico Border, http://www.usembassy-mexico.gov/eng/eborder_mechs.html (accessed 14 December 2008).

Engbersen, G. (2001) The Unanticipated Consequences of Panopticon Europe: Residence Strategies of Illegal Immigrants, in V. Guiraudon and Ch. Joppke (eds), *Controlling a New Migration World*, Routledge: London, pp. 222–46.

Federal Office for Refugees (Swiss) (undated), *Die Berner Initiative*, Bern: FOR.

Fragomen A.T. (1997) The Illegal Immigration Reform and Immigrant Responsibility Act of 1996: An Overview, *International Migration Review*, 31(2), 438–60.

Garcia, J.R. (1980) *Operation Wetback*, Westport, CT: Greenwood Press.

Garson, J.-P. (2004) Migration in Europe: Trends and Perspectives, Paper prepared for Workshop on International Migration and Labour Markets in Asia, Tokyo: Japan Institute for Labour Policy and Training, http://www.jil.go.jp/foreign/event_r/event/documents/2004sopemi/2004sopemi_e_session2.pdf.

Global Commission on International Migration (GCIM) (2005) *Migration in an Interconnected World: New Directions for Action*, Geneva: GCIM.

Guardian, The (2008a) Secret EU Security Draft Risks Uproar with Call to Pool Policing and Give US Personal Data, 7 August 2008.

——(2008b) Ministers Fight Ban on Migrant Checks, 7 August 2008.

Guiraudon, V. (2000) European Integration and Migration Policy: Vertical Policy-Making as Venue Shopping, *Journal of Common Market Studies*, 38(2), 251–71.

Hansen, R. (2010) *An Assessment of Principal Regional Consultative Processes on Migration*, Geneva: IOM.

Hanson, G.H. (2007) *The Economic Logic of Irregular Migration*, CSR 26, New York: Council on Foreign Relations.

High Level Working Group (HLWG) (1999) Draft Action Plan for Afghanistan, Brussels.

Hollifield, J. (1994) The Migration Challenge: Europe's Crisis in Historical Perspective, *Harvard International Review*, 16(3), 26–33.

Holm, U. (2004) The EU's Security Policy towards the Mediterranean: An (Im)possible Combination of Export of European Political Values and Anti-Terror Measures? Danish Institute for International Studies Working Paper No. 13, DIIS.

Horiuchi, M. (1999) Opening Address, IOM International Symposium on Migration: Towards Regional Cooperation on Irregular/Undocumented Migration, Bangkok, 22 April 1999, http://www.ilo.int/public/english/region/asro/bangkok/public/speeches/yr1999/mh_apr1.htm.

International Centre for Migration Policy Development (ICMPD) (2002*a*) *About ICMPD*, Vienna: ICMPD.

——(2002*b*) *The Activities of ICMPD*, Vienna: ICMPD.

——(2008*a*) *ICMPD Activities by Topic*, Vienna: ICMPD, http://www.icmpd.org/work_bytopic.html.

——(2008*b*) *Irregular Labour Migration*, Vienna: ICMPD, http://www.icmpd.org/irregularlabourmigration.html.

——(2008*c*) *MTM Map on Mediterranean and African Irregular Migration Routes*, Vienna: ICMPD, http://www.icmpd.org/fileadmin/ICMPD-Website/MTM/New-Map-MTM_Poster-Landscape_EN_v1.pdf (accessed 10 May 2009).

——(2010) *Dialogue on Mediterranean Transit Migration*, Vienna: ICMPD, http://www.icmpd.org/906.html?&no_cache=1&tx_icmpd_pi1%5Barticle%5D=922&tx_icmpd_pi1%5Bpage%5D=926.

International Labour Organization (ILO) (1997) International Migration—Protecting the Most Vulnerable of Today's Workers, Tripartite Meeting of Experts on Future ILO Activities in the Field of Migration, Geneva: ILO.

——(2001) *Migration Policies—Assisting Governments to Address Labour Migration in the 21st Century*, Geneva: ILO.

——(2005) Report and Conclusions of the Seventh European Regional Meeting, Budapest, 14–18 February 2005, Geneva: ILO.

International Organization for Migration (IOM) (1995*a*) *Migration Information Program—Irregular Migration in Central Europe: The Case of Afghan Asylum Seekers in Hungary*, Geneva: IOM.

——(1995*b*) *Migration Information Programme—Transit Migration in Turkey*, Geneva: IOM.

——(1998) *IOM and the Government of Azerbaijan Capacity Building in Migration Management Program (CBMMP)*, Geneva: IOM.

——(2003*a*) *World Migration Report*, Geneva: IOM.

——(2003*b*) Statement of Lucca Dall'Oglio. Permanent Observer, United Nations General Assembly 3rd Committee: Questions Relating to Refugees, Returnees and Displaced Persons and Humanitarian Question, Geneva: IOM.

——(2003*c*) Press Briefing Notes, 14 November 2003.

Ivakhnyuk, I. (2008) Transit Migration through Russia, Paper presented to Conference on (Irregular) Transit Migration in Europe, Istanbul, Turkey, 18–20 April 2008.

Jordan, B. and Düvell, F. (2002) *Irregular Migration. Dilemmas of Transnational Mobility*, Cheltenham: Edward Elgar.

Kessel, G. van (2004) IGC as a Regional Process and Comments on International Cooperation, Paper presented at HMI World Congress, http://www.iemed.org/mhicongress/dialegs/tots/papers/kessel.pdf.

Kirisci, K. (2006) The Hague Programme: Challenges of Turkish Pre-Accession in the Area of Asylum, Migration and Border Control, in J.W. Zwaan and F. Goudappel (eds), *Freedom, Security and Justice in the European Union*, The Hague: Asser Press, pp. 164–71.

Koppenfels, A. von (2001) The Role of Regional Consultative Processes in Managing International Migration, IOM Migration Research Series 3, Geneva: IOM.

Koser, K. (2005) *Irregular Migration, State Security and Human Security*, Global Commission on International Migration, http://www.gcim.org/attachements/TP5.pdf.

Koser, K. (2005) Irregular Migration, State Security and Human Security. Paper prepared for the Policy Analysis and Research Programme of the Global Commission on International Migration, Geneva: GCIM.

Luciani, G. (ed) (1993) *Migration Policies in Europe and the United States*, Boston, MA: Kluwer Academic.

Martin, P. (1986) Illegal Immigration and the Colonization of the American Labor Market, CIS Paper 1, Washington, DC: Centre for Immigration Studies.

Morris, D. (2006) Blame NAFTA, 13 April 2006, http://www.alternet.org (accessed 15 December 2008).

Newland, K. (2005) *The Governance of International Migration: Mechanisms, Processes and Institutions*, Geneva: GCIM.

Ngai, M. (2004) *Impossible Subjects: Illegal Aliens and the Making of Modern America*, Princeton, NJ: Princeton University Press.

Organisation for Economic Co-operation and Development (OECD) (1977) SOPEMI. Trends in International Migration, Annual Report 1976, Paris: OECD.

——(1979) SOPEMI. Trends in International Migration, Annual Report 1977, Paris: OECD.

——(1981) SOPEMI. Trends in International Migration, Annual Report 1980, Paris: OECD

——(1986) SOPEMI. Trends in International Migration, Annual Report 1985, Paris: OECD

——(1990) SOPEMI. Trends in International Migration, Annual Report 1989, Paris: OECD.

Papademetriou, D. (2006) Ten Years of NAFTA Fails to Stem Illegal Immigration, Press release, 18 November 2003, Washington, DC: Migration Policy Institute, http://www.migrationpolicy.org/news/2003_11_18.php.

Regional Migration Conference (RCM) (2004) The Regional Conference on Migration (RCM). In Brief: What it is, What it has Done, http://www.rcmvs.org/rcm_en_breve_v13-05-05-eng.

Rohter, L. (1989) Mexico Assisting in U.S. Plan to Cut Illegal Migration, *New York Times*, 17 March 1989.

Sciortino, G. and Colombo, A. (2004) The Flows and the Flood: Public Discourse on Immigration in Italy, 1969–2001, *Journal of Modern Italian Studies*, 9(1), 94–113.

Secretariat of the Budapest Group (1999) *The Relationship between Organised Crime and Trafficking Aliens*, Vienna: Budapest Group.

Shrestha, N.R. (1987) International Policies and Migration Behaviour: A Selective Review, *World Development*, 15(3), 329–45.

Simeánt, J. (1998) *La cause de sans papiers*, Paris: Presses de Sciences Po.

Slaughter, A.M. (2004) *A New World Order*, Princeton, NJ: Princeton University Press.

Söderköping Process (2010) *Who we are*, Kiev: Söderköping Process, http://soderkoping. org.ua/.

Spijkerboer, T. (2007) The Human Costs of Border Control, *European Journal of Migration and Law*, 9(1), 127–39.

Statewatch (2001) European Monitor, 3(1), January 2001.

Statewatch (2002) Creation of a Northern 'Axis', 2(1), January–February 2002.

Stobbe, H. (2004) *Undokumentierte Migration in Deutschland und den Vereinigten Staaten*, Göttingen: Universitätsverlag.

Swarns, R. (2004) US to Give Border Patrol Agents the Power to Deport Illegal Aliens, *New York Times*, 11 August 2004.

Swedish Ministry of Foreign Affairs (2001) High Level Working Group on Asylum and Migration Activities Undertaken During the Swedish Presidency, Memorandum, Stockholm.

Thouez, C. and Channac, F. (2006) Shaping International Migration Policy: The Role of Regional Consultative Processes, *West European Politics*, 29(2), 370–87.

Tuckman, J. (2001) Mexico Woos US with War on Migrants, *The Guardian*, 25 July 2001.

United Nations (1997) International Migration and Development. The Concise Report. Population Division. *Population Newsletter*, No. 63, New York: UN.

United Nations High Commissioner for Refugees (UNHCR) (2007a) *Refugee Protection and Mixed Migration: A Ten-Point Plan of Action*, Geneva: UNHCR.

——(2007b) High Commissioner's Opening Statement, High Commissioner's Dialogue, 11–12 December 2007, http://www.unhcr.org/research/RESEARCH/47fe0e532.pdf.

United Nations Office on Drugs and Crime (UNDOC) (2006) *Organized Crime and Irregular Migration from Africa to Europe*, Vienna: UNDOC.

Vogel, D. (2009) *Size of Irregular Migration*, Policy brief, Athens: ELIAMEP.

Vollmer, B. (2009) *Political Discourses on Irregular Migration in the EU*, Comparative Policy Brief, Athens: ELIAMEP.

Walia, H. and Oka, C. (2008) The Security and Prosperity Partnership Agreement: NAFTA Plus Homeland Security, *Left Turn*, http://www.leftturn.org/?q=node/1160.

Wise, R.D. (2003) Critical Dimensions of Mexico-US Migration under the Aegis of Neoliberal Globalism, Paper presented at International Migration Conference in The Americas: Emerging Issues Conference, York University, September, http://www.yorku.ca/cerlac/migration/Raul_Delgado.PDF (accessed 15 December 2008).

4

International Travel

Rey Koslowski

Introduction

Most of the world's 6.3 billion people have not and probably will not ever leave the country of their birth. Many of us have travelled internationally once, some every now and then, and a few travel internationally on a regular basis. The United Nation's (UN) World Tourism Organization (UNWTO) estimates that in 2008 there were 924 million international tourist arrivals, which includes travel for leisure, business, and to visit friends and relatives (UNWTO 2009). If all of these individuals returned directly home, their return trips and entries as citizens in their home countries add another 924 million border crossings, totalling close to 2 billion border crossings. If some of these individuals enter more than one foreign country on one trip abroad (most likely), there will only be one entry back home for several international tourist arrivals abroad. Therefore, it is fair to say that there are well over a billion border crossings of leisure and business travellers. Additionally, there are millions of students and temporary contract workers who stay for less than one year and a large number of cross-border commuters who may or may not be counted in arrival statistics.

Over the past decade, international travel has grown steadily. From 1995 to 2006, arrivals of international tourists have increased from 535 million to 846 million. Of those 846 million international tourist arrivals, 51 per cent travelled for the purpose of leisure, recreation, and holidays; 27 per cent for purposes such as visiting friends and relatives, religious reasons/pilgrimages, health treatment; 16 per cent for business; and the purpose of the remaining 6 per cent was not specified (UNWTO 2007). It is important to point out that many individuals travel internationally several times per year. Therefore, the 846 million international tourist arrivals does not equate to 846 million individuals who have travelled internationally in one year. Nevertheless, in addition to the world's estimated 191 million migrants (UN 2006), there are probably billions of international border crossings by those who travel internationally for stays of less than one year.

The regulation of international travel by states is a crucial component of the global governance of migration because contemporary migration often begins as tourism, business travel, or study abroad. The relationship between international tourism and migration is born out by the fact that six of the top ten destination countries of international tourists—France, Spain, the United States, the United Kingdom, Germany, and Russia (UNWTO 2007)—are also among the top ten migration destination countries (UN 2006). In contrast to other dimensions of international migration, cooperation among states on international travel is long-standing. States have been cooperating on a global level much longer with respect to passports and visas than they have with respect to refugees, low- or high-skilled migration, or any other dimension of migration examined in this volume save human trafficking.

Although international norms and regulations governing international travel may have a direct bearing on international migration and have a long history, cooperation on international travel takes place within international organizations and fora along with regulatory actions of certain international organizations that are not always considered as international cooperation on migration, per se. In order to help provide a broader understanding of global migration governance, I will first review the development of international norms regarding nationality, passports, and visas, and their codification through the efforts of the League of Nations and then the United Nations International Law Commission (ILC) as well as the regulatory activities of relevant international organizations, such as the International Civil Aviation Organization (ICAO), the International Maritime Organization (IMO), and the UNWTO. I will then examine the politics of international cooperation on international travel, which revolve around the facilitation of increasing flows, the role of travel as a factor of trade and development, the environmental impact of growing travel flows and securing international travel. Finally, I consider the steps towards an increasingly sophisticated framework for the global governance of international travel that include the further adoption of the World Trade Organization (WTO) General Agreement on Trade in Services (GATS) 4 commitments on business travel visas, specific protocols on human smuggling and trafficking within international treaties, cooperation within ICAO to develop a global framework for the exchange of advance passenger information (API) and passenger name record (PNR) data, as well as changing norms among states in favour of deploying technologies such as biometrics and electronic travel authorization (ETA) systems to capture the data of travellers by states for the purpose of securing international travel.

Regulation of international travel at the global level

International travel was travel long before it became international. That is, traders and pilgrims had been travelling long distances before the establishment of the European state system with the 1648 Treaty of Westphalia and its expansion and transformation into a system of interacting nation-states that subsequently embraced the entire world. Similarly, there was migration of individuals, groups, and entire peoples long before it became 'international migration' with the establishment of the international system (see Koslowski 2000). International travel and migration shaped the institutional development of the formal state membership (*Staatsangehoerigkeit*) or nationality that delineates a state's nationals from foreigners (Koslowski 2000), which, in turn, helped constitute the modern system of nation-states itself. The modern institution of nationality has been administratively supported by state deployment of official travel documents such as passports. The development of both nationality and the passport involved the routinization of state practices towards international travellers and migrants and the development of norms of reciprocity with respect to one state's treatment of those who came from other states. Eventually, these routinized state practices, which are often understood in terms of common law, became codified through explicit international cooperation in the early twentieth century. This initial international cooperation on nationality and passports established the foundation upon which subsequent cooperation on international travel rests. Most notably, states subsequently cooperated within INTERPOL, ICAO, and the IMO to ensure the validity of the passport, set format standards, incorporate new technologies, and coordinate requirements in order to facilitate movement through border controls.

Nationality

Nationality refers to the status of being subject to a state's laws, its taxes, and military conscription while enjoying the right of protection by the state even when abroad. During the nineteenth century, the inhabitants of the states received a 'nationality' when states identified those people who belonged to it and those who did not (Grawert 1973; Hammar 1990: 41–9). Due to states' unilateral application of differing principles in the ascription of nationality at birth, conflicts of law emerged that required international cooperation (Koslowski 2001a, 2003). As the number of states adopted either the *jus sanguinis* (ancestral lineage) or the *jus soli* (birthplace) principle of ascription of nationality, conflicts of law resulting from the opposing principles of *jus soli* and *jus sanguinis* caused some individuals to become stateless while others received more than one nationality. Dual nationality led to serious international political, and even military, conflicts. The problem of multiple military obligations associated with dual nationality motivated the United States to negotiate bilateral treaties with European states that recognized US naturalization and limited dual nationality (Bar-Yaacov 1961: 163–6).

The proliferation of bilateral treaties accumulated into a set of norms in customary international law that led League of Nations member states to consider nationality as the first of three topics at the International Codification Conference (see Harvard Law School 1929). The conference produced the 1930 Hague Convention on Certain Questions Relating to the Conflict of Nationality Laws and the accompanying Protocol Relating to Military Obligations in Certain Cases of Double Nationality and Protocol Relating to a Certain Case of Statelessness. The 1930 Hague Convention stated, 'it is in the interest of the international community to secure that all members should recognize that every person should have a nationality and should have one nationality only' (League of Nations 1930, preamble). The Convention has been in force since 1937. As I have explained at length elsewhere (Koslowski 2001a, 2003), the international norm that everyone should belong to a state and one state only established a 'demographic boundary maintenance regime' that helped states differentiate which parts of the world's population belonged to which states.

Passports

The issuance and acceptance of passports by states has supported the perpetuation of the demographic boundary maintenance regime, as the passport has increasingly been used as a 'proof of citizenship' by international travellers presenting themselves to state officials authorized to enforce the states rules of entry and exit at official border crossing points. Much as the institutions of formal state membership gradually developed with the modern international system, the issuance of passports to all nationals who travel abroad and the requirement that all travellers present their passports to officials at borders similarly evolved over time but only became fully established in the early twentieth century.

In the distant past, messengers and officials, traders crossing Eurasia on the Silk Road or travelling to medieval fairs in Europe, and Christian pilgrims travelling to the Holy Land or Muslims going to Mecca travelled from the realm of one emperor or king to the other and were given 'leave' to do so. The possession of a letter from one ruler facilitated the granting of such leave to pass from other rulers and reference to such letters goes back to the Old Testament (Nehemiah 2:7–9). Over time, a norm of reciprocity in the mutual recognition of each other's subjects for the purpose of travel gradually emerged with the development of the international system. Between the middle of the fifteenth and middle of the sixteenth centuries, such letters became routinized in the official document known as the *laissez-passer* that was issued to couriers, diplomats, and traders. 'By the beginning of the eighteenth century, failure to carry such an official document while traveling was already an offense that could attract considerable penalties' (Groebner 2001: 16). As the scale of international travel expanded dramatically during the industrial revolution with the development of passenger rail services and the tenets of liberalism took hold politically, state requirements to carry a *laissez-passer* were increasingly not enforced or eliminated altogether within Europe. It was only towards the end of nineteenth century that the successor of the *laissez-passer*, the modern passport, emerged. During World War I (WWI), states re-established border controls and issued passports in order to identify foreigners from their own nationals and only after WWI, did states generally require that all travellers present passports upon entry (Torpey 2000).

In response to the WWI re-imposition of border controls, the League of Nations convened a series of conferences on international travel regulation in the hopes of facilitating movements across borders that might more closely approximate that of the pre-war era. At the 1920 Paris Conference on Passports and Customs Formalities and Through Tickets, League of Nations signatory states standardized passport and visa formats and adopted the now familiar multi-page book format passport with uniform rules for layout, content valid-ity, and issuing fees (see Lloyd 2003; Salter 2003). Despite passport standardiza-tion, travel was not sufficiently facilitated for over a million Russians who fled the Revolution and found themselves in a Europe whose post-WWI borders now required passports to cross and a home state whose revolutionary govern-ment was not about to issue them the travel documents they needed. In response, Fridtof Nansen was appointed the League's High Commissioner for Refugees and in 1921 he persuaded fifty-two states to accept the 'Nansen Passport' to give Russian refugees limited legal status enabling them to work and apply for permanent residency. The Second International Passport Confer-ence which took place in May 1926 in Geneva added specifications to the standard international passport format but the collapse of the League of Na-tions brought a halt to standardization efforts. It was only after WWII that efforts to improve and standardize passports were reignited with the formation of ICAO as a United Nations specialized agency in 1946.

The practice of state officials examining the travel documents issued by other states to determine a traveller's identity and nationality and asking questions of the traveller to determine admissibility has become central to all states' border control practices. This universally accepted practice is expected by internation-al travellers and is considered a normal, if not quintessential, experience of international travel. The passport can only effectively serve a border control function, however, if the person using the passport is the person to whom it was originally issued. Hundreds of thousands of passports are lost or stolen each year and, in order to reduce the possible travel document fraud, INTERPOL established a database through which member states share information on lost and stolen passports. A growing number of INTERPOL's 187 member states are contributing data to the INTERPOL database, which contains more than 16 million records of lost and stolen passports (INTERPOL 2009).

Visas

The visa is an authorization given by a state to the nationals of another state to travel and present themselves to border control authorities for inspection at ports of entry. Normally, consular officers abroad issue visas by stamping them in the prospective traveller's passport. Travellers may need a visa to enter a country but the visa itself does not in and of itself authorize admission. Only the destination state's border control officials are authorized to grant admission. Visas function as the state's extension of extra-territorial 'remote controls' (Zolberg 1999) over borders by requiring that travellers subject themselves to a visa application process that may involve submission of identity documents, return tickets, bank statements, immunization records, and an interview with consular officials. Visas may also be issued at the port of entry in advance of passport inspection but usually such visas are simply revenue-generating mechanisms.

Historically, the visa evolved together with the increasing use of the passport at the end of the nineteenth century. For example, the US Congress first charged US Consular officers posted abroad to issue visas to certain individuals travelling to the United States in immigration legislation passed on 5 July 1884. State use of visas increased with WWI as, for example, the United States began to require visas of aliens seeking to enter the country. After WWI, the League of Nations endeavoured to facilitate international travel by reducing state recourse to visa issuance when possible and promulgated rules for their use at the 1920 Paris Conference on Passports and Customs Formalities and Through Tickets (Salter 2003, 2006). As states adopted the practice of issuing visas and developed policies to govern issuance, a principle of reciprocity informed the norms of visa policy among states. This was recognized by the League of Nations Technical Committee, which recommended that, 'except in special or exceptional cases, entrance visas should be abolished by all countries, either generally or under condition of reciprocity, each country retaining its full freedom of action in respect to the enforcement of its legislation with regard to police measures for foreigners, the regulation of the labour supply, etc.' (Sub-Committee on the Passport Regime 1925: 6, quoted by Salter 2006: 177). The recommendation that entry visas be 'abolished by all countries' fell on increasingly deaf ears as the Great Depression led to increasingly restrictive immigration polices and diplomatic and political conflicts resulting in WWII augured for increasing travel restrictions. After WWII, states gradually relaxed visa requirements to facilitate international travel with, for example, increasing issuance of multi-entry visas. Other states increasingly reciprocated on a bilateral basis by imposing similar visa requirements and comparable visa application fees on each other's nationals.

The visa was initially developed as a tool of immigration law enforcement but it also became a tool of diplomacy. States use the issuance or denial of visas to individuals, certain groups, or all nationals of particular states in efforts to influence other states' policies. For example, the United States denied visas to known members of the Irish Republican Army (IRA) and Sinn Fein members such as Gerry Adams until 1994 when the United States used issuance of a visa to Adams as a means of signalling progress in the Northern Ireland peace process. There have also been multilateral visa bans, as when the EU and the United States banned the issuance of visas to Robert Mugabe and top members of his government in the run-up to the 2002 election in an effort to persuade the Mugabe regime to stop harassment of opposing candidates and interference with international election monitors (Stringer 2004).

Eventually, many states followed the League of Nations recommendation to lift entry visa requirements 'under the condition of reciprocity'. As the volume of international travel increased in the post-war era, many states eliminated visa requirements for the nationals of other states that were members of international organizations promoting regional economic and political integration (e.g. the 1954 Nordic Passport Union; the 1985 Schengen Agreement; the Economic Community of West African States abolition of visas and entry requirements; East African Community; Association of South East Asian Nations, etc.). Similarly, several states dropped visa requirements for short-term visits on a bilateral reciprocal basis. For example, the US Visa Waiver Program (begun as a pilot programme with the United Kingdom and Japan in 1988 and made permanent in 2000) permits travel to the United States for purposes of business or pleasure for up to ninety days without a visa by nationals of thirty-five states that similarly permit visa-free travel by US nationals. Nationals of EU member states do not need visas to travel to other EU states. All EU member states adhere to a common visa policy that includes a list of thirty-six countries whose nationals may travel to any EU member state without a visa for short stays and 126 countries whose nationals must apply for and receive visas in order to travel. Seven of the top ten international tourist destination states (France, Spain, United States, Italy, United Kingdom, Germany, and Austria) have reciprocal visa-free travel arrangements. It is crucial to acknowledge, however, that while the United States, EU member states, as well as Organisation for Co-operation and Development and other countries with relatively high gross domestic products per capita have increasingly permitted visa-free travel to nationals from similarly wealthy countries, these same countries have maintained visa requirements for the nationals of relatively poorer countries (Neumayer 2006).

States have been cooperating with each other on nationality, passports, and visas for close to a century. Such cooperation among states to enable international travel, even in times of war and political tension, joins the cooperation that enables the sending of mail, transmission of telegraph messages and telephone conversations across international borders that was fundamental to industrialization and expansion of international commerce (Murphy 1994). All too often, such cooperation recedes into the background and goes unnoticed by international relations analysts as well as laypeople. While there has been little international cooperation on migration at the global level, the mere possibility of international travel attests to the routinization of international cooperation in this area of international relations. The growth of international travel over the past few decades to hundreds of millions of people crossing borders by land, sea, and air has involved even more international cooperation and its institutionalization within international organizations, to which I now turn.

Crossing land borders

Given that almost every point along a land border is between only two states, international cooperation on international travel by land border crossing has been primarily bilateral in nature—there is little in the way of multilateral cooperation, let alone global cooperation. Many neighbouring states have entered into a wide variety of bilateral agreements to facilitate international travel across their borders, from flexible travel document requirements (e.g. enhanced drivers' licences as an alternative to passports for travel between the United States and Canada) to special cards that function as permanent multi-entry visas and identification cards (e.g. the US Border Crossing Card for Mexicans and a Mexican border crossing card for Guatemalans) to registered traveller programmes and special lanes of roadways that expedite inspections (e.g. the NEXUS and SENTRI programmes). Similarly, many states have developed bilateral arrangements between border control agencies that allow officials to check passports and inspect passengers on trains that are moving across international borders rather than stopping the train and requiring that all passengers get off the train and cross through pedestrian lanes.

Although land border crossing programmes and arrangements may be bilateral, they can also be identified as 'best practices' by other states and be adopted by many states to establish new sets of norms. On a regional level, the Schengen Code was developed through identification of best practices that were eventually adopted by all EU member states (except the United Kingdom and Ireland). Another vehicle of such sharing of best practices has been the 'land border crossing working group' of the International Border Police Conference wherein border control officials from a variety of countries meet to share their approaches.

Passenger sea travel

Over the course of the late nineteenth and early twentieth centuries, states developed customs and immigration inspection requirements with respect to sea travel but they largely did so independently of one another. Increasing transoceanic passenger travel spurred international cooperation on regulations and inspection of passengers arriving by ship. Freighters, transoceanic passenger ships, or cruise ships typically visit several states in a single voyage and each state might require the shipping company, captain, and passengers to submit information on many official forms. Oftentimes, the information requested by each state was the same but would have to be submitted in a slightly different way. In order to reduce onerous multiple paperwork requirements on commercial shipping, states engaged in international cooperation through the IMO to standardize state inspection information requirements and agreed to the 1965 Convention on Facilitation of International Maritime Traffic. Most importantly, for the international travel of crew members and passengers at posts of call, the Convention limited the documents that public authorities could demand of ships and adopted IMO standardized forms: two of the seven standardized forms are crew lists and passenger lists.

Passenger air travel

As international air passenger travel began to overtake international travel by sea, states stepped up cooperation within ICAO to further the facilitation of air travel and, after a rash of passenger airplane hijacking in the early 1970s, institute standards to increase aviation security. Although the standardization of passports helped facilitate international travel by making it easier for inspectors at border controls to quickly find the information they needed on the passport to make their decisions on admissibility, the 1970 launch of the Boeing 747 and then other wide-bodied jets presented a dilemma to airlines, airports, and border control agencies. The prospect of several planes with more than 500 passengers each landing at an airport at the same time threatened to quickly overwhelm inspection capabilities and facilities and lead to passenger throughput bottlenecks at passport controls that would, in turn, lead to passengers missing connecting flights or the delay of those flights waiting for arriving overseas passengers. Airports could build larger inspection areas and border control agencies could staff expanded passport controls at a level that would accommodate peak arrival flows but this would involve costly infrastructure investments and increased costs to governments and taxpayers. Alternatively, airports could force airlines to stagger arrivals of large international flights but this would come at the expense of flexibility in scheduling connecting flights as well as passenger demand for particular arrival times.

One solution to this dilemma was to increase throughput at passport controls by automating aspects of the inspection process. By digitizing the traveller's biographic data and adding that data to a machine readable zone of the passport, automated passport readers could capture the traveller's data rather than having the inspector take the time to manually type the data into the entry systems used by border control authorities to run watch list checks and assist them in determining admissibility.

In 1980, ICAO member states took a major step by agreeing to standards for the issuance of machine readable travel documents (MRTDs), which most states began to issue in the 1980s and 1990s. Moreover, since the machine readable zone contained the same data printed on the passport, the new machine readable passports were more difficult to alter and use for fraudulent entry. Since then, ICAO's Technical Advisory Group on machine readable travel documents (TAG/MRTD) has continued the work of standardizing passports, increasing the security of the document, and improving the document in ways that facilitate international travel. By the mid-1990s, TAG/MRTD division had established a New Technologies Working Group, which was to plan and implement the long-term development of MRTDs. In 1998, this group began work to establish the most effective biometric identification system and the best way to store biometric data on travel documents. They gravitated towards a contactless integrated circuit (IC) chip, a storage medium which had sufficient capacity to store a digital version of the photo in the passport and/or other biometric data. The contactless IC chip is part of a radio frequency identification (RFID) system in which data on a chip or tag is transmitted via radio waves to a reader. As opposed to MRTDs that contain data on magnetic strips, a passport with an RFID chip can be read by the reader at a short distance (10 cm), therefore allowing faster transfer of data from the passport and faster processing of travellers through passport controls. Most of ICAO's standards work had been completed by 11 September 2001 but the attacks on that day led states to accelerate the process of approving the new technology standards. The passport features added by international cooperation through ICAO intended to facilitate international travel would then be leveraged for increased aviation and border security.

International travel for business and leisure

Emerging out of an international non-governmental organization devoted to the promotion of tourism, the UNWTO has essentially continued that mission but placed tourism promotion within the larger context of economic development. The UNWTO traces back its origin to the International Union of Official Tourist Propaganda Organizations, which was established in 1934. After WWII, this unfortunately named organization was succeeded by the International Union of Official Travel Organizations (IUOTO). The IUOTO initiated efforts for the 1963 United Nations Conference on Tourism and International Travel that adopted recommendations on the simplification of international travel formalities as well as a general resolution on tourism development, including technical cooperation, freedom of movement, and absence of discrimination. Six years later, the United Nations General Assembly called for the creation of an intergovernmental organization on tourism and, in 1970, the IUOTO Special General Assembly adopted the statutes of the WTO. In 1975, the first WTO General Assembly met in Madrid, established its headquarters there, and signed an agreement to become an executing agency of the United Nations Development Programme (UNDP). In 2003, the UN General Assembly approved the transformation of WTO into a United Nations specialized body that itself adopted the initials UNWTO to avoid confusion with 'the new WTO'.

The UNWTO has played an important role in collecting tourism statistics including the number of international tourists and the receipts they generate. These statistics have been used to demonstrate the economic importance of tourism generally and to convince the governments of developing countries that opening their borders to international travellers from developed countries could become a significant driver of economic growth. The UNWTO does not serve as the secretariat overseeing the implementation of any major international treaties that entail major commitments on the part of states with respect to accepting the entry of international travellers. Nevertheless, the WTO General Assembly adopted the Tourism Bill of Rights and Tourist Code (1985), a resolution defining the statistical needs of the tourism industry (1991), Recommended Measures for Security in Tourism (1991), the WTO Declaration on the Prevention of Organized Sex Tourism (1995), and the Global Code of Ethics for Tourism (1999).

The politics of regulating international travel

As the above discussion indicates, international cooperation has primarily focused on measures to facilitate international travel and re-establish international travel flows reduced due to war. A wide array of international organizations have become involved in the facilitation and regulation of international travel and the politics taking place within and around these organizations has revolved around several core issues. The politics of international travel have largely pitted the economic interests of carriers, travel companies, the tourism industries in destination countries, and multinational corporations against states and their citizens concerned more with security. By the 1970s, increasing international tourism generated another political cleavage between proponents of economic liberalization in less developed countries that viewed tourism as a vehicle of economic development and sceptics of economic liberalization who were often concerned about neo-imperialism. By the 1990s, the economic development impact of international travel was widely accepted but environmentalists increasingly opposed international tourism given the proportionately large emission of carbon dioxide (CO_2) of long-haul jet aircraft.

Facilitation vs. security

The politics of facilitation vs. security have played out in changing state passport and visa policies during both world wars and the Cold War. During the Cold War, states' permission to allow travel (of their nationals or those visiting their nationals) became a tool of control as well as a political symbol. International travel also became a factor of 'societal security' (Waever et al. 1993) as it was often viewed by states shaking off European colonialism as a vehicle of neo-imperialism, and differing social mores of Western tourists and cultural differences were considered threats to social (and political) order. The 11 September 2001 attacks on the United States, however, triggered one state's policy response that reverberated around the world and has become an occasion for spurring the most recent round of international cooperation. This cooperation, however, aims at securing international travel while at the same time maintaining travel flows if not facilitating their growth.

As discussed above, states are motivated to cooperate internationally to facilitate travel often by monetary (and fiscal) gains. Likewise, security measures are often resisted due to fears that they may increase international travel costs. For example, international tourism to the United States peaked in 2000 at 51.2 million international arrivals (US$82.4 billion in receipts) then dropped to 41.2 million (US$64.3 billion) in 2003. This was the year that the Department of Homeland Security was formed; that the Iraq War began; that many provisions of the Enhanced Border Security and Visa Entry Reform Act of 2002, such as mandatory interviews for visa applications with submission of biometrics, came into effect; and the United States Visitor and Immigrant Status Indicator Technology (US-VISIT) programme was deployed at all airports and seaports to collect facial and fingerprint biometrics from individuals travelling to the United States on a non-immigrant visa. It has taken six years until 2006 for the United States to regain the level of international tourist arrivals and exceed receipts of 2000 (51.1 million and US$85.7 billion, respectively). In the same six years, the world total of international arrivals increased by 24 per cent; Spain overtook the US's second place ranking as international tourist arrivals to Spain increased from 47.9 million to 58.5 million and arrivals to China increased from 31.2 million to 49.6 million, bringing China within striking distance of surpassing the US's third place ranking. This fact has not been lost on the US tourist industry, which has increasingly lobbied against additional border security measures, that would reduce international travel flows.

Despite the fact that the United States and many other states built up their border control capabilities in the 1990s, they proved insufficient to stop the September 11 attacks, as Al-Qaeda systematically studied and trained to compromise existing border controls. Al-Qaeda operated a 'passport office' at the Kandahar airport to alter travel documents and train operatives, including Mohamad Atta (9/11 Commission 2004a: 169) and at least two, and perhaps as many as eleven, of the September 11 hijackers used fraudulently altered passports. Three of the hijackers had stayed in the United States after their visas expired and several purchased fraudulent identity documents on the black market that primarily services illegal migrants (9/11 Commission 2004b: 138–9). Contrary to much of the early discussions in the media that all of the hijackers entered legally and that border controls were irrelevant to their entry, the 9/11 Commission concluded that '15 of the 19 hijackers were potentially vulnerable to interception by border authorities' (9/11 Commission 2004a: 384).

In the aftermath of the September 11 attacks, many governments, led by the United States, initiated measures to increase the security of international travel but, at the same time, they wished to avoid hindering legitimate travel. It is very difficult, however, to simultaneously facilitate international travel while securing movements of people across borders without multilateral cooperation and many states have adopted policies towards securing international travel with this in mind. Most notably, the European Commission and the US Department of Homeland Security have been taking international cooperation into sensitive areas of state sovereignty dealing with border controls, government surveillance, data collection, and information exchanges that before 11 September 2001 would have been unthinkable. Cooperation on securing international travel is centred in the transatlantic area, developing rather quickly and leading to even deeper and broader global international cooperation on travel document security, passenger data sharing, and ETA (see Koslowski 2006; Meyers et al. 2007).

Although the original objective of ICAO's standards for MRTDs was to enable border control authorities to cope with the increased number of passengers, MRTDs provided increased security because data in the machine readable zone could be checked against the biographical data typed on the document itself, thereby making fraudulent alterations more difficult. In the wake of the September 11 attacks, ICAO became a main forum for international cooperation to secure travel. Shortly after the attacks, the US Congress passed legislation requiring that states in the US Visa Waiver Program issue machine readable passports and in 2002 legislation, Congress required that all passports of Visa Waiver Program countries issued after 26 October 2004 contain biometrics. The US Congress deferred to ICAO on setting the biometric standard and ICAO announced an agreement in May 2003—a facial biometric (digital photo) plus an optional additional biometric (e.g. fingerprints) stored on a contactless IC chip (ICAO 2003). As envisioned, holders of new biometric passports would give their passports to inspectors who would simply bring the passport close to the reader. The reader captures the personal data and the digitized biometric. This information can then be checked against terrorist and law enforcement watch lists. In 2006, over forty states communicated their intention to ICAO that they will upgrade to biometric e-passports by 2008[1] and, by December 2008, it was estimated that over 100 million e-passports had been issued (Martin 2008).

Travel for development

As new states emerged out of the post-WWII waves of decolonization ending in the 1970s, they exercised their sovereignty through the issuance of passports and visas. Most of the first foreign visitors to these states came from neighbouring states and from the region, however, economic and social ties to former European metropoles and new American multinational corporations was increasingly reflected in business and tourist travel to these new states. Foreign investment raised concerns of neocolonialism leveraged by nationalist movements that produced policies of expropriation and increasing barriers to foreign visitors. During the 1980s, the International Monetary Fund (IMF) promoted liberal economic policies and openness to international trade and investment as the means of economic development. As governments of developing countries increasingly adopted IMF 'structural adjustment' programmes, many also turned to international tourism as a source of foreign 'hard' currencies and they adopted policies that would facilitate international travel such as simplifying visa requirements and allowing acquisition of visas upon arrival.

The UNWTO had long promoted international tourism as a source of economic growth in general; however, by the early 1990s the organization increasingly focused efforts to promote tourism as a vehicle of sustainable economic development among developing countries, at which time protectionist economic policies largely fell by the wayside in much of the developing world. The UNWTO has provided analysis of the growth of tourism and the economic impact it has as well as providing direct development assistance to countries in order to help them develop the tourism sectors of their economies. In a 2005 publication, the UNWTO documented the dramatic increase in international tourism by noting that of the 736 million international tourist arrivals that took place in 2004 worldwide, 39 per cent were in developing countries with a total of US$177 billion in tourism receipts to developing countries. Not only has tourism become one of the major export sectors of most developing countries but it became the primary source of foreign exchange earnings in forty-six of the forty-nine least developed countries (UNWTO 2005).

Environmental impacts of international travel

Just as international tourism was growing at an accelerating rate in the 1990s, the linkage between the emission of CO_2 and climate change became increasingly clear. By the end of the 1990s, the Intergovernmental Panel on Climate Change (IPCC) issued a report estimating that aviation accounted for 2–3 per cent of the world's total use of fossil fuels and more than 80 per cent of that was consumed by civil aviation. The report further forecasted that the contribution of aviation to global anthropogenic CO_2 emissions would grow to 3–7 per cent by 2050 (Penner et al. 1999). This and other similar reports triggered a flurry of media reports on the environmental consequences of air travel, particularly long distance international air travel, as well as campaigns within the environmental movement to urge people to restrict their air travel in order to reduce their individual carbon footprint.

UNWTO acknowledges that in consideration of the contribution of tourism to climate change, air transport remains the main challenge. Nevertheless, the UNWTO makes the argument that 'To simply *decrease* air travel frequency would be an unrealistic task to attempt. Moreover, staying at home would also involve consuming energy, through working in the factory or the office, the heating, air conditioning, driving cars, etc. Work must be done to find a middle path as populations of less developed countries would be hugely affected if we deprived them of the economic contribution of tourism.' In order to address the challenge posed by increasing international air travel to the environment, the UNWTO works with ICAO 'in a search for the best options on climate change activities—emissions trading, carbon offsets, incentives and taxes, etc.' (UNWTO n.d.). The environmental movement and the efforts of individual states and international organizations has clearly come into conflict with the international travel promotion of the UNWTO. As in other areas, the UN system's promotion of economic development, 'sustainable development', has become the guiding conceptual framework for the UNWTO and a framework within which to negotiate compromises on state promotion of international travel.

Towards global governance of international travel

Several international organizations have established roles in the regulation of international travel and become loci for international travel politics; however, other international organizations have more recently become engaged in these efforts. In some cases, the politics of facilitation vs. security have spilled over into other venues and international fora, particularly after the 11 September 2001 attacks. In other cases, the broadening scope of issues is related to economic globalization and broader initiatives of global governance as well as the development of new technologies that give states and international organizations new capabilities of governance and regulation implementation. In the past decade, an increasingly sophisticated framework for the global governance of international travel appears to be emerging. Steps towards this framework include the further adoption of WTO GATS 4 commitments on business travel visas, specific protocols on human smuggling and trafficking within an international treaty, cooperation within ICAO to develop a global framework for the exchange of API and PNR data, as well as changing norms among states that facilitate and encourage deployment of technologies such as biometrics and ETA systems. Taken together, these developments in international cooperation are helping to shape state policies with respect to international travel and, in turn, transforming the practicalities of international travel itself.

Business travel

International norms codified under the WTO's GATS help govern a major share of international travel—namely the 131 million international arrivals for the purposes of business in 2006 (UNWTO 2007). The GATS delineates the four possible forms of service delivery covered by the agreement, which includes the 'presence of natural persons', also referred to as 'Mode 4'. WTO members' commitments under Mode 4 are to provide for temporary admission of foreign nationals who provide services, as outlined in the GATS 'Annex on movement of natural persons supplying services under the Agreement' (WTO 1994). The scheduled horizontal Mode 4 commitments made by some 100 member states are irrevocable and primarily deal with business visitor visas that are generally limited to 90-day stays (WTO 1998: 13).

In contrast to the proliferation of visa-free travel arrangement extended on a reciprocal basis among relatively rich countries, the commitments to offering business visas under the GATS are more universal. The GATS commitments of states to issuing business visas are, however, limited to travel of people who, in most countries, tend to be from higher socio-economic classes and must, in any event, provide sufficient proof to consular officers that their proposed travel is truly for business purposes and that they have sufficient resources and reasons to return to their origin countries after the term of their visa expires. The GATS Mode 4 provisions have increasingly been considered a wedge that could be leveraged for increasing international cooperation with respect to labour migration; however, the commitments are still primarily oriented towards business travel that takes place in periods of less than one year.

Cooperation on human smuggling, trafficking, and return of illegal border crossers

International cooperation on human trafficking emerged out of the anti-slavery movement of the nineteenth century in an effort to better manage the realities of post-slavery 'coolie' labour and the movements of prostitutes that serviced coolie workforces within overseas European colonial economies (Scully 2001). While international cooperation to combat 'white slavery' within the League of Nations was not international cooperation on travel or migration per se, over time states returned to the issue of combating human smuggling and trafficking. Although international cooperation in this area is treated elsewhere in this volume as one form of migration, as this cooperation has developed over the past decade, it has focused on border controls that effect all travel—not just migration—and has been negotiated and implemented within the context of international cooperation to combat transnational organized crime.

In November 2000, the 'UN Convention against Transnational Organized Crime', as well as its 'Protocol to Prevent, Suppress, and Punish Trafficking in Persons, Especially Women and Children', and the 'Protocol against the Smuggling of Migrants by Land, Sea, and Air' were adopted by the UN General Assembly. Once receiving a sufficient number of ratifications, the Convention went into effect on 29 September 2003, the anti-trafficking protocol on 25 December 2003, and the anti-smuggling protocol on 28 January 2004. As of June 2009, the anti-trafficking protocol had 117 state parties and the anti-smuggling protocol had 112 state parties.[2] The UN Office on Drugs and Crime (UNODC) functions as the secretariat of the Convention on Transnational Organized Crime. The anti-trafficking and anti-smuggling protocols provide rules for interdicting and boarding ships suspected of carrying illegal migrants, approve of state use of carrier sanctions, encourage information programmes directed at the customers of traffickers and smugglers as well as information exchanges between states that enable more effective law enforcement. The protocols also call on states to strengthen border controls and intensify cooperation among border control agencies by establishing and maintaining direct lines of communication, ensuring the integrity of travel documents that they issue, and responding to requests to verify the validity of those documents (for elaboration, see Koslowski 2001b).

Not only are there limitations on what states can do by themselves to identify and apprehend unauthorized border crossers, states also encounter new challenges when they successfully apprehend unauthorized border crossers and visa overstayers, especially in high numbers. That is, destination states may encounter difficulties returning such individuals without the cooperation of their origin countries, especially if they no longer have valid passports or other travel documents. In some cases, origin countries have opted not to acknowledge the nationality of failed asylum seekers and apprehended illegal border crossers and have failed to supply travel documents necessary for an orderly return of these individuals. Many destination countries have, therefore, negotiated bilateral readmission agreements with origin countries to facilitate the voluntary return of those who were never authorized to enter or had lost their authorization to remain in the destination country.

Except for the commitments of states that have signed and ratified the UN Refugee Convention to not return individuals who have a well-founded fear of persecution, there are no international norms or multilateral agreements on readmission at the global level. Nevertheless, the international cooperation that has enabled the International Organization for Migration (IOM) to grow in terms of state membership, budget, staffing, and activities has produced an international organization that facilitates readmission by helping states with its practicalities. The IOM offers Assisted Voluntary Return (AVR) services to states and individuals that provide 'pre-departure, transportation and post-arrival assistance to unsuccessful asylum seekers, migrants in an irregular situation, migrants stranded in transit, stranded students and other persons under similar circumstances. . . . The assistance typically provides information, referral, arrangement of travel to the home location and limited support towards reinsertion' (IOM 2008). On its website, the IOM lists 128 AVR projects involving destination countries such as the United States, Australia, Mexico, Switzerland, Norway, and a majority of EU member states, including Austria, Belgium, Denmark, Finland, France, Germany, Greece, Ireland, Italy, the Netherlands, Romania, Slovenia, Spain, Sweden, and the United Kingdom.

Cooperation on advance passenger information and passenger name records

In order to facilitate and secure international travel, a growing number of countries require carriers to electronically submit API and PNR data before passengers arrive at their destinations. Border control authorities want to know who is coming to their ports of entry well in advance of their arrival. Such knowledge allows authorities to conduct watch list checks, review traveller, conveyance, and route information to detect suspicious anomalies in advance of travellers' arrival, select individuals who may need additional screening upon arrival, and expedite the movement of other travellers through border controls. International organizations are playing a growing role in setting guidelines for data exchanges and becoming a forum for cooperation on standard setting that facilitates information exchange agreements.

API includes information found on the biographic page of the passport, such as full name, gender, and country of passport issuance along with an electronic manifest. In order to cope with a dramatic growth in passenger traffic, in the early 1990s, customs and border control authorities of several countries cooperated with the airline industry to develop API systems that enabled airlines to electronically submit data while planes were in flight so that these data would be available to inspectors in advance of passengers' arrival. In 1993, the World Customs Organization (WCO) worked with the International Air Transport Association (IATA) to issue guidelines on API to help member states implement this system. Initially, airline submission of advance passenger data was voluntary; however, after the 11 September 2001 attacks, the US Congress passed legislation to require such data submissions by airlines for US-bound flights. Several other countries such as Canada, the United Kingdom, Japan, Mexico, Spain, India, and China followed suit. In March 2003, ICAO joined the WCO and IATA to review the API guidelines in consideration of new developments with respect to security, data protection, and mutual administrative assistance and then issued revised guidelines.

A similar dynamic developed with respect to requirements for the submission of PNR data; however, the move to international cooperation on PNR data at the global level was spurred by protracted transatlantic negotiations over US requirements. The 2001 US Aviation and Transportation Security Act required that airlines with US-bound international flights submit electronically a passenger manifest and mandates that 'the carriers shall make passenger name record information available to the Customs Service upon request' (US GPO 2001: Section 115). PNR data is created each time a passenger books a flight and it is stored in the airlines' reservation systems. To comply with these regulations, US-based airlines gave access to their PNR databases to the US Customs Service.[3] Many opted to simply give database passwords to US Customs, which allowed Customs to 'pull' all PNR data rather than select and 'push' a subset of that data which met specific Customs' requests. The US Customs Service also requested PNR data from European-based airlines, but several resisted, contending that it would be a violation of EU data protection rules. Essentially, European airlines were presented with the choice of either breaking US laws, facing fines, and potentially losing landing rights, or violating EU and EU member state data protection laws and facing fines. After a series of interim agreements on the exchange of PNR data between the European Commission and the US Department of Homeland Security that kept data flowing were challenged by the European Parliament in the European Court of Justice, an agreement with a firm legal basis was finally reached in June 2007.

The evolution of transatlantic cooperation on PNR data directly led to increasing cooperation at the global level. Such data collection and exchange requires acceptance of mutual constraints on the range of state action in the area of border control—one of the defining aspects of territorial sovereignty. International cooperation may be limited by differing legal regimes governing privacy and personal data protection. Given the increasing concerns of the European Parliament (and national parliaments) over the privacy of PNR data, it became clear that there may be major limitations to further transatlantic PNR data transfer without global multilateral agreements. Partly motivated by the fact that Canada and Australia, in addition to the United States, also passed legislation requiring advanced submission of PNR data, the European Commission opted to take a global approach to the issue. Ireland, on behalf of the EU, put forward a proposal for an international framework for the transfer of PNR data to the ICAO (Ireland 2004). ICAO subsequently developed a set of guidelines for PNR data transfer that went into effect as a 'recommended practice' on 11 July 2005 (ICAO 2005).

A future of ETA and biometric entry–exit systems

The next frontier of border controls may be ETA systems, first pioneered by Australia in the mid-1990s and increasingly adopted by a growing number of states. ETA systems enable border control authorities to acquire data directly from travellers without relying on airlines or dealing with difficulties arising from conflicts over differing regulations imposed by states on airlines as has been the case with PNR data. Individuals intending to travel to Australia must electronically submit the biographical data on their passports either through travel agents or by themselves through a web portal. Automated watch list checks are executed and usually within minutes an authorization for travel to Australia is issued or the applicant is referred to apply for a visa at an Australian consulate.

The US Congress mandated the development of an Australian-style ETA system in 2007 as a condition to reforming the Visa Waiver Program and expanding the number of states in the programme (Koslowski 2009). The US

ETA system has major implications for the development and use of border control information systems globally, as the European Commission has also announced plans that the EU will develop a similar system (European Commission 2008). The proposed US ETA system not only requires transmission of biographical data of travellers (name, date of birth, passport number, etc.), it also requires an 'exit system that records the departure on a flight leaving the United States of every alien participating in the visa waiver program' and that the system shall 'match biometric information of the alien against relevant watch lists and immigration information; and compare such biometric information against manifest information collected by air carriers on passengers departing the United States to confirm such individuals have departed the United States' (US Senate 2007: Section 501). As the United States, EU member states, Canada, Japan, and other countries join Australia in using ETA systems, the resulting advanced passenger data exchange may yield a collective increase in the security of visa-free travel among these states. To achieve this collective increase in security, however, many other border security measures, such as implementing exit controls, may be necessary and be much more difficult to achieve without even more international cooperation.

The development of electronic passports, passenger data sharing agreements, ETA systems, and biometric entry–exit systems by an increasing number of states offers a glimpse of how a future secure international travel regime may operate in practice. Each state would require visa applications to be lodged abroad as before but state officials would also collect biometrics through the visa application process and then again for comparison at the port of entry. States may extend a visa-free travel contingent on nationals of those states issuing passports with biometrics meeting ICAO standards but visa-free travellers would also be required to electronically submit biographical data from their passports in advance of their travel or not be allowed to board. Travellers' biographical data would be checked by destination states using automated watch lists populated with criminal and terrorist data from their state of nationality and/or residence that was acquired though international information sharing agreements among border control authorities. And when travellers arrive in another state, their biographical data and biometrics would be captured and stored upon entry. Border control authorities would amass tremendous amounts of biographic and biometric data in digital format, which could then be mined to detect anomalies that could then be flagged for further investigation. Depending on the level of law enforcement cooperation among origin, transit, and destination countries involved, these investigations of individual travellers may involve additional international law enforcement cooperation. Such collaboration yields its own intelligence on terrorist travel and the sharing of border control best practices that, in turn, increase individual state border control capabilities.

Conclusion

International cooperation on international travel reaches back to the League of Nations but it has generally been overlooked by migration and international relations scholars alike. This cooperation has enabled billions of international border crossings and has maintained the flow of international travel even during wars and major international political conflicts. While largely taken for granted over the years, cooperation on international travel has recently intensified with more international organizations becoming involved, more international initiatives being launched, more international agreements signed, and more new technologies transforming the practices of international travel regulation and, in turn, requiring even more international standard setting and technical cooperation. The increasing intensity of this cooperation signifies the emergence of an international travel regime at the global level.

As I argue elsewhere (Koslowski forthcoming), this emerging international travel regime is part of a set of three interacting global mobility regimes that also includes the existing international refugee regime and a potential international migration regime. The dynamic growth of the international travel regime and a disproportionate interest in promoting tourism and business travel among major migration destination states presents opportunities for linking cooperation on securing international travel advocated by many migration destination states to cooperation that would facilitate labour migration as desired by many migration origin states.

Whether states will link cooperation on labour migration to securing international travel within the context of the global governance of migration is very much an open question. Nevertheless, understanding the extent and dynamics of cooperation on international travel is essential to a complete understanding of the global governance of migration. Moreover, those policymakers and international civil servants who wish to promote cooperation on migration at the global level must also fully engage the international organizations involved in regulating international travel if they hope to be successful.

Notes

1. Andorra, Australia, Austria, Belgium, Brunei, Canada, Czech Republic, Denmark, Finland, France, Germany, Hong Kong Special Administrative Region of China, Hungary, Iceland, Indonesia, Ireland, Italy, Japan, Republic of Korea, Liechtenstein, Lithuania, Luxembourg, Malaysia, Malta, Monaco, the Netherlands, New Zealand, Nigeria, Norway, Pakistan, Portugal, San Marino, Serbia and Montenegro, Singapore, Slovenia, South Africa, Spain, Sweden, Switzerland, the United Kingdom, the United States (ICAO 2006).

2. For treaty texts, signatures and ratifications, see 'UN Signatories to the UN Convention against Transnational Crime and its Protocols' at http://www.unodc.org/unodc/en/treaties/CTOC/signatures.html.
3. The US Customs Service was merged into the Department of Homeland Security (DHS) formed in March 2003 and its former staff and resources are primarily in the Customs and Border Protection and Immigration and Customs Enforcement branches of the DHS.

References

9/11 Commission (2004a) *The 9/11 Commission Report: Final Report of the National Commission on Terrorist Attacks Upon the United States*, New York: W.W. Norton.

——(2004b) *9/11 and Terrorist Travel: Staff Report of the National Commission on Terrorist Attacks Upon the United States*, http://www.9-11commission.gov/staff_statements/index.htm (accessed 19 August 2004).

Bar-Yaacov, N. (1961) *Dual Nationality*, London: Praeger.

European Commission (2008) New Tools for an Integrated European Border Management Strategy, Press Release, MEMO/08/85, 13 February 2008.

Grawert, R. (1973) *Staat und Staatsangehoerigkeit, Verfassungsgeschichte Untersuchungen zur Entstehung der Staatsangehoerigkeit, Schriften zur Verfassungsgeschichte, Band 17*, Berlin: Duncker and Humbolt.

Groebner, V. (2001) Describing the Person, Reading the Signs in Late Medieval and Renaissance Europe: Identity Papers, Vested Figures, and the Limits of Identification, 1400–1600, in J. Caplan and J. Torpey (eds), *Documenting Individual Identity: The Development of State Practices in the Modern World*, Princeton, NJ: Princeton University Press.

Hammar, T. (1990) *Democracy and the Nation-State: Aliens, Denizens and Citizens in a World of International Migration*, Aldershot: Avebury.

ICAO (2003) Biometric Identification to Provide Enhanced Security and Speedier Border Clearance for the Travelling Public, International Civil Aviation Organization, PIO/2003, 28 May 2003.

——(2005) Guidelines on Passenger Name Record (PNR) Data Transfer to States, Air Transportation Committee, 175th Session of the Council AT-WP/1995, 5 May 2005.

——(2006) International Civil Aviation Organization, *ICAO MRTD Report*, 1(1).

INTERPOL (2009) Secure Borders, Document Security and Anti-Counterfeiting Initiatives High on Agenda in Meeting between Ukraine Prime Minister and INTERPOL Secretary General, INTERPOL Media Release, 20 January 2009.

IOM (2008) Return Assistance to Migrants and Governments, International Organization for Migration, http://www.iom.int/jahia/Jahia/pid/747 (accessed 1 March 2008).

Ireland (2004) An International Framework for the Transfer of Passenger Name Record (PNR) Data, Working Paper, Presented by Ireland on Behalf of the European Community and its Member States, Facilitation Division, ICAO Cairo, Egypt, 22 March–2 April 2004.

Koslowski, R. (2000) *Migrants and Citizens: Demographic Change in the European States System*, Ithaca, NY: Cornell University Press.

——(2001*a*) Demographic Boundary Maintenance in World Politics: Of International Norms on Dual Nationality, in M. Albert, D. Jacobson, and Y. Lapid (eds), *Identities, Borders, Orders: Rethinking International Relations Theory*, Minneapolis, MN: University of Minnesota Press.

——(2001*b*) Economic Globalization, Human Smuggling and Global Governance, in D. Kyle and R. Koslowski (eds), *Global Human Smuggling in Comparative Perspective*, Baltimore, MD: Johns Hopkins University Press.

——(2003) Challenges of International Cooperation in a World of Increasing Dual Nationality, in K. Hailbronner and D. Martin (eds), *Rights and Duties of Dual Nationals: Evolution and Prospects*, The Hague: Kluwer Law International.

——(2006) Border and Transportation Security in the Transatlantic Relationship, in A. Dalgaard-Nielsen and D. Hamilton (eds), *Transatlantic Homeland Security? Protecting Society in the Age of Catastrophic Terrorism*, London: Routledge.

——(2009) Transatlantic Visa Politics, Paper presented at the American Political Science Association Annual Meeting, Toronto, 3–6 September 2009.

——(forthcoming) *Global Mobility Regimes*.

League of Nations (1930) Hague Convention on Certain Questions Relating to the Conflict of Nationality Laws (12 April 1930), 179 League of Nations Treaty Series, 89.

Lloyd, M. (2003) *The Passport: The History of Man's Most Travelled Document*, Stroud, UK: Sutton Publishing.

Martin, Z. (2008) The Next Generation Electronic Passport, *Regarding ID Magazine*, Winter 2008.

Meyers, D.W., Koslowski, R, and Ginsburg, S. (2007) *Room for Progress: Reinventing Euro-Atlantic Borders for a New Strategic Environment*, Migration Policy Institute, October 2007.

Murphy, C. (1994) *International Organization and Industrial Change: Global Governance Since 1850*, New York: Oxford University Press.

Neumayer, E. (2006) Unequal Access to Foreign Spaces: How States use Visa Restrictions to Regulate Mobility in a Globalized World, *Transactions of the Institute of British Geographers*, 31, 72–84.

Penner, J., Lister, D., Griggs, D., Dokken, D., and McFarland, M. (eds) (1999) *Aviation and The Global Atmosphere*, A Special Report of IPCC Working Groups I and III. Published for the Intergovernmental Panel on Climate Change, Cambridge: Cambridge University Press.

Salter, M.B. (2003) *Rights of Passage: The Passport in International Relations*, Boulder, CO: Lynne Rienner Publishers.

——(2006) The Global Visa Regime and the Political Technologies of the International Self, *Alternatives: Global, Local, Political*, 31(2), 167–89.

Scully, E. (2001) Cold War Traffic in Sexual Labor and Its Foes: Some Contemporary Lessons, in D. Kyle and R. Koslowski (eds), *Global Human Smuggling in Comparative Perspective*, Baltimore, MD: Johns Hopkins University Press.

Stringer, K.D. (2004) The Visa Dimension of Diplomacy, Discussion Papers In Diplomacy, No. 91, Netherlands Institute of International Relations (Clingendael), http://www.clingendael.nl/publications/2004/20040300_cli_paper_dip_issue91.pdf.

Sub-Committee on the Passport Regime (1925) Sub-Committee on the Passport Regime, Advisory and Technical Committee for Communications and Transit, in Minutes of the 3rd Session, Paris, 2–5 October 1925 (C.699.M.252. 1925 VIII).

Torpey, J. (2000) *The Invention of the Passport: Surveillance, Citizenship and the State*, Cambridge: Cambridge University Press.

UN (2006) Trends in Total Migrant Stock: The 2005 Revision, United Nations Department of Economic and Social Affairs, Population Division, POP/DB/MIG/Rev.2005/Doc, February 2006.

UNWTO (2005) Sustainable Tourism as an Effective Tool for Eliminating Poverty, UN World Tourism Organization leaflet, http://www.unwto.org/sdt/fields/en/pdf/Tourism_poverty-leaflet_JULIO2005-eng.pdf.

——(2007) *Tourism Highlights*, UN World Tourism Organization.

——(2008) *UNWTO World Tourism Barometer*, Vol. 6 (No. 1), UN World Tourism Organization (January).

——(2009) International Tourism Challenged by Deteriorating World Economy, UN World Tourism Organization Press Release, 27 January 2009.

——(n.d.) FAQ—Climate Change and Tourism, http://www.unwto.org/climate/faq/en/faq.php?op=4.

US GPO (2001) *Aviation and Transportation Security Act*, Public Law 107-71, 19 November 2001, Washington, DC: Government Printing Office.

US Senate (2007) Improving America's Security Act of 2007, S.4.

Waever, O., Buzan, B., Kelstrup, M., and Lemaitre, P. (1993) *Identity, Migration and the New Security Agenda in Europe*, New York: St Martin's Press.

WTO (1994) Annex on Movement of Natural Persons Supplying Services Under the Agreement, World Trade Organization, http://www.wto.org/English/tratop_e/serv_e/8-anmvnt_e.htm.

——(1998) Presence of Natural Workers (Mode 4), Background Note, Secretariat, World Trade Organization, Council for Trade in Services, S/C/W/75, 8 December 1998.

Zolberg, A. (1999) Matters of State: Theorizing Immigration Policy, in C. Hirschman, P. Kasinitz, and J. Dewind (eds), *The Handbook of International Migration: The American Experience*, New York: Russell Sage Foundation.

5

Lifestyle Migration*

Caroline Oliver

Introduction

Lifestyle migration is an emerging phenomenon, which has been subject to very little attention in governance of global migration. In charting the degree of governance facing different migration forms, lifestyle migration occupies a place at the least regulated end of the continuum. This chapter considers why this is so, despite the increasing social, environmental, and economic impact of the phenomenon. It argues that this outcome reflects the characteristics of lifestyle migration as a nascent and emergent migration form which is intrinsically different to other types of migration. It is an anomaly in the scheme of policy categories which normatively frame migration in mainstream policy discourse. Essentially, this is because lifestyle migrants are driven by consumption rather than production. Furthermore, their movement is predominantly North–North, or in some cases North–South. These unique characteristics have led to a neglect of governance of such migrants, especially given no apparent need for regulation on humanitarian, security, or other grounds. From this perspective, any case for introducing further regulation would rest only on its desirability on efficiency grounds or to mitigate the excesses of free market forces. The chapter debates this conclusion, suggesting it becomes questionable when considering the governance of lifestyle migration in a comparative sense. Then, one is provoked into questioning the limited degree of governance on the grounds of equity and social justice for all.

The chapter begins with a discussion of what constitutes lifestyle migration (hereafter referred to as 'LM'). This question is pertinent because understanding the phantasmagoric nature of the phenomenon helps shed light on the limited nature of its regulation (considered in the discussion from page 134). The third section of the chapter explores the political aspects of LM governance, considering whose interests have been served in the current institutional framework.

Finally, it considers how the current apparatus might require critical reflection in the wider contexts of governance of global migration.

What is lifestyle migration?

The term 'lifestyle migration' is applied to a growing number of migrations that are largely undertaken for lifestyle reasons and which do not fit into traditional, existing policy categories of migration. LM is a migration form which is difficult to conceptualize and measure as it blurs with many other mobilities and migration categories. For these reasons, some commentators may consider it debatable whether it is even an adequate or necessary categorization at all. While this section does not minimize the difficulty in defining LM, it argues nevertheless that this is a wholly necessary process to engage with, precisely because the abstract features and specific characteristics of LM explain to a degree the current limited system of governance. First, I outline the phenomenon and give examples of LM and its scope, before considering the unique features of LM.

There is growing evidence of migration processes undertaken for lifestyle reasons across the globe. Although insignificant when considered in relation to labour migration or migration on humanitarian grounds, LM is nevertheless emerging as an important mobility form. Using Britain as a case study, a report by the Institute of Public Policy Research (Sriskandarajah and Drew 2006) shows that at least 5.5 million British people—almost one in ten British citizens—live abroad, while half a million live abroad for part of the year. The Office for National Statistics (2007) also estimates that 400,000 people, of which half were British citizens, left Britain in 2006 to destinations including Australia, New Zealand, France, Spain, or the United States. The British casestudy exemplifies a wider trend of movement abroad in search of a certain lifestyle that as Benson and O'Reilly (2009) argue, has hitherto been overlooked in migration studies. Migrations undertaken under a lifestyle rubric have been explored via other lenses, including the studies of tourism, counter-urbanization and international retirement migration (IRM). Yet, they argue, none of these categories are fully inclusive or unite the various trends found in LM, a phenomenon which for Benson and O'Reilly should be more broadly defined as movement to places which (for those migrants) signify a better way of life (Ibid.).

Related to its nascency, LM has only recently gained academic attention. One sub-theme attracting attention has been retirement migration, a growing phenomenon arising from the global ageing population. For example, Longino observes that between 1995 and 2000, an estimated 2 million people in the United States aged 60 or over had moved across state lines (Longino 2006, cited in Sunil et al. 2007).

Studies also document the experiences of Northern Europeans retiring to the Mediterranean (King et al. 2000; Gustafson 2001; Helset et al. 2004; Oliver 2007 among others). Recently, attention has been paid to other streams of retirement migration, such as from the United States to Panama, Mexico, and Costa Rica (Truly 2002; MPI 2006) as well as the emergence of IRM markets in countries in Southeast Asia, such as Thailand (Koch-Schulte 2008).

There are however many other variants of LM which are also, to some degree, motivated primarily in terms of lifestyle. Alternative cases of retirement migration are found, for example, in the return movement to their home country of older Jamaicans from the United Kingdom (Horst forthcoming 2011) or in the multi-local residential strategies exhibited by Moroccans in pendulum migration between European states and Morocco (de Haas 2006). Some attention has also been paid to counter-urbanization and rural relocations within countries, a phenomenon which has also taken on an international dimension (Benson and O'Reilly 2009). Thus, other scholars have focused on British lifestyle migrants on the Costa del Sol (O'Reilly 2000), Mallorca (Waldren 1996), and France (Benson 2007; Geoffroy 2007). Yet there is also interest in many other diverse forms of LM including expatriates in Florence (Trundle 2009) and bohemian 'extended tourists' in Vara-nasi, India (Korpela 2009 and see Benson and O'Reilly 2009 for more examples).

Despite the apparent growth of the phenomenon, LM involves fluid populations which are difficult to pin down and count with accuracy. Often few data exist on absolute numbers of LM (as the Migration Policy Institute(MPI) observes in relation to Panama and Mexico, for instance). Drake and Collard refer also to the 'notoriously hard-to-quantify' but 'numerous and stealthy' numbers of Britons emigrating to France (Drake and Collard 2008: 216). There are many reasons for this deficiency. In large part, it is related to the way migrancy patterns in LM often extend from pre-existing tourist circuits (see King et al. 2000; O'Reilly 2000). Gustafson thus summarizes in the case of retirement migration in Spain that migrant behaviours exhibit a 'continuum of mobility' (Gustafson 2008: 453) ranging from a short period of transient sojourning to permanent to long-term or permanent residency abroad (O'Reilly 2000). In these circumstances, many lifestyle migrants fail to register as residents (see examples in Spain in King et al. 2000; O'Reilly 2000 and India in Korpela 2009).

Furthermore, immigration authorities' estimates and data do not capture the many lifestyle migrants who come to their destinations on tourist visas, a common practice noted, for example, among lifestyle migrants in India (Korpela 2009) and Mexico (MPI 2006). As such, statistics pertaining to LM are often weak and vastly underestimate its scope, a situation with potentially immense impacts, as discussed later in the chapter.[1] There is however evidence of LM as a growing trend, although the degree varies according to source. For example, using the example of the Central American states, the MPI reports that in Panama, the number of visas issued for US citizens in the visa categories used by retirees tripled between 2003 and 2005 (MPI 2006: 43) with Panamanian officials reporting a surge of migration since 2003. In Mexico, Truly (2002) reports that government officials quoted 5,000–6,000 full-time residents, but that in winter, locals' estimates range between 12,000 and 40,000.

In understanding LM, however, there are two clear factors which set LM apart from other migration forms: first, the motivations for LM, and second, the particular characteristics of those engaging in the process. The key analytical difference between the movements loosely defined as LM and other types of migration is that LM relates to *consumption* rather than *production*. While it is recognized that all migrations are driven by mixed motivations and that life-style benefits are likely to be an important factor in many other forms of migration, in LM, the aspiration for a desirable lifestyle is the primary motivator (Oliver 2007). Thus, lifestyle migrants move to the destination directly in order to consume tangible goods, including lower priced property, land, or hospitality, although other inalienable resources such as climate, environment, a less-demanding lifestyle, nostalgia, love, and social and educational capital may be equally persuasive in their motivations. To this end, LM must be understood more fundamentally as a cultural phenomenon (Oliver 2007) related to wider structural, economic, political, and social changes in 'Western' states in the twentieth century (Giddens 1991; Beck and Beck-Gernsheim 2002). This has seen individuals become directed more towards their own self-projects, as 'individual fulfilment is the guiding rationale—or vocabulary of motive—for choice and decision making' (Hockey and James 2003: 107). Travelling abroad to experience a more desirable lifestyle is a process of non-essential consumption viewed as aiding individuals' reflexive search for self (Oliver 2007).

Of course, this definition is open to contestation. It is clear that, for example, consumption is not the only goal of lifestyle migrants and there may be other value-added benefits of moving. Lifestyle migrants may seek economically favourable circumstances to maximize pensions or tax advantages, as discussed in the following section. Likewise, some migrants may subsequently work, often developing their own businesses as self-employed entrepreneurs (see Stone and Stubbs 2007 and Drake and Collard 2008 on LM in France). Yet even in such cases, any economic advantage or employment advancement is typically not the central reason for their movement. It is rather the opposite in many experiences of LM where migrants seek degrading employment, as is evident in the trend towards 'downsizing' and shown in migrants' rhetoric of escaping the rat-race which is common in many examples of LM (Benson and O'Reilly 2009; Oliver and O'Reilly 2010). Yet, consideration of these mixed motivations demonstrates the potential for blurred boundaries with other sorts of migration, particularly labour migrations.[2] However, in the LM cases, it is that *consumption* is the primary motivator over any of the other reasons.

The second feature defining LM is related to the particular characteristics of those migrating. Lifestyle migrants tend to be individuals or families from Northern countries, who move to other Northern states or sometimes to other Southern states. For instance, an examination of one facet of LM, IRM, shows its development as a form of intra-regional migration from Northern European to Southern European countries or from North America to Panama and Mexico. Now it is expanding rapidly, with new lifestyle possibilities for wealthy retirees increasingly marketed in Southern destinations including Egypt, the Gambia, Thailand, Malaysia, Indonesia, and the Philippines. In this sense, patterns of LM are vastly different from the majority of international migration which exemplifies reverse patterns of movement from South to North or South–South.

In terms of characteristics, LM can also be understood as often a form of life stage migration, with consequent impacts on the patterns of mobility lifestyle migrants' exhibit. Thus, as I have mentioned, a large constituent trend of LM is retirement migration, as retirees seek a better climate and fulfilling social environment in which to spend their retirement years. Yet at the other end of the life course spectrum, international student mobility, which has received 'virtually no attention' in standard academic literature on migration, may also be arguably considered another category of LM (King and Ruiz Gelices 2003: 230). The fact that they are driven by investment in their personal capital rather than consumption precludes their inclusion for further discussion in this chapter, although compellingly, there is a growing body of research suggesting international student mobility is motivated by experiential and lifestyle goals rather than strictly economic ones,[3] in which transnational experience gained by studying abroad counts as a form of 'mobility capital' (Findlay et al. 2006: 293; Amit 2008).

Drawing attention to definitional difficulties is not only interesting for its own sake, but of fundamental importance for understanding the limited degrees of governance in this arena. LM—as a consumption driven, North–North movement—reverses the normative assumptions of global migration inherent in much global policy discourse. It is not conceived of as a separate policy category, as in other cases, because it is not perceived to bring the same sorts of problems as other migration forms, especially in terms of migrants' recourse to public funds. Correspondingly, institutional arrangements are framed in a way to enable—rather than restrict—certain people to engage in this apparently unproblematic form of migration. Yet as I shall go on to explain, these governance arrangements expose lifestyle migrants as, in Bauman's useful distinction (1998), exemplars of 'tourists' rather than 'vagabonds', with institutional frameworks adapted to facilitate their mobility. I outline these existing systems of governance in the following section.

Institutions governing LM

This section describes the framework that regulates institutional responses to LM, considering formal and informal structures that contribute to multilateral, regional, interregional, and bilateral regulation.

As referred to previously, LM is largely overlooked in international fora on international migration, provoking at best little more than brief mention as an 'exception' to the other more important dimensions of international migration. Global frameworks for cooperation and coordination on international migration issues have recently been developed in relation to general migration, for example, through the lens of international collaboration or for economic purposes, but they do not consider LM an issue in its own right. For example, the recently published research compendium of the International Organization for Migration (2007) makes only one indirect reference to leisure, tourism, lifestyle, and retirement. The same is true for the report of the Global Commission on International Migration (2005), an agenda for the future on international migration, where there is no meaningful consideration of LM at all.

One reason for its neglect in international fora is that LM is considered adequately governed already through existing regulation of international travel, including consular arrangements and the international visa regime (for a detailed explanation, see Koslowski, this volume). In particular, governance of LM falls under the Vienna Convention on Consular Relations (1963). This long-standing normative framework codified the many bilateral treaties aimed at allowing consulates, by mutual consent, to intervene on behalf of its own nationals in foreign territory. Consulates provide a variety of legal services that may be of relevance to lifestyle migrants. For instance, they may assist with the estate of a citizen who dies abroad or investigate the safety of any citizen. Under this framework, Article 36 requires that any nation which arrests or detains a foreign national allows them to access his or her consulate, who may then work to ensure judicious treatment as well as communicate with family members.

Visas also frame and set down important conditions for migrants to be able to move freely to individual countries, with great variation in the conditions required. Visas are established at a national level—although with some regional agreements as discussed below—and are inclined to the state's national economic interests. For this reason, lifestyle migrants tend to be favoured, because they hold much consumer power. To give an example, in the United States, a country famed for its restrictive immigration policies, there is currently ongoing debate among trade groups about a 'Silver Card' being introduced to ensure more favourable access for lifestyle migrants. The card creates a visa category for foreign citizens who own US property, do not work, and have enough documented income to retire in North American destinations such as California or Florida. The rationale for the card is essentially because these migrants represent potentially millions of dollars of investment income (Moscoso 2008). Such agreements already exist elsewhere at a bilateral or regional level, for example, between Central America and the United States, New Zealand and Australia. In particular, the North American Free Trade Agreement (NAFTA) has led to greater access of US products and services and removed barriers to migration (Truly

2002). Thus, in Panama, the government has created two visas to specifically target US retirees, the *Turista Pensionado* and the *Rentista Retirado*, the first offering indefinite right to remain, and the other which requires five-year visa renewals and the depositing of large amounts of money (around US$225,000) in the National Bank of Panama, which must yield at least US$750 a month in interest (MPI 2006). There are also regional avenues for retirement migration through NAFTA in suggestions for expedited entries of 'trusted travellers' raised by Hufbauer and Vega-Cánovas (2003). This would include a NAFTA retirement visa, allowing retirement in any of the three NAFTA countries.

These governance systems have obvious consequences in terms of equity when viewed in a comparative sense, as they effectively ensure freedom of movement for certain desirable migrants (Bauman's 'tourists'), while keeping out less desirables who cannot meet visa requirements predicated on income (the 'vagabonds'). This is also underlined by the limited degree of enforcement of registration requirements for lifestyle migrants who may aim to be misleading about their residency (Schriewer and Berg 2008). It also comes down to the generous flexibility often given in visas defined as 'tourist visas' (whereby 'tourists' can stay for most of a year or for extended periods) but which in practice, more adequately represent LM. For example, Mari Korpela (2009) discusses the exploitation of exceptionally long 'tourist' visas among bohemian lifestyle migrants in Varanasi, India. Depending on nationality, lifestyle migrants can live under the guise of a tourist visa for up to ten years. Although officially one is expected to reside as a tourist (in hotels, for example) in practice, locals rent rooms to foreigners to gain income, while visa renewals are subject to corruption. Rules for visa renewal, such as having to leave the country every six months, are also loosely interpreted, as Westerners simply pay a visit to the border of Nepal for a few hours and return immediately.

Such examples reveal the ways that the regulation of LM reflects a Northern prejudice. This concurs with Gamlen's observation (this volume) of how bilateral agreements are almost exclusively developed by Northern countries. As he argues, they are often related to unconnected diplomatic rather than domestic agendas and as such are staggeringly ad hoc, with often unjust consequences. A clear example of this, as Gamlen points out, is in relation to the payment of UK pensions to British citizens outside the European Union (EU). Unless the country of residence has reciprocal links with the United Kingdom, state pensions are not index-linked, but frozen at the rate at which the migrant left the United Kingdom or at the rate when they first received it (Age Concern 2007). Such bilateral governance is ad hoc, random, not transparent in motives, and amounts to something of a country-code lottery in migrants' access to services and provisions.

Beyond the visa regime, governance of LM has also been developing regionally, although again, not without certain implications. Perhaps the most obvious example is seen in the multilateral agreements for free travel between European Economic Area member states and the creation of 'the European citizen' via the Maastricht Treaty (1992). As a consequence, any intra-European migrant gains full access to the range of goods and services to which any citizen of the member state would be entitled. However, where regional governance exists, it is not directly addressed at LM governance, but an effect of the principle of freedom of movement (Treaty on European Union, article 39). To this end, governance of welfare, health, benefits, pensions, taxes, electoral rights, etc. is conducted via national legislations, in which lifestyle migrants experience less often the deliberate governance of migration but rather an array of more or less unintended 'side-effects' of national legislation.[4]

One arena where this is evident is in terms of health and social care, in which legislation fails to address the fluid mobility of LM. As Schriewer and Rodes García (2006) point out, legislations were designed for workers and tourists, of which lifestyle migrants (or in their discussion, retirees) fall into neither category. The European legislation on health and social care is also directed to the case of persons with one usual place of residence and excludes the possibility that people may have two or three. Furthermore, there is nothing to address the disadvantages a citizen might confront when confronting 'different worlds of welfare' and the more or less generous national provisions in different member states (Ackers and Dwyer 2002: 8).

In practice, the governance directed at lifestyle migrants is often poorly understood, exposing them to both exploitation or to situations whereby they unwittingly (or in some cases wittingly) contravene national laws. In consequence, there has been the development of an additional layer of ground roots provisions and commercial ventures aimed at smoothing the legal and economic transitions in moving and living abroad for lifestyle reasons. Networks of non-governmental organizations (NGOs) and local migrant welfare associations play important roles in filling in the knowledge gaps around entitlements and responsibilities. For instance, the NGO Age UK (formerly Age Concern) developed an 'easy, helpful, honest' outline (2007) to aid those moving abroad in retirement. And within my own ethnographic research on retirement migration in Southern Spain, foreign branches of national institutions and charities were keen lobbyists in local and regional campaigning. One of the local branches of the British Legion on the Costa del Sol campaigned to national headquarters in the United Kingdom, for example, to improve rights of repatriation for infirm and economically struggling retirees, after a number of cases of their members struggling with the limited care services common in mother–daughter welfare systems of Southern Europe (Oliver 2007). The need for such provisions speaks to the many gaps exposed as a result of reciprocal national provisions for health and social care.

This case explains also the growing number of private sector agencies who are emerging as strong actors in LM provisions, especially in IRM with regard to health care for older retirees. For instance, in the case of intra-European LM, despite the provisions of reciprocal arrangements, retired EU migrants regularly meet their needs via a mixture of public and private provision. As Dwyer (2000) points out, they also do so by weighing up the disparities in standards of public health care on offer in different EU countries. As he also argues, many Northern European retirees living abroad, 'continued to make use of and were keen to retain any rights to public health care in the nations they had left behind' (Dwyer 2000: 366) either by returning permanently or retaining domicile while abroad (see also Gustafson 2001). His work with Ackers (2004) demonstrates the considerable skill used by individuals in negotiating access to resources. Yet Helset et al. also refer to the evolving 'transnational elderly care' (Helset et al. 2004: 93) developing for Norwegian retirees in Spain, including a municipality which provides trainee posts for Norwegian students in social and care work and private home-help services for Norwegian retirees funded by Norwegian authorities or private insurance (cited in Gustafson 2008).

The fact that freedom of movement—which developed on the back of freedom of trade—underlines regional governance of LM demonstrates that little thought has been given to the social and economic consequences in terms of claims placed on systems (Schriewer and Rodes García 2006). In Europe, it is often overlooked, for example, how lifestyle migrants have (in common with other categories of migrants) the right to vote in local and EU elections following the Maastricht Treaty on the European Union (1992, Article 8). Until recently, the fearful anticipation by host countries with sizeable expatriate communities of the election of foreign councillors to represent migrant interests has largely seemed unwarranted. Drake and Collard reveal that British migrants in France showed, 'relatively poor knowledge and understanding' (Drake and Collard 2008: 227) when questioned on the French political system, a situation echoed among lifestyle migrants in Spain (Rodríguez et al. 1998). However, other evidence emerging from Spain points to the 'mushrooming of expat-dominated political parties' (Wood 2007). These have been particularly established in response to perceived poor national regulation of planning laws which have allowed corrupt municipalities to sell land, a process directly impacting lifestyle migrants. Similarly, the clout of expatriate parties is documented by the rapid *volte face* of the French government in 2008 when it retracted its decision to suddenly withdraw access to health care for early retired LM after pressure from expatriate lobby groups and British officials (Samuel 2008).

In summary to this consideration of institutional provisions for LM, it is evident that while there are some indications of emerging forms of regional and even global polycentric governance of aspects of LM, the main regulation for LM is through visas and bilateral agreements. There are few fora or institutions strategically engaging with people migrating for lifestyle reasons. Multilateral governance beyond visa controls is rather embedded in policy focused on other concerns including health/social care and trade. In this sense, governance of LM emerges as a side effect, rather than a deliberate governance strategy. Any future international dialogue for governance would furthermore have to engage with the polycentric nature of LM governance, especially given the emergence of other stakeholders, such as NGOs or, more particularly, private sector actors.

What drives the politics of LM governance?

The final aspect to consider in this debate is why such limited and haphazard regulation of LM has emerged. Essentially, I suggest that the marginalization of LM in the debate about migration in the international community is reflective of the way that LM has developed as a North–North migration, only recently expanding into a West–East and North–South migration. If as Betts argues (this volume), states' interests in international politics are self-oriented and predicated on maximizing their economic and security interests, this direction of movement is neglected because it is normatively viewed as non-problematic or even favourable for all states concerned. The question is, how has the situation arisen that LM is seen as unproblematic? What drives this interpretation? Is the 'benign' interpretation of the phenomenon enough of a plausible justification for the current LM governance arrangements?

First, LM is seen as unproblematic by sending countries. There are no norms of controlling exit by the sending country, and the Northern states so often affected by this phenomenon do not object to the outmigration of their citizens. They may be marginally concerned with the loss of tax income and may wish to stem the resources leaving the country, but it is also the case that lifestyle migrants are often marginal populations. Particularly in the case of retirees, lifestyle migrants are often in- or under-active economically. As such, states may even perceive a benefit to the associated reduced welfare demands levied through outmigration. Their indifference to LM, especially by older migrants may even reflect a general ageist bias of policy-makers who view the ageing society as problematic, with older people constructed as dependent and a burden on states (Phillipson 1982).

Second, LM is considered unproblematic by receiving countries. As amenity-seeking migrants, lifestyle migrants present little in the way of a security threat, particularly in the EU in an era of European integration, when migrants hail from other Northern countries. Yet more important is the fact that lifestyle migrants fall into a category of desirable migrants due to their spending power and as such, receiving countries and their businesses have a strong incentive to encourage LM as part of their export markets. LM can be viewed as a particular form of trade: the consumption of a country's immaterial goods—of climate, environment, educational services, and lifestyle in exchange for investment in property, goods, and services. As a result, the limited regulation around LM has developed very much in response to the demands of private sector actors, especially in real estate, health care, and financial services, who almost dogmatically profess concern for freedom over regulation. The role of real estate corporations is particularly influential, as they target specific LM groups as niche markets and exert pressure on governments for looser restriction and press for states to actively encourage LM through attractive immigration policies. This is evident, for example, in the vocal lobbying by estate agents for the 'Silver Card' visa that would allow foreign citizens to retire in the United States (Moscoso 2008).

The importance of LM for receiving countries' export markets therefore is marked by a proliferation of open-door policies to lure affluent migrants, particularly in developing nations, through the promise of 'lifestyle' and inexpensive domestic labour. To this end, there is emerging evidence of policy initiatives from the developing South to capture this niche market of desirable migrants. For example, Malaysia operates a government-endorsed long-term stay visa programme, the 'My Second Home' Program (MM2H) to overseas retirees. Certain 'desirable migrants'—often early retired and/or economically inactive—can stay in Malaysia on a (renewable) social visit pass with a multiple entry visa, while still retaining their citizenship. For the price of opening a fixed deposit account or show of monthly pension income, they can also benefit from other incentives including tax concessions and the possibility to invest and own businesses in the country. The official sponsor for the programme, Comfort Life Corporation, appointed by the Immigration Department of Malaysia, intones prospective new migrants to 'Retire Early, Retire Rich' (www/12retireinmalaysia.com/index.htm). Similar incentives exist in Panama and Mexico for US retirees and Canadian snowbirds. In Panama, a package of beneficial tax and property ownership policies are offered to those entering the country on pensioner visas, including, for example, the ability to bring household goods and vehicles into the country without paying import taxes. Another example is of retired Canadians in Mexico, who are subject to the Canadian/ Mexico Tax Treaty, which sees those living out of Canada for at least 183 days a year able to reduce their taxes on pensions and investment income by 15 per cent and all future capital gains tax to 0% (www.retiretoajijic.com/Articles. htm).

Such examples demonstrate the way LM is perceived as a lucrative market, in which limited regulation aids a country's economic development. However, the neglect of this apparently non-problematic form of migration is not as benign as first appears. An alternative reading sees LM as the triumph of brute capitalism or 'a new and more efficient form of colonialism' (Chesterman 2008: 39). This is because when Southern states are receiving states, there is little or no scope for them to demand strict conditions for entry, as they are effectively in competition with other developing or developed nations to attract financially secure migrants. This is confirmed by the MPI (2006) study of IRM to the Central American states, where migrants were observed to be cognizant of the variety of options open to them and variations between countries' immigration policies.

Attention can also be drawn to the ways that private interests define the structures of global migration governance in this domain. The private sector plays an important role in lobbying for the existence and further creation of new visa categories to attract 'desirable' and resource-rich migrants to fuel economic development. Some may argue that this freedom of movement is perfectly logical, on both receiving and sending countries' part. But aside from the unforeseen social and environmental consequences of LM, it is clear that this logic does not extend to comparative cases of migration undertaken in a reverse direction, whereby the configuration of interests in the receiving states is markedly different. There, it has rather been the case of strengthening immigration controls against undesirable 'vagabonds' (Bauman 1998). With this comparative perspective in mind, it is necessary to consider finally whether there may be reasonable grounds for global governance of LM.

A normative case for global governance of LM?

The final question the chapter engages with is whether a normative case can or should be made for more international dialogue and governance in relation to LM. Global governance refers to the participation of multiple interest groups in the management of common affairs, to both engage with diverse interests while achieving cooperative action. It relates to shifting the level of human cooperation to the global rather than national level. As I have argued, in the case of LM, there are limited existing institutional structures for governance and this status quo does not seem to be generally regarded as problematic by the states concerned. As conditions prevail, there seems to be little grounds for arguing for more global governance, apart from perhaps, an efficiency case for market regulation. And with surely more pressing issues for global governance currently provoking attention, including human rights, economic development, security, the control and treatment of infectious diseases, and international trade in other fields of migration (where forced, irregular, or exploitative), there may be significant grounds to agree. However, as the chapter has shown throughout, it may be pernicious to acquiesce to this 'logical' conclusion, particularly as it overlooks the equity implications of existing arrangements. In this section, the chapter concludes with a consideration of the basis on which a normative case for global governance of LM can be made.

One obvious argument in support of stronger regulation is that purely the increase and ever-expanding horizons of this form of migration exerts some form of pressure for research and governance. Quite simply, not enough is known about the effects of this emerging migration form. The neglect of LM is particularly puzzling when considering the way that other areas of global governance of international migration, such as the issue-area 'migration and development' is discussed. Here, links of migration and development are interpreted as the beneficial reception of economically active migrants and the knock-on effects of migrants as agents for development in sending states. Interpreting migration and development from an LM perspective posits a very different understanding of these links, as [non-return] migration *to* (rather than from) Southern states can equally be interpreted as an engine for development. Yet this presumption of LM is questionable; it is well documented that the presence of LM often precedes the development of ethnic—not solely native—entrepreneurship in the destination societies as services are developed in response to the needs of the expatriate society (Gustafson 2008). Certainly, more research is required.

However, even if receiving states continue to see LM as an important part of their export market, often less anticipated are the longer term implications related to these poorly registered populations, both in terms of environmental impacts, social integration, and fiscal challenges to the host state (King et al. 1998). While LM—like tourism—is largely welcomed by host communities as a source of economic development, there is (often post-hoc) realization that its economic advantages are accompanied, if unchecked, by irreversible environmental damage, cultural alienation, and economic dependence. This is particularly evident in the Costa del Sol, one of the earliest sites for LM in Europe, where the sprawling developments have led to an increased water runoff and wider impacts in terms of erosion and desertification (Aledo and Mazón 2004). Other effects include the reduction of local biodiversity, deforestation, forest fires, and water pollution. Truly (2002) also documents the environmental impact created in part by the grand homes, swimming pools, and gardens of US lifestyle migrants in the Lake Chapala district of Mexico. As such, many of the concerns of the heritage sector, ministries of culture, and municipal councils around tourist development are relevant to the related issue of LM. Yet, these consequences continue to be subjugated to the positive effects of development, as evident in the fact that Spain—despite the negative impacts witnessed as a result of unchecked development—is still considered uncritically a paradigm case that provides a positive example for imitation elsewhere (Mantecón 2008).

In terms of social effects, some research demonstrates already the limited integration possible in cases of LM, much of which relates to the characteristics of migrants. The migrants have limited integration channels available in other forms of migration, such as through work or schooling (King et al. 2000) and as such, tend to form their own inward-looking communities (O'Reilly 2000; Oliver 2007). In some destinations, there are specific problems related to the migrant populations involved. For example, Koch-Schulte observes how planning in Udon Thani, Thailand, is unique, 'due to the homogeneous make-up of male retirees who bring with them a host of Western cultural values and problems related to bars and sex tourism' (Koch-Shulte 2008: 3). And certainly the combined effects of limited statistics and conflation of lifestyle migrants with tourists has the potential to place unprecedented strain on the welfare resources of receiving countries, particularly when funding allocations for health care are made using a capitation formula (Helset et al. 2004; Schriewer and Rodes García 2006). From this point of view, a laissez-faire approach to the issue radiates a less innocuous hue than first appears. In relation to retirement migration, it could even be considered as the shifting of increasing responsibilities and costs of social and medical care for an ageing population elsewhere.

The effects of limited governance of LM are also often felt at an individual level, providing compelling moral reasons for further attention to governance in this arena. There are numerous sensationalist accounts in the media of 'the dream' turning into a 'nightmare', but stereotypes of lifestyle migrants as wealthy and self-sufficient belie the reality that LMs represent an economically diverse range of individuals, some of whom are not affluent and find themselves subject to foreign legal systems with little social or economic capital with which to negotiate them. O'Reilly draws attention to Northern European lifestyle migrants in Spain who—in contrast to the strata of flexibly working transnational elite—had 'little to lose' (O'Reilly 2007: 282), being unemployed, redundant, or struggling economically. Their move to Spain to 'escape' the United Kingdom was experienced anxiously, as she comments:

> This research revealed extensive evidence of British migrants working in the informal economy, paying no income tax or national insurance contributions, relying on emergency state health provision or inadequate private health insurance, who are confused about what they are supposed to do to be legal residents, who are neither registered with their town hall nor have residence permits, who do not know who to turn to in times of difficulty, who cannot speak the language adequately and come unstuck when they need to call the police or an ambulance.

She documents that in addition to no longer having entitlements, or paying contributions to British social security systems, others find themselves on uncertain legal grounds regarding property and land ownership.

Similarly, in the case of IRM, while Ackers and Dwyer (2002) document the skill of many older retirees in negotiating one or more welfare systems in Europe, there are equally other compelling and less-well-known stories of those who fall between the gaps raised in transnational migration between two or more states. There are a minority of cases in which people find themselves destitute and unable to fund the social and medical care they need (Hardill et al. 2005; Oliver 2007). In my own research, I witnessed a case of a woman of limited financial resources suffering from increasing dementia, with her friends unable to provide the round-the-clock care she needed. They had been discussing how to physically get her on a flight to the United Kingdom, so that she would be cared for by local social services at the British airport. Helset et al. (2004) also point out in relation to Spain, that although immigrants may put pressure on receiving countries' resources, there is equally uncertainty for municipalities in the sending countries as to whether or not large numbers of retirees will return 'home' and unexpectedly demand costly health and social care upon their return. This is particularly borne out by observations that although LM is often planned as a long-term and permanent endeavour, many people return to their home countries as a result of unforeseen circumstances, such as the death of a partner or deterioration in well-being (see Oliver 2007).

The above argument relates to a further rationale for governance, simply that at present, the debate on governance of migration seems to be captured in discourses of political internationalist ideas, functionalist economic rationales, or strategizing between states, rather than being needs based. Moral imperatives direct those interested in global governance to engage with a more grounded understanding of people migrating and receiving, their needs and how they are met. Moreover, following the cultural trend of individualization and competition (Beck and Beck-Gernsheim 2002), public services are increasingly under scrutiny and even diplomatic services will have to take into account the drive towards personalized services. As I pointed out, even within the relatively straightforward case of the EU, states could do much more in terms of information provision about basics, such as repatriation in cases of illness or death. Migrants are often left to the mercies of private health insurance agencies, which have no overriding interests to account for their actions. More clarity in the development of international administrative law would ameliorate the consequences of negotiating complex and specific legal systems, particularly at times of great distress, illness, or death (Oliver 2004).

The examples given here suggest a lack of clarity in legal and administrative systems. But perhaps more strongly they speak of an inability of existing state and welfare systems to adequately respond to the reality of fluid mobility, as exhibited in LM. With increased mobility, the visa regime also encounters new challenges which cannot be answered under existing frameworks. For example, if a dual national lifestyle migrant resides as a lifestyle migrant in a third country, such as Malaysia, when they require care, which state has responsibility for its national? The limited awareness of such issues reflects the absence of a clear picture on LM as a burgeoning yet little-explored phenomenon. Certainly, this justifies at the very least further monitoring in both scope and effects of LM.

This brings me to the final, but perhaps most convincing argument for governance: on ethical grounds. LM shares many characteristics with other types of migrations, but it is clear that lifestyle migrants enjoy freedom of movement through favourable visa regimes. Thus, some of the rarely discussed consequences of LM raised from empirical observation in this section have resonance with the experiences of irregular migrants. Yet it is important to stress that under existing arrangements, because of the origin of the people involved in LM, they are unlikely to be conceived as undocumented migrants, nor treated as such in enforcement. Indeed, there are clear equity implications when considering LM in a comparative sense, particularly when arguments about access to welfare and public funds for other types of migrants are used to justify strict immigration controls. Lifestyle migrants are subject to preferential treatment in visa conditions because they are perceived as a category of 'desirable migrants' who bring significant economic and cultural capital to the receiving state. Their presence is viewed often by host countries in a similar vein as tourism, as a desirable form of economic development. Yet these assumptions frame certain arrangements which discriminate unfairly and on the grounds of wealth alone between the desirable 'tourist' or lifestyle migrant who has enough consumer power to be of interest to the receiving state's export industry and the 'vagabond', who does not.

Conclusion

The chapter draws attention to the emerging and growing phenomenon of LM. The unique characteristics of this migration form as a North–North or North–South movement has meant its marginalization as a legitimate subject in the emerging global fora on migration. At a global level, regulation of LM is through visa regimes, with degrees of mobility dependent on capital. Other regulation at the regional level is often of a very fragmented and embedded nature, with lifestyle migrants subject to ad hoc national legislations on issues including health and social care, pensions, tax, and property ownership. Yet as the chapter has shown, the assumption that there is no need for governance ultimately reflects the unchallenged dominant interests of Northern states in debates on international migration.

In considering the case as to why there would be any benefits gained through developing more global governance in this migration form, beyond efficiency grounds for market regulation, the discussion highlights that there are also moral imperatives that support a normative case for global governance. Ultimately, in terms of interrogating the causes of LM, especially as it expands beyond the confines of North–North migration, questions need to be raised as to the status and consequences of LM. Existing governance responds to an interpretation of the phenomenon as of benign influence, a win-win phenomenon to be encouraged by both sending and receiving countries. Another governance may yet respond to the inequity raised by existing frameworks which privilege only those who have the financial means to choose where to migrate. Or, as Bauman (1998: 86) summarizes most succinctly:

> The dimensions along which those 'high up' and 'down' are plotted in a society of consumers, is their *degree of mobility*—their freedom to choose

where to be. Those 'high up' travel through life to their heart's desire and pick and choose their destinations by the joys they offer. Those 'low down' are thrown out from the site they would rather stay in, and if they do not move, it is the site that is pulled from under their feet.

Notes

* The author would like to thank Alex Betts, Marc Verlot, Karen O'Reilly, Per Gustafson, Michaela Benson, Klaus Schriewer, Joaquin Rodes, and Mari Korpela for their advice on earlier versions of the chapter.
1. As King et al. (1998: 108) argue with regard to international retirement migration in Spain, 'Given that officially registered foreign populations account for more than half the total populations of at least two municipalities in Spain . . . the impact of under-registration in these areas especially, but more generally throughout Mediterranean Spain is potentially immense.'
2. This blurring is evident in labour migration, where lifestyle considerations influence the choice among a number of possible receiving countries. Yet, among lifestyle migrants who subsequently work, the aspirational dimension is the primary driver rather than purely economic considerations.
3. Amit's research (2008) exposes the difference in official and students' interpretations of the benefits of international student travel. Where institutions envisage the process as training or creating, 'a new kind of contemporary citizen', students hold rather more profane visions of the process as 'just . . . something to do', or 'time out' in which they gravitate towards others in the same situation.
4. Thanks to Per Gustafson for this observation.

References

Ackers, L. and Dwyer, P. (2002) *Senior Citizenship. Retirement, Migration and Welfare in the European Union*, Bristol: Policy Press.

Age Concern England (2007) *Planning to Live Abroad*, London: Age Concern.

Aledo, A. and Mazón, T. (2004) Impact of Residential Tourism and the Destination Life Cycle Theory, in F. Pineda and C.A. Brebbia (eds), *Sustainable Tourism*, Southampton: WIT Press.

Amit, V. (2008) The Limits of Liminality: Capacities for Change and Transition among Student Travelers, in N. Rapport (ed.), *Human Nature as Capacity: An Ethnographic Approach*, London and New York: Berghahn Books.

Bauman, Z. (1998) *Globalization: Its Human Consequences*, New York: Columbia University Press.

Beck, U. and Beck-Gernsheim, E. (2002) *Individualization: Institutionalized Individualism and its Social and Political Consequences*, London: Sage.

Benson, M. (2007) There's More to Life: British Lifestyle Migration to Rural France, Unpublished PhD thesis, University of Hull.

——and O'Reilly, K. (2009) Migration and the Search for a Better Way of Life: A Critical Exploration of Lifestyle Migration, *The Sociological Review*, 57(4), 608–25.

Chesterman, S. (2008) Globalization Rules: Accountability, Power and the Prospects for Global Administrative Law, *Global Governance. A Review of Multilateralism and International Organizations*, 14, 39–52.

Drake, H. and Collard, S. (2008) A Case Study of Intra-EU Migration: 20 years of 'Brits' in the Pays d'Auge, Normandy, France, *French Politics*, 6, 214–33.

Dwyer, P. (2000) Movements to Some Purpose? An Exploration of International Retirement Migration in the European Union, *Education and Ageing*, 15(3), 352–77.

Findlay, A., King, R., Stam, A., and Ruiz-Gelices, E. (2006) Ever Reluctant Europeans. The Changing Geographies of UK Students Studying and Working Abroad, *European Urban and Regional Studies*, 13(4), 291–318.

Geoffroy, C. (2007) From 'Chamouni' to Chamonix: The British in the Alps, in C. Geoffroy and R. Sibley (eds), *Going Abroad: Travel, Tourism and Migration. Cross-Cultural Perspectives on Mobility*, Newcastle: Cambridge Scholars Publishing.

Giddens, A. (1991) *Modernity and Self-Identity: Self and Society in the Late Modern Age.* Cambridge: Polity.

Global Commission on International Migration (2005) *Migration in an Interconnected World: New Directions for Action*, Geneva: GCIM.

Gustafson, P. (2001) Retirement Migration and Transnational Lifestyles, *Ageing and Society*, 21(4), 371–94.

——(2008) Transnationalism in Retirement Migration: The case of North European Retirees in Spain, *Ethnic and Racial Studies*, 28(4), 451–75.

de Haas, H. (2006) International Pendulum Migration to Morocco: Multi-Local Residential Strategies of Ageing Migrants in the Todra Valley, Paper presented to the ASEF Workshop 'Pensioners on the Move': Social Security and Trans-Border Retirement Migration in Asia and Europe, 5–7 January 2006, Singapore.

Hardill, I., Spradbery, J., Arnold-Boakes, J., and Marrugat, M.L. (2005) Severe Health and Social Care Issues Among British Migrants who Retire to Spain, *Ageing and Society*, 25(5), 769–83.

Helset, A., Lauvli, M., and Sandlie, H.C. (2004) *Norske Oensjonister og Norske Kommuner i Spania*, Oslo: NOVA/Norwegian Social Research.

Hockey, J. and James, A. (2003) *Social Identities across the Life Course*, Hampshire: Palgrave Macmillan.

Horst, H. (2011, forthcoming) Reclaiming Place: The Architecture of Home, Family and Migration, Special Edition of *Anthropologica*, edited by K. Fog-Olwig and V. Amit, 53(1).

Hufbauer, G.C. and Vega-Cánovas, G. (2003) Whither NAFTA: A Common Frontier? in P. Andreas and T.J. Biersteker (eds), *The Rebordering of North America*, New York: Routledge.

International Labour Organisation, *International Labour Migration and Development: The ILO Perspective*, Geneva: ILO.

International Organization for Migration (2007) *Research Compendium 2005–2007*, Geneva: IOM.

King, R. and Ruiz-Gelices, E. (2003) International Student Migration and the European 'Year Abroad': Effects on European Identity and Subsequent Migration Behaviour, *International Journal of Population Geography*, 9, 229–52.

——Warnes, A.M., and Williams, A.M. (1998) International Retirement Migration in Europe. Editorial Introduction, *International Journal of Population Geography*, 4(2), 91–111.

————(2000) *Sunset Lives: British Retirement Migration to the Mediterranean*, Oxford: Berg.

Koch-Schulte, J.J. (2008) Planning for International Retirement Migration and Expats: A Case-Study of Udon Thani, Thailand, MA thesis, University of Manitoba.

Korpela, M. (2009) When a Trip to Adulthood Becomes a Lifestyle: The Community of Westerners in Varanasi, India, in M. Benson and K. O'Reilly (eds), *Lifestyle Migration. Expectations, Aspirations, and Experiences*, Aldershot: Ashgate.

Longino, C. (2006) *Retirement Migration in America* (2nd edn), Houston, TX: Vacation.

Mantecón, A. (2008) *La Experiencia del Turismo. Un Estudio Sociológico Sobre el Proceso Turístico-Residencial*, Barcelona: Icaria.

Migration Policy Institute (MPI) (2006) *America's Emigrants. US Retirement Migration to Mexico and Panama*, Washington, DC: MPI and New Global Initiatives.

Moscoso, E. (2008) Realtors Pushing 'Silver Card' Visa for Foreign Retirees, *Cox News Service* (17 July 2008), http://www.coxwashington.com/.

Office of National Statistics (2007) Emigration from UK Reaches 400,000 in 2006, News Release (15 November 2007), http://www.statistics.gov.uk.

Oliver, C. (2004) Cultural Influence in Migrants' Negotiation of Death: The Case of Retired Migrants in Spain, *Mortality*, 9(3), 235–54.

——(2007) *Retirement Migration. Paradoxes of Ageing*, New York: Routledge.

——and O'Reilly, K. (2010) A Bourdieusian Analysis of Class and Migration: Habitus and the Individualising Process, *Sociology*, 44(1), 49–66.

O'Reilly, K. (2000) *The British on the Costa del Sol, Transnational Identities and Local Communities*, London: Routledge.

——(2007) Intra-European Migration and the Mobility-Enclosure Dialectic, *Sociology*, 41(2), 277–93.

Phillipson, C. (1982) *Capitalism and the Construction of Old Age*, London and Basingstoke: Macmillan.

Rodríguez, V., Fernández-Mayoralas, G., and Rojo, F. (1998) European retirees on the Costa del Sol: A Cross-National Comparison, *International Journal of Population Geography*, 4(2), 183–200.

Samuel, H. (2008) British Expats Win French Healthcare Battle, *The Telegraph* (29 January 2008), http://www.Telegraph.co.uk/news/worldnews/europe (accessed 12 January 2009).

Schriewer, K. and Berg, I. (2008) Being Misleading About Where One Resides. European Affluence Mobility and Registration Patterns, *Ethnologia Europaea*, 37, 98–106.

——and Rodes García, J. (2006) Los Cuidados Médicos en un Contexto Transnacional. Jubilados Europeos en la Región de Murcia, Paper presented at conference on Migrations and Social Policies in Europe, Universidad Pública de Navarra, June 2006.

Sriskandarajah, D. and Drew, C. (2006) *Brits Abroad. Mapping the Scale and Nature of British Emigration*, London: Institute of Public Policy Research.

Stone, I. and Stubbs, C. (2007) Enterprising Expatriates: Lifestyle Migration and Entrepreneurship in Rural Southern Europe, *Entrepreneurship and Regional Development*, 19(5), 433–50.

Sunil, T.S., Rojas, V., and Bradley, D.E. (2007) 'United States' International Retirement Migration: The Reasons for Retiring to the Environs of Lake Chapala, Mexico, *Ageing and Society*, 27, 489–10.

Truly, D. (2002) International Retirement Migration and Tourism along the Lake Chapala Riviera: Developing a Matrix of Retirement Migration Behaviour, *Tourism Geographies*, 4(3), 261–81.

Trundle, C. (2009) Romance Tourists, Foreign Wives or Retirement Migrants? Cross-Cultural Marriage in Florence, Italy, in M. Benson and K. O'Reilly (eds), *Lifestyle Migration: Expectations, Aspirations and Experiences*, Aldershot: Ashgate.

Waldren, J. (1996) *Insiders and Outsiders: Paradise and Reality in Mallorca*, Oxford: Berghahn.

Wood, D. (2007) Expats a Political Force in Spain, BBC News Channel (12 May 2007), http://news.bbc.co.uk/1/hi/world/europe/6647443.stm.

6

Environmental Migration[*]

Jane McAdam

Introduction

Environmental migration governance, like global migration governance more broadly, suffers from significant fragmentation, both vertically—with actors at the international, regional, and local levels—and horizontally—with the phenomenon addressed in part or, more rarely, as a whole under the auspices of a range of other 'policy categories' and associated institutions. Interests in environmentally driven population movement can be identified across the fields of migration, environment, development, human rights, disaster management, and humanitarian relief. Yet despite (or because of) the plethora of existing as well as potential governance mechanisms, processes, and institutions, there is presently no coherent multilateral governance framework for environmental migration.

The fact that the same is true of global migration governance generally provides the context for the present chapter's examination of environmental migration. The particular features and challenges that it raises must ultimately inform the broader question of whether, and how, a unified global governance system for migration could and should be developed, and whether, and how, the regulation of environmental migration might fit into such a vision.

Environmental migration is not a new phenomenon. Natural and human-induced environmental disasters and slow-onset degradation have displaced people in the past and will continue to do so. Nevertheless, the environmental events and processes accompanying global climate change threaten to dramatically increase human movement both within states and across international borders. The Intergovernmental Panel on Climate Change (IPCC) has predicted an increased frequency and severity of climate events such as storms, cyclones, and hurricanes, as well as longer term sea-level rise and desertification, which will impact upon people's ability to subsist in certain parts of the world (Hegerl et al. 2007; IPCC 2007). Around a fifth of the world's population lives in coastal areas affected by rising seas and natural disasters (especially the Caribbean,

Central America, and eastern China and India) (Council of the European Union 2008: 3).

As far as actual numbers are concerned, there is no doubt that 'current predictions are fraught with numerous methodological problems and caveats' (Biermann and Boas 2007: 9). Norman Myers' suggestion that some 50–250 million people will be displaced by 2050 stems from a very rudimentary methodology (Kniveton 2008; Kniveton et al. 2008; Crisp 1999), yet in the absence of a more rigorous dataset it has become the yardstick adopted in much of the literature, often without question. Despite this, it is interesting to note that Sir Nicholas Stern, in his authoritative review of climate change in 2007, described Myers' estimates (1993: 52) of 200 million as 'conservative' (Stern 2007).[1] More recent empirical analysis suggests that most movement will occur within countries, rather than across international borders (Laczko and Aghazarm 2009), which raises further questions about what kinds of institutional and normative responses are most suitable. As the United Nations High Commissioner for Refugees (UNHCR) has noted, while climate change impacts are likely to drive an anticipated surge in human movement in the coming decades,[2] primary legal responsibility for ensuring people's rights will lie with the states concerned (Guterres 2009). Furthermore, debates about the way poverty, limited natural resources, and political conflict may influence the nexus between environmental stressors and migration necessarily impact on numerical estimates (Kniveton et al. 2008: 32). As Castles (2002) observes, the different methodologies applied by academics in this area has led to very different conclusions about the existence of 'environmental refugees'.

Part of the problem in compiling accurate statistics is how adequately to account for unknown variables, such as precisely when the effects of climate change are likely to be felt most acutely and 'the level of investment, planning, and resources' that will be invested in trying to counter them (Stern 2007: 112). But perhaps the most difficult variable to account for is human adaptive capacity or 'resilience' (Fritze et al. 2008: 13). It is well-documented in refugee literature that it cannot always be anticipated when people will move in response to external triggers such as war or persecution: some flee instantly, some move later, others never move. The line between movement that is 'voluntary' and 'forced' is also very blurred, and many choices will involve a delicate mix of both elements in different proportions.

Even though scientists cannot predict precisely *when* climatic changes may necessitate migration, or in what numbers people may move, it is clear that current international and national structures lack both normative and operational frameworks for dealing with this. From a legal perspective, the numbers of displaced do not affect the normative response to the issue, although they may of course impact on practical responses. This is already seen in refugee law, with mechanisms such as 'temporary protection' and 'prima facie' recognition of refugee status used in mass influx situations. As Gemenne (2009: 20) argues, 'policies play a key role in determining whether displacements occur, and which form they take'.

Evidently, climate-induced movement could usefully be assisted by a multi-lateral institutional response. Yet environmental migration governance represents a significant challenge, not least because the content and parameters of the concept continue to be debated, and because a universal response might downplay the cultural and livelihood needs of displaced communities and local knowledge bases for adaptation. There is at present no internationally agreed definition of what it means to be an environmental 'migrant', 'refugee', or 'displaced person', and, consequently, no common ground on which to systematically progress deliberations about responses. Questions of definition have clear governance implications, informing the appropriate location of environmental migration both procedurally—as an international, regional, or local, developed and/or developing country concern/responsibility—and thematically—for example, within the existing refugee protection framework or under the UN Framework Convention on Climate Change.[3] The viability and value of institutionalizing international cooperation and collaboration on international migration matters generally, and on environmental migration in particular, depends upon how that phenomenon could and should be formulated as a discrete concept in law and policy. Such normative conclusions must be grounded in a thorough examination and assessment of the existing institutions and political processes that impact upon environmental migration and states' responses to them.

Locating the enquiry: what regulation exists?

The potential impacts of climate change on human migration were recognized two decades ago by the IPCC, when it noted that millions of people would likely be uprooted by shoreline erosion, coastal flooding, and agricultural disruption (IPCC 1990). In the IPCC's most recent reports, these factors, along with increasing salinity and temperatures, rising sea levels, increases in the number and severity of extreme weather events, water scarcity, and glacial melting are identified as compromising the continued habitability of different environments worldwide, impacting upon agricultural viability, infrastructure and services, the stability of governance, and human settlement itself (Hegerl et al. 2007). The effects of climate change are likely to induce some level of human displacement in various parts of the world (Nicholls and Tol 2006; Adger et al. 2007: 733–4; Cruz et al. 2007: 484, 488), with the IPCC suggesting that 'migration is the only option in response to sea-level rise that inundates islands and coastal settlements' (Cruz et al. 2007: 492).[4] In some cases, relocation or migration to a third country may be the only option for the continued survival of a community. But this does not necessarily mean that permanent migration is necessary immediately, or that it is appropriate in all regions where environmental harm occurs. For example, studies have shown that droughts in parts of Africa led to decreases in international and long-distance migration, with food scarcity and increased food prices forcing people to spend money on basic needs rather than moving. By contrast, short-distance migration increased as women and children sought work to supplement household incomes through remittances (Henry et al. 2004). Migration is thus used as a coping strategy (Afsar 2003: 2; Leighton 2006; Renaud et al. 2007).

Though in theory a distinction can be made (at least in the social sciences) between 'climate change' as anthropogenic and 'environmental change' as resulting from natural processes, in practice the dividing line is far from neat. Climate change blurs the distinction between 'natural' and 'man-made' hazards (Ehrhart and Thow 2008: 5) and certain environmental problems cannot always be divorced from the political realm (e.g. Darfur) (Gleditsch 1998; Barnett 2000, 2003: 9–10).[5] Castles argues that the focus on 'environment' as a cause of displacement is therefore misleading, since it may obscure underlying socio-political factors which are more familiar to traditional refugee protection (Castles 2002).[6]

Scholars and policymakers consistently lament the absence of sound empirical evidence about the links between environmental degradation and migration, and the numbers of people likely to be affected. Although scientists now attest that '[m]ost of the observed increase in globally averaged temperatures since the mid-twentieth century is *very likely* due to the observed increase in anthropogenic greenhouse gas concentrations', which has *'very likely*...contributed to a rise in mean sea level' (Hegerl et al. 2007: 729; IPCC 2007: 10), it does not necessarily follow that climate change can be described as the sole cause of human movement, or that those who move would attribute their reasons for doing so to it (Mortreux and Barnett 2009).[7] Studies suggest that decisions to move or to stay are influenced by the overall socio-economic situation of those concerned (Meze-Hausken 2000; Haug 2002; Afsar 2003) and, consistent with findings in traditional refugee literature, the poorest or most vulnerable may not have any choice but to stay put, because they may not have the health, skills, or economic ability to move. Despite the scarcity of comprehensive studies in the field of climate-induced displacement, available evidence rebuts the assumption that climate change leads, in a linear way, to migration (Kniveton et al. 2008: 35; Mortreux and Barnett 2009).

At present, there is no authoritative international institution responsible for governing environmental migration. The absence of a coherent body of norms that could properly be described as 'international migration law' (Aleinikoff 2007: 471) means that there is no singular response to global migration governance, and this is complicated in the context of environmentally induced movement given the multifaceted nature of the phenomenon. Accordingly, regulation in this field is extremely fragmented and disparate. In part, this stems from slow recognition of the problem, confusion over how to understand it (migration versus protection), and the multiple and diverse ways in which its impacts may be felt, which both impede and complicate its regulation. If climate drivers are overshadowed by other features such as general poverty, which have traditionally not been seen as giving rise to a protection response by third states, then the situation may be dealt with in an entirely different manner, such as through *in situ* humanitarian assistance.[8]

Working definitions

An underlying stumbling block in the discourse on environmental migration is the inherent difficulty in conceptualizing and accurately describing the phenomenon. For example, is climate-induced displacement properly conceived of as a refugee issue, a human rights issue, an environmental issue, a security issue, a migration issue, or a humanitarian issue (the last two of which are not governed by hard law norms, and thus leave the problem to the political discretion of individual governments and responses outside the law)? The traditional ways in which law and policy have been divided into 'fields' of enquiry and operation, such as 'human rights', 'trade', 'development', and so on, do not reflect the messy, complex interconnectedness of the issue (Betts, this volume). This chapter does not advocate a position on whether environmental displacement should be viewed as a protection or a migration issue—indeed, some combination of responses may be necessary at different times and places—but rather examines the implications of such classification on governance structures.

The use of the term 'environmental' instead of 'climate change' serves a certain function—it broadens the field of enquiry, but may also be viewed as drawing a distinction between anthropogenic and 'natural' causes. The contemporary focus on climate-induced displacement in some ways represents a repackaging of the broader debate in the 1990s about environmental displacement. Furthermore, disagreement about whether climate or environmental changes themselves drive people to move, or whether a multiplicity of drivers is responsible, renders the bureaucratic label problematic. Tensions between 'refugee' and 'migrant' labels strike at the heart of the debate—do (or should) states have international protection obligations towards the displaced, or should they retain the discretion to pick and choose new migrants? Do those who move do so voluntarily or by force? Some have suggested that, like human movement generally, environmental migration is part of a continuum, and the 'environmental refugee' is simply its most extreme manifestation (Hugo 1996; Renaud et al. 2007: 10).

The term 'environmental refugee' was first used in the 1970s but entered bureaucratic discourse in 1985 (El-Hinnawi 1985; Suhrke and Visentin 1991; Myers and Kent 1995; Morrisey 2009). The choice of the term 'refugee' is highly controversial.[9] Though it may provide a useful descriptor, it does not accurately reflect in legal terms the status of those who move (Keane 2004; McAdam 2009). It has very strong political traction and is highly provocative, leading to a backlash from some Pacific island groups to whom it has been applied (Tong 2008; Gemenne 2009; McAdam and Loughry 2009). Kibreab (1997: 21) argued that the term 'environmental refugee' was 'invented at least in part to depoliticise the causes of displacement, so enabling states to derogate their obligation to provide asylum'. His suggestion is that the use of the term 'environmental' detaches the individual's circumstances from any underlying socio-political causes that might indeed fall within the ambit of the 1951 Refugee Convention,[10] and thus may be a way of receiving states seeking to avoid their obligations towards people whose plight can, at least on one view, be characterized in this way. However, in my view this overstates the genesis of the term. The 'environmental refugee' and 'climate refugee' framework stems from the environmental lobby, where it emerged as a politically powerful advocacy tool to draw attention to the disastrous consequences of unchecked development. The ongoing debate between environmental and migration scholars has focused on the fact that, firstly, the term is inaccurate because the specific legal meaning of 'refugee' does not extend to climate-change or environmental-related movement, and secondly, it is generally impossible to isolate environmental factors as 'the' cause of movement because of the interconnected and complex reasons why people move.

This has led to the development of two competing viewpoints on environmental migration (Gemenne 2009). The first is the alarmist approach, most typically embodied by those who approach the issue from an environmental standpoint. Early proponents of this approach include Myers and Kent (1995) and El-Hinnawi (1985). They tend to regard climate change-related movement as a means of raising awareness about the dangers of climate change, and portray the scenario of large numbers of people moving in response to changes to the climate. They often call for an extension of the international protection regime to respond to such flows. By contrast, the sceptics, typically migration scholars such as Black (2001) and Castles (2002), dispute a direct causal link between climate change and migration. Instead, they emphasize the multiple drivers of movement which depend on individuals' broader socio-economic context and adaptive capacity. They generally do not favour refugee-like responses, but more holistic, nuanced approaches.

A displacement typology

While the absence of a formal legal definition may perpetuate uncertainty about the parameters of the phenomenon, and complicate questions of state and institutional responsibility for the displaced, it does not necessarily preclude international responses. For example, 'terrorism' remains without a uniform legal meaning in international law (Saul 2006), yet that has not prevented UN Security Council resolutions and countless treaties from dealing with it. The absence of definition may allow for more flexible responses—ad hoc responses within a formalized framework. It may permit states a limited discretion, either by failing to define the term or by giving it a particular meaning in particular instruments.

Simply for the purposes of a working definition, the International Organization for Migration (IOM) defines 'environmental migrants' as follows:

> persons or groups of persons who, for compelling reasons of sudden or progressive changes in the environment that adversely affect their lives or living conditions, are obliged to leave their habitual homes, or choose to do so, either temporarily or permanently, and who move either within their country or abroad. (IOM 2007: para 6)

People displaced by climate change might be described as a subset of this category, defined as (Kniveton et al. 2008: 31):

> persons or groups of persons who, for compelling reasons of sudden or progressive changes in the environment as a result of climate change that adversely affect their lives or living conditions, are obliged to leave their habitual homes, or choose to do so, either temporarily or permanently, and who move either within their country or abroad.

The dual elements of compulsion and choice reflected in these definitions reveal the complex reasons why people may move, and the degree of choice may fall somewhere on a single continuum.[11] They also highlight the distinctions between sudden and slow-onset disasters, internal and international movement, and temporary versus permanent relocation.[12]

Walter Kälin, representative of the Secretary General on the Human Rights of Internally Displaced Persons, has little time for the semantics of the debate. Instead, he urges 'a thorough analysis of the different contexts and forms natural disaster induced displacement can take' (Kälin 2008). To precipitate this, he has identified five displacement-triggering scenarios. This classification was subsequently adopted by the Inter-Agency Standing Committee Working Group on Migration/Displacement and Climate Change (IASC 2008; IOM 2008: 3–4).

1. *The increase of hydro-meteorological disasters,* such as flooding, hurricanes, typhoons, cyclones, and mudslides, leading predominantly to internal displacement. Internally displaced people (IDPs) should be protected and assisted in accordance with the 1998 Guiding Principles on Internal Displacement.

2. Government-initiated *planned evacuation* of areas at high risk of disasters. This is likely to lead to permanent internal displacement.

3. *Environmental degradation and slow-onset disasters*, such as reduced water availability, desertification, recurrent flooding, and increased salinity in costal zones. Kälin (2008) explains:

> Such deterioration may not necessarily cause forced displacement strictly defined, but instead incite people to move to regions with better income opportunities and living conditions before it becomes impossible to stay at home. However, if areas become uninhabitable because of complete desertification or sinking coastal zones, then population movements would amount to forced displacement and become permanent.

4. *Small island states at risk of disappearing* because of rising seas. At the point at which the territory is no longer habitable (e.g. because of the inability to grow crops or obtain fresh water), permanent relocation to other states would be necessary. Kälin (2008) notes that current international law provides no status for such people, and even if they were to be treated as 'stateless', 'current legal regimes are hardly sufficient to address their very specific needs' (see also McAdam 2010a). For example, although small island states (such as Kiribati and Tuvalu) emit less than 1 per cent of global greenhouse gases, their small physical size, exposure to natural disasters and climate extremes, very open economies, and low adaptive capacity make them particularly susceptible, and less resilient, to climate change (Mimura et al. 2007: 692–3).[13] The IPCC suggests that the overall vulnerability of small island states stems from four interrelated factors: (*a*) the degree of exposure to climate change; (*b*) a limited capacity to adapt to projected impacts; (*c*) the fact that adaptation is not a high priority, in light of other pressing problems;[14] and (*d*) uncertainty surrounding global climate change projections and their local validity (Mimura et al. 2007: 703).

5. *Risk of conflict* over essential resources. Even though the humanitarian community is used to dealing with internal conflict, and people displaced by conflict may be eligible for protection as refugees or assistance as IDPs, resource-based conflicts 'may be particularly challenging' at the operational level. In particular, where the resource scarcity cannot be resolved, 'it will be extremely difficult to reach peace agreements providing for an equitable solution. The likely outcome is both conflict and the displacement of a protracted nature' (Kälin 2008).

The nature of scenarios contemplated here may be divided into what Brown terms climate processes (2, 3, 4) and climate events (1, 5) (Brown 2008: 17 ff.). Humanitarian aid agencies may be more likely to respond to the latter, since climate events are more likely to cause temporary rather than permanent displacement. What is clear is that each involves different kinds of pressures and impacts, which will affect the time, speed, and size of movement, and the nature of solutions. A sudden disaster, such as a cyclone, may precipitate very fast flight, but it may only be temporary, and assistance in the form of humanitarian disaster relief may be a sufficient response.[15] By contrast, climate change impacts that take place over a much longer period, through erosion, salinity, and so on, may ultimately necessitate the relocation of a whole population to another country. In such cases, the planned, long-term relocation of those people must be negotiated with particular states, for example through enhanced migration schemes or bilateral agreements, or through an international burden-sharing agreement.[16] However, relocation attempts in the past have been fraught with problems and this should be an option of last resort (Campbell 2010).

Would existing legal regimes apply?

Does environmental migration need to be regulated discretely? It seems to warrant a *sui generis* response, but on the other hand, many of the underlying motivations for movement are not dissimilar to existing fields of study and regulation. To what extent should the focus be on the ensuing harm, rather than the cause of movement? A protection response might focus on the human rights deprivations were a person to remain rather than leave. By contrast, a migration response might emphasize the absence of employment opportunities in the country of origin as the motivating factor for movement.

The risk, of course, is that nothing is done because no state wants to be the first to offer a solution, lest doing so exposes it to pressure from other affected populations to take them in as well, or perhaps goes towards establishing a duty under customary international law to protect people fleeing environmental harms. The latter is misplaced in the absence of widespread state practice *and* accompanying expressions that such action stems from a legally binding norm, as opposed to a humanitarian gesture. Permanent international protection is not, and never has been, a response to general poverty or disaster, and would not necessarily be the favoured approach by affected communities. Migration must not be divorced from the broader sphere of development; the effects of climate change might otherwise in fact be hastened by depleting communities of their population and culture (Mortreux and Barnett 2009).

This section examines existing international legal frameworks to see how appropriate they are in regulating climate- and environmentally induced displacement.

International refugee law

At the outset, it is important to point out that while international law defines a 'refugee' in a particular way, this does not mean that people outside this definition are unworthy of protection, or necessarily denied it. Definitions serve an instrumental purpose. They are bureaucratic labels that delimit rights and obligations, and which may seek to bolster some kind of ethical claim to protection or assistance as well.[17] Indeed, the creation of a definition inevitably leads to a testing of its boundaries, and sets up the goalposts for re-evaluating and re-defining what it should be. In some ways, it is stultifying, for it entrenches a particular historical or instrumental or political view as a legal threshold, which becomes the benchmark for further development. On the other hand, it at least provides a starting point to which states are willing to agree, and from which subsequent solutions and developments may stem. Compellingly, and importantly, legal definitions bind states in a way that descriptive labels cannot. But the key point here is that the law does not answer or resolve the fundamental problems of definitional debates; it simply provides a set of criteria from which certain rights and obligations flow.

Refugee law does not strictly apply to those forced to move because of climate change. According to article 1A(2) of the Refugee Convention, a refugee is someone who is already outside his or her country of origin, who has a well-founded fear of persecution *for reasons of* his or her race, religion, nationality, political opinion, or membership of a particular social group, and who, on account of that fear, is unwilling to avail him or herself of the protection of that country.[18] On the face of it, there are numerous obstacles to applying that definition to those moving in response to climatic changes.

Firstly, the requirement of exile—being outside the country of origin—poses an immediate problem for people who have not yet moved, or have moved within their own country. As Kälin's typology (2008) above suggests, a large number of displaced people are likely to be IDPs, who remain under the jurisdiction of their own government and are therefore owed the rights and entitlements of ordinary citizens. As far as the role of the international community is concerned, they are the subject of soft law principles rather than binding treaty obligations. This is because the principle of state sovereignty precludes international responses without an express invitation by the state concerned.[19] In this regard, it is important to note that in late 2009, the African Union adopted the Kampala Convention which requires state parties to 'take measures to protect and assist persons who have been internally displaced due to natural or human-made disasters, including climate change'.[20] Although this provision simply elaborates on Principle 1 of the Guiding Principles on Internal Displacement, it does show how soft law can shape and eventually be adopted as a binding obligation.

Secondly, while there is no obstacle to arguing that socio-economic harms, such as those suffered as a result of livelihoods negatively affected by the effects of climate change, can constitute 'persecution' under the Refugee Convention,[21] there is a difficulty in characterizing climate change itself as 'persecution'. While some have sought to argue the case (Cooper 1998; Kozoll 2004), I find their arguments unconvincing. The effects of rising sea levels, salination, and increasingly frequent storms, earthquakes, and floods on people's homes, livelihoods, and health may be harmful, but they do not constitute 'persecution' as it is understood in international and domestic law (Goodwin-Gill and McAdam 2007: 90–134).[22] The difficulty lies in showing that the relevant harm is sufficiently discriminatory to amount to *persecution*. In other words, there must be a differential impact as against the rest of society (e.g. because the group is marginalized) for harm to amount to 'persecution' (Foster 2007: 310).

This is closely linked to the third reason why international refugee law does not generally apply in the climate change context: the absence of a 'persecutor'.[23] Many of the countries most severely impacted by climate change are some of the least responsible for it. They are not developing policies that increase its negative impacts on particular sectors of the population (which could amount to persecution). This presents yet another problem in terms of the legal definition of 'refugee': the government remains *able* and *willing* to protect its citizens.

Fourthly, even if climate impacts alone were considered to amount to 'persecution', a further difficulty would be linking it to one of the five Convention grounds. In order to meet the refugee definition, a person needs to show that he or she is at risk of persecution *for reasons of* his or her race, religion, nationality, political opinion, or membership of a particular social group. This might be established, for example, if a particular ethnic group were denied access to farming land owing to a discriminatory government policy. However, in the absence of some discriminatory element, it would be very difficult to establish because of the indiscriminate nature of climate change.[24] An argument that people displaced by climate change could collectively constitute a 'particular social group' would be difficult to mount, since refugee law requires such a group to be connected by a fundamental, immutable characteristic other than the risk of persecution itself (Goodwin-Gill and McAdam 2007: 79–80).[25]

In the regional context, Edwards has questioned whether the OAU (Organization of African Unity) Convention's broader refugee definition might capture claims based on environmental movement (Edwards 2006: 225–7). Specifically, she suggests that claims relating to 'events seriously disturbing the public order' could encompass environmental catastrophes such as famine and drought, although notes that such an interpretation is not presently supported by the *opinio juris* of African states. Despite the regional practice of permitting people fleeing natural disasters to cross an international border to receive temporary protection, African governments have taken care not to characterize this as an obligation arising under the OAU Convention. She therefore concludes that at most, the practice can be seen as 'contributing to the development of a right of temporary protection on humanitarian grounds under customary international law, rather than under treaty' (Edwards 2006: 227).[26]

Given the difficulties at the international and regional levels of applying refugee law to environmentally driven movement, it is instructive to scrutinize whether protective principles developed in the refugee context, such as the principle of *non-refoulement* (which precludes states from returning people to face persecution or other forms of serious harm), might apply in the context of climate-induced migration. In addition, is the status envisaged for refugees—the rights, entitlements, and protection options flowing from the Refugee Convention—relevant in this context? The chapter therefore turns to examine the role of international human rights law.

International human rights law

There are three main reasons why international human rights law is of importance to the present analysis (McAdam and Saul 2008: 373–80). Firstly, it sets out minimum standards of treatment to which all individuals in a state's territory or jurisdiction are entitled. In this way, it provides a yardstick for measuring which rights might be at risk from climate change, and which domestic authorities are responsible for addressing them. This is related to the second reason: if people do relocate, then human rights law demands a minimum standard of treatment in the host state. This is pertinent to the legal status granted to such people. While at a bare minimum they must not be subjected to inhuman or degrading treatment, states also have a responsibility to ensure that they may enjoy the full range of human rights which the state is bound to provide under international law. Finally, human rights law may provide a basis on which individuals can claim protection in a third state. This is based on the expanded principle of *non-refoulement* under human rights law, embodied in the concept of 'complementary protection' (McAdam 2007).

Climate change potentially affects the enjoyment of the full range of human rights protected under international law. The cumulative effect of climate change impacts on livelihoods, national economies, and government stability may in some cases preclude vulnerable states from fulfilling their positive obligation to protect life. The right to an adequate standard of living, including adequate food, clothing, housing, and the continuous improvement of living conditions,[27] and the right not to be deprived of means of subsistence[28] are independent human rights as well as necessary components of the right to life. These are compromised where global warming leads to the destruction of people's ability to hunt, fish, gather, or undertake subsistence farming.[29]

Human rights law also requires that ethnic religious, linguistic, or indigenous[30] minorities must also be allowed to enjoy their own culture, practise their own religion, and use their own language.[31] Climate change may threaten these rights where people are displaced from their land and spiritual homes. The Inter-American Commission on Human Rights has acknowledged that 'the use and enjoyment of the land and its resources are integral components of the physical and cultural survival of the indigenous communities'.[32] If relocation results in forced assimilation, then the right to culture may be at risk.[33]

States are prohibited from sending people back to places where they risk being tortured, exposed to cruel, inhuman, or degrading treatment or punishment, or subjected to the death penalty or arbitrary deprivation of life (Lauterpacht and Bethlehem 2003; Goodwin-Gill and McAdam 2007: 345–54; McAdam 2007). These obligations arise under treaties such as the Convention against Torture,[34] the International Convenant on Civil and Political Rights (ICCPR) and the European Convention on Human Rights,[35] as well as under customary international law.

But it does not necessarily follow that these protection mechanisms would assist a person displaced by climate change. To date, both state practice and jurisprudence only recognize a handful of rights as giving rise to a protection obligation on the part of the receiving state. While the House of Lords has acknowledged that, in theory, *any* sufficiently serious human rights violation could give rise to such an obligation[36]—a proposition that remains open to testing in the courts—current practice suggests that the accepted limits of the principle of *non-refoulement* under treaty and customary international law are non-return to persecution, torture, cruel, inhuman, or degrading treatment or punishment, and arbitrary threats to life.

Whereas the prohibition on returning someone to torture or cruel, inhuman, or degrading treatment is absolute, most other human rights provisions permit a balancing test between the interests of the individual and the state, thus placing protection from *refoulement* out of reach in all but the most exceptional circumstances. It may therefore be necessary to try to re-characterize the violated human right, such as the right to health, as a form of inhuman treatment, which *is* a complementary protection ground. However, courts have carefully circumscribed the meaning of 'inhuman or degrading treatment' so that it cannot be used as a remedy for general poverty, unemployment, or lack of resources or medical care except in the most exceptional circumstances.[37] This may limit its application in the case of climate-induced displacement. In addition, displacement caused (at least in part) by climate change does not meet the international definition of 'torture', which requires the infliction of severe pain or suffering by a public official for a purpose such as punishment or obtaining a confession.[38]

Finally, the traditional approach to identifying international protection needs through individualized decision-making seems highly inappropriate to the situation of climate-induced displacement. This is in part because responsibility for displacement is highly diffuse (attributable to a large number of polluting states over many years, rather than to direct ill-treatment of a particular person by a certain government) and the scale of displacement may require group-based rather than individual solutions. Whereas refugee protection extends assistance to people fleeing harm inflicted or condoned by the country of origin, protection sought for climate-induced displacement is the opposite: people may demand protection *in* industrialized states precisely because they are regarded as having a responsibility to assist people who have suffered as a result of their sustained emission patterns.[39]

Statelessness

The most extreme threat to self-determination arises in the context of whole-island displacement, where states (such as Tuvalu, Kiribati, and the Maldives) are threatened with extinction due to rising sea levels (McAdam 2010a). The likely scenario is not sudden inundation of the territory, but rather a gradual process whereby land becomes unsustainable and therefore uninhabitable on a permanent basis. The time frame for this is uncertain, and it may be that with resilience, innovation, and gradual adaption, human habitation remains possible for longer than some initial projections. Nevertheless, the permanent displacement of a population threatens not only peoples' right to self-determination,[40] but also the very existence of their state as a matter of international law.

The criteria for statehood in international law are (a) a permanent population, (b) a defined territory, (c) a government, and (d) the capacity to enter into relations with other states.[41] If one or more of those elements ceases to exist, then the continued characterization of the state qua state is called into question. Whereas international law contemplates the disappearance of a state by reason of absorption (by another state), merger (with another state), and dissolution (with the emergence of successor states), whereby the laws of state succession apply, it is unprecedented for a state to physically disappear without its territory being assumed by any other state. If a state no longer exists, then can its (former) inhabitants retain their nationality? Or do they become stateless as a matter of international law?[42]

This eventuality is not anticipated by the two international treaties on statelessness, which premise loss of nationality on its denial, by virtue of the operation of the law of a particular state, rather than through the disappearance of a state altogether.[43] This deliberately narrow and legalistic definition of statelessness does not even extend to the situation of de facto statelessness, where a person formally has a nationality, but which is ineffective in practice.[44] Furthermore, the statelessness treaties are generally poorly ratified and poorly implemented, making reliance on them difficult.

International environmental law

In international environmental law, the global atmosphere and climate are considered a 'common resource' of vital interest to humanity.[45] Under treaty law, states have obligations to implement programmes for mitigating greenhouse gas emissions;[46] to prevent, reduce, and control pollution of the atmosphere and the marine environment;[47] and to conserve biodiversity.[48] The latter are relevant where displacement is due to a loss of livelihood or resources resulting from disappearing plant and animal species. However, whereas there are mechanisms in international and regional human rights law for individual complaints to be made against state conduct, such avenues are far less developed in the international environmental law field, where the plane of legal responsibility is primarily between states alone.

Under customary international law, every state has an obligation not to knowingly allow its territory to be used for acts that are contrary to the rights of other states.[49] This principle is understood in the field of environmental law as requiring states to refrain from using their territory in a way that causes environmental harm beyond their borders. The customary law principle of responsibility for trans-boundary environmental harm is well established:

> no State has the right to use or permit the use of its territory in such a manner as to cause injury by fumes in or to the territory of another or the properties or persons therein, when the case is of serious consequence and the injury is established by clear and convincing evidence.[50]

The concept of sustainable development adds additional specificity to this concept by limiting the manner in which states may seek to realize the (nascent) 'right to development' (Millar 2007: 86 ff.). Principle 3 of the Rio Declaration states that it 'must be fulfilled so as to equitably meet developmental and environmental needs of future generations', implying limits on emissions that may jeopardize the ability of future generations to live and develop in a healthy environment. Principle 2 requires states to ensure that their exploitation of resources does 'not cause damage to the environment of other states or of areas beyond the limits of national jurisdiction', again suggesting limitations on carbon emissions because of their potential damage to vulnerable populations.[51] The Rio Declaration is not formally binding on states, but represents a set of principles which states have agreed should guide their conduct.

The links between a safe environment and the fulfilment of human rights have been formally recognized since the adoption of the Stockholm Declaration in 1972,[52] but the precise relationship between the two, in terms of states' legal obligations, remains in the developmental stages. Although there is an acknowledgement that the realization of human rights is largely dependent on whether the physical environment is capable of sustaining people as rights-bearers,[53] and some rights are dependent on a particular quality of environment, there is not yet an individual or collective 'right to environment' in international law. Two regional human rights treaties do recognize such a right;[54] in the American context, however, the right is not subject to individual petition to the Inter-American Commission on Human Rights, thus hampering the ability of individuals to seek a remedy for a violation.[55]

As alluded to above, the major obstacle in any legal action relating to climate-induced displacement is the question of causation. How can it be legally established that a particular state (or states) has caused damage to a particular individual or group by virtue of its greenhouse gas emissions? It is very difficult to quantify and attribute harm caused by the carbon emissions of any particular state, given that all states have contributed in some way to emissions over time. In December 2005, the Inuit peoples of the Arctic regions of the United States and Canada sought to bring a case against the government of the United States, alleging that its failure to reduce its greenhouse gas emissions was leading to the destruction of their habitat and way of life (Earthjustice 2007: 3).[56] Although the petition was ultimately dismissed, and instead evidence was presented by way of a general hearing on human rights issues rather than as contentious litigation, the case raised yet unanswered questions about whether a state's failure to ratify key international instruments aiming to combat climate change could *inter alia* constitute a breach of human rights law, the principle of good faith in upholding international obligations, and the duty to cooperate in international environmental law.[57] Mere ratification of the relevant treaties is insufficient—states must ensure that the international system is sufficiently strong to protect human rights, both through international collaboration and domestic measures.

What is the normative case for institutionalized cooperation, and what type of cooperation should it be?

Spheres of governance

Because there are numerous cross-cutting and intersecting issues raised by climate-related displacement which relate to a variety of different institutional mandates (such as international protection, human rights, indigenous rights, cultural rights, and the environment), the concept risks being dealt with in an ad hoc and fragmented manner. Partial efforts to respond to this phenomenon at the international level come from (at least) five traditional 'spheres of governance' and their corresponding institutions:

- migration/asylum

  (UNHCR, IOM, the (former) UN Global Commission on International Migration, the Office of the High Commissioner for Human Rights (OHCHR)—Global Migration Group, OHCHR—Special Rapporteur of the Commission on Human Rights on the Human Rights of Migrants, ILO-MIGRANT, The Hague Process on Refugees and Migration, UN Population Fund (UNFPA), Internal Displacement Monitoring Centre (IDMC));

- the environment

  (UN Framework Convention on Climate Change, UN Environment Programme (UNEP), IPCC, International Institute for Sustainable Development (IISD));

- development

  (UN Development Programme (UNDP), UNFPA, IISD, International Labour Organization (ILO));

- disaster response and disaster management

  (UNEP, UNDP, World Food Programme (WFP), Food and Agriculture Organization (FAO), UN Children's Fund (UNICEF), the Red Cross (ICRC/IFRC), UNHCR)

- human rights/humanitarian aid agencies

  (OHCHR—Special Rapporteur of the Commission on Human Rights on the Human Rights of Migrants, Office for the Coordination of Humanitarian Assistance, the Inter-Agency Standing Committee (OCHA), the International Committee of the Red Cross, and UNFPA).

Clearly, a number of these organizations cut across two or more of the issue-areas. The difficulty is that none of them provides a comprehensive and coherent multilateral framework regulating state responses to environmental migration. Moreover, institutions in the various policy fields may have overlapping or conflicting mandates—or alternatively, such a limited/partial perspective that the phenomenon as a whole remains beyond their scope. Difficulties already exist within some of the sectors mentioned above: for example, the system of disaster management alone 'remains highly fragmented, increasingly specialised, and marred by institutional rivalries' (Gemenne 2009: 231).

Indeed, whether a single organization could harness the interdisciplinary expertise required to address all aspects of the phenomenon—from the science, to mitigation and adaptation strategies, and precisely what its mandate would look like—remains unclear.[58] Presumably such an agency would still require the input and cooperation of other expert institutions in implementing policy, which might suggest its role would more appropriately be in identifying risks and formulating possible responses, rather than operational. Precisely because of the complexity of climate-induced displacement, an inter-agency approach with a central UN focal point or coordinator—perhaps the OCHA—would be the more pragmatic, palatable, and resource-efficient approach. Otherwise, the agency would need to become a conglomeration of existing UN agencies (UNHCR, OHCHR, UNEP, etc.) with a specialist focus on climate change. As needed, the additional expertise of inter-governmental agencies such as the IOM could be tasked with specific functions, subject always to appropriate supervision of the human rights implications of their activities. Much as the IDMC serves to monitor conflict-induced displacement worldwide, collating data and then advocating for durable solutions, such an agency could be tasked with identifying areas at risk, and with devising strategies—in consultation with local communities and receiving states—about adaption and migration options. For example, UNEP is developing National Adaptation Programmes for Action in over twelve countries, including Haiti, Liberia, and Tanzania, funded by the Global Environment Facility.

At a meeting of UN agencies, international and local non-governmental organizations (NGOs) in Fiji on climate change and human security in the Pacific in 2008, there was a strong sense that the cross-cutting and global nature of climate change impacts on human rights and human security required a multi-sectoral response.[59] One suggestion was that an agency structure like that of UNAIDS might be appropriate—namely, one that made full use of UN expertise across its associated organizations to create a coordinated global response. UNAIDS is guided by a Programme Coordinating Board, which comprises representatives from twenty-two governments, five NGO representatives, and ten 'cosponsors' (UNHCR, UNICEF, WFP, UNDP, UNFPA, UNODC, ILO, United Nations Educational Scientific and Cultural Organization (UNESCO), World Health Organization (WHO), and the World Bank), each of which has responsibility for at least one technical area (such as UNHCR's role in respect of HIV/AIDS infection among displaced populations). However, while the importance of strong institutional guidance and leadership was recognized, it was also felt essential to provide local communities with access to information, and to learn from local knowledge in order to implement adaptation strategies on the ground to empower local communities (Loughry and McAdam 2008: 51).

The role of UNHCR

While UNHCR might seem the obvious contender as a lead agency on climate-induced displacement, it is already responsible for over 20 million refugees and other people of concern (including asylum seekers, returnees, and IDPs). Each year it relies on donations and the goodwill of states to provide it with funds to carry out its work in over 100 countries, and it has experienced significant budgetary crises over the years. Currently, it has no legal mandate to deal with those displaced for environmental reasons unless they also happen to fit within its areas of concern.

Two areas in which UNHCR's existing mandate may be engaged is in respect of stateless people and IDPs. Firstly, UNHCR has argued that in cases where whole countries are threatened by rising sea levels, and when 'their populations would be likely to find themselves largely in a situation that would be similar to if not the same as if statehood had ceased' (UNHCR 2009a: 2), its mandate to prevent and reduce statelessness would be triggered.[60] It would accordingly have a duty to engage with states about preventing statelessness, providing some degree of institutional advocacy for affected populations.

Secondly, while UNHCR has some institutional responsibility for IDPs, this is presently limited to IDPs displaced by conflict.[61] This is considerably narrower than the operational definition of 'IDPs' in the Guiding Principles, which expressly encompasses people who have fled their homes due to natural or human-made disasters. From a practical point of view, there are also real doubts about whether UNHCR has the resources, expertise, and capacity to assume a protection or assistance function for over double the number of people for whom it already cares.

Nevertheless, in recent years, UNHCR has responded on an operational level to disasters such as the 2004 tsunami, the 2005 Sri Lankan earthquake, flooding in Kenya in 2006, Cyclone Nargis in Burma in 2008, the 2010 Haiti earthquake, and the 2010 floods in Pakistan.[62] This is in part because it is seen as the institution with the greatest experience in the area (although it has also been suggested that UNHCR's willingness to get involved is linked not only to the scale of the disasters, but 'internal motives, which related to the agency's presence in the region and strategic considerations about its future role in the UN system' (Gemenne 2009: 239). Its emergency-response capacity, through its ability to quickly marshal staff and provide shelter and urgent assistance to displaced people, has secured it an active operational role, although in each case it has been clear to stress that its work is purely humanitarian and not within its protection mandate. While, on the one hand, UNHCR's work in relation both to camps and resettlement equips it well to deal with initial displacement as well as durable solutions, on the other, the root causes for environmental displacement can be very different from the situations with which UNHCR is mandated to deal.

Where UNHCR might play a crucial role is in harnessing action at the international level. The present High Commissioner, António Guterres, has taken a keen interest in climate-induced displacement, and seems personally to be driving the institution's engagement with the issue. Describing climate change as 'one of the main drivers of forced displacement, both directly through impact on environment—not allowing people to live any more in the areas where they were traditionally living—and as a trigger of extreme poverty and conflict',[63] he sees UNHCR as having a 'duty to alert states to these problems and help find answers to the new challenges they represent'[64] (though acknowledging that its own legal mandate precludes formal involvement). At the meeting of states at UNHCR's Executive Committee in 2007, the High Commissioner told states that: 'We see more and more people forced to move because of extreme deprivation, environmental degradation and climate change', noting that

> natural disasters occur more frequently and are of greater magnitude and devastating impact. Almost every model of the long-term effects of climate change predicts a continued expansion of desertification, to the point of destroying livelihood prospects in many parts of the globe. And for each centimeter the sea level rises, there will be one million more displaced. The international community seems no more adept at dealing with these causes than it is at preventing conflict and persecution.

171

The High Commissioner has sought to position UNHCR's work within a broader framework of human movement, noting that the effectiveness of its own mandate of protecting, assisting, and finding solutions for refugees and reducing statelessness depends on its 'ability to understand the broader patterns of people on the move in today's world'.[65] UNHCR has developed a number of policy papers on climate change and displacement, and has worked collaboratively with other interested agencies to promote policy responses (UNHCR 2009a, 2009b).

Other actors

IOM might also be viewed as a contender for a lead role on environmental migration. It is not part of the UN system and, unlike UNHCR, does not have a protection function (although its services at times extend to providing humanitarian assistance to refugees and IDPs). As noted in the 'Introduction' to this volume, it has very little normative vision of its own and primarily exists as a service provided to governments in migration management. IOM would not be an appropriate body were the issue primarily conceived as one of international protection.[66] However, more broadly, it has attempted to facilitate international cooperation on migration and has produced a number of significant research reports on the effects of climate-induced displacement, in addition to co-sponsoring workshops and conferences.[67]

Some interesting coalitions have already emerged between organizations whose interests are not traditionally linked. For example, in April 2008, the Climate Change, Environment and Migration Alliance (CCEMA) was formed as 'an informal framework for a global multi-stakeholder partnership on climate change, environment, and migration',[68] comprised of the IOM, Munich Re Foundation, Stockholm Environment Institute, UN Environment Programme (UNEP), UN Office for the Coordination of Humanitarian Affairs (OCHA), UN University Institute for Environment and Human Security, University of Sussex Development Research Centre on Migration, Globalization and Poverty, and World Wildlife Fund.[69] While this network has no separate international legal identity or mandate, it provides a useful space for sharing ideas and developing common policies. Its main aim of 'mainstream[ing] the environmental and climate change considerations into the migration management policies and practice' perhaps already does informally what a UNAIDS-type structure might do more formally.

Despite common calls for a multifaceted, cooperative, or international approach, the literature does not spell out what this would look like or how it would be achieved. Without binding legal norms supporting it, it may be difficult to get states to respond in the desired ways. This is obvious even in areas which are regulated by treaty, such as migrant workers. International law provides important benchmarks and standards to regulate state action; on the other hand, these must be supported by political will and action. As Aleinik-off (2007: 476) concluded in *International Migration Law*, 'there can be no monolithic approach to migration management. Some areas might well benefit from norms adopted by way of an international convention; guiding principles might work best for areas in which a consensus is further away.'

Most authors agree that an early assessment and strengthening of a community's adaptive capacity is crucial. This requires educating communities about the situation, including providing access to information. Some basic principles for the effective management of environmental migration include:

- Ensuring there is a strong scientific basis underpinning planning and policy;
- Increasing awareness, and developing proactive policy and early action;
- Improving legislation, including through bilateral and regional cooperation;
- Giving the means for adequate humanitarian aid;
- Strengthening institutions and policies, with sufficient budgetary support for long-term planning;
- Developing multi-stakeholder partnerships involving public and private service actors, non-governmental and inter-governmental organizations, trade unions, individual migrants, and diaspora associations (Renaud et al. 2007: 33–5; Brown 2008).

In all of this, it is important to bear in mind Mortreux and Barnett's concern (2009) that focusing too strongly on a displacement discourse may have implications for foreign aid and investment in affected countries, leading donors to withdraw adaptation funding. This is of concern to government officials in Tuvalu, for example,[70] although in Kiribati this does not seem to be perceived as an issue of concern.[71] Furthermore, there is a risk that if the need to move is internalized by locals, unsustainable development practices may ensue and 'the impacts of climate change [may] materialise more through the idea of climate change than through material changes in ecosystems driven by climatic processes' (Mortreux and Barnett 2009).

Security

Finally, when discussing institutional responses and normative frameworks, it is important not to overlook the attention that has been given to the security implications of climate change, given the potency this may have in shaping policy. In April 2007, the UN Security Council for the first time considered the impacts of climate change on international peace and security. The President of the Security Council and UK Foreign Secretary, Margaret Beckett, said that climate change was not merely a matter of national security but was about 'our collective security in a fragile and increasingly interdependent world'.[72]

The Secretary General stated that climate-induced movement could lead to major conflict and instability.[73]

In 2009, the UN General Assembly adopted a resolution on 'Climate change and its possible security implications', which called on all relevant UN organs to 'intensify their efforts in considering and addressing climate change, including its possible security implications',[74] and requested the Security Council to 'submit a comprehensive report to the General Assembly...on the possible security implications of climate change'.[75] Whereas the draft text had expressed deep concern that the 'adverse impacts of climate change' could 'trigger population relocation and threaten the territorial integrity and sovereignty of some States',[76] this detail was omitted from the final resolution.

Of particular concern is the way in which the security dimension generally—but perhaps also implicitly in the resolution above—has been 'flipped' away from the 'human security' of the most vulnerable communities affected by climate change impacts, to focus instead on the security of citizens of developed states that may receive climate migrants. Gemenne (2009: 122, emphasis added) characterizes this as part of the 'alarmist' approach to climate change and migration: environmentally induced migration is perceived as a security threat 'exacerbated *and brought to the policy level* by climate change'. Just as the causal link between climate change and migration is complex and multifaceted, so, too, is the connection between climate change impacts and conflict (Reuveny 2007). Yet, advocates of the security approach seize on the speculative forecasts of scholars like Norman Myers (1993, 2005)and reports by NGOs such as Christian Aid (2007), which are pitched at a level of simplistic generality rather than grounded in solid empirical research (Wood 2001; Boano et al. 2007; Morrisey 2009), to generate a sense of fear and uncertainty. Within an already overhyped security climate, this approach easily gains political traction.

For example, in March 2008, the Council of the European Union released a report on 'Climate Change and International Security' which included a section on environmental migration. Although the report documented the predicted security impacts on regions directly affected, it also highlighted the potential economic, political, and social impacts of this for the EU itself. The German Advisory Council on Global Change (2007: 6) suggested that an intensification of migration would make the risk of conflict 'considerable'. A highly controversial 2003 Pentagon-sponsored report described the national security implications of climate change as including border management, global conflict, and economic malaise (Schwartz and Randall 2003: 3), warning of a potential 'flood of refugees to southeast U.S. and Mexico from Caribbean islands' by 2012 (Schwartz and Randall 2003: 17). A report based on the advice of a team of retired US generals and admirals concluded that climate change creates new security challenges for the United States, such as 'increased immigration', and has 'the potential to disrupt our way of life and force changes in how we keep ourselves safe and secure by adding a new hostile and stressing factor into the national and international security environment' (CNA Corporation 2007). In December 2008, the Australian government appointed a National Security Adviser, part of whose mandate encompassed the security implications of climate change for Australia, including 'unregulated population movements'.[77] That the threats to security in each of these examples includes apparent threats to citizens in the EU, United States, and Australia may encourage a politics of fear, such as has dominated asylum debates in the industrialized world for the past decade, which may mould responses to climate-induced movement.

Conclusion

As the foregoing discussion illuminates, it is not yet clear whether a universally applicable definition of those displaced by climate change is necessary or even possible. This is one reason why calls from some quarters for a new treaty to specifically address the needs of people who 'flee' from climate impacts are problematic (McAdam forthcoming 2011).[78] While international consensus about the need to cooperate to address the needs of affected populations is highly desirable, it is not clear whether a treaty that seeks to define climate-displaced people and provide for their protection and assistance is the best approach.

Firstly, what justifies a new protection instrument focusing on a single displacement driver—climate change—rather than poverty, conflict, or natural disaster (Betts and Kaytaz 2009)? And how are interlinked causes to be analysed and determined in assessing protection needs? Secondly, it is questionable whether a protection framework is always the appropriate lens for addressing the needs of people moving in response to climate change. Empirical evidence about movement patterns suggests that it is important for governments to consider enhancing labour, family, and educational migration opportunities to facilitate structured and planned movement, rather than relying on a remedial instrument in the case of spontaneous (and desperate) flight. Thirdly, and related to the second point, it may be more appropriate and culturally sensitive to respond on a regional basis, taking into account the particular features of the affected population, in determining who should move, when, in what fashion, and with what outcome. Staggered migration, circular migration, or the promise of a place to migrate to should it become necessary might be welcome measures that could appeal both to host and affected communities.[79] Finally, there is a more pragmatic reason. States seem to lack the political will to fully implement their existing protection obligations under the Refugee Convention, human rights instruments, and the statelessness treaties, and one might query whether they would be willing to negotiate—and then ratify, implement, and enforce—a treaty requiring them to provide protection to additional (and potentially large) groups of people. While such an instrument would (in theory) help to share the 'burden', and create legal obligations which would add considerable force to calls to protect affected people, in reality it is unlikely to result in sustainable, durable solutions (McAdam forthcoming 2011).

In any event, the failure of the 2009 Copenhagen talks to achieve international agreement on climate change more broadly suggests that national and regional approaches will have to predominate over international ones, at least in the short to medium term. This is not necessarily a bad thing, because it permits gradual and tailored responses to particular scenarios in particular geographical areas, rather than trying to impose a universal solution on a very diverse range of circumstances. Reminding states of their existing obligations under the law relating to refugees, stateless persons, human rights, and the environment will be important, as will be encouraging them to respond proactively to potential movement, in a multifaceted way, through adaptation funding, technical assistance and support, enhanced migration pathways, and a willingness to contemplate new humanitarian strategies. Finally, it is crucial to recognize that environmental migration should not be seen as a sign that adaptation has failed, since 'it may indeed be part of the solution' (Kniveton et al. 2008: 58)—a sign of community resilience and innovation in response to the negative effects of climate change (Zetter 2008: 62).

Notes

* Thank you to Kate Purcell for her excellent research assistance. I gratefully acknowledge the support of the Law Society of NSW's Legal Scholarship Support Fund (LSSF), the UNSW Law Faculty Research Grants Program, and the Australian Research Council.

1. Myers (2005) revised his estimate, suggesting that it could be up to 200 million. Myers has more recently revised this figure as closer to 250 million: interview with Christian Aid (14 March 2007), cited in Christian Aid (2007: endnote 10). Christian Aid (2007: 6) adopted this figure in its own estimates. See also figures in Byravan and Chella Rajan (2006: 247). For an overview of different estimates, see Boano et al. (2008: 12).

2. United Nations High Commissioner for Refugees, António Guterres, in an interview with *The Guardian* (reported by Julian Borger, 17 June 2008), http://www.guardian.co.uk/environment/2008/jun/17/climatechange.food (accessed 20 August 2008).

3. UN Framework Convention on Climate Change (adopted 9 May 1992, entered into force 21 March 1993) 1771 UNTS 107.

4. It has been argued that although adaptation to five metres of sea-level rise is technically possible, a lack of resources mean that realistically this is outside the scope of adaptation for many vulnerable States (Nicholls and Tol 2006).

5. Barnett (2003: 9–10) argues that the suggestion that climate change can cause conflict is 'more theoretically than empirically driven, and motivated by Northern theoretical and strategic interests rather than informed by solid empirical research'.

6. Refugee law recognizes that there may be more than a single cause for flight, and provided that persecution for a Refugee Convention reason is one such cause, others will not negate the need for international protection. See e.g. Foster on 'economic migration' versus 'forced migration' (Foster 2007: 5–21).

7. The present author's own fieldwork in Kiribati and Tuvalu in 2009 reinforces this.

8. There was an interesting suggestion made at the first session of the UN Human Rights Council's Advisory Committee that the Human Rights Council and the Secretary General use their good offices to extend the principle of *non-refoulement* to 'hunger refugees': Report of the Advisory Committee on its First Session (Geneva, 4–15 August 2008), UN Doc. A/HRC/10/2, A/HRC/AC/2008/1/2 (3 November 2008) Recommendation 1/6, 15th meeting, 15 August 2008.

9. Interestingly, the Australian Labor Party has used the term 'climate change refugees', implying a sense of legal recognition and obligation (ALP 2006).

10. Convention relating to the Status of Refugees (adopted 28 July 1951, entered into force 22 April 1954) 189 UNTS 137, art. 1A(2), read in conjunction with Protocol relating to the Status of Refugees (adopted 31 January 1967, entered into force 4 October 1967) 606 UNTS 267.

11. Gemenne (2009: 150) criticizes the IOM definition as not acknowledging the multicausality of movement. While the definition would benefit from expressly acknowledging multicausality, it does not exclude other drivers as it presently stands. See also the definition provided by EACH-FOR (Dun et al. 2007).

12. Renaud et al. (2007: 29–30) have suggested the following distinction: 'An environmentally motivated migrant "may leave" a steadily deteriorating environment in order to pre-empt the worse', whereas a 'forced migrant' is someone who is compelled to leave. Forward-planning could alleviate the incidence of the latter, especially across international borders, although thought needs to be given to how spontaneous arrivals might be received, processed, and accommodated. The question will in each case be whether the receiving State is permitted, as a matter of international law, to return a person to the situation that he or she has fled: i.e. whether doing so would expose him or her to inhuman or degrading treatment through removal.

13. The report additionally lists the impacts of globalization, pressures on infrastructure, a scarcity of fresh water, and, in the Pacific, internal and external political and economic processes, including the imposition of western adaptation models which are not readily transposable to the island context. These features have resulted in some small island States being recognized by the UN as Least Developed Countries or SIDS (small island developing States).

14. As Brown (2008) notes, of the fourteen National Adaptation Programmes of Action (an initiative supported by the United Nations Framework Convention on Climate Change, which aims to assist Least Developed Countries to rank their priorities for adaptation to climate change) that had been submitted by 10 March 2007, not one referred to migration or relocation as a possible policy response. The fourteen States were Bangladesh, Bhutan, Burundi, Cambodia, Comoros, Djibouti, Haiti, Kiribati, Madagascar, Malawi, Mauritania, Niger, Samoa, and Senegal. See http://unfccc.int/national_reports/napa/items/2719.php.

15. It is erroneous to assume that sudden disasters always lead to temporary flight, however. See Gemenne's analysis (2009) of Hurricane Katrina.

16. The former President of the Australian Human Rights Commission, John von Doussa, regarded a burden-sharing treaty as a possible way forward: see 'Climate Change and Human Rights: A Tragedy in the Making' (20 August 2008), http://www.humanrights.gov.au/human_rights/climate_change/index.html (accessed 8 December 2008). The

failure of this principle in addressing the plight of the world's refugees does not augur well, however, for this as a solution.

17. As Gemenne (2009: 148) notes, '[e]nvironmental migration as a social phenomenon is generally apprehended through its definition, which bears high responsibility for the development of normative framework and policy responses'.

18. Refugee Convention, art. 1A(2).

19. Unless the threat could be characterized in such as way as to trigger the Security Council's enforcement powers under Chapter VII of the UN Charter (McAdam and Saul forthcoming 2010).

20. African Union Convention for the Protection and Assistance of Internally Displaced Persons in Africa (adopted 22 October 2009, not yet in force) art. 5(4).

21. It is important to bear in mind that persecution can be constituted by an accumulation of harms, even if individual harms would not, on their own, be sufficient to meet that threshold. The New Zealand Refugee Status Appeals Authority has stated: 'It is recognised that various threats to human rights, in their cumulative effect, can deny human dignity in key ways and should properly be recognised as persecution for the purposes of the Convention': *Refugee Appeal No. 71427/99*, NZ Refugee Status Appeals Authority, 16 August 2000, para 53(a), as cited in Foster (2007: 94).

22. Note, however, that Sweden has chosen to include a category of 'persons otherwise in need of protection' in its Aliens Act (which entered into force 31 March 2006), encompassing *inter alia* people who are 'unable to return to the country of origin because of an environmental disaster': Swedish Aliens Act, Ch. 4, s. 2(3). It is unclear if this would extend to people displaced by climate change, or whether it is intended only to cover people fleeing environmental disasters such as Chernobyl: see Brown (2008: 39), referring to personal communication with Helené Lackenbauer (International Federation of Red Cross and Red Crescent Societies), who stated that parliamentary discussions of this category prior to the passing of the legislation referred to nuclear disasters.

23. This is also said to be a limitation in economic claims: see Foster (2007: 9). Harding (2000: 122) says that refugees generally attract greater international sympathy than economic migrants because there is an identifiable persecutor, as opposed to a general degree of economic difficulty that prevails in some parts of the world.

24. This is not to suggest that discrimination is a necessary element of persecution, but rather that the nexus grounds require persecution to be on account of a (perceived) characteristic setting apart the racial, religious, etc. group from the rest of society: see Goodwin-Gill and McAdam (2007: 90–1, 128–9).

25. Note, however, Foster's remark (2007: 310) that: 'it is clear that the poor can properly be considered a PSG, such that if being poor makes one vulnerable to persecutory types of harm, whether socio-economic or not, then a refugee claim may be established'. Even if this test could be met by certain people displaced by climate change, the difficulty would remain in establishing 'persecution' in the context of climate-induced displacement. Interestingly, the Marshall Islands and Kiribati have both eschewed the refugee label, fearing that it might lead to scattered, individual, and uncoordinated resettlement breaking down cultural integrity, heritage, and—fundamentally—the sense of a State and people: see discussion in Barnett (2003: 12–13) citing Fraser (2000); Pearce (2000: 47).

26. UNHCR similarly made clear that its assistance activities for people displaced by the Boxing Day tsunami did not fall within its formal protection mandate, but rather constituted 'time-limited humanitarian assistance' requested specially by the UN Secretary General: UNHCR, 'Note on International Protection' UN Doc. A/AC.96/1008 (4 July 2005), para 36, cited in Edwards (2006: 227).

27. International Covenant on Economic, Social and Cultural Rights (adopted 16 December 1966, entered into force 3 January 1976) 993 UNTS 3 (ICESCR), art. 11.

28. International Covenant on Civil and Political Rights (adopted 16 December 1966, entered into force 23 March 1976) 999 UNTS 171 (ICCPR), art. 1(2); ICESCR, art. 1(2).

29. See e.g. Petition to the Inter-American Commission on Human Rights Seeking Relief from Violations resulting from Global Warming caused by Acts and Omissions of the United States (7 December 2005), http://www.earthjustice.org/library/legal_docs/petition-to-the-inter-american-commission-on-human-rights-on-behalf-of-the-inuit-circumpolar-conference.pdf.

30. Convention on the Rights of the Child (adopted 20 November 1989, entered into force 2 September 1990) 1577 UNTS 3 (CRC), art. 30. See also Declaration on the Rights of Indigenous Peoples, A/RES/61/295 (adopted 13 September 2007), which is not formally binding.

31. ICCPR, art. 27.

32. *Maya Indigenous Communities of the Toledo District (Belize Maya)* Case 12.053 Inter-American Commission on Human Rights (2004), para 120.

33. See Inter-American Commission on Human Rights, *Report on the Situation of Human Rights of a Segment of the Nicaraguan Population of Miskito Origin* 76, OEA/Ser.L/V/II.62, Doc. 10, Rev. 3 (1983), para II.B.15.

34. Convention against Torture and Other Cruel, Inhuman, or Degrading Treatment or Punishment (adopted 10 December 1984, entered into force 26 June 1987) 1465 UNTS 85 (CAT).

35. Convention for the Protection of Human Rights and Fundamental Freedoms (European Convention on Human Rights, as amended) (4 November 1950).

36. *R* v. *Special Adjudicator ex parte Ullah* [2004] UKHL 26, paras 24–5 (Lord Bingham), 49–50 (Lord Steyn), 67 (Lord Carswell).

37. *D* v. *United Kingdom* (1997) 24 EHRR 423; *N* v. *Secretary of State for the Home Department* [2005] UKHL 31; *N* v.*United Kingdom* (2008 decision of the European Court of Human Rights); *HLR* v. *France* (1997) 20 EHRR 29, para 42; see also the views of Committee against Torture, as in *AD* v. *The Netherlands*, Communication No. 96/1997 (24 January 2000), UN Doc. CAT/C/23/D/96/1997, para 7.2. See discussion in Goodwin-Gill and McAdam (2007: 350–1). See critique of the socio-economic limitation in Foster, (2009).

38. See respectively ICCPR, art. 7; CAT, arts 3 and 1.

39. This is a variation on the argument made in the Inuit petition (Petition to the Inter-American Commission on Human Rights Seeking Relief from Violations resulting from Global Warming caused by Acts and Omissions of the United States); see also Byravan and Chella Rajan (2006).

40. See ICCPR, art. 1(1); ICESCR, art. 1(1).

41. The Montevideo Convention on the Rights and Duties of States (adopted 26 December 1933, entered into force 26 December 1934) 165 LNTS 19 is regarded as reflecting the position in customary international law.

42. See Universal Declaration of Human Rights (adopted 10 December 1948) UNGA Res 217A (III) (UDHR), art. 15; CRC, arts 7 and 8; ICCPR, art. 24(3); American Convention on Human Rights (adopted 22 November 1969, entered into force 18 July 1978) 1144 UNTS 123, art. 20; Convention on the Reduction of Statelessness (adopted 30 August 1961, entered into force 13 December 1975) 989 UNTS 175.

43. Convention relating to the Status of Stateless Persons (adopted 28 September 1954, entered into force 6 June 1960) 360 UNTS 117l, art. 1(1): 'For the purpose of this Convention, the term "stateless person" means a person who is not considered as a national by any State under the operation of its law.' See further McAdam and Saul (2010).

44. Although, as noted below, UNHCR has a mandate for *de facto* statelessness which could be engaged in such a case.

45. See Recommendations of the International Meeting of Legal and Policy Experts, Ottawa, 19 *EPL* (1989), 78.

46. e.g. Stockholm Declaration, principle 21; Convention on Long-Range Transboundary Air Pollution (adopted 13 November 1979, entered into force 16 March 1983) 1302 UNTS 217; Convention for the Protection of the Ozone Layer (adopted 22 March 1985, entered into force 22 September 1988) 1513 UNTS 293; UN Framework Convention on Climate Change (adopted 9 May 1992, entered into force 21 March 1993) 1771 UNTS 107; Kyoto Protocol to the Framework Convention on Climate Change (adopted 11 December 1997, entered into force 16 February 2005).

47. e.g. Stockholm Declaration, principle 21; Declaration of the United Nations Conference on the Human Environment (Rio Declaration) UN Doc. A/CONF/151/26/Rev.1 (1992), principle 2; UN Framework Convention on Climate Change; Kyoto Protocol; United Nations Law of the Sea Convention (adopted 10 December 1982, entered into force 16 November 1994) 1833 UNTS 3, arts 192–5.

48. e.g. Biological Diversity Convention (adopted 5 June 1992, entered into force 29 December 1993) 1760 UNTS 79.

49. *Corfu Channel case (UK v. Albania)* 1949 ICJ 4, 22.

50. *Trail Smelter Arbitration (United States v. Canada)* 1938–41 3 RIAA 1905, 1965; see also Stockholm Declaration, principle 21; Rio Declaration, principle 2; see also the International Law Commission's draft articles on the Prevention of Transboundary Harm from Hazardous Activities (2001), in *Report of the ILC* (2001) GAOR A/56/10; *Advisory Opinion on the Legality of the Threat or Use of Nuclear Weapons* 1996 ICJ 226, para 29.

51. Rio Declaration, principle 2. See also Millar (2007: 71, 86 ff.).

52. Declaration of the United Nations Conference on the Human Environment (Stockholm Declaration) UN Doc. A/CONF/48/14/Rev.1 (16 June 1972).

53. 'The protection of the environment is . . . a vital part of contemporary human rights doctrine, for it is [an indispensable requirement] . . . for numerous human rights such as the right to health and the right to life itself': *Case Concerning the Gabčíkovo-Nagymaros Project (Hungary v. Slovakia)* 1997 ICJ 92 (Separate Opinion of Judge Weeramantry), at para A(b); see also Shelton (2001); Meeting of Experts on Human Rights and the Environment, Final Text (16 January 2002) (see also background papers at

http://www.unhchr.ch/environment). Ramcharan suggests that the right to life implies a right to environment and a concomitant obligation on States 'to take effective measures to prevent and to safeguard against the occurrence of environmental hazards which threaten the lives of human beings' (Ramcharan 1985: 13), as (mis) cited in Asia Pacific Forum (2007).

54. Additional Protocol to the American Convention on Human Rights in the Area of Economic, Social and Cultural Rights (Protocol of San Salvador) (adopted 17 November 1988) OAS Treaty Series 69, art. 11; 1981 African Charter on Human and Peoples' Rights (adopted 27 June 1981, entered into force 21 October 1986) OAU Doc. CAB/ LEG/67/3 Rev. 5, 21 I.L.M. 58 (1982), art. 24.

55. Additional Protocol, art. 19(6).

56. See Petition to the Inter-American Commission on Human Rights Seeking Relief from Violations resulting from Global Warming caused by Acts and Omissions of the United States.

57. See e.g. Stockholm Declaration, principle 24; Rio Declaration, principles 7 and 27.

58. For example, in terms of ascertaining the likelihood of migration as a spontaneous response, it is important to consider 'the socio-cultural-political-economic environment that communities exist in; the cognitive processes of the people experiencing the impact of climate change; the individual, household and community attitudes to migration and migration outcomes; and the type of climate stimulus that migration may be responding to' (Kniveton et al. 2008: 57). Understanding of this kind cannot come from a single discipline, but rather requires true interdisciplinarity.

59. United Nations High Commissioner for Human Rights Regional Office for the Pacific, 'Roundtable Discussion on Climate Change and Human Security in the Pacific' (16 September 2008) (which the author attended).

60. See e.g. UNGA Res 50/152 (9 February 1996), reiterated in UNGA Res 61/137 (25 January 2007), UNGA Res 62/124 (24 January 2008), UNGA Res 63/148 (27 January 2009). The work of the UNHCR extends in some cases to situations of *de facto* statelessness, such as in trying to get 'States to cooperate in the establishment of identity and nationality status of victims of trafficking, many of whom, especially women and children, are rendered effectively stateless due to an inability to establish such status, so as to facilitate appropriate solutions to their situations, respecting the internationally recognized human rights of the victims': Executive Committee of the High Commissioner's Programme, 'Statelessness: Prevention and Reduction of Statelessness and Protection of Stateless Persons' (14 February 2006) UN Doc. EC/57/SC/ CRP.6, para 7. See also UNGA Res 50/152 (9 February 1996) paras 14–15; UNGA Res 3274 (XXIX) (10 December 1974); UNGA Res 31/36 (30 November 1976).

61. There is debate in the literature about the extent to which resource scarcity could itself lead to conflict. While causation is complex, it would nevertheless be a sad irony if UNHCR's mandate were triggered due to inaction, as a non-violent situation escalated to one of conflict: see e.g. Elliott (2010) and Campbell et al. (2007).

62. See 'Emergency Preparedness and Response', http://www.unhcr.org/pages/49c3646cc2. html.

63. Cited in J. Borger, 'Conflicts Fuelled by Climate Change Causing New Refugee Crisis, Warns UN', *The Guardian* (17 June 2008), http://www.guardian.co.uk/environment/ 2008/jun/17/climatechange.food (accessed 20 July 2008). See also Borger (2002: 2).

64. Opening Statement by Mr António Guterres, United Nations High Commissioner for Refugees, at the 58th Session of the Executive Committee of the High Commissioner's Programme (Geneva, 1 October 2007).

65. Ibid.

66. For this reason, Gemenne's appraisal (2009: 241–3) of IOM seems overly optimistic.

67. See e.g. http://www.unitarny.org/en/ccmigration.html; International Conference on 'Environment, Forced Migration and Social Vulnerability' (Bonn, 9–11 October 2008).

68. See 'About CCEMA', http://www.ccema-portal.org/.

69. See http://www.ccema-portal.org/.

70. Author interview with Enele Sopoaga, Secretary for Foreign Affairs, Tuvalu (25 May 2009).

71. Author interviews with various government officials in Kiribati (May 2009).

72. 'Security Council Holds First-Ever Debate on Impact of Climate Change on Peace, Security, Hearing over 50 Speakers' (5663rd Meeting, 17 April 2007), United Nations Department of Public Information News and Media Division.

73. 'Security Council Holds First-Ever Debate on Impact of Climate Change'. For an analysis of the debate, see Sindico (2007).

74. Operative para 1.

75. Operative para 2.

76. See draft resolution on 'Security and Climate Change' (version dated 10 December 2008; copy with author). See also the Niue Declaration on Climate Change (adopted at the 39th Pacific Island Forum, 19–20 August 2008).

77. Prime Minister Kevin Rudd, 'The First National Security Statement to the Australian Parliament', 26 (4 December 2008), http://www.theaustralian.news.com.au/files/security.pdf/.

78. See Republic of the Maldives Ministry of Environment, Energy and Water, Report on the First Meeting on Protocol on Environmental Refugees: Recognition of Environmental Refugees in the 1951 Convention and 1967 Protocol Relating to the Status of Refugees (Male, Maldives, 14–15 August 2006) cited in Biermann and Boas (2008); H. Grant, J. Randerson, and J. Vidal, 'UK Should Open Borders to Climate Refugees, Says Bangladeshi Minister', *The Guardian* (4 December 2009), http://www.guardian.co.uk/environment/2009/nov/30/rich-west-climate-change/print (accessed 8 December 2009); Draft Convention on the International Status of Environmentally-Displaced Persons (CRIDEAU and CRDP, Faculty of Law and Economic Science, University of Limoges) (2008) 4 *Revue Européene de Droit de l'Environnement* 375; 'A Convention for Persons Displaced by Climate Change', http://www.ccdpconvention.com/ (accessed 7 December 2009); D. Hodgkinson and others, '"The Hour When the Ship Comes In": A Convention for Persons Displaced by Climate Change', http://www.ccdpconvention.com/documents/CCDP_Convention_Summary.pdf (accessed 13 March 2010); Md Shamsuddoha and Rezaul Karim Chowdhury, 'Climate Refugee: Requires Dignified Recognition under a New Protocol' (April 2009), http://www.equitybd.org/English/Press%20040409/English%20Position%20paper.pdf (accessed 10 November 2009); Biermann and Boas (2007); see also Biermann and Boas (2008); for criticism of their approach, see Hulme (2008). For another UFCCC-based proposal, see Williams (2008).

79. This is the preferred approach of the government of Kiribati, for example. See e.g. author interview with President Anote Tong (Kiribati, 12 May 2009); comments of Kiribati's Foreign Secretary, Tessie Lambourne, cited in L. Goering, 'Kiribati Officials Plan for "Practical and Rational" Exodus from Atolls', *Reuters AlertNet* (9 December 2009), http://www.alertnet.org/db/an_art/60714/2009/11/9-181804-1.htm.

References

Adger, W.N. and Barnett, J. (2005) Correspondence: Compensation for Climate Change Must Meet Needs. *Nature*, 436(7049), 328.

Adger, W.N. et al. (2007) Assessment of Adaptation Practices, Options, Constraints and Capacity, in M.L. Parry et al. (eds), *Climate Change 2007: Impacts, Adaptation and Vulnerability. Contribution of Working Group II to the Fourth Assessment Report of the Intergovernmental Panel on Climate Change*, Cambridge: Cambridge University Press.

Afsar, R. (2003) *Internal Migration and the Development Nexus: The Case of Bangladesh*, Dhaka and London: Refugee and Migratory Movements Research Unit and DFID.

Aleinikoff, T.A. (2007) International Legal Norms on Migration: Substance without Architecture, in R. Cholewinski, R. Perrechoud, and E. MacDonald (eds.), *International Migration Law: Developing Paradigms and Key Challenges*, The Hague: T. M. C. Asser Press.

Alston, P. (2001) Peoples' Rights: Their Rise and Fall, in P. Alston (ed.), *Peoples' Rights*, Oxford: Oxford University Press.

Asia Pacific Forum (2007) Human Rights and the Environment, Background Paper, APF 12.

Australian Labor Party (2006) *Our Drowning Neighbours: Labor's Policy Discussion Paper on Climate Change in the Pacific*, ALP.

Barnett, J. (2000) Destabilising the Environment-Conflict Thesis, *Review of International Studies*, 26, 271–88.

——(2003) Security and Climate Change, *Global Environmental Change*, 13(1), 7–17.

——(2005) Security and Climate Change: Towards an Improved Understanding. Paper at an International Workshop on Human Security and Climate Change, Oslo, 20–21 June 2005.

——and Adger, W.N. (2003) Climate Dangers and Atoll Countries, *Climatic Change*, 61, 321–67.

Betts, A. and Kaytaz, E. (2009) National and International Responses to the Zimbabwean Exodus: Implications for the Refugee Protection Regime, New Issues in Refugee Research RP No. 175.

Biermann, F. and Boas, I. (2007) Preparing for a Warmer World: Towards a Global Governance System to Protect Climate Refugees. Global Governance Working Paper No. 33 (November 2007).

——————(2008) Protecting Climate Refugees: The Case for a Global Protocol, *Environment* (November–December 2008).

Black, R. (2001) Environmental Refugees: Myth or Reality?, New Issues in Refugee Research Working Paper No. 34, Geneva: UNHCR.

Boano, C., Zetter, R., and Morris, T. (2008) Environmentally Displaced People: Understanding Linkages between Environmental Change, Livelihoods and Forced Migration, Forced Migration Policy Briefing No. 1, Oxford: Refugee Studies Centre, http://www.rsc.ox.ac.uk/PDFs/RSCPB1-Environment.pdf.

Borger, J. (2002) A Critical Time for the Environment, *Refugees*, 127, 2.

Brown, O. (2008) Migration and Climate Change, IOM Migration Research Series No. 31.

Byravan, S. and Chella Rajan, S. (2006) Providing New Homes for Climate Change Exiles, *Climate Policy*, 6, 247–52.

Campbell, J. (2010) Climate-Induced Community Relocation in the Pacific: The Meaning and Importance of Land, in J. McAdam (ed.), *Climate Change and Human Displacement: Multidisciplinary Perspectives*, Oxford: Hart Publishing.

Campbell, K.M. et al. (2007) *The Age of Consequences: The Foreign Policy and National Security Implications of Global Climate Change*, Center for Strategic and International Studies and Center for a New American Security (November 2007).

Castles, S. (2002) Environmental Change and Forced Migration: Making Sense of the Debate, New Issues in Refugee Research Working Paper No. 70.

Christian Aid (2007) *Human Tide: The Real Migration Crisis* (May 2007).

CNA Corporation (2007) *National Security and the Threat to Climate Change*.

Cooper, J.B. (1998) Environmental Refugees: Meeting the Requirements of the Refugee Definition, *New York University Environmental Law Journal*, 6, 480.

Council of the European Union (2008) Report from the Commission and the Secretary-General/High Representative to European Council on Climate Change and International Security, Brussels (3 March 2008).

Crisp, J. (1999) 'Who Has Counted the Refugees?' UNHCR and the Politics of Numbers, New Issues in Refugee Research Working Paper No. 12, Geneva: UNHCR.

Cruz, V.A. et al. (2007) Asia, in M.L. Parry et al. (eds.), *Climate Change 2007: Impacts, Adaptation and Vulnerability. Contribution of Working Group II to the Fourth Assessment Report of the Intergovernmental Panel on Climate Change*, Cambridge: Cambridge University Press.

Dun, O., Gemenne, F., and Stojanov R. (2007) Environmentally Displaced Persons: Working Definitions for the EACH-FOR Project, http://www.each-for.eu/documents/Environmentally_Displaced_Persons_Working_Definitions.pdf.

Durieux, J.F. and McAdam, J. (2004) *Non-Refoulement* through Time: The Case for a Derogation Clause to the Refugee Convention in Mass Influx Emergencies, *International Journal of Refugee Law*, 16(1), 4–24.

Earthjustice (2007) Global Warming and Human Rights: Testimony of Martin Wagner before the Inter-American Commission on Human Rights (1 March 2007).

Edwards, A. (2006) Refugee Status Determination in Africa, *African Journal of International and Comparative Law*, 14(2), 204–33.

Ehrhart, C. and Thow, A. (2008) *Humanitarian Implications of Climate Change: Mapping Emerging Trends and Risk Hotspots*, OCHA and CARE (August 2008).

El-Hinnawi, E. (1985) *Environmental Refugees*, UN Environment Programme.

Elliott, L. (2010) Climate Change and Climate Migrants: What Threat, Whose Security?, in J. McAdam (ed.), *Climate Change and Displacement: Multidisciplinary Perspectives*, Oxford: Hart Publishing.

Foster, M. (2007) *International Refugee Law and Socio-Economic Rights: Refuge from Deprivation*, Cambridge: Cambridge University Press.

Foster, M. (2009) Non-Refoulement on the Basis of Socio-Economic Deprivation: The Scope of Complementary Protection in International Human Rights Law, *New Zealand Law Review*, 2, 257–310.

Fraser, G. (2000) Sea-Level Rise, Hurricanes, It Is No Paradise on Small Islands, *The Earth Times* (15 November 2000).

Fritze, J.G. et al. (2008) Hope, Despair and Transformation: Climate Change and the Promotion of Mental Health and Wellbeing, *International Journal of Mental Health Systems*, 2, 13.

Gemenne, F. (2009) Environmental Changes and Migration Flows: Normative Frameworks and Policy Responses, unpublished PhD thesis, Institut d'Etudes Politiques de Paris and University of Liège.

German Advisory Council on Global Change (2007) *World in Transition: Climate Change as a Security Risk: Summary for Policy Makers*, Berlin: WBGU Secretariat.

Gleditsch, N. (1998) Armed Conflict and the Environment: A Critique of the Literature *Journal of Peace Research*, 35(3), 381–400.

Goodwin-Gill, G.S. and McAdam, J. (2007) *The Refugee in International Law*, 3rd edn, Oxford: Oxford University Press.

Guterres, A. (2009) Bracing for the Flood, *New York Times* (Op-Ed, 10 December 2009), http://www.nytimes.com/2009/12/11/opinion/11iht-edguterres.html?_r=1&emc=eta1 (accessed 14 December 2009).

Harding, J. (2000) *The Uninvited: Refugees at the Rich Man's Gate*, London: Profile Books.

Haug, R. (2002) Forced Migration, Processes of Return and Livelihood Construction among Pastoralists in Northern Sudan, *Disasters*, 26(1), 70–84.

Hegerl, G.C. et al. (2007) Understanding and Attributing Climate Change, in S. Solomon et al. (eds.), *Climate Change 2007: The Physical Science Basis: Contribution of Working Group I to the Fourth Assessment Report of the Intergovernmental Panel on Climate Change*, Cambridge: Cambridge University Press.

Henckaerts, J.M. and Doswald-Beck, L. (2004) *Customary International Humanitarian Law, Vol. 1: Rules*, Cambridge: Cambridge University Press.

Henry, S., Schoumaker, B., and Beauchemin, C. (2004) The Impact of Rainfall on the First Out-Migration: A Multi-Level Event-History Analysis in Burkina Faso. *Population and Environment*, 25(5), 423–60.

Hugo, G. (1996) Environmental Concerns and International Migraton, *International Migration Review*, 30, 105.

Hulme, M. (2008) Commentary: Climate Refugees: Cause for a New Agreement?, *Environment* (November–December 2008).

IASC Working Group on Migration/Displacement and Climate Change (2008) Displacement and Climate Change: Towards Defining Categories of Affected Persons, First Draft of a Working Paper (20 September 2008).

ILC (2001) *Report of the ILC*, GAOR A/56/10.

IOM (2007) Discussion Note: Migration and the Environment', 94th session, Doc. No. MC/INF/288 (1 November 2007).

—— (2008) Migration, Climate Change and the Environment, IOM Policy Brief (May 2009).

—— (2009) *Migration, Climate Change and the Environment*, IOM Policy Brief (May 2009), Geneva: IOM.

IPCC (1990) *Climate Change: The IPCC Scientific Assessment: Final Report of Working Group I*, New York: Cambridge University Press.

——(2007) Summary for Policymakers, in Parry et al. (eds.), *Climate Change 2007: Impacts, Adaptation and Vulnerability*, Cambridge: Cambridge University Press.

Jacobs, R.E. (2005) Treading Deep Waters: Substantive Law Issues in Tuvalu's Threat to Sue the United States in the International Court of Justice, *Pacific Rim Law and Policy Journal*, 14(1), 103–28.

Kälin, W. (2008) The Climate Change–Displacement Nexus (16 July 2008), http://www.brookings.edu/speeches/2008/0716_climate_change_kalin.aspx?p=1 (accessed 2 December 2008).

Keane, D. (2004) The Environmental Causes and Consequences of Migration: A Search for the Meaning of 'Environmental Refugees', *Georgetown International Environmental Law Review*, 16(2), 209–23.

Kibreab, G. (1997) Environmental Causes and Impact of Refugee Movements: A Critique of the Current Debate, *Disasters*, 21(1), 20–38.

Kniveton, D. et al. (2008) Climate Change and Migration: Improving Methodologies to Estimate Flows, IOM Migration Research Series No. 33.

Kozoll, C.M. (2004) Poisoning the Well: Persecution, the Environment, and Refugee Status, *Colorado Journal of International Environmental Law and Policy*, 15, 271.

Laczko, F. and Aghazarm, C. (eds.) (2009) *Migration, Environment and Climate Change: Assessing the Evidence*, Geneva: IOM.

Lauterpacht, E. and Bethlehem, D. (2003) The Scope and Content of the Principle of *Non-Refoulement: Opinion*, in E. Feller, V. Türk, and F. Nicholson (eds), *Refugee Protection in International Law: UNHCR's Global Consultations on International Protection*, Cambridge: Cambridge University Press.

Leighton, M. (2006) Desertification and Migration, in P.M. Johnson, K. Mayrand, and M. Pacquin (eds), *Governing Global Desertification*, Aldershot: Ashgate.

Loughry, M. and McAdam, J. (2008) Kiribati—Relocation and Adaptation, *Forced Migration Review*, 31, 51–2.

McAdam, J. (2007) *Complementary Protection in International Refugee Law*, Oxford: Oxford University Press.

—— (2009) From Economic Refugees to Climate Refugees?, *Melbourne Journal of International Law*, 10(2), 579–95.

McAdam, J. and Loughry, M. We Aren't Refugees, *Inside Story* (30 June 2009), http://inside.org.au/we-arent-refugees.

——(2010a) 'Disappearing States', Statelessness and the Boundaries of International Law, in J. McAdam (ed.), *Climate Change and Displacement: Multidisciplinary Perspectives*, Oxford: Hart Publishing.

——(forthcoming 2011) Refusing Refuge in the Pacific: (De)constructing Climate-Induced Displacement in International Law, in E. Piguet, A. Pécoud, and P. de Guchteneire (eds.), *Migration, Environment and Climate Change*, Paris and Cambridge: UNESCO and Cambridge University Press.

——and Saul, B. (2010) An Insecure Climate for Human Security? Climate-Induced Displacement and International Law, in A. Edwards and C. Ferstman (eds.), *Human Security and Non-Citizens: Law, Policy and International Affairs*, Cambridge: Cambridge University Press.

Meze-Hausken, E. (2000) Migration Caused by Climate Change: How Vulnerable are People in Dryland Areas?, *Mitigation and Adaptation Strategies for Global Change*, 5(4), 379–406.

Millar, I. (2007) There's No Place Like Home: Human Displacement and Climate Change, *Australian International Law Journal*, 14, 71–98.

Mimura, N. et al. (2007) Small Islands, in Parry et al. (eds.), *Climate Change 2007: Impacts, Adaptation and Vulnerability*, Cambridge: Cambridge University Press.

Morrisey, J. (2009) Environmental Change and Forced Migration: A State of the Art Review, *Refugee Studies Centre Background Review* (January 2009).

Mortreux, C. and Barnett, J. (2009) Climate Change, Mitigation and Adaptation in Funafuti, Tuvalu, *Global Environmental Change*, 19, 105–12.

Myers, N. (1993) Environmental Refugees in a Globally Warmed World, *BioScience*, 43(11), 752–61.

——(2005) Environmental Refugees: An Emergent Security Issue. Paper presented at 13th Economic Forum, Prague, 23–27 May.

——and Kent, J. (1995) *Environmental Exodus: An Emergent Crisis in the Global Arena*, Washington, DC: The Climate Institute.

Nicholls, R.J. and Tol, R.S.J. (2006) Impacts and Responses to Sea-Level Rise: A Global Analysis of the SRES Scenarios over the Twenty-First Century, *Philosophical Transactions of the Royal Society A*, 364(1841), 1073–95.

Nurse, L. et al. (2001) Small Island States, in J.J. McCarthy et al. (eds.), *Climate Change 2001: Impacts, Adaptation, and Vulnerability. Contribution of Working Group II to the Third Assessment Report of the Intergovernmental Panel on Climate Change*, Cambridge: Cambridge University Press.

Oliver-Smith, A. (2005) Applied Anthropology and Development-Induced Displacement and Resettlement, in S. Kedia and J. van Willigen (eds.), *Applied Anthropology: Domains of Application*, Westport, CT: Praeger Publishers.

Pearce, F. (2000) Turning Back the Tide, *New Scientist*, 165(2225), 44–7.

Ramcharan, B.G. (ed.) (1985) *The Right to Life in International Law*, Dordrecht/Boston: Martin Nijhoff.

Renaud, F. et al. (2007) Control, Adapt or Flee: How to Face Environmental Migration? *InterSecTions* No. 5.

Reuveny, R. (2007) Climate Change-Induced Migration and Violent Conflict, *Political Geography*, 26(6), 656–67.

Saul, B. (2006) *Defining Terrorism in International Law*, Oxford: Oxford University Press.

Schwartz, P. and Randall, D. (2003) *An Abrupt Climate Change Scenario and Its Implications for United States National Security*, Washington, DC: Global Business Network (October 2003), http://www.edf.org/documents/3566_AbruptClimateChange.pdf.

Shelton, D. (2001) Environmental Rights in P. Alston (ed.), *Peoples' Rights*, Oxford: Oxford University Press.

Shen, S. (2007) Noah's Ark to Save Drowning Tuvalu, *Just Change: Critical Thinking on Global Issues. Going Under: Climate Change*, 10(October), 18–19.

Sindico, F. (2007) Climate Change: A Security (Council) Issue?, *Carbon and Climate Change Law Review*, 1, 26–31.

Stern, N. (2007) *The Economics of Climate Change: The Stern Review*, Cambridge: Cambridge University Press.

Suhrke, A. and Visentin, A. (1991) The Environmental Refugee: A New Approach, *Eco-decision*, 2, 73–4.

Tong, A. (2008) President of Kiribati, Australian National University (19 June 2008), http://news.anu.edu.au/?p=437.

UNHCR, supported by the International Organization for Migration and the Norwegian Refugee Council (2009*a*) Climate Change and Statelessness: An Overview, Submission to the 6th Session of the Ad Hoc Working Group on Long-Term Cooperative Action (AWG-LCA 6) under the UN Framework Convention on Climate Change (UNFCCC), Bonn, 1–12 June 2009.

——(2009*b*) Climate Change, Natural Disasters and Human Displacement: A UNHCR Perspective (23 October 2008, revised 14 August 2009).

Verheyen, R. (2005) *Climate Change Damage and International Law: Prevention Duties and State Responsibility*, Leiden/Boston: Martinus Nijhoff Publishers.

Williams, A. (2008) Turning the Tide: Recognizing Climate Change Refugees in International Law, *Law & Policy*, 30(4), 502–29.

Wood, W.B. (2001) Ecomigration: Linkages between Environmental Change and Migration, in A.R. Zolberg and P.M. Benda (eds.), *Global Migrants, Global Refugees*, New York and Oxford: Berghahn.

Zetter, R. (2008) Legal and Normative Frameworks, *Forced Migration Review*, 31, 62–3.

Zhang, D. et al. (2007) Global Climate Change, War, and Population Decline in Recent Human History, *Proceedings of the National Academy of Sciences of the United States of America*, 104(49), 19214–19.

7

UNHCR and the Global Governance of Refugees[*]

Gil Loescher and James Milner

Introduction

The global governance of refugees differs from, and is more robust than, the governance of other areas of migration. A formal multilateral institutional framework for regulating states' responses to refugee flows has been in place for nearly six decades. Governments have also developed a range of international agreements and norms which are overseen by an international organization, the Office of the United Nations High Commissioner for Refugees (UNHCR). Unlike other migration organizations, UNHCR has a specific mandate from the international community to ensure the protection of refugees and to find a solution to their plight. Following a pattern set by the Office of the High Commissioner for Refugees, created by the League of Nations in 1921, UNHCR has a unique structure with a High Commissioner and staff both at headquarters and in the field.

UNHCR is also the guardian of the wider global refugee regime. The regime comprises a set of norms, rules, principles, and decision-making procedures that help define states' obligations towards refugees. It includes a number of inter-state agreements and practices. The centrepiece of the regime is the 1951 Convention relating to the Status of Refugees (1951 Convention), which provides a definition of who qualifies for refugee status and sets out the rights to which all refugees are entitled. The 1951 Convention also explicitly identifies UNHCR as having supervisory responsibility for its implementation and provides the Office with a normative framework based on international law to carry out its work and to regulate the regime. While a wider range of actors have come to play a more prominent role in the global governance of refugees,[1] UNHCR has remained at the centre of the global refugee regime.

189

This chapter consequently focuses on the mandate and evolution of UNHCR as the central actor of the global refugee regime. As argued in this chapter, UNHCR's role within the regime has changed over time. UNHCR has been a producer of norms within the regime, and has played a significant role in socializing new states in the principles of the regime. At the same time, UNHCR has been an actor in the regime whose power and influence has been eroded as a result of both the changing dynamics of forced migration and the changing interests of states. In addition, a wider range of issue-areas, such as security, the environment and economic concerns, have also influenced state responses to refugees, arguably frustrating international cooperation and compounding UNHCR's challenge of regime supervision.[2] That said, UNHCR remains the only international organization with a clear mandate responsibility for refugees and supervision of the wider refugee regime. It is therefore important to place UNHCR at the centre of any consideration of the global governance of refugees and trace how these broader factors have influenced the evolution of UNHCR and its ability to regulate the regime.

This chapter outlines how the international community has prioritized the human rights protection needs of refugees over other migrants and explains the difficulties that the international organization responsible for refugees has had in persuading states to observe their responsibilities to this group. It begins by identifying the roles and functions of UNHCR and the international refugee regime. It explains how UNHCR has used its powers of persuasion and socialization to influence states and how the regime has institutionally adapted over time in order to respond to an ever-expanding crisis of forced displacement. It then explores the tensions between the regime's normative agenda of promoting refugee protection and achieving solutions to refugee problems and the constraints and challenges of states' power and interests. Finally, the chapter concludes by examining how UNCHR and the international community might respond in the future to meet new and emerging challenges in forced migration and world politics and better adapt to address the ongoing tension between the power and interests of states and upholding refugees' rights.

UNHCR and the 1951 Convention

The growth of an international refugee regime has been a prime example of the increasing importance of global governance over the last sixty years. Contemporary international concern for refugees, centred around the concepts of international protection and human rights, has its origins in the immediate aftermath of the Second World War. The experience of persecution during the 1930s and 1940s, particularly the Holocaust and the emergence of human rights as an important theme of post-war institutions, had a significant impact on the response of states to victims of persecution who fled their home countries and sought refuge abroad.

Reflecting the spirit of the immediate post-war period, Article 14 of the 1948 Universal Declaration of Human Rights provided that 'everyone has the right to seek and enjoy in other countries asylum from persecution'. While this so-called 'right to asylum' was not enshrined in future agreements, significant new steps were taken to improve refugee protection. The UNHCR was created in 1950 in order to protect refugees and to ensure their eventual integration within either their country of origin or another country. The following year the international community formulated the 1951 Convention Relating to the Status of Refugees. Article 1 (A) 2 of the 1951 Convention defines a 'refugee' as 'any person who . . . owing to well-founded fear of being persecuted for reasons of race, religion, nationality, membership of a particular social group, or political opinion, is outside the country of his nationality and is unable or, owing to such fear, is unwilling to avail himself of the protection of that country'.

While the 1951 Convention was originally confined geographically to Europe, it was made universal by the 1967 Protocol to the Convention. More generally, the term 'refugee' has been broadened since the 1950s through regional agreements to cover a variety of people in diverse situations who need assistance and protection. The most notable of these expansions is found in the Convention Governing the Specific Aspects of Refugee Problems in Africa, a regional instrument adopted by the Organization of African Unity (OAU) in 1969, which, in addition to the 1951 Convention definition, defines a refugee as a person fleeing 'external aggression, internal civil strife, or events seriously disturbing public order' in African countries. The Cartagena Declaration of 1984 covering Central American refugees also goes further than the 1951 Convention by including 'persons who have fled their country because their lives, safety or freedom have been threatened by generalized violence, foreign aggression, internal conflicts, massive violation of human rights or other circumstances which have seriously disturbed public order'. In addition, refugee rights have been incorporated in other areas of international and regional law, thus providing a complementary source of legal protection to refugees.

These international human rights norms and regional refugee norms, particularly in Africa and Central America, are in fact much more inclusive and in keeping with the actual causes of flight for the vast majority of the world's refugees than are those of the 1951 Convention. They respond to the reality that most refugees are in fact fleeing generalized violence and severe human rights violations in which it is often impossible for asylum seekers to generate documented evidence of individual persecution required by the 1951 Convention. While causes of specific refugee movements may differ in terms of how they affect the direction, duration, and size of population displacements, most contemporary mass exoduses occur when political violence is of a generalized nature rather than a direct individual threat.

Recognizing these realities, UNHCR has (in practice) interpreted its mandate over the past several decades to include those who have been forcibly displaced from their countries because of internal ethnic or religious upheavals or armed conflicts. However, in recent years there has been great resistance in the West to this pragmatic expansion of the refugee definition and of the UNHCR's mandate. In the global North, the 1951 Convention definition, with its more specific focus on individuals and on persecution, is used for resettlement and asylum purposes, although groups of people at risk of death or grave harm from violence if returned home are often given temporary protection.

UNHCR and the global refugee regime

Today, UNHCR is widely recognized as the UN's refugee agency. The Office's 1950 Statute sets out a clear mandate focusing on two principal areas: ensuring refugees' access to protection and to durable solutions, namely their reintegration within their country of origin or the integration within a new country. UNHCR has also become the principal organization within the global refugee regime, the centrepiece of which is the 1951 Convention as it defines states' obligations towards refugees. The Convention also explicitly identifies UNHCR as having supervisory responsibility for its implementation. UNHCR, therefore, has responsibility for monitoring and supporting states' compliance with the norms and rules that form the basis of the global refugee regime.

In addition, the 1951 Convention defines a list of rights for refugees. Because refugees are individuals who have fled their home country and no longer enjoy the legal protections afforded to citizens of a state, the Convention stipulated that refugees should have access to national courts, the right to employment and education, and a host of other social, economic, and civil rights on par with nationals of the host country. Arguably the most significant right granted to refugees by the 1951 Convention is *non-refoulement*, the right of refugees not to be returned to a country where they risk persecution. *Non-refoulement* remains the cornerstone of global refugee protection and, as a principle of customary international law, is understood to be binding on all states in the international system (Goodwin-Gill 1996: 167–71).

Given the status of the principle of *non-refoulement*, states are generally understood to have a duty to offer, at minimum, temporary protection to refugees on their territory. The responsibility to host refugees therefore falls primarily on those states neighbouring refugee-producing countries, with most states consequently hosting refugees due to an 'accident of geography' (Hathaway and Neve 1997: 141). As a result, there is an uneven distribution of refugees between countries, which results in 'some countries bearing a disproportionate share of the refugee burden, while others bear little or none of these responsibilities' (Rutinwa 1999: 6). To address this unequal distribution, it has been argued that there is an international collective responsibility to uphold the principle of *non-refoulement* through international cooperation and the sharing of the diverse costs associated with granting asylum more equitably among a greater number of states (Milner 2005). This practice, known as 'burden sharing', has been recognized as 'a virtual *sine qua non* for the effective operation of a comprehensive *non-refoulement* policy' (Fonteyne 1983: 175).

The changing political interests of states since 1950 have increasingly frustrated efforts to negotiate and sustain international cooperation and burden sharing in the global refugee regime. UNHCR and the global refugee regime were established in the aftermath of the Second World War, which was a time when principles of human rights played a significant role in the establishment and shaping of global institutions. During the past six decades, however, the international refugee protection regime has faced the difficult challenge of persuading states to meet their obligations towards refugees during a period of rapidly changing world politics. The Cold War, the aftermath of the Cold War, and the so-called post 9/11 era have not only shaped world politics but have also strongly influenced the way states have responded to refugees. In response to this changing international political context, UNHCR faces the challenge of upholding the norms of the regime and encouraging international cooperation while adapting its work to meet the opportunities and constraints posed by the changing context of world politics.

UNHCR's understanding of its mandate has consequently undergone a number of changes, and the scope of its work has been expanded over time thereby expanding the scope of the global refugee regime. In the 1960s and 1970s, for example, UNHCR shifted its focus from providing legal protection to refugees fleeing communist regimes in Eastern Europe and became increasingly involved in refugee situations in the global South. During the 1960s, violent decolonization and post-independence strife generated vast numbers of refugees in Africa. Refugee emergencies during the next decade emerged on all continents. Mass exoduses from East Pakistan, Uganda, and Indochina, highly politicized refugee crises in Chile and Argentina, and the repatriation of refugees and internally displaced persons (IDPs) in southern Sudan expanded UNHCR's mission around the globe. The 1980s saw the Office shift away from its traditional focus on legal protection and assume a growing role in providing assistance in millions of refugees in camps and protracted situations in Southeast Asia, Central America and Mexico, South Asia, the Horn of Africa, and Southern Africa. The 1990s saw it assume a wider role in providing massive humanitarian relief and engaging in repatriation operations across the Balkans, Africa, Asia, and Central America. The late 1990s and early twenty-first century have seen UNHCR take on ever greater responsibility for the victims of some major natural disasters and for the protection of IDPs, who, unlike refugees, have not crossed an international border. The expansion of the Office's work to include these new areas has often been controversial, and there have been concerns that UNHCR has been used by states in ways that may contradict or undermine its refugee protection mandate.

Within this process of adaptation and expansion, UNHCR has had little political power of its own. In the international political system today, states remain the predominant actors. But this does not mean that UNHCR is not entirely without means to uphold its normative agenda. In the past, most High Commissioners and their executive staff have realized that in order to shape state behaviour they had to exert their leadership skills and use the power of their expertise, ideas, strategies, and legitimacy to alter the information and value contexts in which states made policy. The Office has tried to project refugee norms into an international system dominated by states that are, in turn, driven by concerns of national interest and security. Successful High Commissioners have convinced states that they can ensure domestic and inter-state stability and can reap the benefits of international cooperation by defining their national interests in ways compatible with protection norms and refugee needs. In promoting its normative agenda, UNHCR is further supported by non-state actors who act as norm entrepreneurs through developing and disseminating new norms and through political advocacy and persuasion.

UNHCR not only promotes the implementation of refugee norms, it also monitors compliance with international standards. Both the UNHCR Statute and the 1951 Convention authorize the organization to 'supervise' refugee Conventions. This opens up the possibility for the UNHCR to make judgements or observations about state behaviour under refugee law and to challenge state policies when they endanger refugees. For most of its history, the Office has acted as a 'teacher' of refugee norms. The majority of the UNHCR's tactics have mainly involved persuasion and socialization in order to hold states accountable to their previously stated policies or principles. Past High Commissioners have frequently reminded Western states that as liberal democracies and open societies they are obliged to adhere to human rights norms in their asylum and refugee admissions policies. Because the UNHCR possesses specialized knowledge and expertise about refugee law, states often deferred to the Office on asylum matters. This was particularly the case before the 1980s when the UNHCR had a monopoly on information about refugee law and refugee movements. During the early decades of its existence, the Office enjoyed maximum legitimacy as it simultaneously tried to define the refugee issue for states, to convince governments that refugee problems were soluble, to prescribe solutions, and to monitor their implementation.

In recent decades, however, UNHCR has lost its monopoly on information and expertise as states have questioned UNHCR's moral authority or simply ignored UNHCR in the interest of pursuing more restrictive asylum policies. As the scope of the global refugee regime has increased, efforts to ensure international solidarity and burden sharing have been more problematic. As outlined in the next section of this chapter, states, especially Northern states, have sought means of pursuing their interests in the global refugee regime by attempting to shift responsibility to other actors and by avoiding additional responsibilities. While its authority and legitimacy in the realm of asylum has consequently declined, the Office still has an influence on how states respond to refugees. Despite some serious setbacks, states tend to adhere to the core element of the global refugee regime—*non-refoulement*—for a range of political, legal, and ethical reasons, and violations of this principle are generally criticized by other states.[3]

UNHCR has not only acted as a transmitter and monitor of refugee norms but also socialized new states to accept the promotion of refugee norms domestically as part of becoming a member of the international community. This socialization occurred first in the 1960s and 1970s in the newly independent countries of Asia, Africa, and Latin America, and later in the 1990s in the republics of the former Soviet Union. The political leaders of most newly independent governments in Africa, Asia, and the Commonwealth of Independent States care deeply abut their international image and reputation and sought international legitimacy through cooperation with the UNHCR. High Commissioners sought to maximize their influence or leverage to affect the behaviour of states towards refugees, and different High Commissioners have used different strategies with varying degrees of success to accomplish these ends. In addition to exercising moral leverage to gain influence with states, High Commissioners have repeatedly tried to link the refugee issue to states' material interests. Material assistance programmes have provided the UNHCR with significant leverage. Many new states, particularly in the global South, were willing to adapt their behaviour to UNHCR pressures for purely instrumental reasons. International humanitarian assistance has sometimes provided resource-strapped governments with the means to cope with influxes of refugees. Thus, through a mixture of persuasion, socialization, and material incentives, UNHCR has communicated the importance of refugee norms and convinced many new states that the benefits of signing the refugee legal instruments and joining the UNHCR Executive Committee—either as a member or an observer—outweighed the costs of remaining outside the global refugee regime. Thus, while UNHCR is constrained by states, the notion that it is passive in the global refugee regime, with no independent agenda of its own, is not borne out by the empirical evidence of the past half-century.

Constraints on UNHCR: changing state interests and political processes

While UNHCR has demonstrated its ability to act independently, it is important to understand how its activities and evolution have been defined and, at times, constrained by global politics and the interests of influential states within the global refugee regime. As stipulated by UNHCR's Statue, the organization is dependent on voluntary contributions to carry out its work. This gives significant influence to a limited number of states in the global North who have traditionally funded the bulk of UNHCR's operational budget. At the same time, UNHCR works at the invitation of states to undertake activities on its territory. UNHCR must therefore negotiate with a range of refugee-hosting states, especially in the global South. UNHCR is consequently placed in the difficult position of trying to facilitate cooperation between donor states in the global North and host states in the global South (Betts 2008). At the same time, UNHCR works within global changing contexts, with changing dynamics of displacement, and with a range of partners, both within and outside the UN system. This section will trace how these political constraints affect the functioning of the global refugee regime, the ability of UNHCR to fulfil its mandate, and how UNHCR has tried to respond.

While UNHCR frequently finds itself caught between the norms that underpin the global refugee regime and the competing interests of states, these dynamics are further influenced by changes in world politics. For example, the end of the Cold War not only presented UNHCR with an unprecedented opportunity to resolve some of the world's longest standing refugee situations but also presented new challenges to the organization. The optimism that characterized the end of the Cold War quickly evaporated as the international community failed to effectively respond to a number of new crises, including the collapse of Somalia, the break-up of the former Yugoslavia, and genocide in Rwanda. Each of these crises witnessed significant and complex dynamics of forced displacement, and UNHCR was called upon to play a more prominent role. By engaging more directly in debates on new sources of national, regional, and international insecurity and by retooling itself to provide humanitarian assistance in intra-state conflicts, UNHCR sought to encourage sustained international action on behalf of refugees. Instead, governments used humanitarian relief as a substitute for political action to address the root causes of mass displacement. This response placed a significant strain on UNHCR's operational ability to respond while upholding its mandate of ensuring protection.

These challenges were compounded by the fact that states in the global North and South adopted a series of increasingly restrictive asylum policies through the 1990s, placing additional strain on UNHCR and the global refugee regime. In the North, the period since the end of the Cold War has been marked by a shift 'from asylum to containment' (Shacknove 1993), where Western states have largely limited the asylum they offer to refugees and have focused on efforts to contain refugees in their region of origin. In the South, which continues to host the vast majority of the world's refugees, states are also responding to the mass arrival and prolonged presence of refugees by placing limits on the quantity and quality of asylum they offer.

The asylum crisis in the North originated in the 1980s when the number of asylum seekers arriving in developed countries from conflicts in Africa, Asia, the Caribbean, Central America, and the Middle East began to rise significantly. For example, asylum applications in Western Europe rose from 20,000 in 1976 to 450,000 in 1990. While this rise in numbers is clearly significant, some commentators have rightfully concluded that 'rising asylum claims tell us what governments have been reacting to, but they do not tell us why governments have grasped with such alacrity measures designed to restrict and prevent rather than include and manage those striving for asylum' (Gibney 2001: 3). More significant was the fact that the majority of these asylum seekers came from developing countries, many of whom had travelled to the North with false documents and with the help of smugglers. At the same time, large numbers of illegal migrants used asylum channels to gain entry to Western countries. As outlined in Düvell's chapter in this volume, the rise of this so-called 'asylum-migration nexus' placed additional pressures on the global refugee regime.[4]

In response, Western states introduced a series of measures to reduce the number of individuals seeking asylum on their territory. These measures included non-arrival policies, such as carrier sanctions and visa requirements, diversion policies, such as safe third-country agreements, an increasingly restrictive application of the 1951 Convention, and a range of deterrent policies, such as detention of asylum seekers and the denial of social assistance. Over a period of some twenty years, Western states systematically eroded the principle and practice of asylum to the point where some states, like the United Kingdom, openly called for the scrapping of the 1951 Convention and a new global refugee regime, premised on containing refugees within their region of origin.[5]

These moves to contain refugees in their regions of origin, coupled with a rise in global refugee numbers in the early 1990s and the problematic response by the international community, has placed a significant strain on asylum countries in the South, especially in Africa and Asia. As refugee numbers continued to rise in the 1990s, states in the developing world also began to place restrictions on asylum. Some states limited the quantity of asylum they offered to refugees, by closing their borders to prevent arrivals, by pushing for the early and often unsustainable return of refugees to their country of origin, and, in exceptional cases, forcibly expelling entire refugee populations. More generally, states have been placing limits on the quality of asylum they offer to refugees, by denying them the social and economic rights contained in the 1951 Convention, such as freedom of movement and the right to seek employment. Many states in the South now require refugees to remain in isolated and insecure refugee camps, cut off from the local community, and fully dependent on dwindling international assistance.

The crisis of asylum in both the North and South has confronted UNHCR with a nearly impossible task. While mandated by the international community to ensure the protection of refugees and find solutions to their plight,

UNHCR cannot realize this mandate without the cooperation of states. As the global crisis of asylum emerged, states largely excluded UNHCR and increasingly devised their own responses to insulate themselves from the growing number of refugees seeking access to their territories. The lack of cooperation by states, coupled with the global impasse between Northern donor countries and Southern host states, has significantly frustrated UNHCR's activities in recent years.

In response to the decline in asylum in both the North and the South, the growing disillusionment of states with the 1951 Convention and the emergence of clear gaps in the protection framework, UNHCR launched a major initiative in late 2000 to seek a convergence between the protection needs of refugees and the interests of states within the global refugee regime. This process, called the Global Consultations on International Protection, brought together Northern and Southern states, non-governmental organizations (NGOs), recognized experts in refugee law, and UNHCR to 'shore up support for the international framework of protection, and to explore the scope for enhancing protection through new approaches, which nevertheless respect the concerns and constraints of states and other actors' (Feller 2003: 1). Lasting nearly two years, the Global Consultations process considered the broad range of concerns expressed by Northern and Southern states in the previous decade, including issues not specifically addressed by the 1951 Convention.

There were two major outcomes from the Global Consultations process. The first was a Declaration adopted by more than 100 states in December 2001 at a meeting in Geneva to mark the fiftieth anniversary of the 1951 Convention. The Declaration reaffirmed the importance of the 1951 Convention as the cornerstone of international refugee protection, and reaffirmed 'the fundamental importance of UNHCR as the multilateral institution with the mandate to provide international protection to refugees and to promote durable solutions'.[6] The most significant outcome of the process, however, was the Agenda for Protection, endorsed by the General Assembly in 2002.[7] The Agenda for Protection outlines a series of activities and priorities that were intended to meet the concerns of states and strengthen the international protection of refugees and asylum seekers. Structured around five Goals, the Agenda for Protection calls for specific action by UNHCR, states, and NGOs to enhance respect for the principles of the 1951 Convention, respond to the security implications of refugee movements, enhance burden sharing with countries of first asylum, make durable solutions more predictable, and address the specific protection needs of refugee women and children (Feller et al. 2003).

While comprehensive in scope, the Agenda for Protection has been limited in its impact in the years following its adoption. This may be for several reasons. First, the Agenda may have been too broad, addressing a vast range of issues without focusing on individual issues in depth. The Agenda was also not a binding agreement, and consequently suffers from the same limitations as other non-binding international agreements. Finally, the Agenda did not benefit from universal support within UNHCR. The Global Consultations process was widely seen within the organization as an initiative led by the protection sections of UNHCR and a final inheritance from the time of Sadako Ogata, High Commissioner from 1991 to 2000. In fact, elements of UNHCR began to distance themselves from the Agenda before it was formally completed. Shortly after assuming the position of High Commissioner in 2001, Ruud Lubbers announced a new set of initiatives that would begin before the Global Consultations ended, known as Convention Plus. This created significant confusion within UNHCR and frustration on the part of the donor community, who had provided significant financial support to the Global Consultations process. As a result, the status of the Agenda for Protection within the global refugee protection regime remains uncertain, and its potential largely unrealized. Many of the factors that undermined the potential impact of the process point to the need to consider internal and external dynamics that limit UNHCR's ability to show leadership in the global refugee regime, including UNHCR's structures, decision-making procedures, relations to external actors, and the significant role played by donor states.

While UNHCR is the only global organization with a specific mandate to ensure the protection of refugees and to find solutions to their plight, it is unable to pursue its mandate independently. Instead, UNHCR is structurally and operationally linked to a wide range of other actors in the international system, including donor and refugee-hosting states, other UN agencies, international, national, and local NGOs, and a number of other actors. UNHCR is also dependent on voluntary contributions from donors to carry out its work, and the interest and priorities of donor states have consequently played a significant role in the work and evolution of the organization.

UNHCR has worked with donor and host states, other UN agencies, and NGOs since its inception. The Office's relationships with these actors have, however, changed significantly over time, both in response to the changing nature of displacement and in response to UNHCR's evolving interpretation of its mandate. The most important of these relationships remains the Office's relationship with donors, who control the evolution and direction of UNHCR's work through the tight control of the organization's resources. At the same time, UNHCR has increasingly become a complex international organization with a truly global presence. In a wide range of operational contexts, the Office must respond to local political realities, dynamics, and interests as it seeks to advance its mandate.

Also significant is UNHCR's relationship with the wider UN system. The General Assembly resolution that established UNHCR in 1950 not only detailed the place of the new organization within the UN system but also states that the High Commissioner was to act 'under the authority of the General Assembly'.[8] This authority has played a crucial role in the expansion of UNHCR's mandate. While initially given a limited mandate, UNHCR turned repeatedly to the

General Assembly throughout the Cold War to authorize the Office's involvement in emerging refugee situations in Africa and Asia. Notwithstanding this support, there is a widespread perception within the UN system that refugees are UNHCR's 'problem'. This perception, likely a result of the territoriality and competition between UN agencies that dominated the 1990s, has frustrated efforts to articulate a more comprehensive and holistic engagement in issues relating to refugees.

Another significant role played by the General Assembly is in determining the size and membership of the Executive Committee of the Programme of the UNHCR (ExCom).[9] Established by the General Assembly in 1958, ExCom was initially to consist of twenty to twenty-five UN member states, selected 'on the widest possible geographic basis from those States with a demonstrated interest in, and devotion to, the solution of the refugee problem'.[10] While retaining authority over the work of UNHCR, the General Assembly mandated ExCom to perform a number of executive and advisory functions, arguably playing a significant role as the decision-making body of the global refugee regime. Today, ExCom is responsible for approving UNHCR's budget and programme for the following year, for reaching conclusions on international refugee protection policy issues, and for providing guidance on UNHCR's management, objectives, and priorities.

There are, however, a number of concerns about the effectiveness of ExCom as a decision-making body. First, there are concerns about the size of ExCom. As of April 2007, ExCom consisted of seventy-two member states.[11] This represents a significant growth in the number of ExCom members during its fifty-year existence. From twenty-five ExCom members at its first meeting, the number rose slowly in response to the increased membership of the United Nations, to forty-three members in 1988. With the end of the Cold War, however, the number has grown significantly. Almost thirty states have joined ExCom since the end of the Cold War. As a result of this rapid expansion, ExCom has become a large and cumbersome body. Not only are there too many participants but the issues are complex and numerous, and meetings are not really a forum for organizational guidance.

The composition of ExCom has also meant that many of the broad contours of international politics are reflected in ExCom deliberations, especially the increasing divide between industrialized states, who are traditionally the largest donors to UNHCR's programme, and developing countries, who host the overwhelming majority of the world's refugees. In an effort to overcome this North–South divide, ExCom has adopted the practice of a rotating chairmanship between Northern and Southern states. While this is an important step towards addressing some of the tensions that underlie ExCom meetings, more progress is clearly required.

There have also been concerns in recent years about the domestic refugee policies of a number of ExCom members. While member states are expected to have a 'demonstrated interest in, and devotion to, the solution of the refugee problem',[12] critics have argued that the actions of certain members represent some of the more significant breaches of international refugee protection standards. One refugee rights monitoring group found that longstanding member states such as Tanzania and the United States had engaged in *refoulement*, while member states such as Algeria, Bangladesh, and Kenya placed severe limitations on the freedom of movement and right to seek employment of refugees on their territory, notwithstanding the fact that they were all signatories of the major international refugee instruments which prohibits such acts.[13]

Given these shortcomings of ExCom as an authoritative decision-making body, individual donor governments and some key host states, not ExCom, have come to establish the priorities that guide UNHCR's programme. In fact, by far the most important relationship for UNHCR remains its relationship with donor countries. Since its creation, UNHCR has faced the challenge of how to fund its work. According to its 1950 Statute, 'no expenditure other than administrative expenditures relating to the functioning of the Office of the High Commissioner shall be borne on the budget of the United Nations and all other expenditures relating to the activities of the High Commissioner shall be financed by voluntary contributions'.[14] In the early days of the Office, when its work was primarily focused on legal protection in Europe, UNHCR operated on a very modest budget. It was not until the global expansion of the Office in the 1970s and 1980s that UNHCR's budget began to increase dramatically. UNHCR's budget now averages some US\$1 billion per year.[15] Given this dramatic increase in the organization's budget over the past fifty-five years, contributions from the UN Regular Budget now account for less than 3 per cent of UNHCR's annual budget. As a result, UNHCR is almost exclusively dependent on voluntary contributions to carry out its programmes.

This dependence is compounded by the fact that funding has tended to come from a relatively small number of so-called traditional donors, with around three quarters of its budget coming from its top ten donors. The unpredictability of funding and the concentration of donorship have placed UNHCR in a precarious political position. On the one hand, it has attempted to safeguard the integrity of its mandate by being seen to be politically impartial. On the other hand, its existence and ability to carry out its programmes has been dependent upon its ability to respond to the interests of a relatively small number of donor states.

The influence of states is increased through their ability to specify how, where, and on what basis their contributions may be used by UNHCR. This practice, known as 'earmarking', remains commonplace. In 2006, 53 per cent of contributions to UNHCR were 'tightly earmarked' for specific countries and activities, while 28 per cent were 'lightly earmarked' for specific geographical regions and only 20 per cent came with no restrictions (UNHCR 2007). Some states have used earmarking more than others. For example, the United States, the European Commission, and Japan exclusively earmark, while the Scandinavian states and the Netherlands have traditionally earmarked to a far lesser extent.

The practice of earmarking allows donors to exercise considerable influence over the work of UNHCR as programmes considered important by donors receive considerable support, while those deemed less important receive less support. For example, during the late 1990s, while the international community focused attention and resources on the crisis in Kosovo and East Timor, conflict and displacement in Africa were virtually ignored. This pattern continues almost a decade later as donor governments still give vastly disproportionate amounts of aid to a few well-known crises and trivial amounts of aid to dozens of other refugee programmes.

The fact that donors largely contribute to UNHCR on the basis of their own perceived interests makes the concentration of donors all the more problematic. In 2006, the top ten donors were the United States, European Commission, Japan, Sweden, the Netherlands, Norway, the United Kingdom, Denmark, Germany, and Spain, with all other countries accounting for less than a quarter of contributions to UNHCR. As a result, the interests of a relatively small number of Northern states have been highly influential in determining UNHCR's activities.

The most influential of all donor states, however, remains the United States. For decades, the United States has been by far the biggest donor in absolute terms, consistently providing more than 30 per cent of UNHCR's budget. In many ways, the United States represents the global hegemon within the refugee regime. Because of its size and relative power (Suhrke 1998), coupled with the role that refugees have played in US foreign policy since the Second World War (Loescher and Scanlan 1986), the United States has been willing to disproportionately fund the world's refugee protection regime. While the scale of US support has enabled UNHCR to carry out many of its programmes, American dominance has enabled Washington to determine many policy and personnel decisions within UNHCR.

The significant role played by a small number of donors and their interests places UNHCR in a challenging political position. On the one hand, the Office needs to have independent influence on the behaviour of states in order to fulfil its mandate responsibilities for the protection of refugees. On the other hand, UNHCR needs to attract voluntary contributions to pursue its work, and must therefore be seen to be relevant to its key donors and capable of responding to their concerns. Moreover, the belief that UNHCR is beholden to a relatively small number of Northern donors has also had an impact on the way the Office is often perceived by Southern states. These perceptions have further frustrated efforts at ensuring international cooperation within the global refugee regime. Reconciling the need to have an autonomous influence on states and supervising the refugee regime with being responsive to donor interests has been a precarious balancing act for the Office. At many stages in its history it has placed UNHCR on a 'perilous path', navigating between states' interests and the norms that it seeks to uphold (Loescher 2001).

A limited number of countries have also cooperated with UNHCR in the area of refugee resettlement,[16] defined as 'the making available in a third country, on a voluntary basis, permanent residence to a refugee who is in another country, in a manner where the resettled person enjoys...rights similar to nationals' (UNHCR, ExCom 2003: paragraph 6). Resettlement has long been a feature of the international response to refugee crises. During the Cold War, Western governments, led by the United States, used resettlement not only as a tool of protection for those in need but also as a means of highlighting the failures of communist regimes. In this way, large-scale resettlement tended to be focused on particular groups of refugees and driven by the foreign policy of Western states.[17] While the end of the Cold War removed many of these foreign policy motivations, domestic pressures, especially in the United States, sustained global resettlement programmes, and made resettlement activities more geographically diverse. As with financial contributions to UNHCR, the United States is the largest resettlement country. In fact, the United States has resettled more refugees in the past decade than all other countries in the world combined. Between 1975 and 2003, the United States resettled over 2.5 million refugees,[18] an undertaking which has reinforced US hegemony within the global refugee regime.

It is, however, important to note that while refugee resettlement remains a discretionary act of states, resettlement countries and UNHCR have cooperated in recent years to develop new areas of international resettlement policy. These new policies have emphasized the various benefits of resettlement: as a tool of international protection, as a durable solution and as an expression of international solidarity and burden sharing. There is a growing recognition that these benefits of resettlement are most effective when resettlement is approached strategically and in support of broader protection and durable solution strategies. As such, UNHCR has emphasized the 'complementary nature' of the three durable solutions, and the strategic use of resettlement as part of comprehensive responses to protracted refugee situations and the particular needs of various groups (UNHCR 2001). While critics of resettlement emphasize that it facilitates 'brain drain', is susceptible to fraud and abuse, and is an expensive durable solution that benefits only a limited number of refugees, EXCOM Conclusion on International Protection (No. 90 (LII)—2001), commended 'efforts made by States and by UNHCR to ensure the diverse uses of resettlement as an important tool of international protection, as a durable solution to be used strategically along with the other two durable solutions, as appropriate, as part of a comprehensive approach to enhance protection, and as an expression of international solidarity and a means of burden or responsibility sharing, particularly in countries of asylum coping with large numbers of refugees or protracted refugee situations'. In this way, resettlement represents an important and growing area of cooperation between UNHCR and states. While it is still unclear whether the use of resettlement will unlock other possible solutions for refugees left behind in countries of first asylum, resettlement represents an important area of future innovation within the global governance of refugees.

Towards a more effective UNHCR

Over the past five and half decades, the nature and scope of UNHCR's work has changed considerably in response to the changing nature of forced displacement. From a small Office of some thirty staff based mostly in Europe in the early 1950s, UNHCR is now a global organization with a staff of more than 6,500 in 116 countries. UNHCR now works not only with refugees but also with IDPs, returnees, stateless, and a number of other 'persons of concern'. With an increase in the number of persons displaced by natural disasters and a dramatic rise in the number of economic migrants in the world more generally, coupled with predictions that these numbers will rise further with global warming and globalization, the challenge of forced migration is likely to increase in scale and complexity in the future.

While the gradual expansion of UNHCR's activities has allowed the organization to grow and maintain its relevance to the interests of key donor states, it has also increasingly led to an over-expansion of UNHCR's activities, often in potentially contradictory ways. In fact, taking on an expanded role has had potentially negative consequences for protection and solutions. Despite expanding its work, the Office has struggled to ensure that the world's refugees have access to international protection and the range of rights contained in the 1951 Convention. States' unpredictable financial contributions and increasingly restrictive responses to refugees on their territories have meant that protection needs have been inadequately met. Meanwhile, UNHCR has been unable to fulfil the solutions aspect of its mandate, and the average duration of a refugee situation has nearly doubled in the past decade to a staggering eighteen years. In fact, some two-thirds of refugees in the world have been in exile for more than five years. The prevalence of these so-called 'protracted refugee situations' and the duration of their exile highlight the ongoing need to ensure refugees' timely access to durable solutions. These ongoing challenges further demonstrate the ongoing relevance of UNHCR's core mandate and the need to reinvigorate its focus on its central responsibilities rather than expanding into new and potentially contradictory areas.

While the relevance of UNHCR's core mandate therefore remains as salient as ever, the nature of displacement is fundamentally changing at the start of the twenty-first century. In particular, globalization, the 'War on Terror', and the changing nature of conflict represent key challenges for the Office. In all of these contemporary challenges, UNHCR's work is interconnected in complex ways with broader issue-areas such as migration, security, development, and peace building. In order to fulfil its core mandate of achieving protection and solutions for refugees, UNHCR cannot avoid engaging proactively with these areas. However, this is not an argument for UNHCR to infinitely expand its mandate and become a migration organization or a development organization, for example. Rather, it is an argument for a UNHCR that plays a facilitative and catalytic role in mobilizing other actors to fulfil their responsibilities with respect to refugees. In order to fulfil its core mandate of ensuring protection for refugees and a solution to their plight, UNHCR will need to become more focused and strategic in the advocacy, coordination, and facilitation role that it plays. To be able to play such a role, UNCHR will need to overcome some key challenges—its governance, transparency, and ability to secure funding—while developing ways of engaging more effectively with the UN system and the interests of states.

UNHCR's ability to attract funds remains a key political issue. The Office has historically been most successful in fund-raising not in situations in which it has adopted a technocratic approach to programming and appeal, but where it has been politically engaged and has recognized the challenges and opportunities presented at a particular historical juncture. Instances where UNHCR has been able to attract additional donor contributions was based on recognizing and engaging with the wider context of states' interests at the time, and then demonstrating the leadership to persuade states that those wider interests could be met through a commitment to refugee protection. The era of globalization and the post 9/11 context present both challenges and opportunities for UNHCR's donor relations. To be successful in reconciling donor relevance with a commitment to the integrity of its mandate, UNHCR's donor relations must incorporate an ability to recognize and engage with the broader political context within which donors make decisions to meet their interests through UNHCR. Concerns with terrorism, security, and migration control now dominate the concerns of donor states. Serving these interests uncritically risks the integrity of UNHCR's mandate; ignoring them risks UNHCR being bypassed.

Likewise, UNHCR must also consider how its authority and legitimacy can be preserved and bolstered, especially given the important role that UNHCR's moral authority has historically played in influencing state action. In particular, more can be done to increase the transparency and accountability of UNHCR, particularly regarding the decisions and programmes that affect the lives of the millions of refugees and displaced people for whom it works. Improvements can be made in the organization's decision-making regarding asylum seekers' deportation, release from detention, and eligibility for resettlement to a third country or humanitarian assistance. UNHCR too infrequently has structured dialogue and communication with refugee populations or their leadership. Thus, the principal beneficiaries of UNHCR services, the refugees themselves, often have little or no means to influence or recourse in cases where the Office's programmes or policies may be unsatisfactory or many even lead to harmful consequences.

UNHCR's effectiveness could also be enhanced by re-examining the composition and role of ExCom in light of its original mandate, especially given the role that ExCom could play in providing the formal accountability mechanism that UNHCR so desperately needs. To better serve this function, ExCom member states and UNHCR need to streamline the agency's governance arrangements by making ExCom a more assertive advisory body with serious oversight functions and a capacity for organizational guidance. As states scrutinize UNHCR, they need also to become more self-critical in their own roles in refugee protection and assistance. ExCom should reaffirm the core principles of refugee protection through the work of its Standing Committees, and member states should not undermine UNHCR by adopting policies that violate international refugee norms and set undesirable precedents for refugee protection elsewhere. These issues reinforce the potentially significant role that an independent monitoring mechanism could provide in the oversight of both UNHCR's programmes and state activities in refugee protection and assistance.

More generally, however, UNHCR may need to do more by doing less. In other words, UNHCR may be more effective in fulfilling its mandate not by assuming a greater range of responsibilities, but by placing greater emphasis on its ability to play a focused and strategic role in the areas of advocacy, coordination, and facilitation. In this way, UNHCR would play more of a catalytic role, fulfilling its protection and solutions mandate through closer cooperation with other actors in the UN system and international community more generally.

First, ensuring effective protection and access to solutions for refugees relies upon a UN system-wide approach. Although UNHCR is the principal international organization with responsibility for refugees, the refugee regime itself goes beyond UNHCR. Refugees should not be seen as exclusively UNHCR's responsibility. Rather, peace and security actors, development actors, and other humanitarian actors all need to recognize their role in refugee issues. UNHCR therefore needs to develop clearly defined partnerships with these actors and draw upon their expertise. In order for such collaborative agreements to be effective, the Office of the Secretary General and the General Assembly need to offer leadership to ensure that other agencies are aware of their responsibilities towards refugees and the need to work cooperatively with UNHCR. Within this overall framework, UNHCR would have a crucial role to play in coordinating, facilitating, and advocating for the response of the UN system.

Second, in order to ensure that states contribute to ensuring protection and solutions, UNHCR needs to become a more politically engaged actor. Being politically engaged does not require the Office to abandon its Statute obligation to being a non-political organization. Rather, it means that UNHCR should be aware of the highly politicized environment within which it works. This environment is largely determined by the interests and capacities of states. The enduring challenge for UNHCR when working with states is to facilitate and encourage international cooperation and burden sharing that is appropriate in scale, scope, and duration in responding to the global refugee problem.

Whether UNHCR uses issue-linkage to try to channel states' interests in other issue-areas into a commitment to refugee protection, or relies on its moral authority, it is clear that the Office cannot withdraw from recognizing and responding to world politics. Historically, UNHCR has been at its most effective when it has played a politically engaged role, and least effective when it has attempted to take on a passive and technocratic role. The challenge is to appeal to interests and engage with politics without being involuntarily shaped and moulded by political circumstances. Given UNHCR's central role in the global refugee regime, the future success of the regime will largely depend on UNHCR's ability to meet this challenge.

Notes

* This chapter is based on Gil Loescher, Alexander Betts, and James Milner (2008) *The United Nations High Commissioner for Refugees (UNHCR): The Politics and Practice of Refugee Protection into the Twenty-First Century*, New York: Routledge. The authors would like to recognize the equal role that Alexander Betts played in the original development of the arguments presented here.

1. For a discussion of the rise of other actors in the refugee regime, see Martin (2000).
2. For a discussion of the range of issue-areas that influence state behaviour in this area, see Betts (2008, 2009).
3. For a discussion of why these norms tend to be upheld, see Helton (2002).
4. For a useful discussion of the evolution of this issue and possible responses, see also Crisp (2008).
5. For a consideration of these proposals, see Loescher and Milner (2003). As the authors argue, such approaches would 'turn the notion of international solidarity on its head' by 'shifting the refugee burden away from richer, more stable countries and placing more of it on poor and unstable countries that already host the overwhelming majority of the world's refugees'. (2003: 604).
6. 'Declaration of States Parties to the 1951 Convention and/or its 1967 Protocol relating to the Status of Refugees', Geneva, 13 December 2001, HCR/MMSP/2001/09.
7. General Assembly Resolution 57/187, 'Office of the United Nations High Commissioner for Refugees', 18 December 2002.
8. General Assembly Resolution 428 (V), 14 December 1950, Annex, Statue of the Office of the United Nations High Commissioner for Refugees, chapter 1, paragraph 1.
9. For example, see General Assembly Resolution 61/136, 'Enlargement of the Executive Committee of the Programme of the United Nations High Commissioner for Refugees', 19 December 2006.

10. General Assembly Resolution 1166 (XII), 'International Assistance to Refugees Within the Mandate of the United Nations High Commissioner for Refugees', 26 November 1957.
11. UNHCR, 'Executive Committee Membership', http://www.unhcr.org/excom/ 40111aab4.html.
12. General Assembly Resolution 1166 (XII), 'International Assistance to Refugees Within the Mandate of the United Nations High Commissioner for Refugees', 26 November 1957.
13. See US Committee for Refugees and Immigrants (2006).
14. Chapter III (20), 1950 Statute of the Office of the High Commissioner for Refugees, Annex to UN General Assembly resolution 428/5, 14 December 1950.
15. Global Policy Forum, 'UNHCR: Top Ten Donors 1974–2005', http://www.globalpolicy. org.
16. Following is a list of resettlement countries (and their quotas) in 2003–4: Australia (4,000), Brazil (100), Benin (n/a), Burkina Faso (n/a), Canada (7,700), Chile (60), Denmark (500), Finland (750), Iceland (30), Ireland (10 families), the Netherlands (500), Norway (1,145), New Zealand (750), Sweden (1,000), the United Kingdom (500), the United States (70,000). Belgium, France, Spain, and Switzerland resettled individual refugees referred by UNHCR in 2003. As such, the global resettlement quotas for 2003 were approximately 90,000 refugees. See UNHCR, Resettlement Section, 'Easy Guide to Refugee Resettlement Programmes', Geneva: UNHCR, June 2003.
17. See Loescher and Scanlan (1986).
18. See Government of the United States of America, Department of State, Bureau of Population, Refugees and Migration, 'Cumulative Summary of Refugee Admissions: As of October 1, 2003', Washington, DC, 15 November 2003.

References

Betts, A. (2008) North-South Cooperation in the Refugee Regime: The Role of Linkages, *Global Governance*, 14(2), 157–68.
——(2009) *Protection by Persuasion: International Cooperation in the Refugee Regime*, Ithaca, NY: Cornell University Press.
Crisp, J. (2008) Beyond the Nexus: UNHCR's Evolving Perspective on Refugee Protection in International Migration, New Issues in Refugee Research, Working Paper No. 155, Geneva: UNHCR.
Feller, E. (2003) Introduction: Protection Policy in the Making: Third Track of the Global Consultations, *Refugee Survey Quarterly*, 22(2/3), 1–2.
——Türk, V., and Nicholson, F. (eds) (2003) *Refugee Protection in International Law: UNHCR's Global Consultations on International Protection*, Cambridge: Cambridge University Press.
Fonteyne, J.-P. (1983) Burden-Sharing: An Analysis of the Nature and Function of International Solidarity in Cases of Mass Influx of Refugees, *The Australian Yearbook of International Law*, 8, 162–88.
Gibney, M.J. (2001) The State of Asylum: Democratization, Judicialization and Evolution of Refugee Policy, New Issues in Refugee Research, Working Paper No. 50, Geneva: UNHCR.

Goodwin-Gill, G. (1996) *The Refugee in International Law*, Oxford: Clarendon Press.

Hathaway, J.C. and Neve, R.A. (1997) Making International Refugee Law Relevant Again: A Proposal for Collectivized and Solutions-Oriented Protection, *Harvard Human Rights Journal*, 10, 115–211.

Helton, A. (2002) *The Price of Indifference: Refugees and Humanitarian Action in the New Century*, Oxford: Oxford University Press.

Loescher, G. (2001) *The UNHCR and World Politics: A Perilous Path*, Oxford: Oxford University Press.

——and Milner, J. (2003) The Missing Link: The Need for Comprehensive Engagement in Regions of Refugee Origin, *International Affairs*, 79(3), 595–617.

——and Scanlan, J. (1986) *Calculated Kindness: Refugees and America's Half-Open Door Since 1945 to the Present*, New York: Free Press.

——Betts, A., and Milner, J. (2008) *The United Nations High Commissioner for Refugees (UNHCR): The Politics and Practice of Refugee Protection into the Twenty-First Century*, New York: Routledge.

Martin, S.F. (2000) Forced Migration and the Evolving Humanitarian Regime, New Issues in Refugee Research, Working Paper No. 20, Geneva: UNHCR.

Milner, J. (2005) Burden Sharing, in M.J. Gibney and R. Hansen (eds), *Immigration and Asylum from 1900 to the Present*, Santa Barbara, CA: ABC-Clio.

Rutinwa, B. (1999) The End of Asylum? The Changing Nature of Refugee Policies in Africa, New Issues in Refugee Research, Working Paper No. 5, Geneva: UNHCR.

Shacknove, A. (1993) From Asylum to Containment, *International Journal of Refugee Law*, 5(4), 516–33.

Suhrke, A. (1998) Burden-Sharing During Refugee Emergencies: The Logic of Collective Versus National Action, *Journal of Refugee Studies*, 11(4), 396–415.

UNHCR (2001) *New Directions for Resettlement Policy and Practice*, Standing Committee 21st Meeting, EC/51/SC/INF.2, 14 June.

——Global Consultations (2002) *Strengthening and Expanding Resettlement Today: Dilemmas, Challenges and Opportunities*, EC/GC/02/7, 25 April.

——(2003) *The Strategic Use of Resettlement*, Executive Committee of the High Commissioner's Programme (ExCom), EC/53/SC/CRP.10/Add.1, 3 June.

——(2007) *Earmarking Patterns in 2006*, Geneva: UNHCR.

US Committee for Refugees and Immigrants (2006) *World Refugee Survey 2006*, Washington, DC: USCRI.

8

Internally Displaced Persons

Khalid Koser

Introduction

Internally displaced persons (IDPs) are distinct from the other migrant types considered in this volume in three main ways. First, by definition, they have moved within and not across internationally recognized state boundaries. Second, IDPs are almost always citizens of the countries in which they have moved. They are entitled to the full rights of other citizens, as opposed to the limited rights granted to international migrants and refugees. Third, the primary responsibility for fulfilling the rights of the internally displaced falls on their own states, as opposed to host states or the international community.

IDPs share all of these characteristics with internal migrants, and it may be asked why it is legitimate to include a chapter on the former but not the latter in a volume concerned with the global governance of international migration, if for no other reason than that internal migration is a far more substantial global phenomenon than internal displacement. Three reasons are suggested and developed through this chapter. First, arguably, IDPs present a particular protection and assistance challenge for the international community, which is not to deny that some internal migrants experience human rights abuses and are extremely vulnerable. Second, whether or not it is misdirected, the international community has paid far greater attention and indeed developed some quite innovative approaches to developing a global response to internal displacement. Third, and as a result, there may be some, albeit limited, lessons to be learned from the international response to IDPs for the global governance of international migration.

In the first part of this chapter an overview of internal displacement is provided—including the definition of an IDP, current patterns and processes in internal displacement, and the particular vulnerabilities to which IDPs are often exposed. Thereafter, the main sections of the chapter consider the institutional, political, and normative issues pertaining to the governance of internal displacement. In the conclusion, the extent to which there are lessons to learn from international responses to internal displacement for the wider global governance of international migration is considered.

Internally displaced persons

Unlike the case of refugees, there is not a legal definition of an internally displaced person. The description provided in the Guiding Principles on Internal Displacement is descriptive, and is as follows:

> internally displaced persons are persons or groups of persons who have been forced or obliged to flee or to leave their homes or places of habitual residence, in particular as a result of or in order to avoid the effects of armed conflict, situations of generalized violence, violations of human rights or natural or human-made disasters, and who have not crossed an internationally recognized State border. (Guiding Principles on Internal Displacement 1998: 2)

The two defining characteristics of an IDP are therefore that they have moved involuntarily, and that they have not crossed an international border. While IDPs are usually citizens of their own country, this definition also encompasses international migrants who have been involuntarily displaced within their host country. Another distinction from the refugee definition is that the IDP definition is far wider, including a non-exclusive list of examples of causes of displacement that include natural disasters. People displaced by development projects such as the construction of dams or airports, or the clearance of urban slums, are usually also defined as IDPs. At the same time the definition deliberately excludes people moving internally for economic reasons, for example in response to poverty or unemployment.

According to the Internal Displacement Monitoring Centre (IDMC), the most authoritative source for statistics on internal displacement, there were at least 27 million IDPs displaced by conflict at the end of 2009 (IDMC 2010). The largest populations of IDPs were in Sudan (5 million), Colombia (between 3 and 5 million), Iraq (3 million), Democratic Republic of Congo (2 million), Somalia (1 million), Pakistan (1.2 million), Turkey (1 million); and at least 500,000 in each of Azerbaijan, India, Myanmar, and Zimbabwe. Although there are no published statistics, it has often been estimated that there may be a further 25 million people internally displaced by causes other than conflict. A possible total of 50 million IDPs worldwide compares with a current population of about 10 million refugees (UNHCR 2007).

Although it is increasingly disputed, the reason for focusing on IDPs as a special category is that they often experience particular problems as a result of their displacement (Mooney 2005). The sorts of problems faced by IDPs but not usually faced by citizens who are not displaced from their homes or those who move within their countries voluntarily include: lack of shelter and problems related to camps; loss of property and access to livelihoods; discrimination because of being displaced; lack of identity cards and other formal documents that are left behind, confiscated, or destroyed; lack of access to services; lack of political rights; problems relating to the restitution of or compensation for lost property; and challenges relating to return and integration. As a result, IDPs often run a higher risk than those remaining at home or than other internal migrants to have their children forcibly recruited, become victims of gender-based violence, be separated from family members, be excluded from education, be unemployed, and to suffer higher rates of morbidity and mortality.

A gradually increasing body of empirical evidence on IDPs has largely confirmed that they do indeed tend to be particularly vulnerable. At the same time, such studies demonstrate that the vulnerability of IDPs can reduce over time (Brookings-Bern Project on Internal Displacement and Georgetown University 2007), that it is important to distinguish particular vulnerable categories within IDP populations, and that in urban settings it can be difficult to distinguish IDPs from the urban poor in terms of their vulnerability (IDMC 2008). Equally, other research has demonstrated that those displaced internally may not necessarily always be the most vulnerable of conflict-affected citizens—for example, when compared to people who stay at home in conflict areas or in areas controlled by non-state actors (Zeender 2005).

The institutional framework

The Guiding Principles on Internal Displacement comprise the main 'international framework for the protection of IDPs', as affirmed by the 2005 World Summit Outcome Document (2005, para 132). They were compiled under the mandate of the Representative of the UN Secretary General on Internal Displacement (Francis Deng) at the request of the UN Commission on Human Rights (now the UN Human Rights Council) to elaborate an 'appropriate normative framework'.

The conceptual underpinnings for the Guiding Principles are as follows. First, although IDPs have departed from their homes, unlike refugees they have not left the country where they are normally citizens. Second, they can therefore invoke all human rights and international humanitarian law guarantees available to the citizens of that country. Third, the applicability of refugee law is not possible and would be dangerous, in that it would limit the rights of citizens in their own country. Fourth, IDPs experience a very special factual situation and have specific needs. It is therefore necessary, finally, to restate in more detail those legal provisions that respond to the specific needs of IDPs and to spell them out in order to facilitate their application in situations of internal displacement.

The Guiding Principles are, therefore, in essence a compilation of existing human rights and international humanitarian law, and refugee law by analogy, as it applies to situations of internal displacement. Even where language was used that was not found in existing treaty law, no new law was created, rather existing norms were restated in more specific language (Kälin 2006). The Guiding Principles do not comprise binding law—at best they comprise 'soft law'. They were drafted by experts and submitted to the Commission on Human Rights in 1998 as an expert text. They have not been negotiated or agreed by states.

Instead Deng and his successor Walter Kälin (the title of the mandate was changed to Representative of the UN Secretary General on the Human Rights of Internally Displaced Persons) have promoted a 'bottom-up' approach to try to build consensus. In fulfilling their mandates, both have emphasized convincing states and regional organizations to incorporate the Guiding Principles on Internal Displacement into domestic law and to adapt their existing laws (Kälin 2008). Presently, twenty-two governments have passed laws or developed policies relating to IDPs. In Africa these are Angola, Burundi, Liberia, Sierra Leone, Sudan, and Uganda; in Asia: India, Nepal, Sri Lanka, and Tajikistan; in the Americas: Colombia, Guatemala, Peru, and the United States; in Europe: Armenia, Azerbaijan, Bosnia-Herzegovina, Georgia, Serbia, Russia, and Turkey; and in the Middle East: Iraq. In addition, Nigeria and the Philippines are reportedly close to developing laws or policies.

There have been four broad models of legal adoption of the Guiding Principles (Wyndham 2006). One is a brief instrument simply adopting the Guiding Principles, as in the case of Liberia. A second is a law or policy addressing a specific cause or stage of displacement, for example Angola's norms on the resettlement of the Internally Displaced Population. The third is a law or policy developed to protect a specific right of the internally displaced, as in the Turkish Law on Compensation. The fourth model is a comprehensive law or policy addressing all causes and stages of internal displacement, such as Colombian Law 387 and the Ugandan National Policy for Internally Displaced Persons.

In addition to these national laws and policies, there have been several attempts to develop regional instruments that incorporate the Guiding Principles. For example, the Great Lakes Protocol on Internal Displacement includes an Article which requires states to adopt and implement the Guiding Principles on Internal Displacement. On 23 October 2009 the African Union adopted the Convention for the Protection and Assistance of Internally Displaced Persons in Africa.

The Representative of the UN Secretary General's role is primarily advocacy. The mandate has a nominal support office, and no dedicated budget. Both Kälin and his predecessor, Deng, have however maintained a unique partnership with the Brookings Institution in Washington DC, which has allowed them to mobilize funds, commission research, and in general be far more effective than most other representatives, Special Rapporteurs, and other special appointments by the UN Secretary General.

Institutional arrangements for operational assistance and protection for IDPs falls to the international community, but only in support of national authorities. The Guiding Principles are clear that:

> National authorities have the primary duty and responsibility to provide protection and humanitarian assistance to internally displaced persons within their jurisdiction. (Guiding Principle 3(1))

At the same time:

> International humanitarian organizations and other appropriate actors have the right to offer their services in support of the internally displaced. Such an offer shall not be regarded as an unfriendly act or an interference in a State's internal affairs and shall be considered in good faith. Consent thereto shall not be arbitrarily withheld, particularly when authorities concerned are unable or unwilling to provide the required humanitarian assistance. (Guiding Principle 25(2))

The experience of international responses to humanitarian crises in the last few decades has demonstrated serious deficiencies, in part arising from 'institutional gaps' and a failure to coordinate to fill these gaps. While certain categories of people have benefited from the assistance of distinct international organizations mandated to serve their interests (e.g. United Nations High Commissioner for Refugees (UNHCR) for refugees and United Nations Children's Fund (UNICEF) for children), others—in particular IDPs—have fallen into 'protection gaps'. No single agency has specific responsibility to protect IDPs, and the response to situations of internal displacement has tended to be ad hoc, with little predictability (Eschenbächer 2005).

In order to try to rectify this, member states of the UN called in 2005 for more predictable, efficient, and effective humanitarian action, and for greater accountability, when responding to humanitarian crises, especially in situations of mass internal displacement. The context was the wider UN reform process and overall humanitarian reform agenda. The Principals of the Inter-Agency Standing Committee (IASC) agreed as a result to a 'cluster leads' system according to which different UN agencies were appointed as leads in nine 'sectors' or areas of activity according to their areas of specialization. In December 2005, the 'cluster approach' was officially endorsed as a 'mechanism that can help to address identified gaps in response and enhance the quality of humanitarian action' (IASC 2006: para 2). While not limited to IDPs, the new approach did have as one of its major aims to address the need for a more predictable, effective, and accountable inter-agency response to the protection and assistance needs of IDPs.

The intention of the cluster approach is essentially to provide predictable action in analysing needs, addressing priorities, and identifying gaps in specific sectors in the field:

> It is about achieving more strategic responses and better prioritization of available resources by clarifying the division of labour among organizations and better defining the roles and responsibilities of humanitarian organizations within the sectors. (IASC 2006: para 5)

The approach attempts to raise standards in humanitarian response by ensuring that all sectors have clearly identified and accountable lead agencies that are mandated to be the 'first port of call' and 'provider of last resort' for their respective sectors. These responsibilities ultimately entail mobilizing relevant actors in a specific sector, developing response strategies based on needs, priorities, and gaps in that sector, and implementing projects and activities in order to respond to those areas deemed important by the cluster membership. In addition, it is each cluster lead's responsibility to ensure that operational priorities shift with the context, such as from emergency relief to early recovery to development.

A key element in the cluster approach's design is to strengthen strategic partnerships between non-governmental organizations, international organizations, UN agencies, and the International Red Cross and Red Crescent Movement in the field. It is incumbent on the lead agencies to find ways of involving all relevant sectoral actors in a collaborative and inclusive process so that they are given the opportunity fully to participate in setting and participating in the direction, strategies, and activities of the cluster.

Within this system, UNHCR agreed to be the cluster lead for IDPs during conflict-generated emergencies in three areas: protection, emergency shelter, and camp coordination/camp management. UNHCR also joined as a member in several other clusters, such as water/sanitation/hygiene (led by UNICEF), logistics (led by the World Food Programme), and early recovery (led by the United Nations Development Programme).

UNHCR has piloted the cluster approach among IDP populations in five African countries to date: Democratic Republic of the Congo, Liberia, Uganda, Somalia, and Chad. Initial evaluations have been generally positive, although certain challenges have recurred (ODI 2007). Some of these are operational, including identifying and deploying experienced staff; and the security of the environments in which they are working. Coordination between a significant number of partners in complex and dynamic situations has also proved difficult. More conceptual challenges have also emerged. One has been determining which people are of specific concern to UNHCR as an agency, as opposed to defining the target population for the purposes of cluster members as a whole. UNHCR has also been concerned that its activities with IDPs should not undermine its core mandate for refugees, either in terms of distracting resources, or by contradicting the right to asylum by 'anchoring' people in their own country.

The transition from emergency relief to early recovery and development has proved hard to coordinate, in part because of a lack of targeted funding from the international community. Finally, there have been some criticisms that the cluster approach risks replacing the role of national authorities, rather than supporting or supplementing it.

Political context

What drove the emergence of the Guiding Principles on Internal Displacement? Roberta Cohen, who was centrally involved from her base at the Brookings Institution in advocating for an international response to IDPs, has identified a number of factors (Cohen 2002). First, she cited a realization on the part of the international community of the security context for internal displacement; that large-scale internal displacement not only disrupts the stability of the countries affected but also can undermine regional and international security, as was the case in the Great Lakes and Balkans where the effects of national conflicts spilled across borders.

A second reason for the shift identified by Cohen was a change in the notion of sovereignty. Towards the end of the Cold War and in the post-Cold War era, with concerns about superpower retaliation diffused, new possibilities opened up for crossing borders and reaching people in need. In 1989, for example, the UN aggressively negotiated Operation Lifeline Sudan to provide assistance to those displaced internally there. This new notion of sovereignty has been crystallized in recent years in the form of the 'emerging norm' of the 'Responsibility to Protect', as discussed in the next section.

The growth in the numbers of IDPs also played a significant role. In 1982 the number of IDPs was reported at 1.2 million. By 1986 the number had risen to 14 million. In 1995 there were an estimated 20 million; and current estimates of at least 26 million indicate that the trend is upwards.

Finally, the asylum agenda has also been suggested to have influenced new attitudes to internal displacement. The oil crisis and its aftermath reduced the economic argument for resettling refugees, the end of the Cold War brought to an end political advantages, and rising numbers of refugees only compounded concerns to limit their numbers. Protecting and assisting people within their own borders came to be viewed as the first line of defence against refugee flows and rising asylum applications.

Such factors produced what Roberta Cohen has described as 'an emerging international responsibility' towards IDPs, demonstrated through the appointment of Francis Deng as the Representative of the UN Secretary General on Internally Displaced Persons in 1992. Although the position was voluntary and unfunded, it did nevertheless reflect a growing awareness that IDPs needed an international champion.

In 1998, Deng presented the Guiding Principles on Internal Displacement as international standards to help IDPs, and underscoring that governments have primary responsibility towards their own displaced populations, and that if they fail to discharge this responsibility then the international community has a right to become engaged.

Ten years ago there were convincing reasons not to try to develop a binding UN Convention on the human rights of IDPs (Kälin 2009). First, treaty-making in the area of human rights at the UN level had become very difficult and time-consuming. Deng felt that something more immediate was required to respond to the needs of the growing numbers of IDPs worldwide, and wanted to avoid a long period of legal uncertainty resulting from drawn-out negotiations. This approach was, in particular, justified by the fact that the Guiding Principles were not creating new law but restated, to a very large extent, obligations that already existed under human rights and international humanitarian law binding upon states. In this context, there was also a concern that negotiating a text that draws as heavily from existing law as the Guiding Principles might have provided some states the opportunity to renegotiate and weaken existing treaty and customary law.

Furthermore, having a treaty approved would by no means have guaranteed its widespread ratification by states confronted with internal displacement. Finally, there were concerns that to draft a treaty that combines human rights and humanitarian law as do the Guiding Principles was probably premature. In legal, institutional, and political terms, the distinction between human rights applicable mainly in peacetime and international humanitarian law for times of armed conflict still was so fundamental that strong opposition from many states and organizations was likely to take any attempt to combine both areas of law in a single UN convention.

The current Representative of the UN Secretary General on the Human Rights of Internally Displaced Persons, Walter Kälin, has maintained that most of these reasons still stand today, and that it would still be too risky to try to formulate a binding UN Convention (Kälin 2008). He has pointed out, for example, that negotiations on the 2005 World Summit Outcome Document showed that while the Guiding Principles were welcomed by all governments, many among them were still not ready explicitly to recognize their binding character.

At the time of the presentation of the Guiding Principles, the governments of China, Egypt, Sudan, and India were particularly vocal in their opposition (Cohen 2002). It was not always easy to discern exactly what they were objecting to: political reactions to the Guiding Principles on Internal Displacement cannot be divorced from reactions to the wider issues of the appointment of a Representative, and from his advocacy for the idea that the international community has the right to intervene where states fail to protect their own displaced populations. The government of China, for example, has regularly argued that no other state should interfere with the internal affairs of a sovereign state in the name of humanitarian assistance. Egypt, Sudan, and India have expressed concerns that humanitarian intervention may become the precursor for wider interference of powerful countries in the affairs of weaker states. These latter three countries have also questioned the purpose of and process for developing international standards on IDPs.

Resistance also emerged among certain humanitarian groups. Some objected to the breadth of the IDP definition, preferring to limit it to those to be defined as refugees if had they crossed an international border. Proponents of the wider definition, however, argued that people displaced by natural or human disasters were often also in need of assistance and protection and ran the risk of neglect or discrimination by their governments. The International Committee of the Red Cross expressed reservations, which it still holds, that the Guiding Principles may risk privileging displacement over vulnerability, by focusing attention on IDPs rather than other war-affected civilians in their country (Droege 2009). The response has relied on the growing body of empirical evidence demonstrating the particular needs and vulnerabilities for the internally displaced, and cited above.

A recent assessment also demonstrates how the political context often determines the impact of the Guiding Principles (Ferris 2009). In Burma they have been used to raise awareness about displacement and mobilize humanitarian assistance; on the other hand, they have offered little diplomatic or political leverage with which to influence national authorities there. During elections in Bosnia and Herzegovina and Kosovo, the Guiding Principles focused attention on the right to political participation for IDPs; still worldwide IDP political participation remains inconsistent. They have inspired the peace agreement between the Government and the Maoists in Nepal, but an effective IDP strategy is still not in place there. They informed the drafting of the African Union Convention for the Prevention of Internal Displacement and the Protection of and Assistance to Internally Displaced Persons in Africa; but its effectiveness will entirely depend on the level of compliance and degree of monitoring. They were issued to all members of the Ministry of Refugees and Accommodation, designated by the Government of Georgia to provide assistance to IDPs resulting from the recent conflict there; although the response of the government to the crisis has been criticized. They form the basis for Uganda's National Policy for Internally Displaced Persons; but there is still a very significant implementation gap in that country (Koser 2006).

The normative framework

Fundamentally, what underlies resistance to a binding Convention on IDPs, and forms the backdrop for the limited impact by the international community in terms of either advocacy or operations, is that most states are clear that internal displacement is a sovereign issue, and thus the preserve of states and not the international community.

In response, Deng and colleagues developed the notion of 'sovereignty as responsibility' (Rothchild et al. 1996). Focusing on conflict situations in Africa, this stipulated that when governments are unwilling or unable to fulfil their responsibilities towards their own displaced citizens, they should be expected to request—and accept—outside offers of assistance. If they refuse, or deliberately obstruct access and put large numbers at risk, the international community has a right—and even a responsibility—to intervene. Such intervention can range from diplomatic dialogue to negotiation of access, to political pressure and sanctions; or in exceptional cases to military intervention.

This idea has been elaborated, expanded, and formalized in the 'Responsibility to Protect' (R2P) concept, which has been the most significant normative development for responding to the needs of the internally displaced (Murthy 2007). R2P relates to a state's responsibilities towards its population and to the international community's responsibility in case a state fails to fulfil its responsibilities. One important aim, among others, is to provide a legal and ethical basis for 'humanitarian intervention': the intervention by external actors (preferably the international community through the UN) in a state that is unwilling or unable to prevent or stop genocide, massive killings, and other significant human rights violations (Evans and Sahnoun 2002).

The R2P concept was developed by the International Commission for Intervention and State Sovereignty (ICISS), responding to former UN Secretary General Kofi Annan's challenge to the international community to chart a more consistent and predictable course of action when responding to humanitarian crises, particularly when international intervention on humanitarian grounds and the violation of state sovereignty are at odds. In essence, the Commission proposed a change in terminology and perspective from the notion of the international community's 'right to intervene', which was inherently flawed according to the principles of state sovereignty, to newly understanding it as their 'Responsibility to Protect', which substantively makes it incumbent on the international community to provide 'life-supporting protection and assistance to populations at risk' (ICISS 2001: 17).

According to the Commission, the 'Responsibility to Protect' entails the 'responsibility to prevent', the 'responsibility to react', and the 'responsibility to rebuild'. When discussing the 'responsibility to react', the Commission argued that the R2P approach above all else requires that the international community reacts immediately to cases of compelling need for human protection. As its fundamental premise, the responsibility of the international community to react should take place when prevention measures fail and deadly conflict erupts imperilling the lives of citizens. The Commission strongly stated that all measures other than the deployment of military force—diplomacy, sanctions, arms embargoes, and so on—should be duly and comprehensively undertaken in an effort to resolve the population's suffering prior to considering military intervention.

The R2P framework has gained widespread international accreditation. The UN Secretary General's High Level Panel on Threats, Challenges, and Change in 2004 endorsed it as an 'emerging norm' to protect civilians from large-scale violence, and the Secretary General also supported the concept in his 'In Larger Freedom' report. In the 2005 World Summit Outcome Document, Heads of State also clearly and unambiguously accepted the collective international responsibility to protect populations from crimes against humanity. UN Security Council Resolution 1674, adopted on 28 April 2006, 'Reaffirm[ed] the provisions of paragraphs 138 and 139 of the 2005 World Summit Outcome Document regarding the responsibility to protect populations from genocide, war crimes, ethnic cleansing and crimes against humanity' and commits the Security Council to action to protect civilians in armed conflict. One concrete output has been that UN Peacekeeping Missions have increasingly been mandated with a 'Chapter 7 mandate' to aggressively protect civilians in conflict.

Supporters of R2P view it as a method of establishing a normative basis for humanitarian intervention and its consistent application. Detractors argue that R2P is a breach of the system of state sovereignty. Beyond the debate about its conceptual validity, the real challenge that confronts R2P is implementation. In two recent cases, genocide in Darfur, and Cyclone Nargis in Burma, the responsible states were either culpable for or at least failed to respond to the assistance and protection needs of affected populations, including those internally displaced, but at the same time refused international intervention. The R2P concept was invoked in both cases, but ultimately intervention was limited and largely ineffective.

Conclusion

While noting significant reservations, the preceding sections have nevertheless described a rather innovative response to the challenge of protecting and assisting IDPs, combining the development of 'soft law', a 'bottom-up' consensus-building approach, a unique relationship between a UN Representative and a research institution, a concerted effort at better institutional coordination, and considerable political momentum towards a normative framework to legitimize intervention. Bearing in mind the very significant differences between IDPs and international migrants, outlined in the introduction to this chapter, it is worth nevertheless considering whether there are any lessons to learn for the global governance of international migration.

The Guiding Principles 'model', namely to collate into a single, accessible document the variety of existing laws, principles, and norms that apply to a given situation in order to provide guidance to states, has been cited by several commentators as one way to address the challenge of protecting vulnerable international migrants. The Global Commission on International Migration, for example, observed in its final report that:

> the legal and normative framework affecting international migrants is dispersed across a number of treaties, customary law provisions, non-binding agreements and policy understandings. As a result, the provisions relevant to the protection of migrants' rights are not articulated in a clear and accessible manner; this has added to the difficulties of consistent implementation of the provisions and thus respect for migrants' rights. The Commission sees the value of articulating the legal and normative framework in a single compilation of all treaty provisions and other norms that are relevant to international migration and the human rights of migrants.

Alexander Betts has been more specific, proposing the compilation of the 'Guiding Principles on the Protection of Vulnerable Irregular Migrants' (Betts 2008). He has identified two particular migrant categories that currently fall within 'protection gaps', much as have IDPs, namely: irregular migrants with protection needs resulting from conditions in their country of origin unrelated to conflict or political persecution (such as those fleeing the effects of climate change), and irregular migrants with protection needs arising as a result of movement (e.g. stranded migrants).

The experience of the 1990 International Convention on the Protection of the Rights of All Migrant Workers and Members of Their Families reinforces the argument for such a 'soft law' approach to irregular migrants. The 'Migrant Workers' Convention'—a binding UN Convention—already sets out in a single instrument the rights to which migrants are entitled; most of these rights having also already been accepted by states through their ratification of the six other core human rights treaties and ILO labour standards. But unlike the Guiding Principles on Internal Displacement, in a few instances the 'Migrant Workers Convention' extends existing rights contained in other 'core' treaties. Furthermore, although the Convention distinguishes between migrant workers with regular and irregular status, and specifies certain rights only for regular migrants, it protects the fundamental rights of all migrant workers. Relatively few states (thirty-seven to date) have ratified the Convention, and among the reasons cited is: because it provides migrants (especially those who have moved in an irregular manner) with rights that are not to be found in other human rights treaties, and because it generally disallows differentiation between migrants who have moved in a regular or irregular manner (GCIM 2005).

Betts has also suggested that the 'cluster approach' as applied to protecting and assisting IDPs is also instructive for trying to fill an institutional gap in responsibility for protecting vulnerable irregular migrants. In the context of 'mixed flows' and the 'asylum-migration nexus', it can be hard to discern what category such migrants fall into and which institutions are mandated to respond to their needs. In particular, what is required is greater clarity concerning which organization is responsible at a field level.

At the level of advocacy, there may also be lessons to learn from the relationship developed between the Representative of the Secretary General and the Brookings Institution. There would appear to be the opportunity for similar relationships to develop between a number of migration-oriented Special Representatives or Special Rapporteurs, and burgeoning policy-oriented research centres on refugees and migration issues.

Finally, it is worth considering the implications for the global governance of international migration of the growing political consensus around the R2P. For example, might the concept encompass, and expand, recent initiatives by origin states for migrants to extend protection to their citizens overseas, for example through the exercise of consular protection.

Although it has not been its primary purpose, this chapter has also elaborated on the reasons presented in the 'Introduction' to justify a focus on internal displacement—but not internal migration—in a volume concerned with international migration. At the same time, the analysis here does open up a debate about to the extent to which internal migration is also an area that might require an international response. Some internal migrants are certainly very vulnerable—for example those trafficked inside their own countries—and some experience direct discrimination and even persecution by their own states. What is more, in certain settings, such as movements arising from the effects of climate change, it may become more and more difficult to clearly distinguish voluntary from forced migration. Certainly, there is no reason why the R2P concept cannot be invoked to protect internal migrants or indeed non-mobile citizens in their own countries. The Guiding Principles on Internal Displacement explicitly exclude voluntary migration and could not be extended to cover internal migration more widely, but the way in which they have been formulated and articulated would provide a valuable template for protecting vulnerable internal migrants.

All of this is not by any means to say that international responses to protecting and assisting IDPs have necessarily always been effective or successful, and some of the reservations have been posted through the chapter. What is more, the protection and assistance of IDPs faces its own new challenges. The rights of the majority of the 25 million people already internally displaced by conflict and many millions more by natural disasters and development projects are poorly protected now, and the effects of climate change will almost certainly increase their number and further test protection in law and practice.

References

Betts, A. (2008) Towards a 'Soft Law' Framework for the Protection of Vulnerable Migrants, New Issues in Refugee Research 162, Geneva: UNHCR.

Brookings-Bern Project on Internal Displacement and Georgetown University (2007) *When Displacement Ends: A Framework for Durable Solutions*, Washington, DC: Brookings-Bern Project on Internal Displacement.

Cohen, R. (2002) Nowhere to Run, No Place to Hide, *Bulletin of the Atomic Scientists*, 58(6), 36–45.

Droege, C. (2009) Developments in the Legal Protection of IDPs, *Forced Migration Review*, Special Issue: Ten Years of the Guiding Principles on Internal Displacement, 8–9.

Eschenbächer, J.-H. (2005) The Global Internal Displacement Crisis: Recent Developments and Perspectives for an Improved International Response, *Refugee Survey Quarterly*, 24, 49–60.

Evans. G. and Sahnoun, M. (2002) The Responsibility to Protect, *Foreign Affairs*, November/December.

Ferris, E. (2009) Assessing the Impact of the Principles: An Unfinished Task, *Forced Migration Review*, Special Issue: Ten Years of the Guiding Principles on Internal Displacement, 10–11.

Global Commission on International Migration (GCIM) (2005) *Migration in an Interconnected World: New Directions for Action*, Geneva: GCIM.

Inter-Agency Standing Committee (IASC) (2006) *Guidance Note on Using the Cluster Approach to Strengthen Humanitarian Responses*, Geneva: IASC.

Internal Displacement Monitoring Centre (IDMC) (2010) *Global Overview of Internal Displacement in 2009*, Geneva: IDMC.

——(2008) *Internal Displacement to Urban Areas: The Tufts-IDMC Profiling Study*, Geneva: IDMC.

International Commission on Intervention and State Sovereignty (ICISS) (2001) *The Responsibility to Protect*, New York: ICISS.

Kälin, W. (2005) The Guiding Principles as International Minimum Standards and a Protection Tool, *Refugee Survey Quarterly*, 24, 27–36.

——(2006) The Future of the Guiding Principles on Internal Displacement, *Forced Migration Review*, Special Issue: Putting IDPs on the Map: Achievements and Challenges, 5–6.

——(2008) The Future of the Guiding Principles, *Forced Migration Review*, Special Issue: Ten Years of the Guiding Principles on Internal Displacement, 38–40.

Koser, K. (2006) Concluding Statement, Workshop on the Implementation of the Republic of Uganda's National Policy on Internally Displaced Persons, http://www.brookings.edu/speeches/2006/0704humanrights.aspx.

Mooney, E. (2005) The Concept of Internal Displacement and the Case for IDPs as a Category of Concern, *Refugee Survey Quarterly*, 24, 9–26.

Murthy, J. (2007) Mandating the Protection Cluster with the Responsibility to Protect, *Journal of Humanitarian Assistance*, October.

Overseas Development Institute (ODI) (2007) *Cluster Approach Evaluation*, London: ODI.

Rothchild, D., Deng, F., Zartman, I.W., Kimaro, S., and Lyons, T. (1996) *Sovereignty as Responsibility: Conflict Management in Africa*, Washington, DC: Brookings Institution Press.

United Nations High Commissioner for Refugees (UNHCR) (2007) *Statistical Yearbook 2007*, Geneva: UNHCR.

World Summit Outcome (2005) UN Dov A/60/L.1.

Wyndham, J. (2006) A Developing Trend: Laws and Policies on Internal Displacement, http://www.brookings.edu/articles/2006/winter_humanrights_wyndham.aspx.

Zeender, G. (2005) Engaging Armed Non-State Actors in IDP Protection, *Refugee Survey Quarterly*, 24, 96–111.

9

Human Trafficking and Smuggling

Susan Martin and Amber Callaway

Introduction

In recent years, the trafficking of people for sexual exploitation and forced labour has become one of the fastest growing areas of international criminal activity and one that is of increasing concern to the international community. Trafficking is generally thought of as the movement of a person across national borders, but trafficking within countries is also common, and perhaps occurs to an even greater extent than transnational trafficking.

This chapter begins with background information on human trafficking. It continues with descriptions of the legal and institutional frameworks for combating trafficking. We argue that using a combination of international instruments, particularly the Protocol to Prevent, Suppress and Punish Trafficking in Persons, Especially Women and Children, the United Nations(UN) Convention Relating to the Status of Refugees, and the Guiding Principles on Internal Displacement, creates a stronger framework for protecting victims of trafficking than using the Protocol on its own. The August 2010 launch of the UN Global Plan of Action against trafficking represents a promising step in combatting these practices, but to be effective, it will necessitate improved cooperation with the international community. We also argue for a more effective mechanism to ensure that the multifaceted international and regional responses to trafficking are coordinated, monitored, and assessed.

Background

Human trafficking affects millions of people around the globe and reaps billions in profits. Trafficking is considered one of the most pressing human rights issues in the world today.[1] Recognizing the growth in trafficking operations, states adopted the Protocol to Prevent, Suppress and Punish Trafficking in Persons,

Especially Women and Children (hereafter called the Palermo Protocol) in 2003, which supplements the UN Convention against Transnational Organized Crime.[2] The trafficking Protocol provides the first common normative definition on trafficking in human beings. It requires cooperation from states in combating trafficking and encourages them to pass preventative trafficking measures. The Protocol defines trafficking (which includes trafficking within countries) as:

> The recruitment, transportation, transfer, harboring or receipt of persons, by means of the threat or use of force or other forms of coercion, of abduction, of fraud, of deception, of the abuse of power or of a position of vulnerability or of the giving or receiving of payments or benefits to achieve the consent of a person having control over another person, for the purpose of exploitation. Exploitation shall include, at a minimum, the exploitation of the prostitution of others or other forms of sexual exploitation, forced labour or services, slavery or practices similar to slavery, servitude or the removal of organs.

Therefore, the defining elements of trafficking are the activity, the means, and the purpose, where: (a) the *activity* refers to some kind of movement either within or across borders, (b) the *means* relates to some form of coercion or deception, and (c) the *purpose* is the ultimate exploitation of a person for profit or benefit of another (IOM 2004). Where people are vulnerable because of ignorance, need, war, poverty, crisis, desperation, marginalization, and fear, they are at risk of falling into the hands of those who wish to exploit them. Internal trafficking, and trafficking in general, often goes undiscovered and underestimated, which presents a specific challenge to understanding the scope and magnitude of its occurrence.

A wide range of estimates exists on the number of trafficking victims around the world. The US Department of State (2007) estimated that 800,000 people are trafficked across national borders each year; however, when trafficking within borders is included, estimates increase to 2–4 million people annually (Miko 2006). In 2005, the International Labour Organization (ILO) estimated that there were at least 2.45 million people in forced labour as a result of internal and transnational trafficking, which represents 20 per cent of total forced labour around the world (Belser et al. 2006). Figure 9.1 displays the ILO

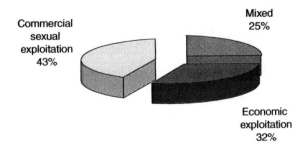

Figure 9.1. Trafficked forced labour by form

Table 9.1. Forced labour outcome of trafficking

	Total number of victims
Industrialized economies	270,000
Transition economies	200,000
Asia and the Pacific	1,360,000
Latin America and the Caribbean	250,000
Sub-Saharan Africa	130,000
Middle East and North Africa	230,000
World	2,450,000

estimates of both internal and transnational trafficking by form, and Table 9.1 displays the ILO estimates for the number of victims by geographical region.

Causes and consequences of human trafficking

Trafficking can often be described as migration gone terribly wrong (Feingold 2005). There is a great deal of confusion between trafficking and migration; although inter-related, they are two separate and distinct issues. Migration is generally thought of as the movement of people from poorer to wealthier countries; however, many more people migrate within their own borders, usually from rural to urban or high-tourist areas (ILO 2003). As is true of international migrants, internal migrants usually move in search of work, to flee persecution, or just because they want to live somewhere else. Migrants can be skilled and educated professionals attracted to better opportunities, or un-skilled, uneducated, and unemployed individuals trying to escape the poverty trap. When people choose to move and the result is a life free from exploitation and coercion, they are migrants and not trafficking victims. However, where migration takes on elements of coercion, force, or exploitation, it becomes trafficking. The connection of trafficking and migration tends to be linked to the vulnerability of people once they are isolated from their homes and families, and therefore displaced.

Trafficking takes many forms. Women and young girls are lured from their homes and forced into prostitution in large cities, sex tourism areas, or near military bases. Men and women of all ages are forced to work in commercial agriculture, fishing industries, mines, and sweatshops. Sometimes they are lured from their homes by recruiters who promise well-paying jobs, a brighter future, or an exciting life in the big city. In other cases, poor families who are unable to support their children may sell them into forced marriages, domestic servitude, or prostitution in exchange for money or to pay off debts. They are subsequently forced to toil under the control of marketers, touts, and pimps in the streets and marketplaces of large urban areas under conditions that seriously threaten their health, safety, and development. In many cases, their most basic rights, such as freedom of movement, are suppressed and thus they become both trafficking victims and displaced persons.

More specifically, trafficking for labour and sexual exploitation takes the following forms.

Domestic servants

Trafficking of women and girls, particularly, to work as domestic servants is common throughout the world. Because domestic workers live within the confines of private homes, they are perhaps the most invisible of all trafficking victims (Fyfe 1989). Both adults and children are implicated. Save the Children (2007) estimates that there are 200,000 child domestic workers in Kenya, 550,000 in Brazil, 264,000 in Pakistan, 100,000 in Sri Lanka, and 150,000 in the Peruvian capital, Lima. Child domestic servants, usually girls, are sold or given to families or distant relatives to serve as household help. They generally work extended hours and often experience sexual abuse by their employers. Often they are not paid for their services. While most domestic servants would not be considered to have been trafficked, if their passports are taken away, they have limited or no opportunity to leave the home, are not paid the promised wage, or are otherwise exploited, then trafficking has occurred.

Slavery and bonded labour

Bonded labour is prevalent in many countries; whereby individuals are indebted to their employer and unable to stop working until the debts have been cleared. It occurs throughout the world, although concrete data is hard to come by due to the fact that it is often found in informal, unregulated, or illegal sectors of the economy. Entering debt bondage to pay for smuggling fees is particularly common. Although those who are smuggled are distinguished from those who are trafficked in that they voluntarily enter into an agreement with the smuggler, when debt bondage occurs, smuggling may well turn into trafficking.

In some countries, such as Niger and Mali, caste-based slavery practices rooted in ancestral master–slave relationships are present in isolated parts of the country. In fact, an estimated 8,800 Nigerians are reported to live in conditions of traditional slavery.[3] Slavery and bonded labour is most common among the economically vulnerable and uneducated members of society, such as minority ethnic or religious groups, or the lowest classes or castes. In some cases, parents accept money in return for their children working, and these children are forced to live with the money-lender in their workplace until the debt is completely repaid. In other cases, entire families are enslaved as the debt passes from generation to generation. They live in extreme poverty, isolated from the rest of the society, and have absolutely no control over their own lives. Many are illiterate and therefore unable to understand how much they owe and how long it should take to pay off their debt.

The farm sector constitutes a large amount of bonded labour. Children and families in rural areas are recruited in the farm sector to work in remote areas long distances from their home, within or outside of their country of origin. Recruiters deceive families into believing they will make higher wages than those actually offered at the work site. Once they arrive at the work site, however, they are isolated and far from home, and at the complete disposal of their employer. Forced bonded labour in the farming sector occurs in many countries and many industries, including small-scale farms in South Asia; fishing industries in Indonesia, Sri Lanka, India, Pakistan; the harvesting of rattan in the Philippines; sugar cane and rubber in Brazil and the Dominican Republic; vegetables in Honduras; cocoa farms in West Africa; and many more.[4] Trafficking of workers into exploitative agricultural activities in the United States and other developed countries is also common.

Sex trafficking

Commercial sexual exploitation has generally received a great deal of attention in the trafficking literature, largely because the plight of millions of people, mostly women and girls, who enter into the global sex trade every year, is significant. Adult sex workers who have been coerced or deceived into migrating fall within the trafficking definition. The trafficking Protocol considers 'consent' irrelevant in the case of children; therefore, sexual exploitation of children in the sex industry is considered trafficking in persons. Children are sold, induced, tricked, or enticed into prostitution, and are often too young to fully comprehend or consent to the acts they are forced to perform. They are taken far from their homes or sold by their parents, and held in confinement where they are abused into submission and exposed to severe health risks including HIV infection and AIDS, other sexually transmitted diseases, drug abuse, and physical and psychological abuse. As is the case for most forms of trafficking, there are not adequately documented figures on the number of people who are sexually exploited. The clandestine nature of the industry makes it impossible to move beyond general estimates. However, an estimated 1.8 million children work in the sex trade every year (ILO 2002).

Most trafficking victims are forced into sexual exploitation because recruiters promise jobs or marriage, after which they transfer the trafficked to brothels far away from their homes and hold them in debt bondage. Parents are also compelled to sell their children into commercial sexual exploitation, which may be used as a survival strategy, or may be used for material gains.

Forced marriage, either through outright abduction, for purposes of receiving a bride price, or through arrangements for debt release is one of the most widespread, yet hidden forms of human trafficking. Girls as young as 4 are removed from their homes and families and taken to the living quarters of their new husbands; their freedoms are removed by another individual who benefits via sexual and domestic services. Around the world, an estimated 100 million girls will marry before their 18th birthday over the next decade; many of them forced into marriage by their parents or extended family members (Clark 2004).

Begging

One of the most celebrated trafficking cases in the United States involved fifty-one deaf Mexicans who were brought to the United States and forced into begging. They had been beaten, tortured, and forced to turn over all of their profits to the traffickers. In Senegal, religious teachers (*marabouts*) often exploit students (*talibés*); bringing them from rural areas to urban centres and forcing them to roam the streets and beg for money from as early as 6 o'clock in the morning until well after dark. If they return to the school (*daaras*) without a sufficient amount of money, they are beaten and abused. A representative from Save the Children Sweden remarked that there are *daaras* in Senegal that 'resemble slave houses' (Moens et al. 2004).

Conflict

Conflict also precipitates, and is inextricably linked to human trafficking. Conflict often causes massive displacement of populations, resulting in extreme vulnerabilities, which often lead to abuse, exploitation, and trafficking. Displacement has profound effects on family and community networks, and social and cultural ties. It strips away economic opportunities, terminates dependable employment arrangements, disrupts educational opportunities, induces extreme forms of isolation and poverty, and destroys social structures. Many refugees and internally displaced persons (IDPs) struggle to survive with inadequate shelter, little or no access to food or basic health care, and no protection. They are cramped together in makeshift dwellings, often in unhy-gienic conditions, leaving them disoriented and less able to resist exploitation as they desperately search for a means of survival. Whether the victims of conflict cluster in camps, flee into the countryside for refuge with friends or relatives, or immerse into a community of the equally poor and dispossessed, they are among the most vulnerable populations in the world.

Displaced women and children are particularly vulnerable to trafficking, which is likely to be related to gender-based violence in camp situations. Since women and children make up 75 per cent of camp populations, they often become the sole source of income for their families. A lack of income-generating activities often forces them, either on their own accord or on that of their parents and/or husbands who barter their bodies into prostitution and trafficking as a means of survival. Regardless of the reason for their displacement, they are forced into extreme poverty without the resources or assistance they need in order to provide for their children. Their vulnerability creates opportunities for male-dominated leadership structures within the camp, and traffickers outside the camp to carry out persistent violations of their rights and human freedoms.

Trafficking becomes more commonplace in areas where conflict strips away economic opportunities and breaks down law and order. The transformation of conflict to protracted, intrastate warfare is marked by violence that indiscriminately kills, violates, abducts, terrorizes, and explicitly targets civilian populations. Areas of conflict are easy targets for those interested in plundering a country's resources, including its people. The actors involved, including governmental and non-governmental military forces, thrive on and create war economies relying on violent and illegal activities, such as trafficking and slavery. The following discussion focuses on the specific forms of trafficking that are inexorably linked to conflict itself.

Child soldiers

Child soldiering is a unique and severe manifestation of human trafficking. Images of young boys carrying AK-47s and stories of forced conscription into the ranks of a country's military or rebel group pervade the popular press and have shed light on the unfortunate plight of millions of children around the world. As a result, a significant and growing body of international law and standards has emerged to prevent child recruitment and its potential links to displacement. The Convention on the Rights of the Child entitles all children under 18 to the right of personal security. Its Optimal Protocol on the Involvement of Children in Armed Conflict and ILO Convention 182 on the Worst Forms of Child Labour deal with trafficking of children into armed forces as well. Despite efforts by the international community, the recruitment of displaced children by national armed forces and/or militias has continued unimpeded in many countries including Burundi, Colombia, Côte d'Ivoire, Chad, the Democratic Republic of Congo (DRC), Iraq, Burma, Nepal, Philippines, Somalia, Sri Lanka, Sudan, and Uganda (IDMC 2007). Worldwide, over half a million children under the age of 18 have been recruited into government or rebel armed forces in more than eighty-five countries. It is estimated that at any one time, more than 300,000 of these children are actively fighting.[5]

Some children join voluntarily as a means of survival in a war-torn region whose economy has been destroyed. In Colombia, girls as young as 12 have submitted themselves to paramilitary forces as a means of defending their families against other groups. However, most are abducted and forcibly exposed to the brutalities of war. They are used as combatants, spies, messengers, porters, servants, to lay or clear land mines or, in the case of girls, they are raped and forced into sexual slavery. To the leaders involved in the conflict, these children are seen as cheap, expendable, and easily manipulated, and as such they are forced or coerced to take up arms in a struggle which they cannot even comprehend.

Children who are separated or displaced from their families and communities are at the greatest risk of recruitment and abduction by armed forces and rebel groups. At the same time, however, children who have been abducted or coerced into the ranks of government or rebel groups are displaced, usually internally, as a result of their abduction. They are physically relocated, often at great distances from their homes, and placed in harm's way. They also lack both the freedom and the means to return to their family or community, and are most at risk of subsequently becoming displaced upon their return. All too often their families have been killed and their homes destroyed, leaving them lost in a world full of people willing to exploit their vulnerabilities. In many cases, abductors force the children to commit atrocities against their own family and community members, therefore making children both the primary victims and the primary perpetrators in the conflict. They are forced to return to a world whose fundamental tenets they were made to violate, and whose categories they have defied. In some cases the violations they have committed leave them unaccepted by the very people whom they run to for help and protection, their families. This leaves thousands of children around the world doubly at risk of recruitment and displacement, and sometimes trapped in a vicious cycle between the two (Alfredson 2002).

Just as child soldiers are displaced, they are also victims of trafficking. The Trafficking Protocol acknowledges the recruitment, transportation, transfer, harbouring, or receipt of a child for the purpose of exploitation as 'trafficking in persons'. Therefore, whether displacement precedes abduction, or whether recruitment or abduction is the cause of displacement, those who are forced or coerced to serve in government or rebel groups are trafficking victims as well as displaced persons.

Sexual exploitation by military and peacekeepers

In conflict situations, sexual violence is often deliberately employed as a war strategy, making women extremely vulnerable to trafficking, particularly when the general level of violence against women is high (GTZ 2004). Women and girls may be abducted and used as combatants, labourers, spies, trainers, or sex slaves, yet no matter the purpose, sexual violence is almost always part of their exploitation.

Unfortunately, human trafficking does not stop when the conflict ends. In fact, post-conflict regions offer ideal conditions for traffickers, as they are frequently characterized by the absence of law, political instability, increased criminal activity, and dysfunctional law enforcement institutions. This highly volatile environment, coupled with social disintegration, destruction of livelihoods, and a lack of economic activities following a war, offer a large collection of highly vulnerable people who are struggling to reconstruct their lives. Former militia, ex-combatants, or warlords may turn to trafficking in human beings as a way to replace revenue losses caused by the cessation of the war (GTZ 2004). The end to conflict may cause a reduction in trafficking in women and children. Finally, sexual violence often continues and even increases with an end to official fighting. Many returning soldiers and fighters often use violence in order to regain control and authority within the family. Other times, they have been socialized into violence and merely continue this behaviour back home. Gender-based violence and a lack of law enforcement institutions create insecurity and contribute to trafficking women in post-conflict settings.

A sudden increase in trafficking for sexual exploitation often occurs when foreign or international peacekeeping or civilian forces are deployed. Foreign soldiers bring money and time to post-conflict settings where both are regarded as priceless commodities. With an increase in demand for sexual services comes an increase in supply. The arrival of peace support missions often directly coincides with an increase in local sex markets around military and peacekeeping camps. Traffickers and local authorities in post-conflict regions are quick to enter and benefit the emerging lucrative market, which represents an economic opportunity in a situation where few other opportunities to earn an income exist.

The deployment of peacekeeping forces to Sierra Leone, Kosovo, Eritrea, and Bosnia, for example, created huge local sex markets (GTZ 2004). In Bosnia and Herzegovina, an explosive growth in 'sex slaves' was fuelled by the arrival of tens of thousands of predominately male NATO and UN personnel in the wake of the signing of the Dayton Peace Accords by Bosnia, Croatia, and Yugoslavia in 1995.[6] The United Nations High Commissioner for Refugees (UNHCR) estimated that 30 per cent of those visiting brothels in Bosnia were UN personnel, NATO peacekeepers, or aid workers. Other research estimates that since 1995, 70 per cent of traffickers' income in Bosnia came directly from peacekeepers.[7] Amnesty International reported that international personnel represented 20 per cent of the people using trafficked women and girls less than three months after the deployment of international forces and police officers, even though they comprised less than 2 per cent of Kosovo's population. In the DRC, the international media reported allegations of a soldier-run prostitution ring involving girls as young as 15 in the South Kivu area. In Mozambique, following the signing of the peace treaty in 1992, soldiers of the United Nations Operation in Mozambique (ONUMOZ) recruited girls as young as 12 into prostitution. In six of the twelve countries on sexual exploitation of children conducted by the United Nations (1996), the arrival of peacekeeping forces has been associated with a rapid rise in child prostitution.

International peacekeeping personnel have purchased trafficked women and children for sex or domestic labour, have permitted trafficking rings to flourish, and have themselves engaged in trafficking persons (Picarelli 2002). Regardless of their involvement, the implications for peacekeeping missions around the world are profound. Peacekeeping forces are deployed to provide peace and security to regions that have sustained brutal conflicts in which civilians are often targeted as a war strategy. Many civilians have been displaced and subject to brutal atrocities and abuses, which frequently includes trafficking, by both sides of the conflict. Every ounce of dignity they once possessed has been stripped away and destroyed by those who wish to benefit from their vulnerability. The arrival of peacekeeping missions is often marked by relief and hope from those who believe their suffering has finally come to an end. When the very people who are meant to provide them protection become just another group who wishes to exploit them, any sense of hope is quickly annihilated. The participation, or even the mere perception that peacekeepers are involved in trafficking, both directly and indirectly, creates distrust within the community and directly impedes the mission's effort to bring sustainable peace. The very essence of what the peacekeeping operation is meant to embody is destroyed, or compromised at best.

International legal framework for protection

No one international Convention or Protocol addresses the full range of protection issues affecting individuals who are at risk of or who have been trafficked. Taken together, however, a number of international instruments provide a framework for protection. Each has strengths and weaknesses that are balanced by other instruments. Three such instruments stand out—the Palermo Protocol, the UN Convention Relating to the Status of Refugees, and the Guiding Principles on Internal Displacement—although others such as the Convention on the Rights of the Child also pertain.

As binding international law ratified by more than ninety countries, the Trafficking Protocol requires states to take specific actions to prevent trafficking and prosecute traffickers, including those who prey on the internally displaced. The Protocol has provisions related to the protection of trafficking victims, but the language is generally weaker in assigning responsibilities to governments. State parties, for example, 'shall endeavour to provide for the physical safety of victims of trafficking in persons while they are within its territory'. The Protocol specifies that 'in appropriate cases and to the extent possible under its domestic law, each State Party shall protect the privacy and identity of victims of trafficking in persons, including, *inter alia*, by making legal proceedings relating to such trafficking confidential'. In this context, 'each State Party shall ensure that its domestic legal or administrative system contains measures that provide to victims of trafficking in persons, in appropriate cases:

(i) Information on relevant court and administrative proceedings;

(ii) Assistance to enable their views and concerns to be presented and considered at appropriate stages of criminal proceedings against offenders, in a manner not prejudicial to the rights of the defence.'

The Protocol is more direct in regards to potential compensation, presumably from traffickers: 'Each State Party shall ensure that its domestic legal system contains measures that offer victims of trafficking in persons the possibility of obtaining compensation for damage suffered.'

It encourages but does not require state parties to adopt provisions to help trafficking victims to recover: 'Each State Party shall consider implementing measures to provide for the physical, psychological and social recovery of victims of trafficking in persons.' Among the areas to be considered are: appropriate housing; counselling and information; medical, psychological, and material assistance; and employment, educational, and training opportunities. For internationally trafficked persons, the Protocol also encourages states to 'consider adopting legislative or other appropriate measures that permit victims of trafficking in persons to remain in its territory, temporarily or permanently, in appropriate cases'. And, also in the case of the internationally trafficked, the Protocol includes specific provisions regarding return and reintegration of trafficking victims to their home countries. By contrast, it includes no provisions related to the return or reintegration of internal trafficking victims to their home communities.

The UN Refugee Convention does not deal with trafficking directly but it affords protection to persons who are outside of their home countries and cannot or will not return home because of a well-founded fear of persecution based on their race, religion, nationality, political opinion, or membership in a particular social group. Individuals who have been trafficked may fit the social group category if they have a well-founded fear of persecution by traffickers in their home country and the government is unwilling or unable to provide sufficient protection to the returnees. It should be noted that the Refugee Convention would not be an appropriate vehicle for protection if the threat of persecution was from traffickers in the destination country. The victim would also have to show that the threat from the traffickers rose to the level of persecution, requiring, for example, threats of death, dismemberment, or even re-trafficking into slave-like conditions. If the victim is able to meet the refugee test, she would be afforded all of the protections included in the Refugee Convention, including protection from *refoulement* (involuntary return) and access to most benefits accorded to legal immigrants and citizens. The Refugee Convention has been ratified by almost 150 countries, making it one of the most widely ratified international treaties.

By contrast, the Guiding Principles are not binding international law (although drawn from human rights and humanitarian law) but they are more detailed than the Trafficking Protocol in setting out the type of measures that are needed to protect and assist those who have been internally displaced by traffickers, and it includes principles related to long-term solutions such as return, local integration, or resettlement. Unlike the Refugee Convention, the Guiding Principles pertain to internal trafficking. Significantly, there is evidence of a growing interest in converting the Guiding Principles into binding national and regional law. In October 2009, for example, the African Union adopted a Convention for the Protection and Assistance of IDPs in Africa, which will go into force when fifteen states ratify it.

The Guiding Principles specifically call for protection of IDPs from many forms of trafficking, including acts of gender-specific violence, forced prostitution, slavery (including sale into marriage, sexual exploitation, and forced labour of children), and recruitment of displaced children to take part in hostilities. They also have important provisions regarding the rights of the internally displaced that are particularly important for internal victims of trafficking. For example, the Guiding Principles specify that 'internally displaced persons shall be protected from discriminatory arrest and detention as a result of their displacement'. Since internal trafficking victims who are forced into prostitution and other illegal activities are often arrested and detained for these coerced actions, this provision would help establish the principle that the victims, as distinct from the perpetrators, should not be subject to prosecution. Interestingly, the Trafficking Protocol is not specific on this point.

The Guiding Principles also specify that IDPs have 'the right to be protected against forcible return to or resettlement in any place where their life, safety, liberty and/or health would be at risk'. This would benefit internal trafficking victims who may be returned to their home communities without an adequate assessment of the risks that they may face. The Protocol encourages states to take these factors into account in determining whether to repatriate international victims, but it has no comparable language for internal victims of trafficking.

The Guiding Principles specify that 'internally displaced persons who have returned to their homes or places of habitual residence or who have resettled in another part of the country shall not be discriminated against as a result of their having been displaced. They shall have the right to participate fully and equally in public affairs at all levels and have equal access to public services'. This provision is particularly important given the stigma that often applies to the victims of trafficking, particularly those who have been forced to engage in prostitution.

Other provisions in the Guiding Principles relate particularly to children who have been trafficked internally:

> Families which are separated by displacement should be reunited as quickly as possible. All appropriate steps shall be taken to expedite the reunion of such families, particularly when children are involved. The responsible authorities shall facilitate inquiries made by family members and encourage

> and cooperate with the work of humanitarian organizations engaged in the task of family reunification.

The Guiding Principles also reiterate the right of children to an education, which is important both in preventing trafficking for labour exploitation and to help victims gain access to education once rescued from traffickers.

Since traffickers often take documentation from their victims in order to enforce their control, the Guiding Principles that relate to the responsibilities of states in this regard are also useful:

> the authorities concerned shall issue to them all documents necessary for the enjoyment and exercise of their legal rights, such as passports, personal identification documents, birth certificates and marriage certificates. In particular, the authorities shall facilitate the issuance of new documents or the replacement of documents lost in the course of displacement without imposing unreasonable conditions, such as requiring the return to one's area of habitual residence in order to obtain these or other required documents.

Taken together, the Protocol, the Refugee Convention, and Guiding Principles provide a good normative framework for protecting trafficked persons but they still lack strong legal enforcement measures. The Protocol's provisions related to protection of trafficking victims are far more tentative than those related to the prosecution of traffickers. Even where states are encouraged to take measures to protect the victims, the language is very general and is often framed in a way that refers more specifically to those trafficked across borders, leaving much greater government discretion with regards to internal trafficking victims. The Refugee Convention pertains only to those outside of their home country, and it has no enforcement measures against states that violate its provisions. The Guiding Principles fill many of the gaps in setting out a legal framework for addressing the protection of the internally trafficked, but they are not legally binding, except to the extent that the Principles are based on existing international law or adopted into national or regional law. Enforcing compliance in the case of internal trafficking runs into the same sovereignty constraints as is true with other forms of internal displacement.

International institutional framework to address trafficking

A wide array of international organizations have policies and programmes aimed at combating trafficking through efforts to prosecute traffickers, prevent trafficking, and protect the trafficked. The principal actors within and outside of the United Nations include the United Nations Office on Drugs and Crime (UNODC), the International Organization for Migration (IOM), the UNHCR, and the UN High Commissioner for Human Rights (UNHCHR). UNODC serves as the Secretariat of the Conference of the Parties to the UN Convention against Transnational

Organized Crime and its Protocols. As such, UNODC is required to 'ensure the necessary coordination with the secretariats of relevant international and regional organizations'. UNODC's Global Programme to Combat Trafficking in Persons comprises data collection, assessment, and technical cooperation.

IOM is largely an implementing agency. It has launched almost 500 projects related to trafficking in eighty-five countries since 1994 and has provided assistance to approximately 15,000 trafficked persons. IOM also conducts both quantitative and qualitative research on trafficking to better inform its work and the work of others. Specific areas of focus have included human trafficking routes and trends and the causes and consequences of human trafficking.

UNHCR has a responsibility to ensure that refugees, asylum seekers, IDPs, stateless persons, and other persons of concern do not fall victim to trafficking. Additionally, the office has a responsibility to ensure that those who have been trafficked and who fear being subjected to persecution upon return to their country of origin, or individuals who fear being trafficked, whose claim to international protection falls within the refugees definition contained in the 1951 Convention and/or its 1967 Protocol related to the status of refugees are recognized as refugees and afforded the corresponding international protection.

The Office of the High Commissioner for Human Rights (OHCHR) has been carrying out an anti-trafficking programme entitled Eliminating Trafficking and Protecting the Rights of Trafficked Persons under the Agency's Voluntary Fund for Technical Cooperation and in the Field of Human Rights. Through bi-annual resolutions on trafficking by the Commission on Human Rights, OHCHR is mandated to address human trafficking at the international, regional, and national levels.

A number of other international organizations focus on the relationship between trafficking and the populations they serve. For example, the ILO focuses on the relationship between trafficking and forced labour. The ILO Governing Body created a Special Action Programme to combat Forced Labour (SAP-FL), as part of broader efforts to promote the 1998 Declaration on Fundamental Principles and Rights at Work and its Follow-up. Since its inception, SAP-FL has been concerned with raising global awareness of forced labour in its different forms. Several thematic and country-specific studies on human trafficking have since been undertaken.

The United Nations Children's Fund (UNICEF) focuses particularly on protection of children from trafficking. UNICEF's Innocenti Research Centre also hosts a Child Trafficking Research Hub. The UN Development Programme (UNDP) aims to identify the factors that increase women's and girls' vulnerability to trafficking and to develop responses for the facilitation of safe mobility. They also seek to increase national capacity and sub-regional cooperation to strengthen and reform legislation, policies, and enforcement of laws to respond to trafficking. The United Nations Development Fund for Women (UNIFEM) addresses the trafficking of women within the context of violence against women as a violation of their human rights and as a development issue. They also focus on improving data and information systems related to trafficking in women, as well as strengthening regional and national coalitions. The United Nations Education, Cultural and Scientific Organization (UNESCO) undertakes policy-oriented research on specific factors leading to the trafficking of women and children in pilot countries in Africa and Asia. Recognizing the impact of sex trafficking, in particular, on the spread of HIV/AIDS, the Joint United Nations Programme on HIV/AIDS (UNAIDS) promotes law enforcement and other activities to prevent trafficking, protect victims, punish traffickers, and reduce demand for the services of trafficked workers, women, and girls.

As seen from this brief review of institutional responsibilities, it is clear that a broad array of organizations participate in anti-trafficking programmes, ranging from the law enforcement community represented by UNODC to the more specialized agencies that focus on women, children, and HIV/AIDS issues. The IOM, which is outside of the United Nations but cooperates with the UN agencies, has had the longest history of involvement in human trafficking programmes and is by far the most operational agency in implementing trafficking-related programmes.

Recognizing the complexity of the international system, the UN Global Initiative to Fight Human Trafficking (UN.GIFT) was launched by UNODC in 2007 to help coordinate these efforts. It is managed in cooperation with ILO, IOM, UNICEF, UNHCR, and a regional body, the Organization for Security and Cooperation in Europe (OSCE). UN.GIFT's mission statement describes the aim as:

> The United Nations Global Initiative to Fight Human Trafficking (UN.GIFT) aims to mobilize state and non-state actors to eradicate human trafficking by (i) reducing both the vulnerability of potential victims and the demand for exploitation in all its forms; (ii) ensuring adequate protection and support to those who do fall victim, and (iii) supporting the efficient prosecution of the criminals involved, while respecting the fundamental human rights of all persons. In carrying out its mission UN.GIFT will increase the knowledge and awareness on human trafficking; promote effective rights-based responses; build capacity of state and non-state actors; and foster partnerships for joint action against human trafficking.

UN.GIFT's strategy focuses on three elements. The first involves building awareness of human trafficking, particularly through support for innovative public–private partnerships: The second strategy is to increase the knowledge base about trafficking: 'The research component of UN.GIFT aims to deepen understanding of human trafficking by better data collection, analysis and sharing, as well as joint research initiatives.' The third element is technical assistance, helping states develop more effective policies and programmes, including through the development of a standardized methodology to collect and analyse national data on human trafficking.

While a useful endeavour, UN.GIFT does not focus on coordination among the international organizations themselves. UNODC has that responsibility, but anchored in a law enforcement agency, it does not have the capacity to address gaps in protection of trafficking victims. UNHCR has a limited role, only in respect to refugees and in a more limited way, IDPs. OHCHR does not have the physical presence or operational capacity in many countries that would be needed to address protection issues. Issues of sovereignty remain major constraints on developing an effective protection capacity, particularly for internal trafficking victims. Yet, as is the case with other vulnerable populations, relying totally on state protection is inadequate as well. This is especially the case when organized criminal elements corrupt government officials in order to benefit from trafficking.

Conclusion

The international regime to address human trafficking is in its infancy. The principal legal framework for combating modern-day trafficking went into force in 2003, and the institutional structures to help states implement the Palermo Protocol are only now being fully developed. It appears that states do recognize the need for multilateral cooperation in combating trafficking, which explains the relatively rapid ratification of the Protocol. This is in sharp contrast to the UN Convention on the Rights of Migrant Workers and Members of their Families, which less than forty countries have ratified since it was adopted in 1990. However, unlike the more well-established refugee regime, which is focused primarily on the rights and protection of those who are forced to flee because of persecution, the trafficking regime is relatively weak in providing protection to the victims of trafficking. As this chapter has demonstrated, a large number of international organizations have developed programmes during the past decade to address trafficking issues. As the issue gains greater attention and improvements are made in understanding the causes, consequences, and solutions to human trafficking, it will be essential to monitor these institutional developments to ensure that the efforts underway to protect victims and prevent future trafficking are monitored and assessed to identify strengths and weaknesses and fill gaps.

Notes

1. http://www.HumanTrafficking.com; Human Trafficking 101.
2. http://www.ohchr.org/english/law/protocoltraffic.htm.
3. US Department of State (2007).

4. US Department of Labor, 'Bonded and Forced Child Labor', http://www.dol.gov/ilab/media/reports/idlp/sweatz/bonded.htm.
5. http://www.amnesty.org.
6. http://www.refugeesinternational.org.
7. http://www.refugeesinternational.org.

References

Acharya, A.K. (2004) Agrarian Conflict, Internal Displacement, and Trafficking of Mexican Women: The Case of Chiapas State, UNAM, Mexico for the 2004 Annual Meeting of Population Association of America, Boston.

Alfredson, L. (2002) Child Soldiers, Displacement, and Human Security, *Disarmament Forum*, 3, 17–27.

Belser, P., Cock, M., and Mehran, F. (2006) *ILO Minimum Estimates of Forced Labor in the World*, Geneva: International Labour Organization.

Blackburn, M. (1994) A Tradition of Slavery, in *Anti-Slavery Reporter*, London: Anti-Slavery International.

Brown, E. (2007) *The Ties that Bind; Migration and Trafficking of Women and Girls for Sexual Exploitation in Cambodia*, Geneva: International Organization for Migration.

Carroll, R. (2003) Child Laborers Rescued from Nigerian Quarries, *The Guardian*, 17 October.

Carson, J. (1993) Young's Town: 'Prison Camp' and Slave Dungeon for Child Workers, *Child Workers Philippines*, Vol. 1 (No. 1), Manila: Kamalayan Development Center, Inc.

Children at Work: A Report Based on the ILO and UNICEF Regional Training Workshop on Programmatic and Replication Issues Related to Child Labour and Street Children, Bangkok: UNICEF.

Clark, B. (2004) The Implications of Early Marriage for HIV/AIDS Policy, Brief based on background paper prepared for the WHO/UNFPA/Population Council Technical Consultation on Married Adolescents, New York: Population Council.

Feingold, D. (2005) Human Trafficking, *Foreign Policy*, September/October.

Fitzgibbon, K. (2003) Modern-Day Slavery: The Scope of Trafficking in Persons in Africa, *African Security Review*, 12(1), 81–9.

Fyfe, A. (1989) *Child Labor*, Oxford: Polity Press.

Gargan, E. (1992) Bound to Looms by Poverty and Fear, Boys in India Makes a Few Men Rich, *New York Times*, July 9.

Deutsche Gesellschaft für Technische Zusammenarbeit (GTZ) (2004) *Armed Conflict and Trafficking in Women: Desk Study*, Eschborn: Sector Project against Trafficking in Women.

Guerrero, E. (1994) *Bonded Labor of Children on Rise in Philippines, Associated Press*, 7 June.

Human Rights Watch/Asia (1995) *Contemporary Forms of Slavery in Pakistan*, New York: Human Rights Watch.

Internal Displacement Monitoring Center (IDMC) (2007) *Internal Displacement: Global Overview of Trends and Developments in 2006*, Geneva: Internal Displacement Monitoring Center.

International Labour Organization (ILO) (1995) *In the Twilight Zone: Child Workers in the Hotel, Tourism and Catering Industry*, Geneva: International Labour Organization.

——*A Future without Child Labour*, Geneva: ILO.

International Organization for Migration (IOM) (2004) *Trafficking in Persons: An Analysis of Afghanistan*, Geneva: IOM.

Mahmood, Z., Riaz, S., Nazeer, M.A., and Haq, M.E. (1991) *Child Labour in Brick Kiln Industries*, Lahore: University of Punjab.

Miko, F. (2006) Trafficking in Persons: The U.S. and International Response, Congressional Research Service Report for Congress, Code Order RL30545.

Moens, B., Zeitlin, V., Bop, C., and Gaye, R. (2004) Study on the Practice of Trafficking in Persons in Senegal, Development Alternatives, Inc. Report for U.S. Agency for International Development.

Pearson, E. (2003) *Study on Trafficking in Women in East Africa; A Situational Analysis Including Current NGO and Governmental Activities, as well as Future Opportunities, to Address Trafficking in Women and Girls in Ethiopia, Kenya, Tanzania, Uganda, and Nigeria*, Eschborn: Deutsche Gesellschaft für Technische Zusammenarbeit.

Physicians for Human Rights (2002) *War-Related Sexual Violence in Sierra Leone. A Population-Based Assessment with the Support of UNAMSIL*, Boston/Washington, DC.

Picarelli, J. (2002) Trafficking, Slavery, and Peacekeeping: The Need for a Comprehensive Training Program, Conference Report, Turin, Italy: UN Interregional Crime and Justice Research Institute.

Polania, F. (2003) Analysis on the Relation between Trafficking in Humans and Drugs in Colombia, Programme Coordinator Trafficking in Persons at IOM Colombia.

Save the Children, UK (2007) *The Small Hands of Slavery*, London: Save the children.

Sayre, K. (2007) India Struggles Against Trafficking: Many Women, Girls Sold into Prostitution, *Washington Post*, 17 June, p. A12.

Sekar, A. (n.d.) *A Study of Granite Export and Bondage of Stone Cutters in Tamilnadu*, India: The Association of the Rural Poor.

Suwal, B. and Amatya, T.L. (2002) *Internal Trafficking Among Children and Youth Engaged in Prostitution in Nepal*, International Labour Organization and International Program on the Elimination of Child Labor-Trafficking in Children-South Asia (TICSA), No. 3.

UNICEF (2001) *Profiting from Abuse: An Investigation into the Sexual Exploitation of our Children*, New York: UNICEF.

UNICEF Innocenti Research Centre (2000) Domestic Violence Against Women and Girls, *Innocenti Digest 6*, Florence.

——(2001) Early Marriage, Child Spouses, *Innocenti Digest 7*, Florence.

UNICEF and Government of Pakistan (1992) *Child Labour in the Carpet Weaving Industry* in Punjab, Punjab: UNICEF.

United Nations (1996) Promotion and Protection of the Rights of Children: Impact of Armed Conflict on Children, A Note by the Secretary General; Fifty-First Session: Item 108 of the Provisional Agenda.

University of British Columbia, Canada (2005) *Human Security Report 2005: War and Peace in the 21st Century*, Human Security Center, Oxford University Press.

US Department of State (2007) *Trafficking in Persons Report*.

10

Remittances

Anna Lindley

Introduction

The recent debates on global migration governance, and the categories of migration dealt with in previous chapters, have mainly focused on the regulation of the movement of people. But the movement of people is often followed by the movement of migrants' capital (money and resources) back to their country of origin. These remittances are also subjected to complex forms of regulation and have captured the attention of global policy communities in recent years.

The geography of the remittance process offers various governance opportunities. Actors may seek to shape the remittance process in terms of remittance sending from the host country, the transnational passage of remittances, and/or the intermediation of remittances in the country of origin. But insofar as remittances are a trans-boundary phenomenon, attempts to shape one aspect of the remittance process invariably has implications elsewhere, meaning that one state's interventions in the remittance process at the domestic level are likely to have ramifications beyond the borders of that state.

Remittances may be viewed from a variety of perspectives. The insights of development economists, rural micro-economists, businesspeople, social development analysts, security specialists, and financial experts studying remittance flows usually focus on different aspects of the phenomenon. Remittances may be seen, depending on your perspective, as household income, a hard-earned transnational family livelihood, a macroeconomic flow, potential dirty money, a source of development finance, or a business opportunity. Thus, remittances emerge as an issue in different areas of policy.

The governance of remittance flows is fragmented into two main issue-areas, namely crime/security and socio-economic development. First, remittances, as a component of global financial flows, are subject to complex and changing global-, regional-, and national-level financial regulation, aimed at preventing criminal and terrorist use of the global financial system. Second, migrants' remittances are also increasingly the subject of analysis and action by development actors seeking to mediate these flows in ways that are intended to accomplish particular socio-economic development goals in migrants' countries of origin. This chapter considers in turn the institutions and politics of each issue-area in terms of how they relate to remittances and the case for global governance.

Governing international financial flows to prevent crime and terrorism

As an international financial transfer, remittances are caught up in the global financial regime. A variety of financial intermediaries facilitate the transfer of remittances to migrants' countries of origin, ranging from couriers and bus and taxi drivers, to banks, specialized money transmitters including hawala (value transfer) operators, post offices, business people with migrant links, mobile phone companies, microfinance institutions, and pre-paid card companies. Some intermediaries are specialized in the business of transferring migrants' remittances, some do it as a convenient sideline to their main business. Some of this economic activity is formal, and some operates beyond state regulations. Globally, remittance transfer is a multi-billion dollar business. In 2006, immigrants in the United States were expected to send over US$20 billion to Mexico and spend around US$948 million in fees and other costs on getting it there (Amuedo-Dorantes and Pozo 2005).

The intermediaries connecting host countries financially to countries of origin have in recent years become increasingly entangled in complex and changing financial regulations. Of course, financial regulation is not new: most states regulate their financial sectors in some way, determining which firms can engage in particular types of business and the terms on which their dealings—including international transfers—are allowed. This is done as a matter of macroeconomic policy, to facilitate government control of the economy. It is done to protect the public from losses through fraud and bankruptcy among financial institutions, and to maintain confidence in the financial sector. It is also done to prevent the use of financial institutions for criminal purposes (e.g. drugs smuggling, illegal arms sales, tax evasion, secreting away the proceeds of political corruption, the funding of criminal or terrorist activities) and money laundering (passing funds acquired through criminal activities such as drugs trade through the financial system so that they appear to have been acquired legitimately).

It is the anti-crime agenda—rather than the macroeconomic or customer protection agenda—that dominated financial regulation debates from the 1990s. The opening up in the 1980s and 1990s of international financial markets provided new opportunities for crime. The international dimension of many of the criminal activities listed above, particularly the laundering of drugs money, prompted the recognition among states of the need for international collective action.

The main source of global financial governance is the Financial Action Task Force (FATF), an intergovernmental body with the mission of developing and promoting policies to combat money laundering and terrorist financing at national and international levels. Established in 1989 by a G7 Summit in Paris, initially to develop measures to deal with money laundering, there are currently thirty-four members, including thrity-two countries[1] and two regional organizations,[2] plus observers.[3] Membership criteria emphasize the strategic importance of the member country, indicated by the size of gross domestic product and the banking sector. This means that the global financial governance is basically determined by the interests of wealthier countries.

The FATF has three main jobs. The first is standard setting. In 1990 the FATF published a series of anti-money laundering (AML) Recommendations (subsequently revised in 1996 and 2003) (FATF 1990). These Recommendations set out a broad framework for AML efforts, which is intended to be universally applied by states. For example, these standards emphasize the importance that financial institutions identify their customers, report large or suspicious cash transactions, and keep records that can be called up by police if necessary. Its second job is the monitoring of members' own implementation of the Recommendations through a system of peer review, and the general monitoring and promotion of counter-measures globally. Third, the FATF is tasked with reviewing money laundering methods and counter-measures to help countries to keep abreast of contemporary developments.

Following the extremist attacks in the United States in September 2001, the drive of powerful states to monitor global financial flows was substantially reinvigorated and further politicized. Value transmission systems serving Muslim migrant communities (commonly known as hawala) came in for particular scrutiny, with the US government initially claiming that these types of system were used to transfer funds to finance the attack on the World Trade Towers. Announcing to the public that his administration had blocked the US assets of individuals and organizations connected to Al Barakaat, the largest Somali money transmitter, President Bush declared a 'financial war on terror' (Bush 2001):

> By shutting these networks down, we disrupt the murderers' work. Today's action interrupts al Qaeda's communications; it blocks an important source of funds. It provides us with valuable information and sends a clear message to global financial institutions: you are with us or you are with the terrorists. And if you're with the terrorists, you will face the consequences. We fight an enemy who hides in caves in Afghanistan, and in the shadows within our own society. It's an enemy who can only survive in darkness. Today, we've

taken another important action to expose the enemy to the light and to disrupt its ability to threaten America and innocent life.

The FATF, as the main multilateral organization focusing on the prevention of financial crime, duly responded to the changing geopolitical environment. FATF reports on money laundering typologies in 1996, 1999, 2000, and early 2001 had already begun to consider the issue of whether existing AML measures were adequate to combat the financing of terrorism or not. But it was in the aftermath of 9/11 that action was taken, the FATF expanding its mandate to include, specifically, combating the financing of terrorism (CFT). Its set of nine *Special Recommendations on Terrorist Financing*, which non-member countries were also strongly encouraged to follow, aimed to provide a basic framework 'to detect, prevent and suppress the financing of terrorism and terrorist acts' (FATF 2001).

Two Recommendations in particular had direct impact on migrant remittance systems. First, Special Recommendation VI on 'Alternative Remittance' recognized that a range of institutions other than regulated banks were engaging in money or value transmission and required that all such people and organizations should be licensed or registered and subjected to all the FATF measures applying to banks and non-bank financial institutions. The accompanying Best Practices paper indicated that a primary concern is that unregulated money or value transfer services may allow funds to be sent anonymously with few or no records, serving the interests of money launderers and terrorist financiers (FATF 2003). It suggests best practices for licensing and registration; strategies for identifying informal money and value transfer operators and raising awareness of the regulations; requirement for customer identification, record keeping, and suspicious transaction reporting; compliance monitoring; and sanctions in the event of non-compliance. The aim was to even out the widely varying regulation of money transfer businesses between different jurisdictions.

Second, Special Recommendation VII on Wire Transfers requires that financial institutions, including money remitters, retain the name, address, and account number (or unique reference number) for the senders of funds transfers, and forward this information through the payment chain. It required countries to ensure that financial institutions, including money remitters, carry out greater scrutiny of suspicious funds transfers without the complete originator information. While it encourages countries to 'aim for the ability to trace all wire transfers and . . . minimise thresholds taking into account the risk of driving transactions underground', it also states that 'it is not the intention of the FATF to impose rigid standards or to mandate a single operating process that would negatively affect the payment system', and ultimately suggests a minimum threshold of US$1,000 below which countries may not require financial institutions to identify, verify, record, or transmit originator information on cross-border transfers.

Although the 40+9 recommendations are technically soft law, they have considerable 'teeth', and have succeeded in driving changes through the financial regulation of many states around the world, with implications for remittance facilitation.[4] There are processes of peer review by members and the listing of 'Non-Cooperative Countries and Territories'.[5] Any financial institution doing business with US financial institutions—a vast number, given the fact that the US dollar is a global medium of exchange—is expected to uphold the international standards. Thus there are considerable political and economic pressures on non-complying countries. With global governance efforts backed up by regional initiatives, while some countries have been slower than others, most have begun to incorporate FATF standards in some way into their regulation of the financial sector and remittance transfer.

At the regional level, several initiatives were also launched aimed at preventing the use of the financial system for criminal or terrorist purposes. The FATF incorporates, as Associate Members or Observers, several regional bodies dedicated to a similar AML mission.[6] For example, FATF's awareness-raising activities on money laundering in the Asia/Pacific region led to the establishment of the FATF Asia Secretariat in 1995, with Australian funding, with the aim of obtaining regional commitment to AML policies and the establishment of a more permanent regional body. At the Fourth Asia/Pacific Money Laundering Symposium in 1997 in Bangkok, the Asia/Pacific Group on Money Laundering (APG) was established by thirteen states, as an autonomous regional AML body funded by all the member jurisdictions, with a Secretariat in Sydney.[7] Membership grew to thirty-eight jurisdictions by 2008, from Afghanistan to Canada. Seven members are also members of the FATF. The aims include to coordinate mutual evaluation of members; coordinate technical assistance and training from donors to improve member compliance; to research money laundering and terrorist financing trends; and contribute to global AML and CFT policy through Associate Membership in the FATF. Organizations like the APG have played a role in pushing FATF's AML principles down to national level and offering regionally appropriate guidance and technical assistance to member jurisdictions.

Another example of regional-level cooperation is found in Europe. When the FATF Special Recommendations were issued, there was still considerable variation between EU member states on the regulation of money transmission. But the process of translating the FATF's international standards and best practices into regional European Community legislation soon began. One of the most important legal frameworks is the Payment Services Directive (PSD),[8] accompanying the creation of a Single European Payments Area, which aimed to develop a more integrated and competitive European financial market. The PSD which came into European Law in December 2007 (to be passed into national law by member states by November 2009) and provides the legal framework within which all payment service providers, including remittance services, are expected to operate. The aim is to make payments markets more competitive and secure by harmonizing rules across the European Union for which types of organizations can provide payment services (apart from banks) and on what terms, incorporating the FATF's latest AML/CFT recommendations into Community legislation. In addition, Regulation (EC) No. 1781/2006 of the European Parliament and of the Council on Information on the Payer Accompanying Transfers of Funds requires that money transfers (over a 1,000 euro threshold) not made from an account should carry certain traceable information about the sender (or that such information is easily retrievable), incorporating Special Recommendation VII into European law.[9] Several other European legislative changes have also supported the regulation of remittances, for example the Third Money Laundering Directive adopted in September 2005, which requires member states to have a licensing or registration system for money transmitters that includes a 'fit and proper' test for directors.

Against the background of this renewed drive to govern financial flows at global and regional level, since 9/11, around the world, states began to enforce existing financial regulations more vigorously and impose new regulations on money transfer activities. Thus, the national-level governance of remittances, as a key component of global financial movements, is increasingly harmonizing around core principles agreed by the relatively privileged members of the FATF.

What are the politics—constellations of power, interests, and ideas—behind the global governance of remittances as a component of international financial flows? From the point of view of some states, the transborder element in much criminal and terrorist activity makes it important to seek international collective action to tackle these problems. Uncoordinated action by some states and not others can interfere in the smooth functioning of international payment systems, hindering international business and finance between countries, which represent powerful constituencies in many states, and can have much wider economic ramifications for society.[10] States have an interest in coordinating their own regulatory frameworks to allow their financial sector to interface efficiently across financial jurisdictions, particularly with important trading partners or migrant-hosting countries. Collective action through the FATF to develop and encourage minimal principles of financial regulation to which states can refer, and its power to sanction non-compliant countries are in principle potentially very useful to this end. However, the ways that the global governance of remittances has been playing out is not as harmonious as this might imply, but has also thrown up some thorny political issues.

First the rationale for the focus on intervention in micro-scale transfers of migrants' cash is far from clear. The central, much-vaunted association between alternative remittance systems and terrorism is rather dubious. Non-bank ethnic niche money and value transmitters, particularly those serving Muslim traders and migrant communities, have come in for particular scrutiny. There has been in recent years a discursive—and in some cases literal—criminalization of hawala. Yet evidence to support the widespread suspicion of connections between this particular culturally embedded form of economic activity seems rather thin.[11] It is true that many hawala dealers were operating without appropriate licences and that many use techniques of settling debt at international levels in ways (netting off debt, over- and under-invoicing trade shipments) that infringe regulations designed to benefit the states concerned. There are general concerns that hawaladars do not keep records and therefore there is no paper trail to follow for those investigating crime—despite some evidence to the contrary from academic experts like Roger Ballard (2003). Noted transnational economic crime expert Nikos Passas has pointed out that in fact no informal value transfer system was used in the 9/11 operation (Passas 2006). The bulk of transactions went through formal banks, credit card accounts, and wire transfers run by US and British institutions. According to Spanish financial investigators, the Madrid bombers did not use hawala for their operation either (although ironically they did use it to remit money to family in Africa). Moreover, Passas' interviews with financial investigators around the world suggest that even if the FATF's nine recommendations *had* been implemented prior to 9/11, this would not have red-flagged the hijackers' financial transactions. Most FATF prosecutions of alternative remittances have been carried out on grounds of non-compliance—there have been relatively few prosecutions that clearly link small money transmitters to extremist activity. Success in combating terrorism is notoriously hard to measure, but there are few concrete examples of the effectiveness of existing measures regarding alternative remittance systems (Vleck 2006).

Some even suggest that the drive to govern alternative remittance systems is part of a much broader effort by powerful states of the global North to contain the challenge posed by globalization 'from below'.[12] Roger Ballard suggests that the USA Patriot Act, from which flowed much of the financial regulation aimed at combating terror, could not have been prepared in the short time between 9/11 and its passage through Congress, implying that (Ballard 2007: 12):

> regulatory enthusiasts within the administration took advantage of the chauvinistic post 9/11 uproar to fold a whole series of ready-made measures at which Congress might otherwise have balked into the new measure, which was promptly enacted as law with little or no discussion or scrutiny.

The second major issue to consider is that even in those states best motivated and best equipped to implement global standards regarding remittance transfer may do so in a counter-productive way. Heavy regulation can drive providers out of business, or drive legitimate business underground (where it may be easier for criminals to make use of their services), thereby reducing competition in the formal sector (Passas 2006). This, combined with the fact that regulatory systems are expected to be to a large degree self-financing, and the costs of regulation are often passed on to the consumers can contribute to raising money transfer fees.

The banking sector may use the regulatory excuse to close down money transmitters' accounts when they are really interested to capture more of the retail money transmission market (instead of the wholesale only market). There are also fears in some quarters that regulations requiring the forwarding of information about the payer through the payment chain will make personal information on migrants and their families accessible to receiving countries in ways that facilitate taxation in ways that mainly benefit elites in government, bribe-seeking and corruption, and even possibly harassment of asylum-seekers' families (Vleck 2006).

Finally, the fervour to tackle extremism may be leading policymakers to make rash decisions with damaging collateral impact. What happened to Al Barakaat, formerly a successful Somali business empire and the leading money transmitter, illustrates this point (9/11 Commission 2004). In the aftermath of 9/11, the US government claimed US$25 million was skimmed from the company's network for terrorist operations and that the owner was a 'friend and supporter' of Bin Laden. Reactions around the world were swift, with all the key countries in Al Barakaat's network freezing its bank accounts. The United Nations Security Council added Al Barakaat to its list of suspected terrorist supporters. But by August 2002, it was clear that US agents' investigations in the United Arab Emirates were not producing evidence to substantiate the major intelligence claims and the company was taken off the US list of terror-supporting organizations. With hindsight, the 9/11 Commission found that the designation of Al Barakaat had been precipitated by the policy goal to conduct 'A public and aggressive series of designations to show the world community and our allies that the United States was serious about pursuing the financial targets... Treasury officials acknowledged that some of the evidentiary foundations for the early designations were quite weak' (9/11 Commission 2004: 79). Alternatively, in the rather more direct words of one Treasury official, 'we were so forward leaning we almost fell on our face' (9/11 Commission 2004: 79).

In the end, Al Barakaat agents were actually only charged *in court* with undertaking money transfer informally, plus one case of low-level welfare fraud in Minneapolis. This episode on the financial 'war on terror' was certainly backed by the military, political, and economic might of the United States, but the Somali money transmitter was in many respects an easy target. It seems unlikely that the United States would have designated money transmitting giants such as MoneyGram or Western Union, let alone Swiss banks renowned for dealing with 'sensitive' clients, based on such limited evidence as appears to have been available in the Al Barakaat case. Meanwhile, the closure sent shockwaves through the Somali economy, and led to considerable upheaval in money transmission networks on which many relied for survival (Lindley 2009). Moreover, the targeting of alternative remittance systems like Al Barakaat often implies the criminalization of the economic mechanisms used by particular ethnic groups, fomenting alienation and mistrust between those groups and the authorities (Passas 2006). The effective criminalization of all small-scale money transmission, as has been the case in Norway, for example, negatively rebounds on those immigrant communities who have no other choice but to use these systems to send funds home (e.g. Somalis and other nationalities which have non-existent or corrupt banking systems in their country of origin) (Pieke et al. 2007).

Whose interests are served by increased financial regulation of remittances as it has unfolded since 2001? While it is a clear national security priority for many countries in the global North and South affected or potentially affected by terrorist actions to prevent the use of their financial systems by extremist groups of various kinds, many countries in the global South have far more pressing national security concerns, and in some cases the regulations recommended directly conflict with their national economic development priorities. For example, in some countries, new regulations further restrict access to financial services, when expanding access is a major development priority.[13] The FATF, the major source of global financial governance, is not a multilateral global institution, but rather represents some of the largest economies and richest economies in the world (particularly the United States) which have driven the development of the prevailing regulatory norms, and through the threat of sanction (particularly by US financial institutions) are effectively imposing them on much poorer and smaller states. In this sense, the FATF is an example of an ad hoc non-multilateral global institution which serves to reinforce asymmetric power relations. While not worth risking sanction by international financial institutions, the consequences of poorly adapted financial regulation in specific national contexts can nevertheless be serious. Years of deregulation of financial markets and rolling back of the public sector mean that in many smaller and poorer states even if new regulations are incorporated into national legislation, overstretched state bureaucracies find it difficult to impose them effectively. It may simply drive yet more financial activity into the informal sector and offer additional opportunities for rent-seeking behaviour by civil servants.

The perceived need to defend remittances against over-zestful and blunt financial regulation which might hinder legitimate flows to migrants' families has led to growing calls to ditch a one-size-fits-all approach, in favour of risk-based approaches that take account of the socio-economic context (Ballard 2005; Passas 2006). These calls have been heeded to an extent, with the FATF producing guidance on how to develop approaches to regulation that ensure that measures to combat crime are commensurate to the risks posed by particular transactions and systems (FATF 2007).

However, the global governance of remittances is certainly not limited to policy initiatives aiming to combat crime and terrorism through financial regulation; it also includes interventions aimed at enhancing their impact on socio-economic development. The next section explores the emergence of the remittances-for-development policy agenda, and its articulation with financial governance efforts.

Governing remittances for socio-economic development

The linkages between migration and development processes in migrants' places of origin have long been the subject of analysis and academic debate, particularly among micro-economists interested in rural–urban migration and macro-economists interested in global capital flows. However, since 2001, there has been a boom in interest, with an emphasis on the potentially positive effects of migration and finding policy mechanisms to link migration to particular policy goals in the global South. Effects of the movement of people on labour markets, inequality, macroeconomy, human capital and 'social remittances' of ideas, norms, and values are all aspects of the relationship between migration and development of countries of origin and have been receiving due scrutiny. But remittances have taken a particularly prominent place in contemporary migration-development policy debates, to the point of becoming a 'new development mantra' (Kapur 2004). This is due to a constellation of factors.

First, there is the clear economic significance of remittances in many poorer countries around the world. This was partly drawn to the attention of analysts by the notable growth in recorded volumes of remittances[14] in the last two decades and their macroeconomic significance. In 2007, developing countries received official remittances[15] of US$251 billion, double official aid and two-thirds of foreign direct investment (World Bank 2008). Unrecorded remittances may amount to as much as 50 per cent of the recorded amount as official records fail to capture the often large transfers through informal channels and often even exclude transfers made through regulated non-bank channels (World Bank 2006). Remittances are clearly an important a source of income for some poorer countries and has a major impact on the balance of payments, and on processes of social change at community, regional, and national level.

Second, the fact that remittances occupy a popular place in contemporary debates also reflects contemporary development fashions relating to the free market and the rolling back of the state, promotion of 'self-reliance', and interest in local–global linkages, as outlined by Devesh Kapur (2004: 7):

> Remittances strike the right cognitive chords. They fit in with a communitarian, 'third way' approach and exemplify the principle of self-help. People from poor countries can just migrate and send back money that not only helps their families, but their countries as well. Immigrants, rather than governments, then become the biggest provider of 'foreign aid'. The general feeling appears to be that this 'private' foreign aid is much more likely to go to people who really need it. On the sending side it does not require a costly

government bureaucracy, and on the receiving side far less of it is likely to be siphoned off into the pockets of corrupt government officials.

Third, the complex and changing global regulation of international financial flows drew attention to the relationship between remittances and financial sector development issues. At the macro level, the increases in recorded remittances to some countries following crack-downs on 'alternative remittance systems' served to demonstrate untapped potential for remittances to drive the expansion of the formal financial sector in countries of origin, increasing the availability of capital and credit. At the micro level, extending access of poorer people to more institutionalized and formal financial services (credit, savings, insurance) is seen as a way to help them manage and improve their livelihoods, and there are hopes that remittance flows can be utilized to plug poor people into financial services, which in turn will help them maximize the benefits for themselves and their communities.

Against this background, all kinds of policy goals and measures have been discussed regarding remittances, as indicated by Carling's inventory (2007) given in Table 10.1.

The popularity of different policy measures varies across countries and over time. Overall, there has been a general trend from either neglect, or policies aimed at rather heavy-handed control, towards softer 'remittance management' policies aiming to attract remittances by lowering costs, offering a range of incentives, or more broadly fostering good state-diaspora relations.[16] The policy of imposing taxation or other levies on incoming remittances has become less popular, due in part to evidence that this either discourages remittances or encourages leakage of remittances into the informal sector (World Bank 2006). The securitization of future remittance flows and issuance of diaspora bonds have been used as yet in rather a limited number of cases but may well increase in the future as governments seek ways to raise investment capital (World Bank 2006; Ketkar and Ratha 2007). Increasing officially channelled volumes of remittances (by means of transparency initiatives and fostering competition) and financial intermediation opportunities have also proved popular policy initiatives.

Remittances have long been recognized as a development policy issue by countries of origin with large numbers of emigrants, for example El Salvador, Mexico, Morocco, the Philippines, Sri Lanka, and micro-states in the Pacific. But in recent years, it is not only major labour-exporting countries that play a role in governing remittance flows, as states in the global North have also become involved in debating these issues, in their capacities both as host countries and as donors. Moreover, there is increasing interest also from intergovernmental organizations, international organizations, financial institutions, and civil society actors in using global mechanisms to shape remittance flows.

Table 10.1. Policy goals and measures regarding remittances

Intermediate objectives	Specific objectives	Examples of measures
Increase the volume of current remittances	Maximize the volume of remittances sent from abroad	Promote short-term labour migration
	Minimize the depletion of remittances by transfer costs	Low barriers to market entry for transfer service providers
	Increase financial returns to remittance deposits	Foreign currency accounts with premium interest rates
Promote the channelling of remittances directly to development purposes	Divert a proportion of remittances to be used by the state	Direct taxation of remittance transfers
	Promote donations by remittance senders	Voluntary check-off for charitable donations on transfer forms
	Stimulate development financing by hometown associations (HTAs)	Matched funding for HTAs
Stimulate direct investment of remittances	Outreach through the infrastructure of microfinance institutions	Small-scale credit for remittance receivers
	Outreach through migrants' service bureaus	One-stop-shop for emigrant investors
	SME schemes (financial, infrastructural, or innovative)	Tax break on imports of capital goods
Stimulate indirect investment of remittances	Promoting transfers through financial institutions	Cross-subsidization of transfer services by banks
	Increase financial returns to remittance deposits	Foreign currency accounts with premium interest rates
Stimulate development-friendly consumption	Promoting consumption of local goods and services	Tariffs on imported goods with locally produced alternatives
	Enabling migrants to spend on their relatives' behalf	Health insurance for non-migrants marketed to emigrants
	Address the social impact of remittance-fuelled business sectors	Surveillance of employment conditions in the construction sector
Stimulate sound management of remittances	Stimulate banking unbanked senders and receivers	Cross-subsidization of transfer services by banks
	Promoting financial literacy among senders and receivers	Financial education programmes through community organizations
	Promoting transfers through financial institutions	Cross-subsidization of transfer services by banks
Secure future remittances	Promote continued migration	Bilateral labour migration agreements
	Promote diaspora engagement	Exchange programmes for children of emigrants

Source: Carling (2007).

253

Prompted by growing information on the scale of global remittance flows and the potential of remittance-fuelled, private sector-led development, the G8 Sea Island Summit in June 2004 made remittances a key point in its Action Plan on Applying the Power of Entrepreneurship to the Eradication of Poverty (2004). This galvanized and guided the efforts of the major industrialized democracies in recent years in engaging with remittances as an international development issue.[17] Encouraged by such cues, many government development aid donors in the global North have engaged in a range of policy initiatives and programming activities regarding remittances, both at the domestic level and in their target countries (including the UK's Department for International Development (DFID), Agence Française de Développement, the United States Agency for International Development, Germany's Gesellschaft für Technische Zusammenarbeit (GTZ), Netherland's NOVIB).

During the last decade, nearly every major international development organization has shown some form of interest in the issue of remittances. Some now have dedicated staff or whole teams responsible for research activities or policy initiatives on the issue of remittances. For example, the World Bank, which has taken a prominent role, has engaged in considerable policy-focused research on the development impact of migration and remittances, working on improving statistical data on remittances, reducing transaction costs, and enhancing the integrity of money transfer systems, as well as providing input into its own Country Assistance Programs.

Regional development banks have also taken considerable interest in remittances as a source of development finance, as well as a financial flow to be regulated. For example, the Inter-American Development Bank's (IADB) Multilateral Investment Fund (MIF) provides financing aimed at increasing the development impact of remittances, particularly focusing on reducing transfer costs and increasing the rural outreach of formal banking services.

Finally, at national, regional, and global level, there are also private sector actors (e.g. Western Union and other global financial firms, and industry associations such as World Council of Credit Unions) and civil society actors (e.g. home town associations (HTAs) and their umbrella networks) that are engaging in shaping remittance flows.

What are the global-level mechanisms used by these actors in their attempts to govern remittance flows?[18] International legal instruments that regulate various aspects of migration generally have little to say about remittances. In the International Labour Organization (ILO) Convention No. 97 concerning Migration for Employment (Revised 1949), ratified by forty-seven states including many major migrant-sending and migrant-hosting countries, Article 9 requires parties 'to permit, taking into account the limits allowed by national laws and regulations concerning export and import of currency, the transfer of such part of the earnings and savings of the migrant for employment as the migrant may desire'.[19]

However, other global governance mechanisms are more prominent in the shaping of remittances as a development issue than these international legal frameworks, including global information-sharing and policy coordination platforms, codes of voluntary standards or principles, and remittance-related development programmes funded by international donors.

First, there has been the formation of platforms for the exchange of information and practices and the coordination of policy. Like many development policy hot topics, a vast amount of energy, money, and hope has been invested in a mushrooming global knowledge industry and information exchange around remittances. There has been a dramatic growth of organizational and expert networks and information-sharing platforms,[20] as well as conferences and other events.[21] A variety of ad hoc or semi-permanent forums have arisen to facilitate interaction.

For example, the Global Forum for Migration and Development which, as outlined in other chapters, emerged from the UN High-Level Dialogue on Migration and Development in 2006, describes itself as 'a platform for policy-makers to share information on ideas, good practices and policies regarding migration and development, and to explore new initiatives for international cooperation and multi-stakeholder partnerships'. The focus was explicitly on the socio-economic development implications of migration, rather than immigration management issues.[22]

In July 2007, representatives of 156 nations and numerous international organizations and civil society groups met in Brussels to discuss human capital development and labour mobility, remittances and diaspora resources, and enhancing policy and institutional coherence and partnerships. Discussions about remittances focused on policies and practices to enhance remittance services competition, ways to support financial institution partnerships, new technologies to reduce costs, and sharing best practices (e.g. on migrant financial literacy, migrant investment support, remittance data collection and creditworthiness, and securitization of future remittance flows and issuing of diaspora bonds).

Another example of a global policy coordination mechanism more specifically focused on remittance issues is the Inter-Agency Remittances Taskforce, co-chaired by the DFID and the World Bank and including the IADB, the Asian Development Bank, the Consultative Group to Assist the Poor, International Organization for Migration (IOM), ILO, NOVIB, and others, and which was founded to coordinate research and programming activities among these organizations. Building on such exchange platforms, a consensus has emerged on several principles regarding remittance, for example, the importance of recognizing that remittances are private money, and the counter-productive outcomes of taxing incoming remittances.

The second type of mechanism used in the global governance of remittances as a development policy issue has been the development of several codes of voluntary standards with various developmentally inspired aims. For example, the Core Principles for the Remittance Market in Latin America and the Caribbean, developed by a committee convened by the IADB's MIF, lay out some key broad principles of development-friendly remittance policies, intended to focus the collective efforts of a range of actors: remittance institutions (improve transparency, promote fair competition and pricing, apply appropriate technology, seek partnerships and alliances, and expand financial services), public authorities (do no harm, improve data, encourage financial intermediation, promote financial literacy), and civil society (leverage development impact and support social and financial inclusion) (Orozco and Wilson 2005).

Another example focuses more closely on the issue of the payment systems that facilitate remittances. A taskforce led by the Bank for International Settlement's Committee on Payments and Settlement Systems and the World Bank, composed of various central banks and international institutions, formulated the General Principles for International Remittance Services, focusing on transparency, competitiveness, consumer protection, efficiency of payments infrastructure, and appropriate legal frameworks. Again, the aim was to focus the efforts of states and international organizations working to maximize the development impact of remittances.[23]

The third global governance mechanism is remittance-related development programming by international donors. For example, the MIF, in partnership with the UN's International Fund for Agricultural Development, established a Financing Facility for Remittances in 2006 to promote inclusive financial systems and innovative partnerships between rural financial institutions and remittance operators that reduce remittance costs and open up more options for rural families to deploy their capital profitably.[24]

Another initiative is bilateral partnerships between countries of origin and host countries on migration and remittance issues. For example, in 2001, the United States and Mexico launched a 'Partnership for Prosperity', 'a private-public alliance to harness the power of the private sector to foster an environment in which no Mexican feels compelled to leave his home for lack of jobs or opportunity',[25] which includes in its Action Plan lowering the cost of sending money home by increasing competition and promotion of financial literacy. In 2004, DFID initiated 'Remittance Country Partnerships' with Bangladesh, Ghana, and Nigeria, countries receiving large volumes of remittances from the United Kingdom, with the aim of removing impediments to remittance flows, improving access for low-income and rural people to remittances and other financial services, and strengthening the capacity of the financial sector to provide efficient remittance services.

Other popular investments include initiatives in host countries aimed at increasing migrants' financial literacy and access to financial services, and reducing the costs of remittances. This is demonstrated by the growth of remittance price comparison websites to improve market transparency—Mexico's

'Quién es quién en el envío del dinero' has been followed by several host country-financed projects including the United Kingdom's 'Send Money Home' and 'MoneyMove', France's 'Observatoire des coûts d'envoi d'argent à l'étranger', Germany's 'Geldtransfair', and the Dutch 'Geldnaarhuis', and the Norwegian 'Sendepender'.[26]

Beyond the institutional framework, what are the politics of these global-level attempts to govern remittances? It is important to note that emigration states have played a role in and benefited from the creation of the global-level institutional frameworks described above that focus on remittances as a development issue for migrants' countries of origin. Emigration states, with the keen support of a development industry hypnotized by the new-found faith that remittances can galvanize developing economies, have made a space at global level to debate an issue of major import to their economies.

However, the heavy focus on remittances in recent years within what is a potentially wider (and indeed widening) migration-development debate is in part symptomatic of the interests and power relations underlying cooperation on this issue. From the perspective of host states in the global North, remittances are a secondary issue to the much thornier issue of immigration, which raises issues of state sovereignty. Remittance outflows are rarely significant enough in these economies to concern their economists or public. Promoting policy aimed at reducing obstacles to remittance transfers or enhancing the impact of remittances on the home country development of existing immigrants, is unlikely to ruffle the feathers of the electorate. The host-state-side policy goals which have really taken off in some European countries and North America—of improving transparency and reducing costs, improving migrants' financial literacy and financial access, and promoting HTAs—overlap with domestic goals of consumer protection, financial inclusion, and civil society promotion and are relatively achievable and uncontroversial. Major host countries are happy to discuss remittances, but frequently effectively veto discussions about opening up migration opportunities. It is interesting that although, as already mentioned, anticipated remittances are the rationale behind many emigration states' policy stances on labour migration, the links between the two are often not coherently articulated in recent global policy initiatives—although this may be changing as a resurgence of bilateral circular migration programmes is predicted.

Furthermore, there are important issues in the relationship between the 'remittances-for-development' agenda and the drive to govern international financial flows—which are far from entirely separate, articulating in interesting ways. First, there are important contrasts in institutional terms. The financial crime/security agenda tends to use stronger and more formal forms of intervention, mobilizing legal and regulatory tools to filter international financial flows, to prevent the criminal or terrorist use of the financial system. In contrast, the socio-economic development agenda tends in recent years to use softer forms of influence, building on non-binding voluntary standards, informal information exchange, and development programming to shape remittance flows in ways that are intended to maximize their positive impact in receiving countries. The ways in which remittances are mobilized for development also foreground private sector and civil society actors' roles much more.

Second, there is the question of timing: the process of exchanging information and building consensus around remittances at the global level has in some ways been prompted by the financial regulatory activity that drew attention to remittances, and has acted as a counter-balance to this in producing calls from some development actors (emigration states, and civil society and international organizations) for the moderation of overzealous regulations or adaptation to specific contexts.

Third, there are institutional interfaces. For example, national governments regulate their financial sector but also have to deal with development policy. The two agendas find their most obvious global institutional interface in the Bretton Woods institutions, which promote global monetary and financial stability, and provide loans, grants, and advice to countries in economic trouble. Their policy-making process has been criticized for the strong includes of the G7, because they represent the largest donors, and it seems that the way the 'remittances-for-development' debate has unfolded may have been influenced by this. For example, Ballard (2007:14) has pointed out that,

> if the Bank had actively followed through the implications of the arguments [articulated in its research reports, i.e. that remittances are a major source of relatively stable external finance to developing countries and that promoting migration can have major beneficial effects on poorer countries] . . . it would in effect have put the institution on a collision course with respect a set of issues of intense concern to its principal sponsor.

Ballard argues that the Bank, DFID, and other donors have resolved this tension, under pressure, by focusing on transmission costs, financial sector development issues, and moving remittances into formal channels, goals that do not conflict with the interests of Northern states.

Conclusions

Migrants' remittances have been subject to perhaps the most dramatic changes in global governance efforts of any of the areas of migration tackled in this book. A few years transformed remittances from a relatively arcane issue for many policymakers, concerning mainly emigration states, into a global financial governance issue close to the heart of the geopolitical moment.

The governance of remittances is fragmented into financial crime/security and broader socio-economic development agendas, which as we have seen are rather differently structured in institutional terms. In terms of financial regulation, states are key actors, but the last two decades have seen growing levels of regional- and global-level cooperation between states. The primary governance mechanisms in this area remain legislation and regulation. Meanwhile, regarding the development agenda, while emigration states have historically been the main actors in efforts to mobilize remittances towards national development goals, non-state actors, as well as state in the global North, have come to play a prominent role. In contrast to the legislative and regulatory approaches used by financial capital regimes, the 'remittance-for-development' agenda has been marked in recent years by a proliferation of informal and non-binding initiatives.

In terms of politics, emigration states have tended to find themselves as the 'takers' of global financial regulation—the FATF basically serves the interests of powerful nations. The government of the United States has proved particularly active in pursuing the financial 'war on terror', taking with it other powerful states, and catching up in its wake under threat of sanction a large number of smaller and poorer states that struggle to implement global standards effectively, but know that they must play the game to retain access to global financial markets. These asymmetric power relations have been formalized at global level through the norm-making activities of the FATF, a non-multilateral intergovernmental institution, and its regional subordinates.

In the global development policy arena, the power dynamics are less clear. Emigration states have found more opportunities to give voice to their concerns. But this has taken place in a more diffuse global arena, involving more non-state actors, dominated by much softer forms of cooperation—for example, the elicitation of statements of commitment to encouraging voluntary standards (rather than agreements to implement legislation). In focusing on remittances, some Northern state donors have found a way to engage in the global migration-development debate while avoiding some of the issues (such as low-skilled migration opportunities) less palatable to their governments' home affairs agendas.

Migrants might be forgiven for feeling confused: on the one hand, financial regulators scrutinize their remittances en route in case they might be 'dirty money', and on the other hand, global policymakers rub their hands at the possibilities offered by this private 'development capital'. The case for global-level intervention in remittance flows has several dimensions, which have some merits, but also weaknesses, at least from the perspective of migrants and the global majority. The most emphasized aim is the combating of crime and terrorism, which has shown to be a rather dubious rationale for targeting alternative remittance systems, with sometimes counter-productive and damaging results. Recent events in global banks suggest that the emphasis in recent years on alternative migrant remittance systems as a destabilizing element in the global system was rather misplaced.

Another aim of global governance sometimes cited has been to include remittances, as an important aspect of the economy, in Balance of Payment data for developing countries,[27] no doubt a source of satisfaction among macroeconomic planners and bureaucratic elites, but at first sight a rather distant concern to many migrants, and their communities. The formalization of remittances does suggest opportunities for financial intermediation to a range of private sector actors who may benefit themselves and whose involvement can bring—hopefully but in no way certainly universally—wider benefits for the communities and countries of origin.

A further argument marshalled in favour of the global governance of remittances has been that it can lead to improvements in remittance services from the point of view of migrants—and while financial regulators have not tended to emphasize customer protection and service standards, development policy initiatives have.[28] Migrants themselves tend to emphasize speed, availability, and cost: aside from 'mature corridors' like United States–Mexico, more evidence is needed to substantiate development policymakers' frequent claim that current interventions have led to improvements from migrants' perspectives (Ballard 2007).[29]

Finally, many remittance-related development projects have been met with vocal enthusiasm by many migrant associations (often involved in project implementation), and undoubtedly have considerable merits, but we need more evidence on the overall effectiveness of the many remittance-related development projects and initiatives spawned by global development policy actors.

This remains a contradictory and shifting subject of study. The global constraints on the mobility of labour have often been contrasted with the increasing liberalization of the movement of capital. The constraints on the global movement of people are often contrasted with the liberalization of the movement of capital. Yet the micro-transfers of migrants' capital has been subject to growing regulation in recent years, with systems emerging to tag and filter migrants' cash in ways that parallel border regimes with their visa controls and passports (Ballard 2007). While remittances have attracted the attention of policy-makers in powerful states much later in the day than migration, there has been an impressive flurry of global-level governance activity in the last decade. Indeed, compared with other dimensions of migration considered in this book, remittances in fact seem to be subject to much more comprehensive and clearly articulated global governance.

Notes

1. Argentina, Australia, Austria, Belgium, Brazil, Canada, China, Denmark, Finland, France, Germany, Greece, Hong Kong China, Iceland, Ireland, Italy, Japan, Netherlands, Luxembourg, Mexico, New Zealand, Norway, Portugal, Russian Federation, Singapore, South Africa, Spain, Sweden, Switzerland, Turkey, United Kingdom, and United States.
2. European Commission and the Gulf Co-operation Council.
3. India and the Republic of Korea have observer status, as do major international financial institutions, including regional development banks, and global and regional anti-crime bodies.
4. For more detailed analysis see Passas (2006) and Ballard (2005).
5. The latter demands that financial institutions pay special attention to financial relationships involving these countries and that states apply counter-measures against persistent offenders.
6. Eastern and Southern Africa Anti-Money Laundering Group (ESAAMLG); Intergovernmental Action Group against Money-Laundering in Africa (GIABA, for West Africa); Middle East and North Africa Financial Action Task Force (MEAFATF); Eurasian Group (EAG), Asia/Pacific Group on Money Laundering (APG); Financial Action Task Force on Money Laundering in South America (GAFISUD); Caribbean Financial Action Task Force (CFATF); Council of Europe Select Committee of Experts on the Evaluation of Anti-Money Laundering Measures and the Financing of Terrorism (MONEYVAL).
7. http://www.apgml.org (accessed 8 September 2004).
8. Full name: Directive 2007/64/EC of the European Parliament and of the Council of 13 November 2007 on Payment Services in the Internal Market.
9. Although it is unclear to what extent this will initially apply to transfers to locations outside the EU.
10. See mention of this point in Regulation (EC) No. 1781/2006 of the European Parliament and of the Council of 15 November 2006 on Information on the Payer Accompanying Transfers of Funds.
11. The word 'hawala' has been increasingly used as shorthand for all informal value transfer systems. There is an important distinction made in literature on informal economies between illicit and licit informal trade—activity that does and does not infringe criminal law. Prior to 9/11, in most financial jurisdictions (exceptions are India and Pakistan, where hawala has been illegal for some time), a distinction was made by law enforcers between 'white hawala' (the use of the hawala system to make legitimate international transfers, e.g. migrant remittances and legitimate trade transfers) and 'black hawala' (the use of the system for transfers that are considered illegitimate in most jurisdictions, for example a part of narcotics trafficking or fraud). But after 9/11, hawala has been increasingly presented in the media and the financial and law enforcement worlds as, at best, particularly *vulnerable* to use for illegitimate purposes, and at worst, expressly *designed for* illegitimate purposes. See Jost and Sandhu (2000).
12. i.e. in contrast to globalization from 'above'. See Smith and Guarnizo (1998).

13. For example, in South Africa an important component of the post-apartheid Black Economic Empowerment agenda was the extension of access to financial services—less than half the population had bank accounts in 2004—so that even the poorest people in society could access basic savings, credit, and insurance facilities to help them manage their livelihoods. But opening up access to financial services to poor black people was initially stalled by commitments South Africa made in its Financial Intelligence Centre Act, which required international best practice in the identification and verification of account holders. According to the 2001 Census, one-third of South Africans did not have a formal address, living in traditional dwellings or informal structures, which under the Act would have made it impossible for them to access bank accounts. In the end, a basic bank account (Mzansi) with exemptions was authorized to get around this problem. See Koker (2006).

14. This is only partly accounted for by the migration of funds into formal channels under regulatory pressure since 9/11.

15. 'Official remittances' are calculated by combining three items in the International Monetary Fund's *Balance of Payments Yearbook*: (*a*) 'workers' remittances', that is amounts received from people resident abroad throughout the year, (*b*) 'compensation of employees', that is wages, salaries, and other benefits of border, seasonal, and other non-resident workers, and (*c*) 'migrants' transfers', that is the net worth of the migrant transferred at the time of migration.

16. For example, in Morocco, a state that long recognized the importance of remittances and long feared a decline in flows, years of attempted 'remote control' of migrants to maintain remittance flows and quell political opposition gave way in the 1990s, in a climate of broader political and economic reforms, to policies that rather sought to attract remittances by courting migrant communities (providing support to migrants working overseas and on holiday in Morocco; changing fiscal and monetary policies favouring migrants which decreased remittance transaction costs and made sending money home more attractive; on the private sector front, Moroccan bank networks expanded through Europe and international money transfer firms expanded through Morocco providing efficient official channels for remitting). See de Haas (2007) and de Haas and Plug (2006).

17. G8 Action Plan: Applying the Power of Entrepreneurship to the Eradication of Poverty, Sea Island, 9 June 2004, http://www.g8.utoronto.ca/summit/2004seaisland/ poverty. html. The G8 laid out a broad agenda, focusing on making it easy for people to send remittances, reducing the costs, improving coherence and coordination among international organizations working on remittances, strengthening local financial markets and financial access by encouraging cooperation between various types of financial institutions, encouraging local development funds to facilitate the productive investment of remittances, and addressing infrastructure and regulatory impediments.

18. It is not possible to capture here all the many initiatives underway; the key initiatives, and some particularly interesting ones are given by way of illustration.

19. http://www.ilo.org/ilolex/cgi-lex/convde.pl?C097. Regular migrants' capacity to remit of course depends considerably on their circumstances in the host country and can be enhanced when they are treated no less favourably than nationals, in terms of remuneration, accommodation, social security, and employment taxes, which is also provided for in Article 6 of Convention No. 97. See also ILO (2007).

20. http://www.remesas.org, http://www.remittances.eu, http://remesasydesarrollo.org/, http://www.elremesero.com, http://www.dmassocs.com/dril, the DFID/USAID-sponsored Migrant Remittance Newsletter, the Research Consortium on Remittances in Conflict and Crises (http://isim.georgetown.edu/pages/RCRCC%20BIOS.html).

21. Recent issues of the Migrant Remittances Newsletter suggest that there is at least one remittance-related workshop or conference around the world each week.

22. http://www.gfmd-fmmd.org. The website declares that: 'The GFMD should also ensure that development is not instrumentalized for migration management purposes, and avoid that migration is seen as an alternative to development at either individual or country levels'.

23. http://www.bis.org/publ/cpss76.pdf. There are other principles and guidance developed, often as an element in broader agreements, for example see ILO (2006).

24. http://www.ifad.org/ruralfinance/remittance/call.htm.

25. http://www.state.gov/p/wha/rls/fs/8919.htm.

26. http://www.sendmoneyhome.org (funded by DFID) and http://www.moneymove.org, http://www.profeco.gob.mx/envio/envio.asp (Mexican Procuraduría Federal del Consumidor), http://www.envoidargent.org (Agence Française de Développment), http://www.geldtransfair.de (Deutschen Gesellschaft für Technische Zusammenarbeit, GTZ), http://www.geldnaarhuis.nl (IntEnt and NCDO), http://www.sendepenger.no (Norwegian Ministry of Foreign Affairs and the Norwegian Agency for Development Cooperation). All accessed 15 September 2008.

27. This is done more easily through the development of globally standardized methodologies and data collection and comparison.

28. Failure to deliver remittances is not such a key issue for migrants—given global telecommunications, it tends to be apparent fairly quickly which services may be trusted and people adjust their behaviour accordingly. Discussions with Roger Ballard were invaluable in clarifying some of the points in this paragraph.

29. See also Pieke et al. (2007).

References

9/11 Commission (2004) *Monograph on Terrorist Financing*, Washington, DC: 9/11 Commission.

Amuedo-Dorantes, C. and Pozo, S. (2005) On the Use of Differing Money Transmission Methods by Mexican Immigrants, *International Migration Review*, 39(3), 554–76.

Ballard, R. (2003) *A Background Report on the Operation of Informal Value Transfer Systems (Hawala)* (Unpublished edited version of an expert report prepared for the defence in one of the 'Hawala'/money laundering prosecutions mounted by UK Customs and Excise).

——(2005) Coalitions of Reciprocity and the Maintenance of Financial Integrity within Informal Value Transmission Systems: The Operational Dynamics of Contemporary Hawala Networks, *Journal of Banking Regulation*, 6(4), 319–52.

——(2007) Continuing the Challenge of Transnational Networking from Below: Post 9/11 Initiatives, Paper given at the Conference on Transnationalism and Development(s): Towards a North South Perspective, University of Bielefeld, 31 May–1 June 2007.

Bush, G. (2001) President Announces Crackdown on Terrorist Financial Network, Washington, DC: Whitehouse Press Release (7 November 2001).

Carling, J. (2007) Interrogating Remittances: Core Questions for Deeper Insight and Better Policies, in S. Castles and R. Delgado-Wise (eds), *Migration and Development: Perspectives from the South*, Geneva: IOM.

——Bivand Erdal, M., Horst, C., and Wallacher, H. (2007) *Legal, Rapid and Reasonably Priced? A Survey of Remittance Services in Norway*, Oslo: International Peace Research Institute.

Financial Action Task Force (FATF) (1990) *The Forty Recommendations*, Paris: FATF.

——(2001) *Special Recommendations on Terrorist Financing*, Paris: FATF.

——(2003) *Combating the Abuse of Alternative Remittance Systems: International Best Practices*, Paris: FATF.

——(2007) *Guidance on the Risk-Based Approach to Combating Money Laundering and Terrorist Financing: High Level Principles and Procedures*, Paris: FATF.

de Haas, H. (2007) Between Courting and Controlling: The Moroccan State and 'Its' Emigrants, Centre on Migration, Policy and Society Working Paper, No. 54, University of Oxford.

——and Plug, R. (2006) Cherishing the Goose with the Golden Eggs: Trends in Migrant Remittances from Europe to Morocco 1970–2004, *International Migration Review*, 40(3), 603–34.

International Labour Organization (ILO) (2006) *Multilateral Framework on Labour Migration: Non-Binding Principles and Guidance for a Rights-Based Approach to Labour Migration*, Geneva: ILO.

——(2007) *Rights, Migration and Development: The ILO Approach. Background Note for the Global Forum on Migration and Development*, Geneva: ILO.

Jost, P.M. and Sandhu, H.S. (2000) *The Hawala Alternative Remittance System and Its Role in Money Laundering*, Lyon: Interpol General Secretariat.

Kapur, D. (2004) Remittances: The New Development Mantra?, G-24 Discussion Paper Series, No. 29, New York and Geneva: United Nations Conference on Trade and Development and Intergovernmental Group of Twenty-Four.

Ketkar, S. and Ratha, D. (2007) *Development Finance via Diaspora Bonds: Track Record and Potential*, Policy Research Working Paper 4311, Washington, DC: World Bank.

de Koker, L. (2006) Money Laundering Control and Suppression of Financing of Terrorism. Some Thoughts on the Impact of Customer Due Diligence Measures on Financial Exclusion, *Journal of Financial Crime*, 13(1), 26–50.

Lindley, A. (2008) Between Dirty Money and Development Capital: Somali *Xawilaad* Under Global Scrutiny, Draft paper.

Orozco, M. and Wilson, S. (2005) Making Migrant Remittances Count, in D. Terry and S. Wilson (eds), *Beyond Small Change: Making Migrant Remittances Count*, Washington, DC: IADB.

Passas, N. (2006) Fighting Terror with Error: The Counter-Productive Regulation of Informal Value Transfers, *Crime, Law and Social Change*, 45, 315–36.

Pieke, F., Van Hear, N., and Lindley, A. (2007) Beyond Control? The Mechanics and Dynamics of 'Informal' Remittances between Europe and Africa, *Global Networks*, 7(3), 348–66.

Smith, M.P. and Guarnizo, L.E. (1998) *Transnationalism from Below*, New Brunswick, NJ: Transaction Publishers.

Vleck, W. (2006) Development v. Terrorism—Migrant Remittances or Terrorist Financing? Challenge Working Paper, London: Institute of Commonwealth Studies.

World Bank (2006) *Global Economic Prospects. Economic Implications of Remittances and Migration*, Washington, DC: World Bank.

——(2008) *Migration and Development Brief, No. 3 and 5*, Washington, DC: World Bank.

11

Diasporas

Alan Gamlen

Introduction

This chapter discusses the governance of diasporas as a facet of 'global migration governance'. Its basic brief is to outline the institutions and politics of the global governance in this area and make a case for how it should look, and the chapter is divided into three sections accordingly. It also aims to contribute to the wider discussion by asking what the governance of diasporas reveals about the meaning of 'global migration governance' generally.

Alex Betts describes a conventional view of 'governance' as 'regulation' in the absence of 'a single authoritative rule-maker' (Betts 2010: 4). What of the more familiar terms 'migration' and 'global'? Elsewhere, these terms are often conceived in a state-centric way that overlooks diasporas and transnationalism. Remembering two points helps to avoid this: firstly, 'migration' includes not just immigration but also emigration, and secondly, 'global' includes not just international but also transnational—and other—dynamics (e.g. see Agnew 2001). To highlight these points, this chapter looks at the regulation of emigration, diasporas, and transnational relations, which has become central to discussions of global migration governance (e.g. see GFMD 2007, 2008; GMG n.d.). This regulation is characterized by interactions among grass-roots translocal organizations, 'migration and development' policies made by development aid agencies and international organizations, and most importantly, the extra-territorial reach of emigration-state policies.

This approach highlights how global migration governance is not only an additional layer of regulation over and above the level of the nation-state but also a 'fragmented tapestry of overlapping, parallel and nested institutions' (Betts 2010: 2)—or as I shall phrase it, a 'multi-layered patchwork' of institutions and practices at, below, above, and across the nation-state level.

Diasporas and diaspora engagement

The term 'diaspora', while not as watered down as its harshest critics claim, has been subject to the kind of conceptual inflation that plagues many good and important ideas (e.g. see Tölölyan 1994; Cohen 1997; Safran 1999; Brubaker 2005). The current consensus seems to be that the essential features of a diaspora group are dispersion to two or more locations, ongoing orientation towards a 'homeland', and group boundary maintenance over time (Butler 2001; Brubaker 2005). This definition is broad enough to encompass both archetypal and more recent manifestations, yet specific enough to preserve the term's analytical value.

Perhaps the most interesting questions in diaspora theory now are the explanatory ones (raised e.g. by Stéphane Dufoix, 2008), which focus on how and why diaspora communities emerge and dissipate, rather than on whether or not they conform to an ideal type at any given moment. Because governance itself is constitutive of group identity and activity, the policies and politics of a variety of institutions form a complex set of explanatory variables in these processes of emergence and dissipation. Thus, like many of the concepts that form the chapter headings in this book, 'diaspora' is not merely an object of policy but also a function of it.

With these debates in mind, I approach 'diaspora' as an umbrella term for the many extra-territorial groups that, through processes of interacting with a variety of state institutions at, below, and above the nation-state, are attributed with various 'thicknesses' of 'diasporic membership' (Smith 2003a) in their home country. These groups include temporary or transnational migrants who spread their time between several places in which they hold some or other status (e.g. citizen, denizen, or visitor). They also include longer term but still first-generation emigrants settled in another country, and descendants of emigrants who—in certain places at certain times—identify as diasporic or even as members of a fully fledged diaspora 'community'.

Thus, the focus of the chapter is on the multi-layered patchwork of policies and politics that constitute these disparate groups as 'diaspora'. These are sometimes referred to as 'diaspora engagement policies' (e.g. see Newland and Patrick 2004; Van Hear et al. 2004; Gamlen 2006). The term 'diaspora engagement' is used in several different senses. In the first, it refers to the bottom-up, grass-roots trans-local activities of migrants and their associations. In this sense, it is something that diasporas do—that is, they engage to a greater or lesser extent in the economic, political, and social life of their home country. Secondly, the term is used in the context of top-down attempts by aid agencies and international organizations to encourage this kind of engagement. In this sense, diaspora engagement is both something diasporas do, and something that is done to them—that is, they are engaged or seconded into the process of aided development. In the third sense, diaspora engagement refers to the policies of migrant-sending states towards their diasporas. At one level, a diaspora engagement policy is a deliberate effort by a government or administration to promote the diaspora's continued existence and involvement at home. However, at another level such a policy breaks down into numerous micro-level initiatives and ad hoc practices across a range of different state agencies. Moreover, these micro-level practices typically exist whether or not there is any macro-level effort to coordinate them, and therefore terms like 'policy' or 'strategy' can sometimes be misleading. Instead, it may be useful to think of a particular portion of the state system as connected to the diaspora, whether or not this portion is organized in a deliberate or coherent way. I refer to this portion as 'the emigration state' system (Gamlen 2008a).

Institutions

A number of writers have emphasized the importance of a multi-level perspective on transnational relations (e.g. see Østergaard-Nielsen 2003b; Shain and Barth 2003; Délano 2010). In this section I explore how institutions at the local, national, and international levels interact and pressure nation-states to 'engage the diaspora'.

Local

Even though only a relatively small proportion of migrants are often involved in transnational activities (Portes et al. 2002), as migration increases—for whatever reason—so does the significance of local-level groups and institutions that identify with and connect to a foreign place of origin. Important work on trans-local migrant associations is currently being carried out at a number of leading institutions, including the International Migration Institute at the University of Oxford, and the Centre for Migration and Development at Princeton University.

Perhaps the key organizations within 'engaged' diaspora communities—with whom national and international organizations are partnering—are hometown associations (HTAs). Manuel Orozco and Rebecca Rouse describe HTAs as 'organizations which allow immigrants from the same city or region to maintain ties with and materially support their places of origin' (Orozco and Rouse 2007). They note that HTAs are found in most migrant-receiving countries, and estimate that, worldwide, around 3,000 Mexican HTAs, 1,000 Filipino groups, and 500 Ghanaian organizations were active in 2007. HTAs are typically built around core groups of emigrant organizers who coordinate events and collective donations, mobilizing wider and more diverse networks at particular moments. For example, the authors found that even though Guyanese HTAs in the

United States typically receive donations from over 100 people, the core groups themselves usually comprise fewer than twenty actual members.

However, in addition to HTAs, there is a wide variety of types of trans-local organizations, ranging from sporting and cultural clubs and societies, through to professional associations, chambers of commerce, philanthropic networks, and lobby groups. Individual organizations differ widely in the extent to which they identify with, and actively connect to, a region of origin. However, in general it is fair to say that such associations play a significant role in the mobilization and governance of migrant communities in receiving locations, and sometimes also in the governance of trans-local communities. Often such groups cluster, socially if not always geographically, around the local diplomatic post of their origin country. For example, the large Korean community in the New Malden suburb of London is thought to have formed around the former residence of the Korean Ambassador in neighbouring Wimbledon.[1]

National

Perhaps the most important institutional developments in terms of diaspora engagement are currently occurring at the national level—to the extent that Levitt and de la Dehesa (2003) suggest that a 'redefinition of the state' is taking place. On one hand, national institutions are adapting as transnational activities transform governance of localities. On the other hand, these adaptations are eliciting responses from agencies within migrant-receiving states and from multilateral institutions. These responses at the international level are in turn creating pressures on states to interact with and regulate the conduct of 'their' diasporas in particular ways. Thus, the pressure to 'engage diasporas' (e.g. see de Haas 2006; Ionescu 2006) currently converges on policy-makers in national-level institutions.

States respond to these pressures and deal with emigrants and their descendants through a diverse range of mechanisms. Østergaard-Nielsen (2003a) and Chander (2006) distinguish between states' economic, political, and cultural devices. Barry (2006) identifies legal, economic, and political instruments. Levitt and de la Dehesa (2003) distinguish between bureaucratic reforms, investment policies, political rights, state services abroad, and symbolic politics. I identify two types of diaspora policy mechanism: one type which cultivates and recognizes a fairly thin identification and orientation among emigrants and their descendants towards home-country institutions, and another type which extends a thicker form of membership involving various privileges and responsibilities extra-territorially (Gamlen 2008a).

'Diaspora building' is the label I use for institutions and activities that cultivate diasporic identities and communities, and/or formally recognize them. In cases where emigrants and their descendants are not as organized as state officials might like, the latter may try to cultivate feelings and expressions of attachment to 'home', organizing national celebrations abroad, convening diaspora congresses, using flattering rhetoric, or handing out patriotic awards. State agencies often actively support or facilitate public broadcasting and media abroad, or organize concert tours, cultural exhibitions, and courses targeted at 'diaspora' audiences. They may even take an active role in organizing HTAs or other expatriate associations around particular local issues or interests.

In cases where diaspora communities are more organized, they may pressure state institutions for formal recognition in various ways. Such recognition may come in the form of claims by government to represent the diaspora, and in some cases even constitutional amendments or similar statutes. Governments may commission surveys or studies to enshrine the diaspora in statistics. An increasing number of countries are expanding their consular structures or establishing bureaucratic units dedicated to relations with diaspora communities—for example, a review of sixty-four states found 76 per cent had some kind of bureaucratic structure for dealing with expatriates (Gamlen 2008a).

'Diaspora integration' is my label for mechanisms which bind emigrants and their descendants into what Jagdish Bhagwati (2003) describes as 'a web of rights and obligations' with their home country. There has recently been an international trend towards greater tolerance of dual citizenship (Bauböck 2005), but there is still wide variation both among and within states with regard to the extent of civil, social, and political rights granted to particular sectors of the 'diaspora'.

As Rainer Bauböck (2003: 709) notes, disinterest towards the diaspora is the default normative position of home states. However, in empirical terms, expansive political rights are neither new nor unusual: they are widespread and long-standing in states of all kinds. In a sample of 144 countries, Collyer and Vathi (2007) found that 115 (80 per cent) allowed extra-territorial electoral participation in some form, and that this result could not be explained merely by ratios of residents to non-residents or remittances to gross domestic product.

Origin states can protect the civil and social rights of diasporas through consular service and bilateral agreements. The Vienna Convention on Consular Relations (UN 1963) broadly specifies the lower and upper bounds of accepted practice, but allows considerable latitude for states to use their discretion when 'protecting and safeguarding the interests of nationals', or 'helping and assisting' them. In practice, therefore, the content of consular service differs widely among different states and among the consular districts maintained by each individual state. In cases where consular posts are maintained at all, it is typically not domestic policy but either foreign policy or the discretion of the most senior officer that dictates whether the post merely provides minimal notarial services to an exclusive group, or acts as a secretariat for a thriving diaspora community. Between these extremes lies a range of relatively unmapped consular activities, which includes but is not limited to maintaining and using consular databases, lobbying for the rights of prisoners or undocumented migrants, issuing diaspora identity cards, and even offering supplementary health-care and education services for emigrants and their descendants.

Bilateral agreements on social security benefit portability form another set of tools states have at their disposal for extending extra-territorial social rights. The Ministry for Overseas Indians, for example, has a special unit dedicated to bilateral issues (Gurucharan 2009). Like that of consular service, the scope of bilateral agreements is not standardized: except in comparatively integrated regions such as the European Union (EU), agreements rarely follow a common multilateral template (Holzmann et al. 2005: 23–4). They can therefore be a complex and patchy area of international regulation, characterized by gaps and overlaps which lead to inefficiencies and injustices. Migrants may pay into schemes from which they cannot benefit (e.g. see Clark 2002). One state may receive contributions while the other state bears the burden of social care (Holzmann et al. 2005: 20–31). Only some 20–25 per cent of migrants are covered by bilateral or multilateral social security agreements (which currently represent best practice in social security portability), and most of these agreements are between developed countries (Holzmann et al. 2005: 35).

Though they lack extra-territorial authority to enforce obligations, states may play on feelings of responsibility or loyalty in their diasporas in order to socially (rather than coercively) enforce membership obligations. Thus, for example, though formal expatriate taxes[2] such as the USA's are relatively rare, informal expatriate taxes such as Eritrea's war-time 'healing tax' (Koser 2003)—enforced by social expectations rather than by law—appear to be more widespread. States which cannot enforce taxation either legally or socially may attempt to 'woo' remittance senders and channel their private contributions into the public purse through a mixture of incentives, marketing techniques, and patriotic appeals. Some of the best-known mechanisms in this policy space are matching fund programmes, duty-free import schemes, incentives such as free passport issuance or preferential interest rates, and foreign-currency bank accounts. Some states target larger scale expatriate investments as part of targeted foreign direct investment campaigns, or financial products such as foreign-currency-denominated 'diaspora bonds' (Chander 2001). Public tourism agencies frequently attempt to boost tourist revenues by targeting 'roots' tourists among emigrants and their descendants. Research and education bureaucracies are increasingly encouraging highly skilled expatriates to contribute ideas and know-how towards economic growth at home—not only by returning but by remaining connected through networks and online skills banks—while publicly funded universities and schools frequently seek to supplement their endowments through philanthropic donations from alumni luminaries. In addition to soliciting economic contributions, a number of states co-opt well-positioned sectors of the diaspora as lobbyists or informal ambassadors who can speak up for their home country.

International

Diaspora engagement is also on the international agenda. In the bilateral arena, for example, development aid agencies such as Britain's Department for International Development (DFID) and the United States Agency for International Development (USAID) now promote the transnational engagement of UK-based or US-based diaspora groups in order to 'intensify the flow of knowledge and resources of Diaspora to their home countries to promote economic and social growth'.[3]

One of the most useful overviews of diaspora engagement activities in the multilateral arena is provided by the United Nations Secretary General's 2008 Report on International Migration (UNGA 2008). The report notes that informal 'regional consultative processes' such as the '5+5 Dialogue' on Migration in the Western Mediterranean, the 'Colombo Process' on Overseas Employment and Contractual Labour in Asia, and the 'Lima' and 'Puebla' Processes on Migration in Latin America and the Caribbean have all been examining ways of facilitating the developmental contributions of emigrants to their home countries. It also notes the 'ad hoc' consideration given to the role of diasporas in homeland development, by the 'Söderköping Process' on border management in Eastern and Central Europe; the Intergovernmental Consultations on Migration, Asylum, and Refugees; and the Inter-Governmental Asia-Pacific Consultations on Refugees, Displaced Persons, and Migrants (UNGA 2008: 17).

Formal regional cooperation forums are also encouraging diaspora engagement. For example, the European Commission and United Nations Development Programme (UNDP) have established a 10 million euro fund to encourage remittance and knowledge transfer initiatives from diaspora and other small groups,[4] while the African Union's 2006 'Migration Policy Framework' aims to 'mitigate the effects of the emigration of highly skilled professionals and to maximize the mobilization and use of migrant remittances' (UNGA 2008: 15). The 2008 'common approach on migration' of the Economic Community of West African States (ECOWAS) included an agreement to support and develop transnational ties and return migration (UNGA 2008: 15), while the 2007 'Declaration on the Protection and Promotion of the Rights of Migrant Workers' adopted by the Association of Southeast Asian Nations (ASEAN) specifies the obligations of sending countries to protect emigrants rights.[5] A similar approach of encouraging sending states to create 'enabling environments', for example through attention to dual citizenship provisions, pension portability, and issues surrounding taxation and remittances, characterized the 2008 'consultative meeting' on 'Mobilizing the African Diaspora for Development' convened by the African Union, along with the African Development Bank, USAID, the International Finance Corporation (IFC), and the World Bank.[6]

In addition, a myriad of specialized international agencies and non-governmental organizations have shifted their aid strategies towards encouraging developmental engagement between diaspora communities and their home countries.

For example, the Dutch arm of Oxfam International (Oxfam Novib) published a report entitled 'Engaging Diasporas' in 2006 (de Haas 2006), and works with the African diaspora in the Netherlands to fund HTA economic development projects in places like Somalia, Ghana, and Burundi (Orozco and Rouse 2007). The International Labour Organization (ILO) makes various efforts to 'optimize' remittance usage and returnee integration, while the World Bank conducts research on remittances and recommends ways of improving remittance infrastructure (World Bank 2005; UNGA 2008: 13), in addition to supporting several country-level projects to build and maintain databases and networks of skilled emigrants (Kuznetsov 2006). In 2008 the Bank signed a five-year memorandum of understanding with the African Union covering assistance for African governments engaging their diasporas.[7] The United Nations Educational, Scientific and Cultural Organization (UNESCO) has looked at the homeland developmental impact of expatriate 'knowledge networks' (Meyer and Brown 1999; Turner et al. n.d.), while the International Organization for Migration (IOM) consistently advocates engaging diaspora communities as development partners (e.g. see Ionescu 2006).

The Secretary General's report notes increasing activity related to diaspora engagement at the core of the United Nations system. For example, various regional commissions are initiating studies and projects on diaspora engagement. The Economic Commission for Africa (ECA) and the Economic and Social Commission for Asia and the Pacific (ESCAP) are looking into remittances and development, and the latter is also interested in 'transnational entrepreneurship' and diaspora technology transfers (UNGA 2008: 10). In addition, the United Nations Conference on Trade and Development (UNCTAD) and the UNDP have both offered advice to policy-makers on policies to improve the developmental impact of remittances and diaspora contributions (UNGA 2008: 11), while the International Fund for Agricultural Development (IFAD) has also spearheaded work with HTAs, teaming up with the Multilateral Investment Fund of the Inter-American Development Bank to fund the work of HTAs in Mexico, Honduras, and Haiti (Orozco and Rouse 2007).

Perhaps most importantly, diaspora engagement has become a central theme for newly formed and forming bodies such as the Global Forum on Migration and Development (GFMD 2007, 2008) and the Global Migration Group (GMG n.d.). Both organizations represent a growing movement—at least partly galvanized by the Global Commission on International Migration (GCIM 2005)—for coherence and coordination concerning migration issues across the international system.

Politics

As suggested above, there is currently a convergence of pressures on institutions at the national level to 'engage their diasporas'. This section begins to outline the political processes that have led to this pressure.

Various authors have demonstrated that national-level diaspora engagement policies are nothing new (e.g. see Thunø 2001; Smith 2003a; Cano and Delano 2007). For example, Rachel Sherman (1999) observes that the Mexican state has gone through periods of 'introversion' and 'extension' with respect to emigrants and their descendants, and that changes in orientation are prompted by 'crises of legitimacy'.

I attempt to build on this approach in two ways. Firstly, for ease of analysis I modify Sherman's idea of 'introverted' and 'extended' incorporation, viewing the portion of the state which deals with emigrants as an analytical unit—the emigration state system—which undergoes periods of expansion and contraction. Secondly, I generalize about what kinds of domestic and international political debates cause expansion and which cause contraction. To be specific, on one hand, I suggest that pressure for recognition from diaspora groups at the local level, along with international pressure to achieve 'migration and development', is stimulating the creation and expansion of diaspora-related institutions and activities within migrant-sending states. On the other hand, I suggest that 'territorial' factors—in both the domestic and international spheres—tend to restrict expansion in the emigration state system.

Local

Alejandro Portes writes, 'grass-roots transnationalism is seldom initiated by governments from the sending countries, ... governments enter the picture as the importance of the phenomenon becomes evident' (Portes 1999: 466–7). According to this perspective, migrants engaged in transnational activities remain a relatively small proportion of all migrants, but as their absolute number increases with migration, they become more organized and active in transnational politics. As part of this process they gradually push for recognition from institutions in their home country, either through political parties or through direct lobbying of state agencies, often emphasizing their transnational contributions through remittances, investments, expertise, and political support. This pressure prompts responses from institutions in the home country. The Mexican case certainly supports the 'reactive' hypothesis, as Carlos Gonzalez-Gutierrez, Executive Director of the Institute for Mexicans Abroad, explains:

> Like other homelands and other diasporas, we wanted to believe that migrants go just for a time and then they will come back, they will not take their families. And [the] 1986 [Immigration Reform and Control Act] broke with that illusion, because almost from Monday to Tuesday 2.3 million Mexicans became legal in the US and therefore could come and go. And that by itself multiplied societal relations and links between Mexican organizations and Mexican leaders in the US and Mexico. And I think that the government realized that a lot of processes were not controlled and then

they had to do something. It was a process that the state didn't control: they [had] to react.[8]

However, there is also evidence to support a 'proactive' hypothesis about the role of home states in grass-roots transnational activities. As a number of writers have highlighted, states may also take the lead, assuming an active role in community organization (e.g. see Margheritis 2007). This is currently occurring in a number of states as particular agencies, or groups of agencies, are encouraged (by 'migration and development' thinking) to perceive a strategic interest in transnational activities. While they are certainly not the be all and end all of state-diaspora relations, as Wendy Larner notes (Larner 2007), such 'diaspora strategies' have become increasingly common in recent years.

In reality there are probably pressures from both sides in any particular case. Migrant associations are often established with or by consular and diplomatic officers; the officers move on but organizations mature and become independent, and eventually seek new and expanded forms of recognition from new officers. In New Zealand, for example, government has funded the 'Kiwi Expats Assocation' (Kea New Zealand), a global network headquartered in New Zealand, to collect data on expatriates and employ Regional Managers to act as community organizers in key locations worldwide. As groups have cohered, typically around social and professional networking events, they have become increasing involved in discussions of expatriates' voting rights and behaviour.[9] Robert Smith describes a similar back-and-forth dynamic opening up 'transnational public spheres' in the Mexican, Italian, and Polish cases (Smith 2003*b*).

State responses recognizing or encouraging grass-roots trans-local organization are more or less constrained by factors relating to territoriality. One of these is the potential conflict of interest between residents and non-residents. Residents tend to complain when scarce public resources are spent on programmes, activities, or institutions dedicated to non-taxpayers, or when non-residents are given voting rights or influence in government decisions that they do not have to live with. A territorially bounded conception of society is also at the heart of second argument that sometimes constrains the expansiveness of state-diaspora relations: the argument that diaspora policies of various sorts represent a kind of state interference in the lives of individuals who have decided to leave and should therefore be left alone. A third territorial constraint is that imposed by receiving states, who may veto diaspora policies which they perceive to be infringements on their sovereignty—as did Hungary's neighbours when it tried to enact its Status Law earlier this decade (Ieda 2004). Finally, lack of extra-territorial capabilities can restrict the expansion of emigration regimes as much as these types of normative arguments (e.g. see Levitt and de la Dehesa 2003; Østergaard-Nielsen 2003*a*). Exercising control at a distance can be costly—especially when options are limited and brute force is ruled out—and this imposes resource constraints on emigration regimes.[10]

International

One of the most important expansionary pressures on emigration states is currently found at the international level and consists of the activities (outlined above) promoting 'migration and development'. According to migration and development theory, migration is not necessarily a zero sum game: migrants, receiving countries, and sending countries may all simultaneously win. In economic terms, migrants win through higher wages. They bring down excessive labour costs in receiving states and excessive unemployment in sending states. In theory, their labour power is not monopolized by receiving-country employers, but shared with sending countries through remittances, investments, and philanthropy. Similarly, their brainpower is not 'stolen' from sending countries by receiving countries, but rather enhanced and shared through 'circular migration'. Moreover, in theory, migrants' brains and get-up-and-go attitudes make them great unofficial ambassadors for their homelands—if only sending states would stop treating them as deserters. The lynchpin of the theory is that emigrants remain—or can be encouraged to remain—positively engaged both in their host societies and in their homelands through remittances, investments, knowledge transfers, circular migration, and 'soft' diplomacy.

Why has the idea of migration and development recently become so appealing to development agencies and international agencies? One explanation would be that it is politically convenient for these organizations if migration and development theory holds. On one hand, the theory is useful for governments of donor countries: if the theory holds, they can simultaneously pacify pro- and anti-immigration lobbies, arguing that immigration not only boosts the receiving economy but also develops the sending one and thereby eventually eliminates the need for migration—leading to the convenient argument that the best way of preventing migration in the long run is to let it continue. Moreover, if receiving states can promote development in home countries through diaspora engagement, they need no longer fear diaspora groups so much as fifth columnists, and can instead begin courting them with aid funds so that they might help further receiving-state interests vis-à-vis the sending government. To boot, by outsourcing aid provision to diaspora groups, aid agencies may cut their costs and better monitor how aid is spent. Perhaps these factors help to explain why development agencies such as the United Kingdom and the United States are actively promoting the engagement of diaspora groups as partners in the development of their home countries (see above).

On the other hand, the notion of promoting migration and development through diaspora engagement is also useful for international institutions. To these organizations, the theory presents a potential solution to the seemingly inevitable conflicts of interests between migrant-sending and migrant-receiving states; it is an optimistic argument for the international cooperation they exist to promote. Those organizations which favour free market solutions can encourage governments to 'enable' the transnational tendencies of migrants by freeing-up cross-border flows (Kapur 2005: 339). Those favouring interventionist solutions can implement programmes to actively encourage transnational involvements. Perhaps this political economy helps to explain why, on one hand, the World Bank has encouraged governments to free up remittance markets (World Bank 2005), while on the other hand, the European Commission and UNDP have created a 10 million euro fund to support diaspora-led development projects (see above).

Rationales

In this section I discuss what rationales might justify particular types of global governance in the area of diasporas. I make the case for an efficient and equitable style of governance, led by emigration states and moderated by global norms and institutions. At this point it is important to recall that there is a distinction between micro-level diaspora policies, which are more or less ubiquitous but typically ad hoc and often incoherent, and macro-level diaspora policies which aim at coherent 'joined up' or 'whole of government' approaches to emigrants and their descendants. In principle, a policy of 'no policy' (as Mexico had for many years; see Fitzgerald 2006a) or a policy of rejecting the diaspora (as in cases where the diaspora is mired in conflict with the state of origin) could be coherent. However, here I make the case for coherent efforts to 'engage' or 'incorporate' emigrants and their descendants into national society to some degree. Below I outline two possible rationales for this type of policy approach, based on two contrasting views of the diaspora: the first of which sees it as a 'constituency', and the second of which sees it as a 'resource'.[11]

Diaspora as constituency

The extent to which a migrant-sending state should be thought of as having obligations towards emigrants and their descendants is dependent on a particular concept of citizenship. Rainer Bauböck, for example, argues that 'citizenship status and rights should be allocated to individuals who are stakeholders in the future of the political community' (Bauböck 2007: 2446).

> The notion of stakeholding expresses first the idea that citizens have not merely fundamental interests in the outcomes of the political process, but a claim to be represented as participants in that process. Second, stakeholding serves as a criterion for assessing claims to membership and voting rights. Individuals whose circumstances of life link their future well-being to the flourishing of a particular polity should be recognized as stakeholders in that polity with a claim to be represented in collective decision-making processes that shape the shared future of this polity. (Bauböck 2007: 2442)

Such a conception of citizenship leaves room for some members of the diaspora to be seen as legitimate stakeholders in their home country, with concomitant membership rights and obligations.

These rights and obligations arguably generate an imperative to create coherent macro-level diaspora engagement policies, for two reasons. Firstly, as Bhagwati (2003) emphasizes, rights and obligations must go together. It is relatively easy for entitlements to more or less inadvertently spill across borders, driven by policy in unrelated areas. For example, consular service and bilateral agreements may cover some expatriates quite thickly, as a side-effect of foreign policies towards the region where they happen to live. However, it requires concerted efforts to efficiently and equitably impose responsibilities on the recipients of these extra-territorial entitlements, without infringing the sovereignty of the receiving state, over-serving expatriates at the expense of home-country residents, or interfering unjustly with people who have chosen to disassociate themselves with their state of origin. Such concerted efforts imply a coherent macro-level approach of engaging the diaspora.

Secondly, although the dominion of a state is thickest within its own territory, migrant-sending states inevitably exert a thinner form of dominion over their diasporas, and this arguably places them under obligation to treat their diasporas fairly. In this case, I would argue that fairness implies treatment with 'differential but equal' concern—that is, treatment with concern that is different from that accorded to residents who are more thickly dominated, but treatment that is equal across regional and demographic groups within the diaspora. In sum, I would argue that migrant-sending states should make coherent, macro-level diaspora policies based on the aim of differential but equal treatment where rights and obligations are extended in equal measure.

Normative arguments against such an approach are not uncommon. A number of writers make a kind of 'no representation without taxation' argument against diverting attention, decision-making power, and resources away from residents towards emigrants. For example, David Fitzgerald writes, 'emigrants make policies to which they are not as directly subject as resident citizens... [and] it is much easier for emigrants to claim rights of citizenship than for states to enforce the duties of emigrant citizenship' (Fitzgerald 2006b: 116). In a similar vein, Glick Schiller and Fouron write that 'efforts to...portray the diaspora as the hope of the nation channel energy and resources away from struggles for social and economic justice. These efforts also divert attention from the root causes of... continuing economic and political crisis' (Glick Schiller and Fouron 1999: 358). Some authors see such policies as authoritarian or paternalistic insofar as they interfere with people who have chosen to sever ties to their home state. For example, Basch et al. (1994: 269) warn of a situation where 'the nation's people may live anywhere in the world and still not live outside the state... wherever its people go, their state goes too'. Policies of engaging diasporas are sometimes seen as ethnically chauvinistic or discriminatory—for example, Christian Joppke (2005: 243) argues that the 'the bashing of the immigrant and embracing the emigrant bears the unmistakable signature of the political right'. Similarly, some writers see diaspora engagement policies as a type of pernicious 'long-distance nationalism' (Anderson 1992; Glick Schiller 2005), which may even be linked to irredentist ambitions.

However, there are also many strong normative counterarguments. Under Bauböck's 'stakeholder' view of citizenship (see above), emigrants are not necessarily 'outsiders' with separate and less-legitimate interests to those of residents. As Robert Smith writes, 'Migrating to and settling in another state while maintaining various political and other links with one's home state creates the possibilities for creative use of exit, voice and loyalty that would not be available were one to reside within the home state's territory' (Smith 2003b: 301). Those who wish to disassociate themselves from their home state are much more free to do so than had they never left—they may naturalize elsewhere, or at least to avoid contact with the institutions of their nominal homeland. It seems excessive to suggest that diaspora policies are necessarily expressions of ethnic chauvinism and hostility towards immigration; rather, policies of engagement with the diaspora are often part of explicit efforts to recognize diversity (as Irish President Mary Robinson pointed out in her famous 'Cherishing the Diaspora' speech in 1994), or to integrate into supranational groupings like the EU (as Hungarian Status Law framers insisted they were doing, even as they were being accused of long-distance nationalism by ultra-nationalists in neighbouring countries; Ieda 2004). For every case where long-standing ethnic rivalries or territorial disputes engender suspicion of irredentism or fifth column-ism, there is another where bilateral relations are warm enough to accommodate diaspora policies without friction (e.g. see Délano 2010).

Perhaps it is true that diaspora engagement policies may become vehicles for ethnic chauvinism, irredentism, paternalistic treatment of emigrants, or comparative neglect of those who remain in the sending country. However, it would be a mistake to suggest they are necessarily so.

Diaspora as resource

A second rationale for making coherent, macro-level diaspora engagement policies rests on the view that diasporas represent a resource available to the home country. This rationale can be summarized in one phrase: migration and development. As discussed above, migration and development theory asserts that migrant-sending states can gain through the remittances, investments, knowledge transfers, and political influence of their diasporas.

Whether or not this is the case is a matter for empirical research on specific cases. The migration and development case is discussed extensively above, and there is no need to review it again here, except to emphasize that it is prudent to retain some scepticism. Could there really be a grand bargain among sending states, receiving states, and migrants, or is the celebration of remittances and other diaspora effects a way of legitimizing a bargain in which the elites of powerful receiving countries benefit disproportionately? Can national interests actually converge over migration, or is migration and development theory being used to argue that nation-states should be less self-interested and more open to cooperation for a (possibly imagined) global collective interest? Are diaspora groups really the most effective development actors, or is 'diaspora engagement' just a way for aid agencies and international organizations to 'pass the buck' onto migrants? It is important to ask such questions rather than assuming the current celebration of migration and development as politically neutral.

A related argument sees transnational relations less as a policy opportunity and more as a policy imperative. For example, in the realm of economic policy, inward and outward migration patterns condition patterns of investment and labour demand and supply—yet economic policy-makers only collect decent data on inward migration and tend to equate migration policy with immigration policy. Relationships among different types of transnational involvement—cultural, social, economic, and political—interact in ways that most national policy-makers have only relatively recently begun to take an interest in. Similarly, education and health-care policies must grapple with populations spread across national borders, tax systems, and welfare states (Lunt et al. 2006). For example, when children emigrate or parents retire abroad, the burden of caring for dependent youths or elderly people may shift onto other family members or public services. A 'brain drain' may take place, whereby residents take a 'free ride' on national education before emigrating to a foreign tax jurisdiction. The complex, ad hoc international system of benefit portability contains many gaps and overlaps in coverage leading to inefficiencies and injustices both for states and for individual migrants—such as where migrants pay into health-care schemes in one country but get sick in another, or where their pension eligibility is discounted arbitrarily when they retire abroad (Clark 2002).

In short, the impact of diasporas on existing public institutions and policies is complex and far-reaching, but it is typically treated in an arbitrary and ad hoc manner, based on migration data in which the emigrants are invisible.

Conclusion

This chapter has discussed the institutions, politics, and policy rationales reg-ulating transnational relations between diasporas and migrant-sending states. The discussion of institutions focused on three levels: the local, the national, and the international. At the local level, a range of civic organizations—particu-larly HTAs and similar groups—play a role in mobilizing and governing trans-national relations, for example by pooling remittances, organizing cultural activities, and acting as representatives for migrants vis-à-vis institutions in the home and host country. At the national level, domestic policies with an extra-territorial reach play a central role in governing diasporic ties. Clusters of national-level agencies, which I refer to collectively as 'emigration state' sys-tems (Gamlen 2008a), perform various roles in conferring diasporic identities and recognizing diasporic activities, and draw emigrants and their descendants into 'a web of rights and obligations' (Bhagwati 2003). Increasingly, develop-ment aid agencies and international organizations are encouraging these local- and national-level dynamics, hoping to promote 'migration and development' through 'diaspora engagement'.

The discussion of politics focused on how and why these three levels interact, arguing that emigration states expand and contract and that current trends of expansion result from the simultaneous pressure of local and international level dynamics on national administrations. On one hand, sending-state govern-ments 'enter the picture as the importance of the phenomenon [of transnation-alism] becomes evident' (Portes 1999: 466–7), while on the other hand, international actors are encouraging more engagement of this kind between emigrant organizations and the administrations in their sending countries. National governments are responding by extending and thickening their extra-territorial reach—encouraging and channelling more and more diasporic identities and activities. However, this expansionary dynamic is constrained by 'territorial' factors, such as perceived conflicts of interest between diasporas and communities in the homeland, or between administrations in the receiving and sending territories.

The discussion of policy rationales makes two separate cases for coherent diaspora engagement policies in migrant-sending states, one based on the assumption that the diaspora forms a constituency, and the other based on the assumption that it constitutes a resource. The constituency view leads to an argument that it is unjust for states to impact on diasporas in an unplanned way, through ad hoc or purely exploitative measures. The resource view leads to arguments that a policy of engaging the diaspora can help to achieve 'migration and development', or that such a policy is required in order to adapt to increas-ing transnational relations.

Can these discussions add anything to the broader discussion about what 'global migration governance' is, how it has come about, and what it should look like? Potentially yes—at least in terms of emphasizing one of Alex Betts' key points, about the 'fragmental nature of global migration governance. I have emphasized that global migration governance is not merely an additional layer of regulation lying flatly over and above the level of the nation-state. Rather, it consists of cross-cutting interactions among local, national, and international institutions. It is a 'multi-layered patchwork' of institutions and practices that have come into being at different times, for different reasons, and in different locations and levels of governance. This patchwork is not entirely new, though novel elements are being spliced in and old elements are being re-stitched as part of a new round of globalization. Though not the only layer in this patchwork, the nation-state remains the most thickly woven and the least 'leaky'. This is to be welcomed: on one hand, nation-states provide the strongest institutional fabric we have to hold together 'global' society, while on the other hand, we know that strong global and local structures can help loosen this fabric where it is bound too tightly. A global migration governance with self-governing nation-states at its core, sewn together by sub-national and supra-national organizations, is one that seems suited for the current age of migration.

Notes

1. Hall, S. 'With Heart and Soul in the Seoul of Surrey', *The Guardian*, 25 June 2002, http://www.guardian.co.uk/uk/2002/jun/25/worldcupfootball2002.sarahhall. Accessed 2 Feb. 2009.
2. For discussion of expatriate taxes, see Bhagwati (1976, 2003).
3. USAID Global Partnerships, 'Diaspora Engagement: Remittances and Beyond', http://www.usaid.gov/our_work/global_partnerships/gda/remittances.html. Accessed 24 Sep. 2008. Also see DFID (2007).
4. http://content.undp.org/go/newsroom/2008/november/ec-un-launch-initiative-on-migration-and-development.en. Accessed 1 Feb. 2009.
5. 'ASEAN Declaration on the Protection and Promotion of the Rights of Migrant Workers', 13 January 2007, http://www.aseansec.org/19264.htm. Accessed 1 Feb. 2009.
6. 'African Finance Ministers and Donors Meet Chart New Course', *Modern Ghana News*, 14 October 2008, http://www.modernghana.com/newsp/186250/1/pageNum1/african-finance-ministers-and-donors-meet-chart-ne.html. Accessed 9 Jan. 2009.
7. Also see 'The African Union and World Bank: Mobilizing the African Diaspora', 9 October 2008, http://web.worldbank.org/WBSITE/EXTERNAL/COUNTRIES/AFRICAEXT/0,,contentMDK:21936148~menuPK:258649~pagePK:2865106~piPK:2865128~theSitePK:258644,00.html. Accessed 9 Jan. 2009; 'Sierra Leone Diaspora Mobilization Program Takes off', 27 October 2008, http://web.worldbank.org/WBSITE/EXTERNAL/NEWS/0,,contentMDK:21954665~pagePK:34370~piPK:34424~theSitePK:4607,00.html. Accessed 18 Nov. 2008.
8. Interview with the author, Mexico City, 5 Sep. 2007.

9. Moss, I. 'Overseas Voters Change Two Seats in Parliament', Kea Media Release 17 December 2008.
10. Interestingly, this suggests that the emigration regimes of weaker states are more constrained than those of powerful states, despite that most of the scholarly and policy attention has been directed towards the efforts of weaker states. Rhodes and Harutyunyan (2007) and Gamlen (2008*a*).
11. For related discussion see Gamlen (2008*b*, 2008*c*).

References

Agnew, J. (2001) Disputing the Nature of the International in Political Geography—The Hettner-Lecture in Human Geography, *Geographische Zeitschrift*, 89, 1–16.

Anderson, B. (1992) The New World Disorder, *New Left Review*, 193, 3–13.

Barry, K. (2006) Home and Away: The Construction of Citizenship in an Emigration Context, *New York University Law Review*, 81, 11–59.

Basch, L.G., Schiller, N.G., and Szanton Blanc, C. (1994) *Nations Unbound: Transnational Projects, Postcolonial Predicaments, and Deterritorialized Nation-States*, Amsterdam: Gordon and Breach.

Bauböck, R. (2003) Towards a Political Theory of Migrant Transnationalism, *International Migration Review*, 37, 700–23.

——(2005) Expansive Citizenship: Voting Beyond Territory and Membership, *Political Science and Politics*, 38, 683–7.

——(2007) Stakeholder Citizenship and Transnational Political Participation: A Normative Evaluation of External Voting, *Fordham Law Review*, 75, 2393–447.

Betts, A. (2010) Introduction, in *Global Migration Governance*, Oxford: Oxford Univeristy Press.

Bhagwati, J. (ed.) (1976) *The Brain Drain and Taxation: Theory and Empirical Analysis*, Amsterdam: North-Holland.

Bhagwati, J. (2003) Borders Beyond Control, *Foreign Affairs*, 82, 98–104.

Brubaker, R. (2005) The 'Diaspora' Diaspora, *Ethnic and Racial Studies*, 28, 1–19.

Butler, K. (2001) Defining Diaspora, Refining a Discourse, *Diaspora*, 10, 189–219.

Cano, G. and Delano, A. (2007) The Mexican Government and Organised Mexican Immigrants in the United States: A Historical Analysis of Political Transnationalism (1848–2005), *Journal of Ethnic and Migration Studies*, 33, 695–725.

Chander, A. (2001) Diaspora Bonds, *New York University Law Review*, 76, 1005–99.

——(2006) Homeward Bound, *New York University Law Review*, 81, 60–89.

Clark, G. (2002) Country of Residence and Pension Entitlement: The Arbitrary Geography of UK Legal Formalism, *Environment and Planning A*, 34, 2102–6.

Cohen, R. (1997) *Global Diasporas: An Introduction*, London: UCL Press.

Collyer, M. and Vathi, Z. (2007) *Patterns of Extra-Territorial Voting*, University of Sussex.

Délano, A. (2009) From limited to Active Engagement: Mexico's Emigration Policies from a Foreign Policy Perspective (2000–2006), *International Migration Review*, 43, 764–814.

DFID (2007) *Moving Out of Poverty: Making Migration Work Better for Poor People*, London: Department for International Development.

Dufoix, S. (2008) *Diasporas*, Berkeley, CA; London: University of California Press.

Fitzgerald, D (2006a) Inside the Sending State: The Politics of Mexican Emigration Control, *International Migration Review*, 40, 259–93.

——(2006b) Rethinking Emigrant Citizenship, *New York University Law Review*, 81, 90–116.

Gamlen, A. (2006) *What are Diaspora Engagement Policies and What Kinds of States Use Them?*, Oxford: Centre on Migration, Policy and Society, University of Oxford.

——(2008a) The Emigration State and the Modern Geopolitical Imagination, *Political Geography*, 27, 840–56.

——(2008b) Why Engage Diasporas? COMPAS Working Papers, 08–63.

——(2008c) Why is it Important to Know About Diasporas? United Nations Economic and Social Council, ECE/CES/2008/26.

GCIM (2005) Migration in an Interconnected World: New Directions for Action—Report of the Global Commission on International Migration, Geneva: United Nations.

GFMD (2007) Report of the first meeting of the Global Forum on Migration and Development, Belgium, 9–11 July 2007.

——(2008) Protecting and Empowering Migrants for Development, Second Meeting of the Global Forum on Migration and Development, Manilla.

Glick Schiller, N. (2005) Long-Distance Nationalism, in M. Ember, C.R. Ember, and I. Skoggard (eds), *Encyclopedia of Diasporas: Immigrant and Refugee Cultures Around the World*, New York: Kluwer Academic/Plenum Publishers.

——and Fouron, G. (1999) Terrains of Blood and Nation: Haitian Transnational Social Fields, *Ethnic and Racial Studies*, 22, 340–66.

GMG (n.d.) Global Migration Group: Migration and Development Projects and Activities.

Gurucharan, G. (2009) Engaging the Diaspora for Development, Diaspora Strategy Workshop, National University of Ireland.

de Haas, H. (2006) *Engaging Diasporas: How Governments Can Support Diaspora Involvement in the Development of Countries of Origin*, Oxford: Oxfam Novib.

Holzmann, R., Koettl, J., and Chernetsky, T. (2005) Portability Regimes of Pension and Health Care Benefits for International Migrants: An Analysis of Issues and Good Practices, Paper prepared for the Policy Analysis and Research Programme of the Global Commission on International Migration.

Ieda, O. (2004) Post-Communist Nation Building and the Status Law Syndrome in Hungary, in Z. Kántor, B. Majtényi, O. Ieda, B. Vizi, and I. Halász (eds), *The Hungarian Status Law: Nation Building and/or Minority Protection*, Sapporo: Slavic Research Center.

Ionescu, D. (2006) *Engaging Diasporas as Development Partners for Home and Destination Countries: Challenges for Policymakers*, Geneva: IOM.

Joppke, C. (2005) *Selecting by Origin: Ethnic Migration in the Liberal State*, Cambridge, MA; London: Harvard University Press.

Kapur, D. (2005) Remittances: The New Development Mantra? in S.M. Maimbo and D. Ratha (eds), *Remittances: Development Impact and Future Prospects*, Washington, DC: World Bank.

Koser, K. (2003) Long-Distance Nationalism and the Responsible State: The Case of Eritrea, in E. Østergaard-Nielsen (ed.), *International Migration and Sending Countries: Perceptions, Policies and Transnational Relation*, Basingstoke: Palgrave Macmillan.

Kuznetsov, Y. (ed.) (2006) *Diaspora Networks and the International Migration of Skills: How Countries Can Draw on Their Talent Abroad*, Washington, DC: World Bank.

Larner, W. (2007) Expatriate Experts and Globalising Governmentalities: The New Zealand Diaspora Strategy, *Transactions of the Institute of British Geographers*, 32, 331–45.

Levitt, P. and de la Dehesa, R. (2003) Transnational Migration and the Redefinition of the State: Variations and Explanations, *Ethnic and Racial Studies*, 26, 587–611.

Lunt, N., McPherson, M., and Browning, J. (2006) *Les Familles et Whanau sans Frontieres: New Zealand and Transnational Family Obligations*, Wellington: Families Commission.

Margheritis, A. (2007) State-Led Transnationalism and Migration: Reaching Out to the Argentine Community in Spain, *Global Networks*, 7, 87–106.

Meyer, J.-B. and Brown, M. (1999) Scientific Diasporas: A New Approach to the Brain Drain, World Conference on Science UNESCO-ICSU, Budapest, Hungary, Management of Social Transformations Discussion Paper No. 41.

Newland, K. and Patrick, E. (2004) *Beyond Remittances: The Role of Diaspora in Poverty Reduction in Their Country of Origin: A Scoping Study by the Migration Policy Institute for the Department of International Development*, Washington, DC: Migration Policy Institute/Department of International Development.

Orozco, M. and Rouse, R. (2007) Migrant Hometown Associations and Opportunities for Development: A Global Perspective, *Migration Information Source*, February 2007.

Østergaard-Nielsen, E. (2003a) International Migration and Sending Countries: Key Issues and Themes, in E. Østergaard-Nielsen (ed.), *International Migration and Sending Countries: Perceptions, Policies and Transnational Relations*, Basingstoke: Palgrave Macmillan.

——(2003b) The Politics of Migrants' Transnational Political Practices, *International Migration Review*, 37, 760–86.

Portes, A. (1999) Conclusion: Towards a New World—The Origins and Effects of Transnational Activities, *Ethnic and Racial Studies*, 22, 463–78.

——Guarnizo, L., and Haller, W. (2002) Transnational Entrepreneurs: An Alternative Form of Immigrant Economic Adaptation, *American Sociological Review*, 67, 278–98.

Rhodes, S. and Harutyunyan, A. (2007) States and Their Citizens Abroad: Democratization and the Extension of Formal Rights and Obligations to Diasporas, Annual Meeting of the American Political Science Association, Hyatt Regency Chicago and the Sheraton Chicago Hotel and Towers, Chicago, IL.

Safran, W. (1999) Comparing Diasporas: A Review Essay, *Diaspora*, 8, 255–91.

Shain, Y. and Barth, A. (2003) Diasporas and International Relations Theory, *International Organization*, 57, 449–79.

Sherman, R. (1999) From State Introversion to State Extension in Mexico: Modes of Emigrant Incorporation 1900–1997, *Theory and Society*, 28, 835–78.

Smith, R.C. (2003a) Diasporic Membership in Historical Perspective: Comparative Insights from the Mexican, Italian and Polish Cases, *International Migration Review*, 37, 724–59.

——(2003b) Migrant Membership as an Instituted Process: Transnationalization, the State and the Extra-territorial Conduct of Mexican Politics, *International Migration Review*, 37, 297–343.

Thunø, M. (2001) Reaching Out and Incorporating Chinese Overseas: The Trans-Territorial Scope of the PRC by the End of the 20th Century, *The China Quarterly*, 168, 910–29.

Tölölyan, K. (1994) Diasporama, *Diaspora*, 3, 235.

Turner, W.A., Henry, C., and Gueye, M. (n.d.) Diasporas, Development and ICTs, Institute for Research on Development (IRD), http://www.limsi.fr/Individu/turner/DKN/Completed_research/IRD_article.pdf.

UN (1963) Vienna Convention on Consular Relations, *Treaty Series*, 596, 261.

UNGA (2008) International Migration and Development: Report of the Secretary General, Sixty-third session.

Van Hear, N., Pieke, F., and Vertovec, S. (2004) *The Contribution of UK-Based Diasporas to Development and Poverty Reduction*, Oxford: Centre on Migration, Policy and Society (COMPAS), University of Oxford.

World Bank (2005) *Global Economic Prospects 2006: Economic Implications of Remittances and Migration*, Washington, DC: World Bank/The International Bank for Reconstruction and Development.

12

Root Causes

Stephen Castles and Nicholas Van Hear

Introduction

Previous chapters have explored the governance of migration in relation to the forms and consequences of human mobility. At various times over the last forty years or so there have also been attempts to address the forces and factors which generate migration: these attempts have been cast as 'addressing the root causes of migration'. Since the causes of migration are diverse, and a matter of much debate, there is not an explicit set of governance policies and practices that can be said to address them, but rather a slew of approaches that have shifted over time and according to circumstances. We review some of the main approaches to 'root causes' in this chapter.

'Addressing the root causes of migration' became something of a mantra in the 1980s and 1990s, similar in some ways to the 'diaspora engagement' and 'harnessing remittances for development' debates of more recent times. Indeed such an approach sounds like incontrovertible common sense. However, addressing root causes has proved somewhat intractable, not least because ultimately they lie in the imbalances of power and resources in the global political economy, and addressing them would require a major transformation in the distribution of power and resources worldwide.

The notion essentially refers to measures designed to reduce migration (especially South–North migration) by dealing with the supposed driving factors in origin countries, especially violence, human rights violations, disparities in living standards, and poverty. As such, the idea is inextricably bound up with notions of development, poverty alleviation, and conflict reduction. Explicit discourse on 'root causes' appears to have originated in debates on forced migration, but is now widely used in the context of economic migration as well. The use of the term 'root causes' seems to have started in the early 1980s

(Boswell 2003: 624). But if one looks at measures rather than terminology, policies to limit economic migration to Europe through the development of origin regions go back to the 1970s—in fact, just as far as measures to address the 'relief-development gap' in forced migration. Recently, debates on root causes have played a major role in international policy deliberations, notably through the Global Commission on International Migration (GCIM) (2003–5), the UN High-Level Dialogue on Migration and Development (HLD) (2006), and the Global Forum on Migration and Development (GFMD) (2007–10). The question has therefore once again become a key policy concern.

In the case of forced migration, root causes approaches have been concentrated on dealing with violence and human rights violations, through 'humanitarian action' such as conflict prevention, peace-building, and post-conflict reconstruction—and in extreme cases, military intervention. In the case of economic migration, the solution is seen in development policies designed to reduce poverty. One variant of this is the 'co-development' policies (especially used by France, Italy, and Spain), which explicitly link return migration (of 'unwanted' migrants) with development measures.

Since the 1990s, root causes debates have been linked to the realization by governments and international agencies that it has become increasingly difficult to distinguish between forced and economic migrants in certain movements—such as those from South Asia and Africa to Europe. The growing awareness of 'mixed movements' and 'mixed motivations'—often summed up in the concept of the 'migration-asylum nexus'—implies that conflict and poverty are closely linked and often occur in the same places. This in turn has led to a blurring of the distinction between humanitarian action and poverty reduction: developmental approaches have become significant in policies to reduce forced migration, while human rights and good governance are now seen as central to poverty reduction.

In this chapter we track the development of root causes approaches over the last fifty years or so. We first examine the origins of root causes approaches, and then turn to more recent discourses on migration and development, which emphasize the potential of remittances, 'brain circulation', and diaspora engagement to bring about development in regions of origin, and thus—it is hoped—to reduce future migration. As we discuss, the unspoken assumption of most protagonists in such debates is that migration of the poor should be prevented or deterred. By contrast, we argue that migration is (and has always been) a way in which people can develop their human capabilities and improve their livelihoods. We will put the root causes debate in the context of the social transformation of both North and South through neo-liberal globalization. Finally, we will point to possible shifts (both short- and long-term) in root causes approaches as a result of the current global financial crisis.

The unfolding of 'root causes' approaches

In the 1970s and 1980s, root causes approaches at first emerged fairly separately for economic and forced migration, only to become more closely linked from the 1990s. Here we will briefly chart these two strands in the European context, and how they came together as a result of the end of the Cold War and accelerated globalization.

Economic migration 1950s–1980s

From 1945 to about 1973, the core industrial nations of Western Europe all imported labour either from the European periphery (Southern Europe, Ireland, Finland, North Africa, and Turkey) or from former colonies in Africa, the Caribbean, and Asia. The provision of mainly low-skilled labour through migration was part of the political economy of a Western European boom based on Fordist-era mass production plants. However, many development economists argued that labour migration was also beneficial to origin countries, and was an integral aspect of their 'modernization'. Such economists believed that the reduction of labour surpluses (and hence unemployment) in areas of origin and the inflow of capital through migrant remittances could improve productivity and incomes, and help overcome economic backwardness (Massey et al. 1998: 223). The governments of countries like the Philippines, Morocco, and Turkey shared this view, and encouraged their nationals to migrate to North America or Western Europe, claiming that labour export would facilitate economic and social development at home (Castles and Kosack 1973; Castles and Delgado Wise 2008).

However, such positive views on the benefits of labour migration for origin countries were questioned by development scholars influenced by dependency and world systems theories.[1] By the 1970s, research in countries like Turkey was showing that labour recruitment schemes often brought little long-term economic benefit for origin countries (Paine 1974; Abadan-Unat 1988; Martin 1991). The result was a shift amongst policy-makers and analysts to a predominantly pessimistic view that 'migration undermines the prospects for local economic development and yields a state of stagnation and dependency' (Massey et al. 1998: 272).

This shift coincided with a major change in Western Europe: in reaction to the 1973 Oil Crisis, virtually all labour importers stopped recruitment and introduced policies to encourage migrant workers to return home. As is now well known, many migrant workers stayed on and brought in their families, leading to unexpected trends towards permanent settlement and the formation of new ethnic minorities. The Oil Crisis proved to be a turning point in other ways too. Instead of investing in Fordist-type industries in the old industrial areas of Western Europe, corporations became multinationals, and often moved labour-intensive production process to low-wage areas of the South (Froebel et al. 1980).

289

This set the stage for a reassessment of ideas on the costs and benefits of labour migration epitomized in the title of an economic study of the time: *Trade in Place of Migration* (Hiemenz and Schatz 1979). Mainstream economics now argued that free trade was conducive to development of poorer countries, while migration brought few benefits. It was no doubt pure coincidence that free trade and restricted migration were now key policies of this phase of globalization. By the 1980s, the dominant view was that Europe would no longer need migrant workers, and that globalized capital investment would bring about accelerated development in poor regions of the world, leading to a trend towards equilibrium in productivity and incomes between North and South. As we will discuss below, a decade later, when asylum became a key political issue in Europe, governments sought to restrict it partly through strict border control, partly through getting origin and transit countries to cooperate in 'migration management', but also partly through addressing the 'root causes' of flight—defined as impoverishment and violence.

Forced migration 1980s–1990s[2]

Root causes approaches in the area of forced migration developed separately and in parallel with the application of the concept to economic migration. The international refugee regime established by the UN Refugee Convention of 1951 had focused on the situation of Europe in the aftermath of the Second World War, but was quickly adapted to Cold War exigencies, serving as a mechanism for welcoming fugitives from communist countries in Western countries. The numbers were small, due to the exit restrictions of Soviet-Bloc countries, so that generosity towards those who succeeded in traversing the Iron Curtain provided valuable propaganda to the West.

However, from the 1950s, large-scale refugee movements started to develop in the South in response to decolonization and struggles around the formation of new states in Asia, Africa, and Latin America. According to Charles Keely (2001, 2004) and B.S. Chimni (1998), a *dual refugee regime* emerged. A 'Northern regime', run by the United States and Western European states, was designed to resettle Cold War refugees in the West. A 'Southern regime' was developed in response to mass flight from violence. This regime centred on the United Nations High Commissioner for Refugees (UNHCR), which took responsibility for assisting refugees in camps or hosted outside camps by local populations in Africa, Asia, and Latin America. The solution of permanent resettlement on a large scale in developed countries was not seen as appropriate—except for Indo-Chinese and Cuban refugees who fitted the Cold War mould. The objective was repatriation as soon as possible. Assistance was seen as an emergency measure, quite separate from development aid. There was little coordination between relief agencies like the UNHCR and development agencies like the United Nations Development Programme (UNDP). Many of the refugee flows were the result of proxy wars arising from the East–West rivalry, and aid sometimes had the effect of keeping such conflicts going, while hindering escalation into all-out inter-bloc warfare.

The failure to overcome the causes of protracted conflicts led to discussions between key actors, including donor government and UN agencies, about how to bridge the 'relief-development gap'. This related to situations where an immediate conflict or disaster had passed and humanitarian assistance was withdrawn, without the affected populations being integrated into longer term development initiatives. Refugees and other forced migrants often strad-dled the two categories 'relief' and 'development', and were insufficiently catered for by either regime, particularly in situations where they had been displaced for long periods.

Several attempts were made to address this dilemma, and these can be seen as forerunners of more recent 'developmental approaches' to the root causes of forced migration. The 'refugee aid and development' initiatives of the 1970s and 1980s focused on Africa and climaxed in the Second International Conference on Assistance to Refugees in Africa (ICARA II) in 1984, which linked humanitarian aid to refugees in African countries with measures to support economic and social development in these host countries. The later 'returnee aid and development' schemes of the 1990s similarly fell short of expectations because they were not able to adequately address coordination and mandate issues, and because of the mutual suspicions of each other's motives by the parties involved (Crisp 2001; Betts 2004). Refugee-hosting countries wanted recognition of the principle of international burden sharing, not least in the form of compensation for the costs of hosting large numbers of refugees. On the other hand, developed countries were eager to reduce asylum seeker inflows and to reduce expenditure on relief and aid. Donors 'felt that the refugee aid and development concept was being used as a means of mobilising additional development funding for some hard-pressed (and in many cases badly governed) states, instead of consti-tuting a genuine effort to resolve refugee problems' (Crisp 2001).

In any case, the Northern refugee regime was coming under increased pres-sure from the mid-1980s, when the number of asylum seekers started to increase sharply, with many coming from the South. As both government and publics became increasingly hostile to escalating numbers of new arrivals, the asylum debate became highly politicized after the end of the Cold War.

After the Cold War: 'mixed flows' and 'migration management' in the 1990s

Following the collapse of the Soviet Bloc, Europe experienced a rapid increase in migration flows, which included both forced and economic migrants. In the early 1990s, the spotlight was on East–West flows of asylum seekers resulting from the meltdown of the Soviet Union and the former Yugoslavia, as well as states like Romania and Albania. The largest inflows were to states near the fault-lines—especially Germany, which received 438,000 asylum seekers in 1992—as well as Italy and Sweden. This resulted in an upsurge in racist violence and extreme-right mobilization. Germany amended its Basic Law, which had given a right to asylum, while Sweden revised its hitherto welcoming asylum rules. There was widespread panic at the idea of a flood of impoverished people on the march from East to West. European politicians and large sections of the media claimed that many asylum claimants were economically motivated, and were abusing the system. The emphasis of the international refugee regime shifted to containment of refugees in their areas of origin.

Yet it soon became clear that the expected mass flows from East to West were not taking place (Thränhardt 1996). It also became evident that flows were 'mixed'—in more ways than one. First, the increase in mobility to Europe was from the South as well as the East: people were coming from Africa, Latin America, and Asia as well as from Eastern Europe. The growth in migration was as much due to the improved transportation and communication opportunities developing as part of globalization, as to the removal of political barriers. Second, flows typically included not only people fleeing persecution and violence but also labour migrants and family members of previous migrants. Indeed, many of the people moving had 'mixed motivations': they were fleeing violence and persecution (and were thus 'asylum seekers'), but they were seeking to build new lives and to send remittances to dependants back home (so they were also 'economic migrants').

The initial response of European states to the new trends of the 1990s was to strengthen national border control measures. The resettlement-based refugee approach of the Cold War period was largely abandoned. Generosity towards refugees from the East had been based on the 'non-departure' measures of communist states. Now the West shifted to 'non-arrival' measures. European states adopted a range of measures to improve border control, including visa requirements, carrier sanctions, temporary protection systems for refugees, and safe third-country rules. National asylum regimes were tightened up to deter claimants through prohibitions on work, reduced welfare entitlements, and detention of certain groups.

But it soon became apparent that national border control alone was doing little to stop movements of asylum seekers and 'unwanted' migrants. The vast discrepancies between Europe and the South in terms of incomes, welfare, and human rights encouraged migration however high the barriers. European states moved towards cooperation on new systems of 'migration management'. Initial efforts through the Schengen Agreement, the Dublin Agreement, and various European Union measures were designed to improve border protection, prevent 'asylum shopping', and harmonize policies. Inevitably, such steps often made it difficult for genuine refugees to enter a potential asylum country to lodge a claim. An unexpected, though unsurprising, side effect was to force many refugees into the hands of people-smugglers, generating a new and lucrative transnational business opportunity. In any case, border control at the European level proved little more effective than national measures.

The result was a trend towards integration of migration and asylum into the EU's foreign policy. This 'external dimension' of EU cooperation in Justice and Home Affairs (JHA) (Boswell 2003: 619) found expression in a series of European Council[3] statements and in the establishment in 1998 of the High Level Working Group on Asylum and Migration (HLWG), which comprised not only JHA experts but also experts in the fields of foreign, security, development, and economic policies. EU activities in this area, especially the fairly unsuccessful record of the 'country action plans' suggested by the HLWG, have been charted in detail elsewhere (see Van Selm 2002; Castles et al. 2003). The key point in the context of this chapter is, as Boswell (2003) shows, that the 'external dimension' took two very different forms. The first was to gain the cooperation of origin and transit countries in *externalizing border control*: that is getting these countries to deter asylum seekers and irregular migrants from departing, to combat people-smuggling, and to readmit persons who had been deported from the EU. The second form was cooperation with origin and transit states on *preventive measures*: that is measures designed to address the factors that influence people's migration decisions, for instance by improving refugee protection, as well as through measures to promote development, trade, investment, or human rights. Such measures can appropriately be referred to as root causes approaches.

The struggle between proponents of externalization of border control and of root causes approaches has been a constant theme of European migration management since the late 1990s. JHA officials within the Commission, and also in national government departments (like the British Home Office), have advocated strong border control measures both domestically (within Europe) and beyond (in transit and origin countries). Development and foreign affairs officials, by contrast, have often been loath to advocate preventive measures, for fear of making their areas of responsibility into apparent instruments of migration control policy. Governments of transit and origin countries have also tended to reject policies which link migration prevention with development aid, since they see these areas as separate and often have an interest in increased labour migration of their nationals.

Such conflict became evident in the run-up to the Seville European Council of 2002, when proposals were made by the Spanish and the British Prime Ministers to link readmission agreements for failed asylum seekers and migrants to aid and cooperation arrangements with countries of origin. The relevant part of the conclusions adopted by the Seville Council in fact stopped short of imposing economic sanctions on countries of origin, but focused strongly on combating illegal immigration and on the readmission of illegal immigrants including failed asylum seekers. It seemed that the JHA agenda was paramount. This was not surprising in view of the increasingly hostile climate to migration in Europe, and the growing perception, particularly after 11 September 2001, that migrants were a threat to national security (Bigo and Guild 2005).

However, the 'neighbourhood policy' of the EU continues to put forward both control and preventive measures to reduce migration from such countries as Morocco and Ukraine, and development and foreign affairs officials within the Commission and national governments seem more willing to participate in such efforts (Boswell 2003: 636). At the same time, 'co-development' policies put forward by France, Italy, and Spain have in some cases won the cooperation of origin country governments. The notion of co-development envisages development through 'circular migration' to generate both transfers of money in the form of remittances and human capital, as well as knowledge more generally. However, many of the countries of migrant origin targeted by such policies understood the link between migration-reduction and development incentives implicit in the notion of co-development, and are somewhat wary of it, as with other similar interventions.

Root causes and policy developments in the twenty-first century

The rise and fall of the 'migration-asylum nexus'

The struggle between the proponents of border control and those who saw addressing root causes as a more productive approach was accentuated by the mixed migratory flows that gathered momentum in the 1990s and 2000s, as noted above. Researchers and analysts had pointed increasingly to the continuum between 'forced' and 'voluntary' migration from the 1990s (Richmond 1994; Van Hear 1998). This perspective was increasingly taken up in the policy arena, where it found expression as concern with 'mixed migration' and the somewhat grander term the 'migration-asylum nexus', particularly after around 2000.[4]

While it had some currency beforehand, the term the 'migration-asylum nexus' took hold during the Global Consultations on International Protection, launched by UNHCR in 2000 against the background of what the organization saw as a crisis in international protection of refugees at the time of the 50th anniversary of the 1951 Refugee Convention. A major part of that crisis was the increasing perception by the governments and publics of Western countries that large-scale abuses of the asylum system were taking place: the view was that asylum seekers were really economic migrants in disguise. The exploration of the 'nexus between migration and asylum' (UNHCR 2001a: 1) was in part undertaken to address such anxieties, and spawned a number of position papers drafted jointly by UNHCR, ILO, IOM, and other agencies (UNHCR 2001a, 2001b). The notion found its way into the outcome of the Global Consultations, the Agenda for Protection, agreed in 2002, under which states reaffirmed their support for the 1951 Convention and pledged support for the goal of 'protecting refugees within broader migration movements' (UNGA 2002: 10).

This became a key concept in subsequent policy statements. In its report to the UN General Assembly of October 2003, under the heading of 'Asylum and Migration Nexus', UNHCR noted:

> Since the beginning of the 1980s, the attitude of many Governments towards asylum-seekers, refugees and migrants has changed. Their new policies have sought to respond to increasing numbers of asylum-seekers and to the challenges posed as a result of mixed flows, where asylum-seekers are found alongside labour migrants. With many channels of legal migration virtually closed, some migrants fall prey to smugglers and traffickers who misuse the asylum channel as a viable means of entry.... UNHCR must strive to ensure that the needs of refugees and asylum seekers are properly met within the broader context of migration management.... Although different in scope and nature, efforts to develop better systems for migration and for asylum go hand in hand. Asylum systems cannot function effectively without well-managed migration; and migration management will not work without coherent systems and procedures for the international protection of refugees. Asylum and managed migration systems should, however, be based on a clear distinction between the different categories of persons ... It is important to maintain the credibility of asylum systems and regular migration channels. Factors which could contribute to this objective in the asylum area include simplifying asylum procedures, strengthening protection capacities in host countries, as well as promoting durable solutions. (UNGA 2003: 11)

This was a fairly succinct statement of the migration-asylum nexus problematic: it also showed the extent to which UNHCR had endorsed the related and wider notion of 'migration management'. This was also seen in the incorporation of such ideas into a UNHCR major policy initiative of the early 2000s, Convention Plus, whose aims included addressing mixed flows and irregular secondary movements of refugees and asylum seekers (Castles and Van Hear 2005).

The notion also found organizational expression in the European Union, particularly in the HLWG (see above, p. 288). As explained above, the HLWG's responsibility was to develop a framework across such different government interests to improve the EU's approach to asylum and migration policy. While the brief of the HLWG was to seek comprehensive approaches—including for example addressing the root causes of forced movements—in practice the thrust of its approach was the containment of migration, and the cajoling of countries of origin and transit through aid to take steps towards that end (Castles and Van Hear 2005). Immigration and asylum were conflated in major policy statements, such as the conclusions to the Tampere and Seville summits of 1999 and 2002, and the notion underlay policy trends in relations with 'third countries', often in the developing world and notably with respect to readmission agreements for rejected asylum seekers and other returnees (Boswell 2003; Castles and Van Hear 2005).

The growing salience of the notions of mixed migration and the migration-asylum nexus can therefore be seen as an outcome of pressure from two directions. The first was scholarly analysis in the 1990s that highlighted the increasingly common roots of movement, where economic factors were often linked with human rights abuses and violence: this analysis became increasingly integrated into policy circles. The second thrust was acknowledgement by multilateral agencies that governments in the 'global North' (or at least their home or interior ministries) and their publics had reason to believe that the asylum system was being abused and used for immigration purposes on a substantial scale. The adoption of the notions of 'mixed migration' and the 'migration-asylum nexus' by the multilateral aid and relief agencies can then be seen as a liberal response to state concerns (indeed to try to take the steam out of them), as well as to the findings of researchers on refugees and forced migration.

In 2008, UNHCR reconsidered its perspective on the migration-asylum nexus and began to distance itself from the notion (Crisp 2008). While the organization still recognized the importance of mixed migration both in terms of global migration and its particular mandate, it was felt that the discourse associated with migration-asylum nexus could compromise UNHCR's core purpose of refugee protection. The 'more prosaic notion of "refugee protection and durable solutions in the context of international migration"' was now preferred (Crisp 2008: 3).

The principal reasons for this shift were that the migration-asylum nexus discourse had become too closely associated with the agenda of the migrant-receiving countries of the 'global North'—concerns with irregular migration, control of borders, unfounded asylum claims, the return of asylum seekers whose claims for refugee status had been rejected, and so on—an agenda that could conflict with the UNHCR's mandate to protect those fleeing harm. Likewise, the migration-asylum nexus had become too closely associated with movement from the 'global South' to the 'global North', reinforcing the view that the world's most important migration issue was movement of people from poorer parts of the world to more affluent countries. In reality, 'some of the largest migration flows, and the vast majority of the world's refugees, are to be found in developing regions' (Crisp 2008: 3).

Nevertheless, the need to address refuge protection and solutions within the context of the wider international migration arena remained. UNHCR found itself 'engaged in a difficult balancing act':

> On one hand, the organization recognizes the need to underline the distinctive status, rights and obligation of refugees, and is sensitive to charges that it wishes to extend its mandate to broader migration issues that lie beyond its legitimate concern. At the same time, UNHCR is aware that human mobility is growing in scope, scale and complexity, and acknowledges that other stakeholders, especially states, increasingly regard the movement of refugees, asylum seekers and irregular migrants as part of a single (and often unwanted) phenomenon. (Crisp 2008)

The re-emergence of discourse on migration and development

While governments and agencies struggled with the manifestations and consequences of mixed migration, debate on the connections between migration and development re-emerged, and with it a return to the notion of tackling root causes of mobility.

With respect to this discourse, it is worth noting that root causes approaches are based on two assumptions, the first implicit, the second more explicit. The first assumption is that migration—especially of the poor from the South—is a bad thing that ought to be stopped.[5] As Bakewell (2008) has argued, this 'sedentary bias' in migration policy goes back to colonial traditions of trying to stop rural–urban movements, which were perceived as a threat to public order. Development was meant to take place in the village. Similarly, as Zygmunt Baumann (1998) has pointed out, the rich are globally mobile, but the poor are meant to remain at home. In contrast, the history of human development shows that people have always enhanced their capabilities and livelihoods by moving from poor areas to those offering more opportunities (Sen 2001). Today this often means rural–urban migration—both internal and international. In other words, strategies to stop migration through development are misguided, because migration is more likely than immobility to lead to better livelihoods.

The second assumption is that development will in fact reduce migration. This is not a new idea: we have already drawn attention to the idea of 'trade instead of migration' back in the 1970s (Hiemenz and Schatz 1979). This approach was revived in the context of increasing hostility to immigration in Europe. In 1994, the European Ministers for Development Cooperation requested the European Commission to investigate the possibility of using development aid to diminish migration pressures. The idea was summed up in a statement by former Danish Prime Minister Rasmussen in 1995: 'if you don't help the third world…then you will have these poor people in our society' (de Haas 2006). As also pointed out above, this connection was stressed at the 2002 European Council meeting in Seville. France's 'co-development' programmes have been particularly strongly linked to 'return and stay-at home policies' (de Haas 2006: 16).

Plans for using development to reduce migration are based on the idea that migration and refugee movements are driven by poverty, underdevelopment, and unemployment, and that tackling these 'root causes' can help keep people at home. This leads on to the notion of a 'virtuous circle' of migration and development, in which circular migration is used to support development efforts, which will in the end reduce emigration (Bakewell 2008). However, migration researchers have long questioned such simple linkages, and pointed out that development is likely to lead initially to increased emigration rather than to reduce it (e.g. Tapinos 1990).

This has led to the notion of the 'migration hump': economists Martin and Taylor have argued that a chart of emigration shows a rising line as economic growth takes off, then a flattening curve, followed in the long run by a decline, as a mature industrial economy emerges (Martin and Taylor 2001). In other words, development in poor countries leads at first to more migration, and to a decline only in the very long term if sustained economic development takes place. The 'migration hump' approach was first applied to Mexico–US migration in the early 1990s. But the hope that the North American Free Trade Area (NAFTA) would lead to development and hence reduced migration has proved illusory. Indeed mobility from Mexico to the United States has become a way of life, and Mexico has experienced little development as a result (Delgado Wise and Guarnizo 2007). Awareness of this issue on the part of the European Commission has led to a call for measures aimed 'at reducing the time span of the migration hump' (CEC 2002: 20).[6]

This is because people need resources to migrate. Most of the main emigration countries are not amongst the world's poorest, but tend to be middle income countries. For instance, Mexico has reached the World Bank's 'upper-middle' income group, while Turkey, Morocco, and the Philippines are considered to be lower-middle income countries (World Bank 2006). Emigrants from poor countries in Africa or South Asia generally come from families with incomes above the local average, which can pool resources to fund mobility. The very poor usually only migrate if forced to by conflict or disasters, and then mainly move within their own countries or to neighbouring territories. Migrants come mainly from areas already caught up in a process of economic and social transformation. Development actually helps provide the resources needed for migration.

The notion of transforming societies

Root causes approaches are based on the principle of transforming societies, in order to overcome the economic underdevelopment and political instability that are seen as the main determinant of migration and refugee flows. Proponents of human rights may see root causes measures as morally preferable to measures of border control, which are often discriminatory and exclusionary, especially towards the poor and the persecuted. Yet setting out to transform societies is problematic too. It can be seen as a continuation of the 'civilizing mission' argument used to justify colonialism, or of the 'modernization theories' of the 1960s, which argued that less developed countries needed to adopt the values and institutions of the West in order to prosper (Baeck 1993; Portes 1997).

Mark Duffield has argued that there has been a shift from policies of containment and intervention to a 'new humanitarianism': a much more active policy of political, economic, and (sometimes) military intervention designed to transform whole societies. Globalization is marked by persistent underdevelopment in large parts of the South. This is not an economic problem for the North, Duffield argues, because, apart from providing certain raw materials, many Southern countries are largely disconnected from the global economy. However, the South re-connects with the North through the proliferation of transnational informal networks, such as international crime, the drug trade, people-smuggling and trafficking, and migrant networks which facilitate irregular mobility (Duffield 2001). Such phenomena are linked to economic deregulation and privatization in the North, which open up the space for informal economies to thrive.

Underdevelopment has thus become a threat to the North. The result is a fundamental change in the objectives of both development policy and humanitarian action. Containment of forced migration through neutral humanitarianism has failed. Similarly, the 'Washington Consensus'—the neo-liberal credo of the World Bank and the International Monetary Fund that underdevelopment could be countered by economic growth based on foreign investments and export-led growth—has proved mistaken. Humanitarianism and development policy now has a new joint task: the transformation of whole societies in order to prevent conflict and to achieve social and economic change. Such interventions seek to restore peace and achieve economic development at the local level through imposing certain political and economic structures as part of a system of global governance. The price of being connected to global economic and political networks is thus the adoption of Northern economic structures, political institutions, and value systems.

This shift was reflected in a fundamental change in thinking and policy on conflict-ridden societies from the late 1990s.[7] As well as destroying assets and livelihoods, dislocating and disrupting local and national economies, undermining trust and social capital, and displacing large numbers of people, conflict came to be seen as an opportunity for socio-economic transformation—the 'every cloud has a silver lining' argument. By sweeping away social and economic structures that were held inimical to 'development', conflict could open the way for progressive market-led reform and innovation, it was thought.

The new approach was no longer just fire-fighting or simply shoring up societies in parlous straits while halting the export of terrorists, criminals, and unwanted migrants from them. It went beyond this palliation, embracing the notion of the opportunity to transform whole societies. It was interventionist, in contrast to earlier rhetoric about letting market forces work their magic. In the new perspective, conflict and displacement were seen not only as destructive but as holding the potential for the transformation of the economy and society. While conflict was previously seen as regressive, it was now presented as an opportunity for a society's social, political, and economic transformation.

This perspective developed in tandem with growing concern about security challenges posed by what came to be known as 'fragile' and 'failing' states and the so-called 'LICUS' grouping of territories: 'low income countries under stress'

(World Bank 2002). Somalia was a case in point of such state collapse and conflict and the threats and opportunities that it posed. The UNDP's percipient *Human Development Report* of 2001 remarked: 'The prolonged absence of a central Somali government means that Somali society is more directly exposed to both the beneficial and the harmful effects of globalization.... The civil war achieved what the structural adjustment programmes of the 1980s did not, that is, economic deregulation that has enabled the expansion of the private sector' (UNDP 2001: 40–1).

The realization of the 'creative' potential of conflict has been manifested in policy shifts within the World Bank concerning conflict and post-conflict societies. Although it was formed after the Second World War—as the International Bank for Reconstruction and Development—as part of the Marshall Plan to rebuild 'post-conflict' Europe, the Bank had no comprehensive operational policy for post-conflict situations in the developing world until the later 1990s. Indeed, the Bank tended to avoid countries embroiled in armed conflict in favour of those undergoing what it regarded as more conventional development—even though these countries had often experienced conflict and upheaval short of civil war. This changed when the Bank set up its Post-Conflict Unit (PCU), operational by 1997, and established a Post-Conflict Fund which aimed at supporting countries in transition from conflict to sustainable peace and economic development. The PCU transmuted subsequently into the Conflict Prevention and Reconstruction Unit, reflecting an expanding remit (World Bank 1997, 1998).

The new emphasis meant that the Bank now embraced use of conflict situations to promote economic adjustment and recovery, to build institutional capacity, and to revitalize civil society. The Bank cooperated with other agencies engaged in post-conflict activities in which forced migration issues were prominent, notably through the 'Brookings Process', a partnership between the Bank, UNHCR, and UNDP initiated in 1999. This was later revived in 2002 as the '4Rs' initiative—Repatriation, Reintegration, Rehabilitation, and Reconstruction—as an integrated inter-agency 'relief-to-development' approach for countries in transition from conflict (Lippman and Malik 2004).

Critics were wary of this new approach to conflict by the World Bank and other powerful donors. For the critics, such agencies saw 'the terrain of post conflict situations as ripe for implementation of their kind of state, economy and society' (Moore 2000: 14). 'The wake of war leaves the "level playing field" so beloved by...neo-liberal discourses' (Ibid.: 13). Conflict conditions offered opportunities for market-friendly interventions. In this perspective, social and economic structures governing property, labour, and other economic factors which obtained before conflict may well have been impediments to the development of markets: if these structures were destroyed or fatally undermined by conflict, the foundations could be laid for individual property rights and other dimensions of market-friendly 'good governance' (Moore 2000: 11). The dispensers of humanitarian relief could be enlisted to join with those implementing reconstruction and development for these market-friendly purposes. Money was on offer to humanitarian agencies through an array of transition budgets and reconstruction funds, which were increasingly attractive as other sources of humanitarian funds were on the wane.[8]

While this critique of this policy shift as a manifestation of neo-liberalism has some substance, the new interest of the World Bank, and other agencies in conflict-ridden societies in fact coincided with the move from the 'Washington Consensus', promoting structural adjustment and other measures of neo-liberalism up to the 1990s, to the 'Post-Washington Consensus' from the later 1990s (Stiglitz 1998; Maxwell 2005), associated with Poverty Reduction Strategy Papers (PRSPs), the Millennium Development Goals, bringing back the developmental state, and emphasis on good governance, civil society, and so on. In other words, there was a shift in emphasis from 'good markets' to 'good governance', from getting markets to function unfettered by the state to recognizing the imperfections and shortcomings of the market and strengthening social institutions through the nurturing of civil society. The 'Post-Washington Consensus' was certainly still market-friendly, but acknowledged the need for means to counter the harm done by the market and by 'market imperfections': it was the promotion of *liberal* capitalism rather than *neo-liberal* capitalism.

From the point of view of the 'global North' and its development agencies then, conflict-ridden societies are seen as a source of unwanted people, forces, and trends: refugees, fundamentalists, criminals, terrorists, and the export of insecurity generally. But at the same time it has been recognized that such conditions may present opportunities for remoulding society. The emergence of this perspective was accompanied by a rise of interest in the development potential of diasporas, and later of their potential for assisting with recovery in conflict settings. This perhaps at least partly accounts for the interest of the World Bank and other agencies in conflict and possible diaspora influence on it. The notion of enlisting conflict-induced diaspora—as part of 'transnational civil society'—to transform conflict societies into stable, sustainable communities has now become a project of relief and development agencies, and the latest twist on the root causes approach—for if diasporas can be enjoined to help address those root causes of displacement, they may supplement intervention by humanitarian and development agencies, or even supplant the need for them. This shift in thinking is embedded in wider notions of the new importance of diasporas in development: the shift from the 'development through return' option to the 'development through the diaspora' option (Bhagwati 2003; Faist 2008).

Conclusion: root causes and the governance of migration

'Root causes' approaches developed as a reaction to two trends: first, the growth in international movements of asylum seekers and lower skilled workers; and second, the gradual comprehension that border control measures on their own were ineffective in the face of the powerful forces causing mobility, especially from poor to rich countries, in the epoch of neo-liberal globalization. To put it more generally, the 'root causes' notion involves a recognition that migration cannot be dealt with in isolation from other global issues, and that migration policies cannot be separated from other issues of global governance.

Migration is driven by many factors (see Massey et al. 1998), but inequality between different nations and regions is amongst the most important. This refers not only to income inequality but also to differentials in human security and human development. The phase of neo-liberal globalization from the late 1970s to the late 2000s led to a marked growth in such inequalities, and increased human mobility—both as economic and forced migration—was an inevitable result. Northern states sought to manage this mobility through ever-tighter border control. This approach often led to unexpected—and often unwanted—side effects, such as the growth of irregular migration, increases in people-smuggling and trafficking, and the erosion of refugee protection. 'Root causes' approaches implied a recognition that border control measures could not succeed without complementary efforts to address poverty and human rights deficits in origin regions.

Yet 'root causes' approaches still remained limited in at least three respects: first, they did not seek to address fundamental North–South inequalities; second, they remained based on the implicit assumption that the migration of poorer people was a bad thing that should be curtailed; and third, 'root causes' approaches remained poor cousins of the migration control measures, in the sense that governments were willing to spend far more on the latter. Thus, 'root causes' approaches have on the whole failed to bring about substantial changes in migration dynamics, and especially in the unequal power relationships between migrant origin and destination states.

International migration therefore remains an area of international relations in which efforts to achieve global governance are in their infancy compared with such areas as cooperation on international finance or trade. It could be that the current economic crisis will provide opportunities for new initiatives for cooperation based on recognition of the varying interests of various groups in origin and destination countries, and of the migrants themselves. Equally, the crisis may lead to greater pressures for national protectionism in the migration field. In the long run, migration governance needs to go beyond both border control and root causes approaches, to take account of the interdependence of migration with other key areas of global relations, including trade, investment, development cooperation, security, and international politics.

Notes

1. The debates are treated in detail in Castles and Miller (2009: chs. 2 and 3) and Massey et al. (1998a: ch. 2).
2. For more detail and further references, see Castles and Van Hear (2005).
3. The European Council is the regular meeting of prime ministers and other ministers of the EU states, which determines key EU policies.
4. This section draws on and updates in Castles and Van Hear (2005).
5. Note that this generally only applies to asylum and lower skilled labour migration. Highly skilled and entrepreneurial movements are usually not called migration at all but rather labelled as 'professional mobility', 'circulation of brains', or similar positive euphemisms. All developed countries have set up privileged entry systems for the highly skilled, and exclusionary migration systems for the lower skilled. The latter encourages limited temporary contract labour, or, as the current buzzword goes 'circular migration', while excluding most would-be labour migrants. The result has been large-scale irregular migration, which is perhaps not as unwanted as it seems, since right-less workers suit many employers well, while the pretence of exclusion meets the political interests of governments. Indeed, many advanced countries—including the United States, Japan, Spain, Italy, and Britain—make systematic use of irregular migrant workers.
6. Quoted by Boswell (2003: 634–5).
7. This section draws on Van Hear ((2006).
8. This critique has recently been trenchantly restated by Klein (2008) in her exposition of what she calls 'the shock doctrine' and 'disaster capitalism'.

References

Abadan-Unat, N. (1988) The Socio-Economic Aspects of Return Migration to Turkey, *Revue Européenne des Migrations Internationales*, 3, 29–59.

Baeck, L. (1993) *Post-War Development Theories and Practice*, Paris: UNESCO and The International Social Science Council.

Bakewell, O. (2008) Keeping Them in Their Place: The Ambivalent Relationship between Development and Migration in Africa, *Third World Quarterly*, 29(7), 1341–58.

Bauman, Z. (1998) *Globalization: The Human Consequences*, Cambridge: Polity.

Betts, A. (2004) *International Cooperation and the Targeting of Development Assistance for Refugee Solutions: Lessons from the 1980s*, unpublished manuscript, University of Oxford.

Bhagwati, J. (2003) Borders beyond Control, *Foreign Affairs*, 82(1), 98–104.

Bigo, D. and Guild, E. (eds) (2005) *Controlling Frontiers: Free Movement Into and Within Europe*, Aldershot: Ashgate.

Boswell, C. (2003) The 'External Dimension' of EU Immigration and Asylum Policy, *International Affairs*, 79(3), 619–38.

Castles, S. and Delgado Wise, R. (eds) (2008) *Migration and Development: Perspectives from the South*, Geneva: International Organization for Migration.

——and Kosack, G. (1973) *Immigrant Workers and Class Structure in Western Europe*, London: Oxford University Press.

——Loughna, S., and Crawley, H. (2003) *States of Conflict: Causes and Patterns of Forced Migration to the EU and Policy Responses*, London: Institute of Public Policy Research.

——and Miller, M.J. (2009) *The Age of Migration: International Population Movements in the Modern World*, 4th edn, Basingstoke and New York: Palgrave-Macmillan and Guilford.

——and Van Hear, N. (2005) Developing DFID's Policy Approach to Refugees and Internally Displaced Persons, Report to the Conflict and Humanitarian Affairs Department, Oxford: Refuge Studies Centre.

Commission of the European Communities (CEC) (2002) Communication from the Commission to the Council and European Parliament on Integrating Migration Issues in the European Union's Relations with Third Countries, COM (2002) 703 Final, Brussels: Commission of the European Communities.

Chimni, B.S. (1998) The Geo-Politics of Refugee Studies: A View from the South, *Journal of Refugee Studies*, 11(4), 350–74.

Crisp, J. (2001) Mind the Gap! UNHCR, Humanitarian Assistance and the Development Process, *New Issues in Refugee Research*, Working Paper No. 43, Geneva: UNHCR (May 2001).

——(2008) Beyond the Nexus: UNHCR's Evolving Perspective on Refugee Protection and International Migration, *New Issues in Refugee Research*, Working Paper No. 155, Geneva: UNCHR, http://www.unhcr.org/research/RESEARCH/4818749a2.pdf.

Delgado Wise, R. and Guarnizo, L.E. (2007) *Migration and Development: Lessons from the Mexican Experience*, Washington, DC: Migration Information Source, http://www.migrationinformation.org. Accessed 6 February 2007.

Duffield, M. (2001) *Global Governance and the New Wars: The Merging of Development and Security*, London and New York: Zed Books.

Faist, T. (2008) Migrants as Transnational Development Agents: An Inquiry into the Newest Round of the Migration-Development Nexus, *Population, Place and Space*, 14, 21–42.

Froebel, F., Heinrichs, J., and Kreye, O. (1980) *The New International Division of Labour*, Cambridge: Cambridge University Press.

de Haas, H. (2006) Turning the Tide? Why 'Development Instead of Migration' Policies are Bound to Fail, IMI Working Paper 2, Oxford: International Migration Institute.

Hiemenz, U. and Schatz, K.W. (1979) *Trade in Place of Migration*, Geneva: International Labour Organization.

Keely, C.B. (2001) The International Refugee Regimes(s): The End of the Cold War Matters, *International Migration Review*, 35(1), 303–14.

——(2004) The International Forced Migration Regime, Paper Commisioned for the Project, Developing DFID's Policy Approach to Refugees and Internally Displaced People, Oxford: Refugee Studies Centre.

Klein, N. (2008) *The Shock Doctrine: The Rise of Disaster Capitalism*, London: Penguin.

Lippman, B. and Malik, S. (2004) The 4Rs: The Way Ahead? *Forced Migration Review*, 21 (September), 9–11.

Martin, P.L. (1991) *The Unfinished Story: Turkish Labour Migration to Western Europe*, Geneva: International Labour Office.

——and Taylor, J.E. (2001) Managing Migration: The Role of Economic Policies, in A.R. Zolberg and P.M. Benda (eds), *Global Migrants, Global Refugees: Problems and Solution*, New York and Oxford: Berghahn.

Massey, D.S, Arango, J., Hugo, G., Kouaouci, A., Pellegrino, A., and Taylor, J.E. (1998) *Worlds in Motion: Understanding International Migration at the End of the Millennium*, Oxford: Clarendon Press.

Maxwell, S. (2005) The Washington Consensus is Dead! Long Live the Meta-Narrative! Overseas Development Institute, Working Paper 243, London: ODI.

Moore, D. (2000) Levelling the Playing Fields and Embedding Illusions: 'Post-Conflict' Discourse and Neo-Liberal 'Development' in War-Torn Africa, *Review of African Political Economy*, 83, 11–28.

Paine, S. (1974) *Exporting Workers: The Turkish Case*, Cambridge: Cambridge University Press.

Portes, A. (1997) Neoliberalism and Sociology of Development: Emerging Trends and Unanticipated Facts, *Population and Development Review*, 23(2), 229–59.

Richmond, A. (1994) *Global Apartheid: Refugees, Racism and the New World Order*, Oxford: Oxford University Press.

Sen, A. (2001) *Development as Freedom*, Oxford: Oxford University Press.

Spencer, S. (1996) Tackling the Root Causes of Forced Migration: The Role of the European Union, in European Commission DG 10 (ed.), *The European Union in a Changing World*, Brussels: European Commission.

Stiglitz, J. (1998) More Instruments and Broader Goals: Moving Towards the Post-Washington Consensus, World Institute for Development Economics Research Annual Lecture, January 1998, United National University, Helsinki.

Tapinos, G.P. (1990) *Development Assistance Strategies and Emigration Pressure in Europe and Africa*, Washington, DC: Commission for the Study of International Migration and Co-operative Economic Development.

Thränhardt, D. (1996) European Migration from East to West: Present Patterns and Future Directions, *New Community*, 22(2), 227–42.

United Nations Development Programme (UNDP) (2001) *Human Development Report 2001 Somalia*, Nairobi: UNDP Somalia Country Office.

UN General Assembly (UNGA) (2002) Agenda for Protection: Addendum, UN General Assembly 2002, Executive Committee of the High Commissioner's Programme, 53rd Session, A/AC.96/965/add.1, 26 June, New York.

——(2003) Strengthening the Capacity of the Office of the UN High Commissioner for Refugees to Carry of its Mandate, Note by the Secretary-General A/58/410 (3 October 2003).

UNHCR/ILO (2001*a*) The Asylum-Migration Nexus: Refugee Protection and Migration Perspectives from ILO, Presented to the UNHCR Global Consultations on International Protection, Geneva (June).

UNHCR (2001*b*) Global Consultations on International Protection, 2nd Meeting, Refugee Protection and Migration Control: Perspectives from UNHCR and IOM, EC/GC/01/11 31, Geneva (May).

UNHCR (2006a) *Addressing Mixed Migratory Movements: A 10-Point Plan of Action*, Geneva: UNHCR (June 2006).

——(2006b) *The High-Level Dialogue on International Migration and Development: UNHCR's Observations and Recommendations*, Geneva: UNHCR (28 June 2006).

——(2007a) *UNHCR, Refugee Protection and International Migration*, Geneva: UNHCR (January 2007).

——(2007b) Refugee Protection and Durable Solutions in the Context of International Migration, High Commissioner's Dialogue on Protection Challenges, Discussion Paper, UNHCR/DPC/2007 (19 November 2007).

Van Hear, N. (1998) *New Diasporas: The Mass Exodus, Dispersal and Regrouping of Migrant Communities*, London: Routledge/University College London Press.

——(2006) Re-casting Societies in Conflict, in N. Van Hear and C. McDowell (eds), *Catching Fire: Containing Forced Migration in a Volatile World*. Lanham, MD: Lexington/Rowman and Littlefield.

Van Selm, J. (2002) Immigration and Asylum or Foreign Policy: The EU's Approach to Migrants and their Countries of Origin, in S. Lavenex and E. Uçarer (eds), *Externalities of EU Immigration and Asylum Policies*, Washington, DC: Lexington.

World Bank (1997) *A Framework for World Bank Involvement in Post Conflict Reconstruction*, Washington, DC: World Bank.

——(1998) *Post-Conflict Reconstruction: The Role of the World Bank*, Washington, DC: World Bank.

——(2002) *World Bank Group Work in Low Income Countries Under Stress: A Task Force Report*. Washington, DC: World Bank.

——(2006) *Key Development Data and Statistics*, Washington, DC: World Bank, http://web.worldbank.org/WBSITE/EXTERNAL/DATASTATISTICS/. Accessed 23 January 2006.

Conclusion

Alexander Betts

The international institutional framework that regulates states' responses to migration is of a fundamentally different type to the United Nations (UN)-based multilateralism that emerged to regulate other international issues in the immediate aftermath of the Second World War. Although international migration is not a new process, it has only relatively recently been recognized as a significant global issue that requires a debate on the role of international cooperation. The quantitative growth in international migration has contributed to migration becoming an increasingly politicized and visible issue. Meanwhile, the qualitative change in the nature of migration, with increasing South–South movements and the internationalization of labour markets, has led states to seek cooperative ways to maximize the economic benefits of migration, while minimizing the costs associated with undesirable migration. As with other trans-boundary issue-areas, states have increasingly recognized that they are unable to address their concerns with migration in isolation but that forms of collaboration and coordination are necessary.

Yet, with the notable exception of the refugee regime, there is no formal or comprehensive multilateral regime regulating how states can and should respond to the movement of people across national borders, and no overarching UN organization monitoring states' compliance with norms and rules. The majority of the formal rules that do exist in relation to migration pre-date the Second World War. The long-standing passport regime, treaties on labour rights, and the basis of the refugee regime all emerge from the Inter-War Years, and most subsequent formal multilateralism has merely supplemented or updated these institutions. Attempts to develop new formalized cooperation mechanisms in the post-Cold War era have been very limited and generally failed. The limited ratification of the UN Treaty on the Rights of All Migrant Workers and Their Families and the degree of inter-state polarization over the UN High-Level Dialogue on Migration and Development and the Global Forum on Migration and Development's (GFMD) relationship to the UN system highlights the degree of opposition to formal multilateralism.

Yet even though there is no formal, coherent multilateral UN-based governance framework, this is not to say that there has been no global migration governance. In reality there is a rich and fragmented tapestry of global migration governance, much of which has emerged in a historically ad hoc way. It exists at a number of levels. At a first level, there is a thin and incoherent layer of formal multilateralism that builds upon the Inter-War Years framework in areas such as the refugee regime, International Labour Organization (ILO) Conventions, and norms underpinning the use of passports. At a second level, there are a range of international agreements that have emerged to regulate other issue-areas—World Trade Organization (WTO) law, maritime law, human rights law, and humanitarian law for example—which although not explicitly labelled as migration, have implications for how states can and do respond to human mobility. This 'embedded' governance has contributed to a range of international organizations and other actors becoming actively engaged in debates on migration insofar as it touches upon a broader set of mandates. At a third level, as political concern with labour migration and irregular migration has increased, new mechanisms of global migration governance have emerged that are exclusive rather than inclusive and can be subsumed under the notion of 'trans-regionalism'. A cross-cutting layer of bilateral, regional, and inter-regional cooperation has emerged. One of the principal mechanisms through which this has emerged is through the development of informal network governance structures; most notably through Regional Consultative Processes (RCPs), which have enabled groups of like-minded states to discuss issues informally and then develop more formalized cooperation. This model of informal network governance, which is giving rise to a range of formal bilateral, regional, and inter-regional agreements among groups of 'like-minded states', has been promoted and facilitated mainly by the International Organization for Migration (IOM), and is, to some extent, replicated at the global level through the GFMD.

Drawing upon the preceding chapters, this conclusion revisits the questions outlined in the Introduction to the volume. Examining the volume's chapters in depth, it compares the governance of the different areas across the three main questions posed by the volume's introduction: institutional, political, and normative issues. Firstly, it describes how the governance of different areas of migration varies, and attempts to offer an explanation for this variation. Secondly, it assesses the politics of the different areas of migration, identifying the cooperation problems underlying different areas of migration governance. Thirdly, given what we have learned analytically, it asks, normatively, what should be the way forwards for global migration governance. It sets out three alternative visions: informal network governance, formal multilateralism, and coherent plurilaterlism. It suggests that the first option alone is undesirable, the second unrealistic, and that the third option offers the best available vision for global migration governance.

Institutions

The Introduction to the volume outlined the characteristics of global migration governance, taken as a whole, highlighting how it can be analytically identified at three different levels—a thin multilateralism, embeddedness, and trans-regionalism. However, beyond this broad characterization, it is important to recognize that, reflecting the structure of this book, global migration governance is diverse. The overarching typology applies more in some areas of migration than others, and it is important to recognize how governance varies across the different aspects of migration. This section therefore describes the variation in global governance across the different areas of migration and then, drawing upon global public goods theory, offers an explanation for that variation.

Koslowski (forthcoming) has argued that global migration governance can be analytically divided into three broad regimes: the refugee regime (regulating access to protection), travel regime (regulating movement—including irregular migration), and labour migration regime (regulating access to livelihoods abroad). He suggests that these exist on a spectrum in terms of the degree of multilateral cooperation that exists, whereby the refugee regime is the most institutionalized, followed by the travel regime, which has some, and the labour migration regime which is virtually non-existent.

If one goes through the degree of formalized cooperation within each of these broad areas, then there is indeed a spectrum of formalized cooperation. The chapters broadly bear out this claim. However, they nuance the typology in two important ways. Firstly, the typology becomes more nuanced when one distinguishes between two different types of cooperation: collaboration and coordination. Collaboration refers to contributions to collective action, whether through action or inaction, to achieve mutually agreed ends that actors would not otherwise have chosen when acting in isolation. Coordination refers to the adoption of common standards to achieve a given end (Snidal 1985; Hasencleaver et al. 1997). Secondly, the chapters highlight two important aspects of global migration governance that are not included with the global mobility regimes typology, and exist prior to and after the typology: the regulation of the causes and consequences of migration.

The refugee regime remains the area with the greatest degree of multilateral collaboration and coordination. As Loescher and Milner show, states have committed, through the 1951 Convention on the Status of Refugees to provide asylum to refugees, and to have their asylum policies monitored by the United Nations High Commissioner for Refugees (UNHCR), in return for other states doing likewise. Meanwhile they have coordinated at a multilateral level to ensure that states offer broadly the same standards of protection to refugees. Nevertheless, even in the refugee regime, there are limitations to the extent of multilateral collaboration, with no binding norms on burden-sharing to ensure that states contribute to supporting protection and durable solutions for refugees who are on the territory of another state. As Koser shows, this refugee regime has been supplemented by an emerging internally displaced person (IDP) regime to ensure that people in 'refugee-like' situations but who have not crossed an international border nevertheless have access to protection. Although this embryonic regime is reliant upon a 'soft law' framework and a 'cluster' approach allocating responsibility between international organizations, it nevertheless represents a relatively strong multilateral framework in comparison to other areas of migration. Furthermore, as McAdam highlights, a range of human rights norms exist that, although not institutionally consolidated, have the potential to be applied to emerging sources of forced migration such as climate-induced displacement.

In terms of the governance of movement across borders, there is much more limited multilateral collaboration than for refugees. However, there is significant multilateral coordination and collaboration that has emerged on a regional basis. Koslowski's chapter demonstrates the long-standing nature of coordination on travel, dating back to the creation of the passport regime. States have subsequently agreed on the adoption of a range of common standards relating to aspects of travel, most notably through agreeing to common International Civil Aviation Organization (ICAO) standards. In the context of international concerns with security and terrorism, attempts to engage in standard-setting are ongoing. In terms of collaboration, there is less formal multilateral cooperation on the movement of people across borders. However, as Düvell's chapter illustrates, a set of regional regimes have emerged to facilitate collaboration on managing irregular or undocumented migration. The most notable example is collaboration within the European Union (EU) through common contributions to institutions such as the Europe-wide system for the identification of asylum seekers (EURODAC) and the European Union border agency (FRONTEX) within Europe and the adoption of a common external policy relating to irregular migration and border control. As these chapters demonstrate, much of the cooperation that exists in relation to the movement of people across borders has focused on security; however, there is also an important layer of governance in the area of human rights. As Martin and Galloway's chapter highlights, the focus on the securitization of travel has contributed to the emergence of common standard-setting in relation to human trafficking through the adoption of the Palermo Protocol to the United Nations Covention an Transnational Organized Crime (UNTOC). Nevertheless, while irregular migrants have human rights, these rights are rarely adequately operationalized (Koser, this volume; McAdam, this volume).

In terms of labour migration and the regulation of livelihoods across borders, there is even less institutionalized cooperation than for travel. There is no multilateral collaboration and only very limited multilateral coordination through various international standards. States are far more likely to act unilaterally or to engage in bilateral agreements in relation to labour migration. As Kuptsch and Martin show, low-skilled migration is subject to a range of common standards, set out within International Labour Organization (ILO) and UN human rights treaties; however, these are frequently over-ridden by states' economic and security interests. High-skilled labour migration is arguably even less regulated at the global level, with states generally competing with one another to secure skilled labour in accordance with their own interests. Nevertheless, as Betts and Cerna show, forms of coordination have emerged to reduce the transaction and information costs of skilled migration through, for example, the reciprocal recognition of qualifications.

Aside from this limited coordination on labour migration, the majority of state behaviour in relation to labour migration is unilateral. Nevertheless, much of the unilateral behaviour might also be interpreted as a source of global governance insofar as it constrains or shapes the actions of other states. Gamlen, for example, demonstrates how states' emigration policies vis-à-vis their diaspora may be unilateral but nevertheless have important political effects in the receiving countries. Similarly, in looking at lifestyle migration, Oliver shows how in the absence of institutionalized cooperation between states, the politics of lifestyle migration is largely determined by the unilateral choices of receiving states.

The chapters also serve to highlight two important areas of global migration governance that cannot easily be subsumed within the refugee-travel-labour migration regimes typology: the regulation of the causes and consequences of migration. These areas are especially interesting because there is limited cooperation explicitly in these areas. However, they are characterized by 'embedded' governance in other issue-areas. In terms of causes, Castles and Van Hear show how a growing array of ad hoc initiatives have emerged to engage with the 'root causes' of migration. While no formal institutional collaboration or coordination exists, the global governance of a range of other issue-areas—development, security, trade, and the environment—all have implications for the underlying causes of movement. Furthermore, Lindley's chapter serves to illustrate the range of transnational consequences, of which remittance is just one, that result from migration. As she demonstrates, remittances have come to be regulated by global governance in a range of other issue-areas, most notably security and economic governance.

Beyond description, a particular challenge is to explain this variation. Many authors express surprise at the incoherence and arguable under-development of migration governance (Ghosh 2000; Bhagwati 2003; Hollifield forthcoming). However, from the perspective of states, there is a certain underlying logic to this spectrum of migration governance. The question of 'why there is so little global migration governance' is actually a fairly straightforward one to answer on the basis of a mainstream institutionalist understanding of international relations, and relates primarily to the nature of the externalities involved within the three broad categories of migration.

The 'demand' for international regimes is generally understood in relation to the type of externalities involved—in other words, to what extent are different states affected—positively or negatively—by a given trans-boundary movement (Keohane 1982). In issue-areas in which one finds 'global public goods' (i.e. goods for which (*a*) the benefits or costs are non-excludable between actors and (*b*) the benefits are non-rival between actors), one would expect it to be in the mutual interest of states to reciprocally cooperate to ensure the provision of global public goods and the mitigation of global public bads. One would expect the degree of formalized cooperation that exists to be a function of the extent to which externalities are non-excludable and non-rival between states.

It has been claimed by James Hollifield (forthcoming) that there should be a collective interest in the development of a global migration regime because it would represent a global public good, the benefits of which would be non-excludable, in the sense that all states would benefit from its existence irrespective of their own contribution, and non-rival, in the sense that one state's enjoyment of the benefits would not diminish those available to another state (Kaul et al. 1999; Barrett 2007). For Hollifield, the public good nature of the benefits of 'orderliness and predictability' that come from global migration governance underlie the rationale for an inclusive, possibly UN-based framework.

However, this characterization misrepresents the nature of migration governance. To be strictly accurate about this point, one can divide migration into three broad areas: refugees, irregular and low-skilled migration, and high-skilled migration.

1. The governance of refugee protection and IDP protection represent, to some degree, a global public good. Although the benefits of refugee protection being provided (in terms of security and human rights) are asymmetrically distributed among states, the benefits accrue to all states to some extent and the enjoyment of those benefits by one state is largely undiminished by another state's enjoyment. One would therefore expect a multilateral regime.

2. The governance of irregular and low-skilled labour migration, on the other hand, is not a global public good. It represents a 'club good' in the sense that while regulating irregular movement has benefits that are 'non-rival', the benefits are to some extent excludable in the sense of being largely geographically confined benefits. Hence one would expect cooperation within 'clubs', whether regional, inter-regional, or trans-regional.

Table C.1. Migration as a public good

Type of migration	Dominant level of governance	Type of good
Refugees/IDPs	Multilateral	Public good
Irregular/low-skilled	Regional	Club good
High-skilled	Unilateral/bilateral	Private good

3. The governance of high-skilled labour migration, on the other hand, is different. Like the governance of irregular migration, its cost benefits are highly excludable, accruing almost exclusively to the sending state, the receiving state, and the migrant. Unlike the governance of irregular migration, though, in the case of skilled labour, at least, the benefits of labour migration are rival because skilled labour has finite supply. In that sense, it is a private good. One would therefore expect the dominant form of cooperation to be through unilateral liberalization or bilateralism.

This recognition of the different nature of the type of goods that different aspects of migration governance represent (see Table C.1) is fundamental to any understanding of why migration governance is structured as it is, and the desirability—from a state perspective—of reform. It implies that the status quo may be less surprising and 'irrational' than is often implied in the emerging debates on international cooperation and migration. While this 'justification' of the status quo is from a narrowly state-centric perspective, it contributes to an understanding of why it is that we see the type of variation that exists in the degree of formalized institutional cooperation.

Politics

Explaining the international politics of migration is crucial to understanding why we see the institutions that we see, and what prevailing sets of interests, power, and ideas have led to the creation of different degrees of institutionalized cooperation on migration. Combining the insights of the chapters with insights from international relations allows us to identify the nature of the central cooperation problems that exist in relation to international migration and the conditions under which they might be overcome. Two broad cooperation problems emerge from the literature, which implicitly re-occur throughout the chapters. As has been argued above, international cooperation, divides between the areas of (a) coordination (the adoption of common standards for achieving a given end) through, for example, ICAO and (b) collaboration (contributions to collective action, whether through action or inaction, through contributing to a mutually agreed end) through, for example, agreeing to regional or international treaties that reduce the degree of border controls.

Both problems can be represented game theoretically—the main coordination problem in migration can be represented by a 'battle of the sexes game'; the main collaboration problem in migration can be represented by a 'suasion game'.

Firstly, one of the main forms of cooperation in migration is the rather prosaic and banal issue of standardization: adopting common practices among states. Standardization takes place in a range of areas of world politics, most obviously through the work of the International Standards Organization and within regional integration (Mattli 1999). Within migration, it is especially important in areas such as travel, in which ICAO facilitates the adoption of common standards (Koslowski, this volume) or within labour migration in terms of the adoption of standard recognition of qualifications (Betts and Cerna, this volume). Within the type of regional cooperation on asylum standards or irregular migration controls, standardization also takes place (Düvell, this volume). Standardization is regarded as important to states because it can offer significant possibilities for reducing transaction costs or providing economies of scale in addressing externalities.

Mattli (1999) highlights the nature of the coordination problem relating to the adoption of common standards and policies. The Coordination Dilemma involves a choice between multiple stable and efficient equilibria. It is based on the analogy of the 'battle of the sexes' game in which a man and woman both wish to spend the day together but he wants to go to the football and she wants to go to the theatre. His first preference is for them to spend the day together at the football, her first preference is to spend the day at the theatre; however, both would prefer to spend the day with the other than to spend it alone. The challenge is therefore to choose between the multiple, competing equilibria. In other words, it is to decide whose standards should be adopted, even though both actors recognize that they would be better off with common standards than without.

In Figure C.1, CC represents the repeated outcome of the iterated game. State A gets its optimum outcome; however, state B receives its second-best outcome.

		Actor B	
		C	D
Actor A	C	4,3*	2,2
	D	1,1	3,4

Figure C.1. Coordination problem: number left (right) of comma refers to A's (B's) preference ordering (1 = worst outcome, 4 = best outcome), * = equilibrium

Since the Coordination Dilemma involves agreement on which equilibrium to move to, it has distributional consequences. One actor may have to sacrifice its optimum scenario for coordination in deference to the preference of another. The challenge of coordination, then, is to create the conditions under which a set of actors will agree to defer to the standards of a dominant actor, even though it is their 'second-best' scenario.

Mattli (1999) identifies that coordination requires strong leadership; it will occur under two conditions. Firstly, it requires strong leadership at the inter-state level by, for example, actor A. In other words, an authoritative hegemon is needed whose standards might be accepted and adopted. Secondly, strong domestic leadership will be needed—especially by actor B—to sell the second-best outcome to its domestic political constituencies. Indeed, where coordination has taken place in the area of migration, it has tended to be under these conditions. In the areas of travel or trafficking, for example, it has tended to be US standards that have been adopted as the basis of common international standards. In these areas, the collective gains have been recognized as sufficiently great for other states to shift to adopt the US standards. In contrast, at the regional level, it has been especially challenging to adopt EU common standards on asylum and migration in the absence of clear hegemonic leadership.

Secondly, the main characteristic of the international politics of migration is power asymmetry. Whether on a global or regional level, asymmetric power relations represent the principal barrier to international collaboration. In the area of labour migration, and related areas such as remittances, there is a fundamental power asymmetry between predominantly migrant-sending and migrant-receiving states. At the global level, this takes on a significant North–South dimension. Voting patterns at the UN General Assembly on incorporating the GFMD within the UN system or ratifications of the UN Convention on the Rights of All Migrant Workers and Their Families illustrate this fundamental division. Northern receiving states are generally reluctant to engage in collaboration that constrains their unilateral discretion; Southern sending states frequently push for greater institutionalized collaboration through the UN system. This global sending/receiving division is frequently replicated at the regional level with regional hegemons such as South Africa often being reluctant to commit to institutionalized regional collaboration that reduces their sovereignty in the area of migration.

This collaboration problem can be illustrated by the game theoretical analogy of a 'suasion game' (Martin 1993; Hasencleaver et al. 1997; Betts 2009). The game involves two actors: one stronger (B) and one weaker (A). Because of their different relative power, the two actors have different interests. *Either* A has a dominant strategy to cooperate (C), which B can exploit by defecting *or* B has a dominant strategy to defect (D), while the other must cooperate in order to avoid an even worse outcome. In either case, the weaker actor's preferred strategy is to cooperate—either because non-cooperation is not practically viable or because it

Actor B

		C	D
	C	4,3	3,4*
Actor A			
	D	2,2	1,1

Figure C.2. Suasion game: number left (right) of comma refers to A's (B's) preference ordering (1 = worst outcome, 4 = best outcome), * = equilibrium

would lead to even greater costs. However, the stronger actor is in a position to choose to not cooperate and that is likely to be its preferred position. An instance of unrequited cooperation (CD) is consequently the only stable outcome of the game. Suasion games have only a single equilibrium outcome, which satisfies only one actor and leaves the other aggrieved. The stronger actor B will exploit the weaker actor A. The only alternative strategy available to actor A would be to scupper cooperation entirely by choosing outcome DD, which could be an effective strategy if the game was repeated over time such that harming itself in the short run led to actor B, enhancing its long-run bargaining power in a manner that might lead to outcome CC (Figure C.2).

In the case of labour migration, actor A represents a migrant-sending state and actor B represents a migrant-receiving state. B's defecting strategy (D) will be to maintain unilateral control over immigration policy; its cooperative strategy (C) will be to pool sovereignty in the area of immigration policy. A's cooperative strategy (C) will be to allow emigration and its defecting strategy (D) will be to place restrictions on emigration. A's dominant strategy is cooperation (C) because, whether or not B cooperates, it is likely to be better off allowing labour emigration than prohibiting emigration. B's dominant strategy is defection (D) because it will generally prefer to maintain a unilateral position and not constrain its discretion to determine entry on to its territory. The outcome is therefore likely to be box CD in which the sending state seeks cooperation, and the receiving state shuns cooperation. This leads to a logic in which migrant-receiving states are likely to be 'makers' of global migration governance and migrant-sending states are likely to be 'takers'.

In the case of the refugee regime, actor A represents a host country of first asylum in the South; B represents a donor or resettlement state in the North. As Loescher and Milner (this volume) note, the refugee regime has established norms relating to asylum (states' contributions to protection on their territory) but it lacks established norms relating to burden-sharing (states' contributions to protection of refugees who remain on the territory of another state). In the refugee regime, B's defecting strategy (D) will therefore be to contribute limited or no burden-sharing; its cooperative strategy (C) will be burden-sharing. A's cooperative strategy (C) will be to provide asylum and its defecting strategy (D) will be to not provide asylum. A's dominant strategy is likely to be to cooperate by providing asylum, irrespective of whether B contributes to burden-sharing. Consequently, the equilibrium position will almost certainly be CD in which the strong state exploits the weak.

The suasion game problem therefore dominates cooperation on refugee protection and labour migration and other areas such as remittances and diaspora which, like labour migration, are characterized by a sending/receiving as takers/takers logic. Lifestyle migration also engenders a sending/receiving dynamic. However, as Oliver (this volume) notes, much lifestyle migration is North–South or North–North and so it frequently leads to situations in which materially weaker Southern states become the 'makers' of global migration governance, and Northern states often find themselves as the 'takers'. So under what conditions can collaboration take place and can the suasion game logic be overcome? Two factors seem to make cooperation across sending/receiving or North–South lines possible: issue-linkage and interdependence.

Issue-linkage offers a recognized means to overcome the suasion game logic (Haas 1980; Martin 1993; Betts 2009). By linking cooperation on migration to issues or issue-areas in which the dominant states have an interest, then incentives for cooperation might emerge. Indeed, migration is increasingly being negotiated alongside issue-areas such as development (at the GFMD), trade (through the WTO), and the environment (in climate change adaptation discussion), in ways that create incentives for cooperation across a range of issues. Examples of potentially cooperation-enhancing linkages in migration include: linking travel security to privileged labour market access (Koslowski forthcoming), linking refugee burden-sharing to travel security (Betts 2010), and linking development assistance or trade concessions to irregular migration control (Paoletti 2008).

Interdependence seems to be a means through which stronger actors might develop an interest in more formalized cooperation (Keohane and Nye 2001; Rudolph 2008). If the interests of receiving states are tied to what happens in sending states, then this may create a basis for international bargains that are in the mutual interests of states on different sides of the power asymmetry. Indeed, as the chapters by Gamlen and Lindley demonstrate, the emergence of transnationalism in areas such as remittances and diaspora is contributing to a greater interdependence across states and between North and South. Economic and security interests increasingly transcend the ability of individual Northern states to address unilaterally, and, in that sense, the emergence of transnationalism may have the potential to transform the nature of power relations between states and to transcend the sending/receiving state dichotomy (Gamlen 2008; Court 2009).

Normative

The final issue that each of the chapters has addressed is the question of how global migration governance should look in each area. As the Introduction highlighted, academic work on global governance in general has struggled with normative issues. There are often implicit normative assumptions about 'more' global governance or more cooperation being inherently more desirable, when in fact cooperation by itself is not inherently normatively desirable or undesirable. This begs the question of what 'good' global migration governance would look like, and on what basis it might be assessed. As the Introduction highlighted, concepts such as legitimacy, efficiency, and equity offer a basis for having some kind of normative criteria. However, a definitive answer to the question of how global migration governance should look is beyond the scope of this book. The study of global governance as a whole needs to develop a better set of analytical concepts for normative analysis, and to establish what a desirable institutional architecture would look like, would require serious engagement with moral and political philosophy.

Nevertheless, the chapters highlight notable 'gaps' in the global governance of different areas of migration, and provide some justification for why institutionalized cooperation or its absence may or may not be desirable in that area. For example, Düvell highlights the absence of a protection framework for irregular migrants, which Koser in turn suggests could learn lessons from the IDP experience by creating a 'soft law' framework on the protection of vulnerable irregular migrants. Martin and Calloway argue that the existing trafficking regime has focused too much on prosecution to the detriment of developing a protection framework for victims of trafficking. Loescher and Milner argue that UNHCR needs to evolve to meet the imperatives of the contemporary era by playing a more politically engaged role and through 'doing more by doing less', catalytically engaging other parts of the UN system. Castles and Van Hear highlight the importance of seeing migration in its broader context, as part of not only 'migration governance' but also that of security, development, and trade governance, all of which impact upon the underlying causes of human mobility. McAdam highlights the need to reflect on where to institutionally locate debates on environmental displacement, suggesting it to be an important component of both climate change adaptation and migration debates. In that sense the chapters offer a wide range of normative proposals for reform and a starting point for a more in-depth and comprehensive normative debate about the future contours of global migration governance.

Furthermore, though, the chapters help to identify the major normative trade-offs that exist in selecting between different types of global governance. This takes use beyond assertions that 'more cooperation is good' and highlights what might be gained and lost (and for whom) as a result of different types of

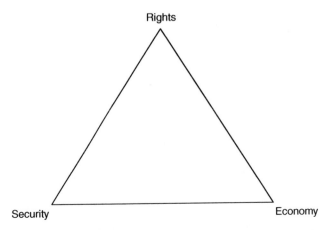

Figure C.3. Normative trade-off triangle, within which institutions governing migration face a choice about how to choose between competing priorities

institutional design. Collectively, the chapters point to three particular norma-tive areas, across which there are trade-offs resulting from different types of institutional structure: *rights*, *security*, and the *economy*. Across nearly all of the areas of migration, a shift towards or away from a certain type of governance involves trading off across these three concepts, and a choice about which to privilege or sacrifice. The three concepts need not be zero sum but there nevertheless seem to be trade-offs and hence choices that global migration governance needs to confront, which can be crudely illustrated in Figure C.3, within which institutions governing migration will all inherently have to locate themselves.

The normative trade-off is most clearly articulated in Kuptsch and Martin's chapter, in which they outline the 'rights versus economy', trade-off that normatively characterizes the governance of low-skilled labour migration. On the one hand, economic imperatives privilege 'numbers' of migrants; however, once significant rights obligations are extended to low-skilled workers, the number that will be economically, socially, and politically acceptable will di-minish. In their chapter, they characterize this trade-off as 'liberalism versus neo-liberalism', and identify how this trade-off is also manifest at the institu-tional level through, for example, the ILO and UN promoting rights while the WTO promotes numbers.

The 'security versus economy' trade-off is highlighted by numerous chapters. Lindley, for example, demonstrates how the governance of remittances is divided between these two areas, and how they often coexist in tension to one another. On the one hand, there is a strong economic and developmental case for allowing the unfettered movement of capital across borders. On the other hand, in the context of the 'War on Terror' and concern with transnational organized crime, remittances have come under increasing international scrutiny and been subject to ever greater regulations deriving from security imperatives.

The same trade-off is perceptible within Koslowski's analysis of the travel regime. On the one hand, the facilitation of the free movement of people for business and tourism, for example, represents an important economic flow which contributes to states' economic growth. On the other hand, however, unimpeded movement poses risks relating to terrorism and organized crime. Many of the standards adopted through ICAO have been conceived in an effort to address possible security threats while causing minimal economic disruption.

The 'rights versus security' trade-off comes out in numerous chapters. Düvell shows how the development of regional responses to irregular migration has been driven by a security logic that has sidelined developing an institutional framework to ensure the human rights of irregular migrants. Loescher and Milner demonstrate the omnipresence of this trade-off within the refugee regime, in which states constantly balance their asylum provision with concerns about national security in ways that impel UNHCR to be politically responsive to states' concerns. Meanwhile, Martin and Calloway argue that the existing regime for addressing human trafficking has been conceived partly out of states' concerns with security and transnational crime, and has consequently focused far more on prosecution and prevention than it has on protection.

Of course, these trade-offs are a crude representation. They need not be zero sum; in some cases, it may be possible to identify policies or institutional frameworks within which rights, security, and economic imperatives are mutually compatible and reinforcing, rather than contradictory. However, identifying and articulating the major trade-offs is an important normative starting point for recognizing the choices that can and do exist within global governance and the sacrifices that are often implicitly made by privileging one imperative over another.

The way forwards

This begs the question of what type of global migration governance do we want? This question has partly motivated former UN Secretary General Kofi Annan to commission both the Doyle Report and then the Global Commission on International Migration. However, ultimately, both of these initiatives but fell short of laying out a coherent vision for global migration governance. There are currently two principal areas in which states are engaging in ongoing debates about the possible contours of global migration governance. On the one hand, there is the 'migration and development' debate taking place within the UN system and the GFMD. On the other hand, there is the International Organization for Migration (IOM)-led debate, mainly focused on irregular migration, which is taking place through the RCPs. These two sites of debate have little interaction with one another and neither has attempted to come up with a single, coherent vision for global migration governance. This section does not attempt to fill this gap by outlining a single vision of global migration governance. However, it attempts to provide a starting point for thinking through this question by outlining the broad visions for global migration governance that are implicit within ongoing debates and discussing their relative merits. It suggests that the competing visions can be subsumed under two broad areas: informal network governance and formal multilateral governance. However, it posits that there is a third, alternative vision which is likely to be the most desirable and politically feasible balance between these extremes: coherent plurilateralism.

Informal network governance

As things stand, the current trend within global migration governance is the development of exclusive, informal groups of 'like-minded' states engaged in regional and inter-regional dialogues on issues of mutual concern. As with a growing range of other issue-areas of global economic governance, informal networks are being seen by states as an efficient way in which small 'coalitions of the willing' can avoid and bypass the perceived inefficiencies and binding obligations of the UN system while still achieving the types of coordination and collaboration that maximize their perceived interests in relation to migration. The RCP model, propagated by IOM has spread rapidly to become the modus operandi of global migration governance. Northern states have shunned formal multilateralism through the UN in favour of 'clubs' within which they can discuss and develop good practice. Rather than being tied to formal multilateral agreements, informal network governance is focused on creating the conditions in which sovereign states may engage in coordination and collaboration on a selective and ad hoc basis, mainly through bilateral agreements.

While informal network governance conceived on a trans-regional basis may offer efficiency and its more exclusive basis may favour frank and open exchanges on an issue of political sensitivity, its consequences may be more ambiguous in terms of rights, equity, and accountability. As an exclusive forum, closed to the public, and generally without documentary record of its proceedings, the RCP model does not foster inclusive global migration governance. Furthermore, it may represent a model which reinforces existing power asymmetries between states. Indeed the existing structures of governance may entrench inequalities of power by enabling materially stronger or migrant-receiving states to systematically include and exclude prospective partner states on a strategic basic. Indeed the existing informal network and trans-regional governance structures create opportunities for forum-shopping and a 'divide and rule' approach by the North towards prospective Southern partner states.

Certainly, the informal network model raises a lot of questions about the relationship between networks and power. As Woods and Martinez-Diaz (2009) show, informal networks have an important relationship to power by serving a range of functions: agenda-setting, consensus-building, policy coordination, knowledge production and exchange, and norm-setting and diffusion. However, it remains ambiguous whether, in the case of migration, the RCP model transfers these functions towards otherwise weaker Southern states or, alternatively, creates a model through which Northern states or regional hegemons assume ever greater control of these functions. The fact that many developing countries are actively arguing for more inclusive and open forms of multilateral governance would suggest that they regard the existing RCP model, by itself, to be inadequate to meet their needs and concerns.

Formal multilateral governance

The main competing vision is for formal multilateralism à la 1945, perhaps based around a new UN migration organization (Bhagwati 2003). Politically, it is a vision shared by many developing countries keen to create binding commitments from Northern states to admit their workers and provide them with rights. The principal argument in favour of such a framework is based on equity and rights. The UN system provides an inclusive and open forum in which all states can participate in a frank dialogue. It also allows for the creation of binding rules and norms in ways that can bring rights-based concerns to the fore. However, many states argue that this form of inclusive multilateralism is inefficient and unresponsive to the realities of migration. Indeed, debate on migration at the UN has been stunted by North–South polarization, with Northern states reluctant to make major binding concessions in the area of migration.

Many areas of migration are, of course, within the UN system—issues relating to refugee protection, human trafficking, and environmental displacement, for example, are strongly entrenched within a range of the UN system and are debated within UN forums. However, there has been great reluctance among mainly Northern states, and particularly the United States, to countenance binding, UN-based regulation in the area of labour migration. The prospects for a coherent, UN-based governance framework in relation to labour migration therefore appear remote, primarily because of North–South polarization. Voting at the UN on the GFMD, ratifications of the UN Convention on the Rights of All Migrant Workers and Their Families, and the polarized discussions at the first High-Level Dialogue on Migration and Development (HLDMD), all exemplify the extent to which North–South polarization is inhibiting the emergence of UN-based governance structure in the area of labour migration.

This is not to say that a coherent UN-based governance structure is impossible but that, at the moment, the most powerful states in the UN system do not appear to have an appetite for such a system. It is possible that this may change.

The United States is increasingly more positive about multilateralism than in its recent past. China and India may become increasingly vocal actors in global migration governance in ways that may reshape global migration governance. Furthermore, in other issue-areas such as trade and the environment, it is worth noting that states took many years to develop the contours of multilateral governance. Although the General Agreement on Tariffs and Trade was created in the post-war era, it was not until the creation of the WTO in the 1990s that states made significant concessions to their sovereignty in the area of trade. Given that debate on global migration governance only really began with the International Conference on Population and Development ICPD in Cairo in 1994, it may be too early to definitively rule out a significant UN role in migration. Nevertheless, the UN itself faces a significant challenge of credibility and authority and will need to reform if states are to regard it as a more viable and efficient way of addressing labour migration than the alternative, and currently more efficient, option of resorting to informal network governance.

Coherent plurilateralism

The current trend in global migration governance is towards the creation of a cross-cutting tapestry of bilateral, regional, inter-regional institutions to complement pre-existing multilateral institutions. States engage selectively in institutionalized cooperation at different speeds and on different 'tracks' in accordance with their own preferences and the constraints of power. It seems likely that this trend of plurilateralism—that is the coexistence of different modes and levels of governance—will continue to define global migration governance.

However, the idea that global migration governance must be a choice between informal network governance, on the one hand, and formal multilateralism, on the other hand, represents a false dichotomy. There is an alternative third path, which attempts to strike a balance between the flexibility and efficiency of network governance, on the one hand, with the respect for equity, rights, and inclusivity offered by the UN system. This alternative—coherent plurilateralism—stems from a dual recognition. On the one hand, informal and trans-regional mechanisms of governance alone may not be desirable for addressing the needs of the developing world or migrants' rights. On the other hand, a purely multilateral track may not be feasible and may not always adequately respond to the particular needs of smaller 'clubs' of states.

The immediate challenge is to balance the fragmented tapestry of cross-cutting institutions, and the eclectic way in which different areas of migration are subject to their own institutional architectures, with greater coherence. There is a need for greater coordination across existing institutions and, as many of the chapters point out, a greater emphasis on rights across the board. The creation of the Global Migration Group, the creation of an inter-RCP meeting, and the existence of the GFMD, all represent a welcome acknowledgement of the need for greater coherence across both levels of governance and across areas of migration. However, in practice, these mechanisms have yet to achieve the type of coherence they purport to nurture and policy-makers' responses to questions suggest dissatisfaction with the achievements of existing coordination mechanisms.

As a starting point, one way of setting out a vision for developing global migration governance based on coherent plurilateralism would be to first identify what functions global migration governance should fulfil. Based on the assumption that an international institutional framework should enable states to identify areas of preference convergence and facilitate international cooperation in these areas, five broad functions of global migration governance can be identified. Yet within each area there are important gaps.

FUNCTION 1: NORMATIVE OVERSIGHT

One of the biggest gaps in existing governance is the absence of an institutional authority to oversee implementation of states' existing obligations under international migration law. IOM has no clearly defined normative role, and, in contrast to UNHCR's role in overseeing international refugee law or the International Committee of the Red Cross (ICRC)'s role in overseeing international humanitarian law, there is no organization with a similar normative role in relation to migration. This is a particularly problematic gap in relation to the human rights of migrants, which frequently fall between the mandates of different international organizations.

FUNCTION 2: FORUM FOR DIALOGUE

The GFMD currently provides the most inclusive forum for dialogue on migration available to states. However, it is not yet totally inclusive in terms of either its participants (states or non-state actors) nor in terms of the range of migration topics that it covers. Meanwhile, the UN High-Level Dialogue on Migration and Development has created opportunities for the entire international community to convene, but with a seven year gap between its first meeting in 2006 and its second scheduled meeting in 2013. There is therefore an ongoing need to consider the appropriate context for a universally inclusive forum for dialogue on migration.

FUNCTION 3: SERVICE PROVISION

A range of organizations support capacity-building for states in the area of migration, most notably IOM. However, capacity building tends to focus on issues relating to border control, travel documentation and forensics, to the neglect of capacity-building in other areas. To take one example, the author's interviews on migration capacity-building in East Africa reveal that many IOM-trained border guards were often familiar with identifying fraudulent documents but did not know the definition of a 'refugee'.

FUNCTION 4: POLITICAL FACILITATION

An important role that international institutions can play for states is in overcoming collective action failure through facilitation. By identifying areas of mutual interest and putting forward a vision for collaboration or coordination, international organizations play an important role in many policy fields. However, this function is largely missing in the area of migration. IOM, for example, has little capacity at headquarters to engage in political facilitation and other institutions working on migration lack the personnel and resources to play this role. Yet it is a crucial function if leadership and vision are to emerge.

FUNCTION 5: KNOWLEDGE CAPACITY

In order to identify areas in which international cooperation is needed, global migration governance needs to have a knowledge capacity that can engage analytically with developments in migration—in terms of both the issue, and its wider political and institutional context. However, at the moment none of the major institutions working on migration have significant capacity in this area. One or a group of international organizations need to develop a much stronger knowledge capacity in the area of migration. The World Bank, for example, might be one option for a lead organization in this role given its growing work on international migration and its aspiration to serve as a 'knowledge bank' as well as a 'money bank'. In its initial stages, this might involve convening an international panel of experts, similar to that which emerged in the area of climate change.

Identifying these functions does not offer a single, unified vision for migration governance. However, it sheds light on the procedural purpose of global migration governance in ways that can help identify gaps and shortcomings in the existing institutional tapestry. In the short run, at least, it is not realistic to expect a 'blank slate' to emerge on which a single multilateral framework can be built. Instead, there is a need to make existing institutions work better in the interests of both states and migrants. Global migration governance will not be based on a 'one-size fits all' vision of UN-based multilateralism. However, it can and should strive to make the complex tapestry of existing institutions more coherent and responsive to the challenges of an increasingly mobile world.

References

Aleinikoff, A. (2007) International Legal Norms on Migration: Substance Without Architecture, in R. Cholewinski, R. Perruchouf, and E. MacDonald (eds), *International Migration Law: Developing Paradigms and Key Challenges*, The Hague: TMC. Asser Press, pp. 467–80.

Alter, K. and Meunier, S. (2009) The Politics of Regime Complexity Symposium, *Perspectives on Politics*, 7(1), 3–24.

Appadurai, A. (ed.) (1986) *The Social Life of Things: Commodities in Cultural Perspective*, Cambridge: Cambridge University Press.

Barrett, S. (2007) *Why Cooperate? The Incentive to Supply Global Public Goods*, Oxford: Oxford University Press.

Betts, A. (2009) *Protection by Persuasion: International Cooperation in the Refugee Regime*, Ithaca, NY Cornell University Press.

——(2010) The Refugee Regime Complex, *Refugee Survey Quarterly*, 29(1), 12–37.

Bhagwati, J. (2003) Borders Beyond Control, *Foreign Affairs*, Jan.–Feb.

Court, E. (2009) India as 'Rule-Taker' and 'Rule-Maker' in the Politics of International High Skilled Migration: Methodological Challenges Integrating What Happens Between, Within and Across States, Paper presented at the Graduate Research in Progress Seminars for the Social Sciences, May 2009, Nuffield College, Oxford.

Gamlen, A. (2008) Why Engage Diasporas? ESRC Centre on Migration Policy and Society Working Papers No. 63, WP-08-63, University of Oxford.

Ghosh, B. (2000) *Managing Migration: Time for a New International Regime*, Oxford: Oxford University Press.

Haas, P.M. (1980) Why Collaborate? Issue-Linkage and International Regimes, *World Politics*, 32(3), 357–405.

Hasencleaver, A., Mayer, P., and Rittberger, T. (1997) *Theories of International Regimes*, Cambridge: Cambridge University Press.

Hollifield, J. (forthcoming) Migration as a Global Public Good, in R. Koslowski (ed.), *Global Mobility Regimes*.

Kaul, I., Grunnberg, I., and Stern, M. (eds) (1999) *Global Public Goods: International Cooperation in the 21st Century*, Oxford: Oxford University Press.

Keohane, R. (1982) The Demand for International Institutions, *International Organization*, 36(2), 325–55.

Keohane, R. and Nye, J.S. (2001) *Power and Interdependence*, New York; London: Longman.

Koehler, J. (2008) What States Do and How They Organize Themselves in Regional Consultative Processes (RCPs), Paper presented at the workshop Migration and International Cooperation: South–South Perspectives, 7–8 August, IOM, Geneva.

Koslowski, R. (ed.) (forthcoming) *Global Mobility Regimes*.

Martin, L. (1993) The Rational State Choice of Multilateralism, in J. Ruggie (ed.), *Multilateralism Matters: The Theory and Praxis of an Institutional Form*, New York: Columbia University Press, pp. 91–121.

Mattli, W. (1999) *The Logic of Regional Integration*, Cambridge: Cambridge University Press.

——(2003) Public and Private Governance in Setting International Standards, in M. Kahler and D. Lake (eds), *Governance in a Global Economy*, Princeton, NJ Princeton University Press, pp. 199–225.

Nielsen, A.-G. (2007) Cooperation Mechanisms, in R. Cholewinski, R. Perruchouf, and E. MacDonald (eds), *International Migration Law: Developing Paradigms and Key Challenges*, The Hague: T.M.C. Asser Press, pp. 405–26.

Paoletti, E. (2008) Bilateral Agreements on Migration and North–South Power Relations: The Case of Italy and Libya, Doctoral thesis, submitted to Oxford University.

Raustiala, K. and Victor, D.G. (2004) The Regime Complex or Plant Genetic Resources, *International Organization*, 58, 277–309.

Rudolph, C. (2008) Globalization, Interdependence and Migration, Paper presented at the Annual Meeting of the International Studies Association, 26–29 March 2008, San Francisco, CA.

Sahlins, M. (1974) *Stone Age Economics*, London: Tavistock Publications.

Slaughter, A.-M. (2000) Governing the Global Economy Through Government Networks, in D. Held and A. McGrew (eds), *The Global Transformations Reader: An Introduction to the Globalization Debates*, Cambridge: Polity, pp. 189–203.

——(2004) *A New World Order*, Princeton, NJ; Oxford: Princeton University Press.

Snidal, D. (1985) Cooperation Versus Prisoners' Dilemma: Implications for International Cooperation and Regimes, *American Political Science Review*, 79, 923–42.

Wilk, R. (1996) *Economies and Cultures: Foundations of Economic Anthropology*, Boulder, CO: Westview Press.

Woods, N. and Martinez-Diaz, L. (2009) *Networks of Influence? Developing Countries in a Networked Global Order*, New York: Oxford University Press.

Index

Index